Communications in Computer and Information Science 685

Commenced Publication in 2007
Founding and Former Series Editors:
Alfredo Cuzzocrea, Dominik Ślęzak, and Xiaokang Yang

More information about this series at http://www.springer.com/series/7899

Xiaokang Yang · Guangtao Zhai (Eds.)

Digital TV and Wireless Multimedia Communication

13th International Forum, IFTC 2016
Shanghai, China, November 9–10, 2016
Revised Selected Papers

 Springer

Editors
Xiaokang Yang
Shanghai Jiao Tong University
Shanghai
China

Guangtao Zhai
Shanghai Jiao Tong University
Shanghai
China

ISSN 1865-0929 ISSN 1865-0937 (electronic)
Communications in Computer and Information Science
ISBN 978-981-10-4210-2 ISBN 978-981-10-4211-9 (eBook)
DOI 10.1007/978-981-10-4211-9

Library of Congress Control Number: 2017934327

Printed on acid-free paper

This Springer imprint is published by Springer Nature
The registered company is Springer Nature Singapore Pte Ltd.
The registered company address is: 152 Beach Road, #21-01/04 Gateway East, Singapore 189721, Singapore

Preface

The present book includes extended and revised versions of papers selected from the 13th International Forum of Digital TV and Wireless Multimedia Communication (IFTC 2016), held in Shanghai, China, during November 9–10, 2016.

IFTC is a summit forum in the field of digital TV and multimedia communication. The 2016 forum was co-hosted by SIGA, the China International Industry Fair 2016 (CIIF 2016), and co-sponsored by Shanghai Jiao Tong University (SJTU), IEEE BTS Chapter of Shanghai Section, Shanghai Institute of Communication, and the Shanghai Society of Motion Picture and Television Engineers (SSMPTE). IFTC serves as an international platform for exchanging the latest research advances in digital TV and wireless communication around the world as well as the relevant policies of industry authorities. The forum also aims to promote technology, equipment, and applications in the field of digital TV and multimedia by comparing the characteristics, frameworks, significant techniques and their maturity, analyzing the performance of various applications in terms of scalability, manageability, and portability, and discussing the interfaces among varieties of networks and platforms.

The conference program included invited talks delivered by seven distinguished speakers from China, France, and the USA, as well as oral sessions of ten papers and a poster session of 28 papers. The topics of these papers range from image processing and audio processing to image and video compression as well as telecommunications.

This book contains 38 papers selected from IFTC 2016. We would like to thank the authors for contributing their novel ideas and visions that are recorded in this book.

November 2016

Xiaokang Yang
Ping An
Weisi Lin
Guangtao Zhai
Jia Wang
Jiantao Zhou
Kai Li

Organization

General Co-chairs

Xiaokang Yang	Shanghai Jiao Tong University, China
Ping An	Shanghai University, China
Weisi Lin	Nanyang Technological University, Singapore

Program Chairs

Guangtao Zhai	Shanghai Jiao Tong University, China
Jia Wang	Shanghai Jiao Tong University, China
Jiantao Zhou	University of Macau, Macau, SAR China
Kai Li	Shanghai University, China

International Liaisons

Patrick Le Callet	Nantes University, France
Soren Forchhammer	Denmark Technical University, Denmark
Nam Ling	Santa Clara University, USA

Finance Chairs

Yi Xu	Shanghai Jiao Tong University, China
Lianghui Ding	Shanghai Jiao Tong University, China

Publications Chairs

Yue Lu	Eastern China Normal University, China
Qiudong Sun	Shanghai Secondary Polytechnic University, China

Publicity Chairs

Xiangyang Xue	Fudan University, China
Dingxiang Lin	Shanghai Institute of Visual Art, China
Byeungwoo Jeion	Sungkyunkwan University, Korea

Industrial Program Chairs

Yijun Zhang	SSV Co. Ltd, China
Shengjun Jin	Digi-Graphic Co. Ltd, China
Guang Tian	Bocom Co. Ltd, China

Local Arrangements Chairs

Cheng Zhi   Shanghai Image and Graphics Association, China
Jun Zhou   Shanghai Jiao Tong University, China

Contents

Image Processing

Audio Processing

Image and Video Compression

Telecommunications

Image Processing

Color Constancy Using Illuminant-Invariant LBP Features

Yan Xia and Chen Yao[✉]

The Third Research Institute of Ministry of Public Security, Shanghai, China
yaochensing@126.com

Abstract. Color constancy is a problem related to how to make captured image color closer to biological vision, which is important for a lot of vision application including image stitching, visual tracking etc. Color constancy consists of light source color estimation and image white balance processing. Although, color constancy is ill-posed problem, there still are much study on it. In this paper, we try to solve this problem from illuminant invariant pixel estimation angle. LBP (Local Binary Pattern)-based statistical method is adopted as key tool for light source color estimation. Finally, experimental results demonstrate our algorithm advantage.

Keywords: Color constancy · Ill-posed · Illuminant invariant · LBP

1 Introduction

Images captured by CMOS (Complementary Metal Oxide Semiconductor) or CCD (Charge Coupled Device) often show different color under variant light source. Color constancy can be used to remove color cast which is resulted from different light source. Essentially, color constancy processing is to make image color more conformed to human biological visual system, which is also meant chromatic adaption. Color constancy has many applications, including video surveillance, object recognition, image stitching and visual tracking etc. [1].

Because of unknown light source in captured images, color constancy is a typical ill-posed problem. Generally, it includes light source color estimation and canonical image transform. Color constancy related research has been developed for many years. For most color constancy algorithm, an assumption of image regularity is used for illumination estimation such as gray world, average or maximum of RGB, grey edge etc. Based on the assumption, illuminant color can be computed by the average color of image pixels or image gradients. Concretely, generalized norms is utilized to model or infer illuminant color. In the generalized norms, image spatial distribution and color histograms are often used. During the inferring of key points color, PCA (Principal Component Analysis) and ICA (Independent Component Analysis) can be used for reasoning. Additionally, color gamut based statistical method is used for chromatic adaption [2–5].

The above mentioned methods are all classical image statistical-based. Another kinds of color constancy computation method are learning-based. Distribution of colors

© Springer Nature Singapore Pte Ltd. 2017
X. Yang and G. Zhai (Eds.): IFTC 2016, CCIS 685, pp. 3–11, 2017.
DOI: 10.1007/978-981-10-4211-9_1

are learned from training data. Generative models are all implemented in statistical and learning methods. In learning-based methods, high-level image feature description is used for universal illuminant estimation. Some of learning-based algorithm are more suitable for specific scene category. These algorithms application is constrained, which can not be applied in a wild environment. With biological-vision development, recent advances have been made for color constancy computation. Totally, learning-based ways are more depended on training data selection and illumination labeling [6–9].

In this paper, our method is related to statistical one. We assume that there are some illuminant invariant pixels in image. We use a simple local LBP [10] to position illuminant invariant pixels color and white balance image color. In the rest part of this paper, LBP and color constancy scheme will be reviewed and introduced in Sect. 2. Experimental results are provided in Sect. 3. And finally Sect. 4 concludes the paper.

2 Proposed Algorithm

In this paper, we assume that there exits some intrinsic illuminant-invariant pixels. These LLP (illuminant-invariant pixels) can be used for light source color estimation. Therefore, the key challenging problem is how to localize these pixels' position. Logarithmic transform, LBP statistics and local variance sorting techniques are combined to find LLP in our paper.

The captured image can be described as product of the illuminant and surface reflectance. Considering the computational convenience between neighboring pixels, logarithmic transform is used. After logarithmic transform, differences of pixels are less variables related. Logarithmic transform is done as following,

$$I_{LOG} = LOG(I_{R,G,B}). \tag{1}$$

Where, $I_{R,G,B}$ is an input image. I_{LOG} is logarithmic transformed image. LOG is image logarithmic operator. Then, LBP computation is performed in three different RGB channels, which can be described as following,

$$I_{LBP}(\text{R}) = LBP(I_{LOG}(\text{R})),$$
$$I_{LBP}(\text{G}) = LBP(I_{LOG}(\text{G})), \tag{2}$$
$$I_{LBP}(\text{B}) = LBP(I_{LOG}(\text{B})).$$

Where, I_{LOG} is logarithmic transformed image. LBP is image local binary pattern operator. In order to explain the whole algorithm more clearly, LBP image operator is reviewed as following. The current image pixel binary-valued LBP can be described as

$$LBP(I_C) = \sum_{i=0}^{P-1} 2^i sgn(I_i - I_C). \tag{3}$$

Where, the parameter P is the number of central pixel neighbors. I_c and I_i are the gray level values at central pixel and its neighbors. sgn is an simple binary function for the difference between I_c and I_i, which can be formulated as

$$sgn(x) = \begin{cases} 1 & x \geq 0 \\ 0 & x < 0 \end{cases}. \tag{4}$$

LBP represents similarity between central pixel and neighboring pixels. It can be a good describer for different texture in image [10]. In our paper, we assume that illuminant invariant points existing different texture area. Therefore, LBP is chosen for the computation of illuminant invariant points. The basic LBP process is illustrated in Fig. 1. From Fig. 1, LBP formulates a correlation between neighboring pixels. The final value means smoothness in a patch. And, LBP computed results are shown in Fig. 2.

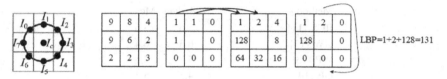

Fig. 1. LBP computation illustration

(a)   (b)

Fig. 2. LBP results (a) original image.(b) LBP results for one channel

Fig. 3. Variance statistical results

After image LBP computation, we can highlight pixel difference in image. Furthermore, a variance statistical method is used for narrowing LLP range, which can be described as

$$STD = \frac{1}{3}\sum_{i=R,G,B} \frac{\left(LBP_i - \overline{LBP}\right)^2}{\overline{LBP}}. \tag{5}$$

In Fig. 3, variance statistical results is obtained from LBP binary value. Next, ascent sorting is adopted for variance analysis. We select 0.01% pixels among least variance

Table 1. Performance statistics of various methods

Method	Median	Mean
IICS [11]	13.6	13.6
GW [12]	6.3	6.4
WP [13]	5.7	7.5
GE [14]	4.5	5.3
Our proposed algorithm	**2.8**	**5.1**

Fig. 4. Color constancy test data. The first row are original images, the second row are ground truth images.

points. Then, image color is recomputed using the selected pixel value, which is illustrate as

$$I_{new} = \frac{1}{n} \sum_{i \in std} I_{R,G,B}(i)./I_{R,G,B}. \qquad (6)$$

Fig. 5. Color constancy results. The first row are our processed results, the second row are gray world algorithm results, the last row are gray edge algorithm results.

Where, $I_{R,G,B}$ is unprocessed image. I_{new} is white balanced image. The whole algorithm procedure can be formulated as following

Step1   Read image data
Step2   Image logarithmic transform
Step3   LBP binary value statistics
Step4   Image variance computation
Step5   Key points sorting
Step6   Image white balancing

3   Experimental Results

In this section, the proposed algorithm was compared with different methods on single illuminant dataset including 568 high dynamic linear indoor and outdoor natural images. Four various algorithms are considered for comparison include inverse-intensity

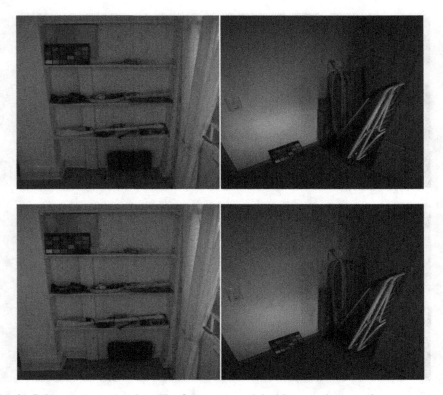

Fig. 6. Color constancy test data. The first row are original images, the second row are ground truth images.

Fig. 7. Color constancy results. The first row are our processed results, the second row are gray world algorithm results, the last row are gray edge algorithm results.

chromaticity space (IICS) [11], Grey world (GW) [12], White patch (WP) [13] and Grey edge (GE) [14]. Meanwhile, angular error is chosen as error metric, which is formulated as

$$\varepsilon = arccos((I_{NEW} \cdot I_{GT})/(\| I_{NEW} \| \cdot \| I_{GT} \|)). \tag{7}$$

Where, $I_{NEW} \cdot I_{GT}$ is the dot product of light source color estimation I_{NEW} and the ground truth illumination I_{GT}. $\| \cdot \|$ is Euclidean norm of a vector. Median and mean angular error are adopted for final algorithm evaluation.

In Table 1, our proposed algorithm is compared with method [11–14]. The median and mean angular error are shown in Table 1. From the results, we can find that our proposed algorithm demonstrates superior performance over traditional methods. In this comparison, statistical-based methods are used for comparing. And, we don't compare with learn-based methods. We think statistical-based method has more unconstrained than learning-based method. Especially, statistical-based way will show better performance without training data. In order to better illustrate our advantage, we give two results comparison in Figs. 4, 5, 6 and 7. In Figs. 4 and 6, the first row is input image. The second row is ground truth image with correct light source color. In Figs. 5 and 7, the first row are our processed results and the second row are gray world algorithm results, the last row are gray edge algorithm results. It can be shown that our results are quite close to ground truth image. In this paper, our algorithm is more related to single illumination color constancy. However, there are much multi-illuminant application in practice. So, we will focus on LBP-based multi-illuminant problem solvent. In some special application, we will try to combine learn-based method to solve practical problem.

4   Conclusion

In this paper, we present a novel color constancy algorithm built on LBP-based illuminant invariant feature selection strategy. We build a sequential framework through introducing LBP and variance statistics. Finally, best selected feature points are forwarded into white balance computation. Experiments demonstrate the effectiveness and efficiency of LBP-based color constancy algorithm.

References

1. Barnard, K., Martin, L., Coath, A., Funt, B.: A comparison of computational color constancy algorithms. ii. experiments with image data. IEEE Trans. Image Process. **11**(9), 985–996 (2002)
2. Gao, S., Yang, K., Li, C., Li, Y.: A color constancy model with double-opponency mechanisms. In: IEEE International Conference on Computer Vision, pp. 929–936. IEEE (2013)
3. Gao, S.-B., Yang, K.-F., Li, C.-Y., Li, Y.-J.: Color constancy using double-opponency. IEEE Trans. Pattern Anal. Mach. Intell. **37**(10), 1973–1985 (2015)

4. Gijsenij, A., Gevers, T., Van De Weijer, J.: Computational color constancy: survey and experiments. IEEE Trans. Image Process. **20**(9), 2475–2489 (2011)
5. Gijsenij, A., Gevers, T., Van DeWeijer, J.: Improving color constancy by photometric edge weighting. IEEE Trans. Pattern Anal. Mach. Intell. **34**(5), 918–929 (2012)
6. Bianco, S., Schettini, R.: Color constancy using faces. In: CVPR (2012)
7. Gijsenij, A., Gevers, T.: Color constancy using natural image statistics and scene semantics. In: TPAMI (2011)
8. Gehler, P., Rother, C., Blake, A., Minka, T., Sharp, T.: Bayesian color constancy revisited. In: CVPR (2008)
9. Taskar, B., Chatalbashev, V., Koller, D., Guestrin, C.: Learning structured prediction models: a large margin approach. In: ICML (2005)
10. Ojala, T., Pietikainen, M., Maenpaa, T.: Multiresolution gray-scale and rotation invariant texture classification with local binary patterns. IEEE Trans. Pattern Anal. Mach. Intell. **24**(7), 971–987 (2002)
11. Tan, R.T., Nishino, K., Ikeuchi, K.: Color constancy through inverse-intensity chromaticity space. JOSA A **21**(3), 321–334 (2004). IICS
12. Buchsbaum, G.: A spatial processor model for object colour perception. J. Franklin Inst. **310**(1), 1–26 (1980). GW
13. Land, E.H., McCann, J.J., et al.: Lightness and retinex theory. J. Opt. Soc. Am. **61**(1), 1–11 (1971). WP
14. Van De Weijer, J., Gevers, T., Gijsenij, A.: Edge-based color constancy. IEEE Trans. Image Process. **16**(9), 2207–2214 (2007). GE

A New Source-Side De-interlacing Method for High Quality Video Content

Yulai Bi$^{(\boxtimes)}$, Xiaoyun Zhang, and Zhiyong Gao

Institue of Image Communication and Network Engineering,
Shanghai Jiao Tong University, Shanghai 200240, China
yulaibi9351@gmail.com, {xiaoyun.zhang,zhiyong.gao}@sjtu.edu.cn

Abstract. Traditionally, de-interlacing is implemented at the terminal-side as a post processing step, however this paper proposes a novel and advanced source-side de-interlacing method for high quality video content. It is an adaptive integration of texture-based intra-interpolation and inter-field motion compensation. Firsty, intra-interpolation based on texture similarity is proposed for wider search scope and better reconstruction performance. Motion compensation is strictly limited by vertical motion conditions and uniform motion check. Then, adaptive intra or inter mode decision is presented to further remove the compensated artifacts. Experiments show that the proposed technique can produce more convincing de-interlaced videos with less artifacts on both subjective and objective evaluation in comparison with other methods, including the leading multimedia tool ffmpeg. The parallelism nature of the proposed technique also makes it suitable for acceleration implementation on GPUs and thus is applicable for real time systems.

Keywords: De-interlacing · Texture-based · Motion compensation · Adaptive integration

1 Introduction

Interlacing was once widely used as the standard of TVbroadcast in analog television systems to meet the limit requests of transmission bandwidth and scanning frequency. De-interlacing is thus a necessary and important technology for displaying interlaced video on progressive scan displays without obvious visual artifacts, such as edge flickers and jagged effects.

In digital television system, the terminal-side de-interlacing has been widely used and implemented in the post-processing chips or set-top boxes. Due to the cost and hardware limitation of terminal devices, most video post-process chips in TVs make a tradeoff between computation complexity and video quality when developing de-interlacing algorithms.

With the development of broadcasting, Internet transmission and display technique, progressive video signal can be transmitted directly and displayed on all kinds of progressive displays. However, there are still a great amount of legacy

© Springer Nature Singapore Pte Ltd. 2017
X. Yang and G. Zhai (Eds.): IFTC 2016, CCIS 685, pp. 12–23, 2017.
DOI: 10.1007/978-981-10-4211-9_2

interlaced video, such as 1080/50i, which are very popular and valuable content for audience. Hence, it is essential and worthwhile to conduct a high-quality de-interlacing process at the source-side, and the de-interlaced progressive video is transmitted and displayed directly for consumers.

Generally, de-interlacing methods can be classified into three categories: intra-field de-interlacing, inter-field de-interlacing, and adaptive de-interlacing. They differ on how spatial and temporal information is exploited to calculate the missing pixels.

The intra-field de-interlacing methods only use the information within the current field to interpolate the missing pixels. A well-known intra-field de-interlacing method is the edge-based line-averaging (ELA) [1], which interpolates the missing pixels after a simple edge direction estimation. It generally provides satisfactory results at the regions where edge detection can be estimated accurately. Many optimized algorithms (eg. [2,3]) based on ELA have been proposed and widely used in early digital televisions because of the low computation. In addition, other intra-field de-interlacing methods based on edge pattern or texture similarity (eg. [4–6]) have also been proposed.

The inter-field de-interlacing methods, also called motion compensation methods (MC), reconstruct the image using temporal information in adjacent fields. In these methods (eg. [7–9]), a local motion vector is first estimated. And temporal interpolation is then performed. However, the motion compensation methods involves a heavy calculation burden, and the quality is not robust since it is difficult to keep the accuracy of motion estimation in rotation, zooming and fast motion scenarios.

The adaptive de-interlacing methods can be sub-classified into two categories: motion adaptive (MA) and motion compensated adaptive (MCA). MA methods exploit inter-field information in static areas and intra-interpolation in moving areas to reconstruct vertical resolution. And MCA (eg. [10–13]) further make use of inter-field information in both statics and some specific moving areas. The key point in adaptive methods is to obtain reliable motion vectors and make mode decision correctly.

In this paper, we propose a novel source-side de-interlacing framework based on software implementation and GPU acceleration for high quality video content application, such as IP-based video on demand. In the proposed method, intra-interpolation is based on local texture similarity, and motion compensation is strictly limited by vertical motion conditions and uniform motion check. More importantly, an adaptive integration based on the reliability of motion compensation is used to further reduce visual artifacts. Experimental results show both subjectively and objectively that the proposed technique can produce convincing de-interlaced videos in comparison with other state-of-art techniques.

This paper is organized as follows. The motivation for the proposed de-interlacing method is discussed in Sect. 2. The proposed algorithm is presented in Sect. 3. Section 4 shows the experimental results. And Sect. 5 gives the conclusion.

2   Motivation

2.1   ELA and Its Jagged Effects

In this section, we introduce the traditional intra-interpolation algorithm, ELA. The ELA-based algorithm is widely used because of its simple calculation. It interpolates the missing pixels using edge directional correlations between two neighboring lines $j - 1$ and $j + 1$. The ELA$5+5$ algorithm using 5 directions is shown in Fig. 1. Pixel $X(i, j)$ represents the missing pixel and is interpolated along the best direction with the smallest difference.

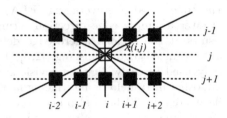

Fig. 1. ELA structure

The ELA method provides a good performance in regions where the edge direction can be detected accurately. However, interpolation errors usually exist since it only focuses on recovering a single pixel that is the most similar to its neighbor pixels without considering the texture structure in its region. And wider search such as 9 directions are generally used for finer edge interpolation in ELA, but it also tend to bring more incorrect results with visual artifacts.

Figure 2 shows a graduated black edge Fig. 10(a), and its interlaced field Fig. 10(b). The white lines represent the missing lines of the current field. Pixel represents the pixel to be interpolated, and a black pixel for is expected according to the ground truth Fig. 10(a). But the ELA algorithm selects a wrong direction along the red line and interpolates a light gray pixel for in Fig. 10(c), which we call jagged effects.

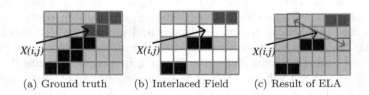

(a) Ground truth   (b) Interlaced Field   (c) Result of ELA

Fig. 2. Jagged effects of ELA (Color figure online)

Thus, in order to avoid jagged effects and get better edge direction estimation with wider search area for small angle edge directions, an intra-interpolation based on texture structural similarity is needed and will be proposed in Sect. 3.1.

2.2   Artifacts Introduced by Motion Compensation

The intra-interpolation can recover the missing pixel lines using the existing pixel lines of the current field. But it may cause blurring and distortion, especially in static areas. Thus motion adaptive is proposed to reconstruct the real missing information in static and slow motion areas using the neighboring fields. The key and difficult point of motion adaptive is to decide whether motion compensation is used. In most adaptive algorithms, the missing pixels are reconstructed by motion compensation if the compensated information is found in the searching scope. And in other regions, intra-interpolation is applied.

Theoretically, the adaptive method provides better performance by using neighboring fields, especially in static and slow motion areas. However, in practice, more artifacts are caused because of the worse robustness in motion compensation. Statistics show that the artifacts are related to the severity of compensation conditions. If we strictly control the compensation conditions, artifacts rate is low, but the compensated information we get is less, and the motion adaptive de-interlacing is basically the same with intra-interpolation de-interlacing. On the contrary, if we relax the conditions, more compensated information can be found, but more artifacts may be introduced. Thus, the accuracy of motion estimation and compensation need to be improved, and a trade-off criterion is required to integrate the intra-interpolation and compensated information adaptively.

3   The Proposed Method

3.1   Texture-Based Intra-interpolation

In order to improve the accuracy of edge estimation, we proposed a new intra-interpolation method using block-based texture similarity, which was first introduced by direction-oriented interpolation (DOI) algorithm [4]. DOI introduces a spatial direction vector (SDV) so that finer resolution and higher accuracy of the edge-direction can be obtained. In Fig. 3, we re-illustrate the concept of SDV and introduce the concepts of upper matching block (UMB) and lower matching block (LMB).

In Fig. 3, the white pixels represent the missing lines, the black and gray pixels represent the reference lines, and the black pixels represent the texture structure. Pixel $X(i,j)$ represents the current pixel to be interpolated. B_X is the local block centered at $X(i,j)$. The blue block upon line $j-3$ and $j-1$, that best matched with B_X, called Upper Matching Block (UMB). The upper SDV, SDV_U (the blue vector), is the vector that points from B_X to UMB. The LMB (the green block) and SDV_L (the green vector) are defined in a similar way.

The UMB and LMB are selected according to the smallest sum of absolute differences (SAD), and then SDV_U and SDV_L are calculated from the location of UMB and LMB. In this framework, more candidate directions can be searched, and 21 candidate directions is used in our algorithm, which can bring much better interpolation results along small angle edges.

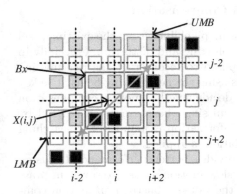

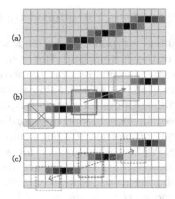

Fig. 3. Intra-texture-interpolation (Color figure online)

Fig. 4. An example at the ends of a line

In case of edge regions, there are two kinds of relationship between these parameters. In normal edge regions like Fig. 3, the directions of SDV_U and SDV_L are nearly opposite, which means the sum of these two vectors is close to 0. In this case, the edge direction is explicitly estimated. And $X(i,j)$ is interpolated according to the direction via Eq. 1.

$$X(i,j) = \frac{1}{2}[X(i+\frac{1}{2}SDV_{Ux}, j-1) + X(i+\frac{1}{2}SDV_{Lx}, j+1)] \tag{1}$$

In some edge regions like Fig. 4, the current block is located near the end of texture. In this case, only UMB (or LMB) can be found, as shown in Fig. 4(b). So SDV_U and SDV_L are absolutely not opposite. Here, we use the estimated direction of the pixels next to it as a reference direction vector (SDV_{ref}), shown in Fig. 4(c). If SDV_U (or SDV_L) is correlated to SDV_{ref}, we interpolate $X(i,j)$ using the SDV_U or SDV_L instead.

The edge direction estimation above is built on the hypothesis of non-horizontal edge regions. By using the texture structural similarity, the edge direction can be estimated more accurately, and the reconstruct performance in non-horizontal edge regions is perfect. However, there still exist horizontal edge regions and smooth regions. Thus, a pre-processing is needed before edge estimation for these regions.

$$X(i,j) = \frac{1}{2}[X(i,j-1) + X(i,j+1)] \tag{2}$$

In edge direction estimation shown in Fig. 3, horizontal edge is ignored. And in horizontal edge regions, no correct similar blocks can be found. So we also need to consider horizontal edge direction before edge estimation by calculating the SAD between current block and the left block (the right block). If SAD_{left} and SAD_{right} are both small enough, then the texture is considered to be horizontal and line averaging in Eq. 2 is applied.

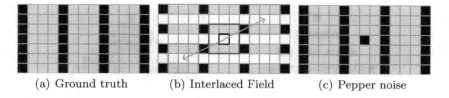

(a) Ground truth   (b) Interlaced Field   (c) Pepper noise

Fig. 5. The salt-and-pepper problem in smooth regions

For smooth regions, edge estimation may cause unwanted pepper noise. As shown in Fig. 5, similar blocks in non-local areas may be found, then wrong edge direction is estimated at a smooth region. In this case, unwanted pepper noise may be interpolated, as shown in Fig. 10(c).

Thus, we calculate the variance within a local region to distinguish smooth area. If the variance is small enough, then we consider it as a smooth region, and $X(i,j)$ is interpolated by region averaging in Eq. 3.

$$X(i,j) = \frac{1}{6} \sum_{k=-1}^{k=1} [X(i+k,j-1) + X(i-k,j+1)] \qquad (3)$$

With the texture based framework above, the proposed methods not only increase the accuracy of direction estimation, but also provide a good framework for wider searching scope, which make it have better performance in both smooth regions and edge regions (including small angle edge regions), without jagged effects in small angle edges and pepper noise in smooth regions.

3.2 Motion Compensation

The texture based intra-interpolation performs well in reconstructing a single interlaced image without jagged effects and pepper noise. However, the problem of edge flickers still exists. The reason lies in the fact that different information may be absent in neighboring odd and even fields, so the texture based intra-interpolation may result different de-interlaced frames for the neighboring odd and even fields. Then edge flicker is caused when watching such de-interlaced frames continuously. Figure 6 shows an example of a stationary texture region with edge flicker.

To solve the problem of edge flickers, motion compensation (MC) algorithm is needed, in which motion estimation and compensation decision are two important parts.

In order to improve the accuracy of motion estimation, many algorithms calculate the sum of absolute difference (SAD) or the mean absolute difference (MAD) between the current block and candidate blocks in the same parity neighboring fields. Different search methods have also been proposed to decrease the computational complexity.

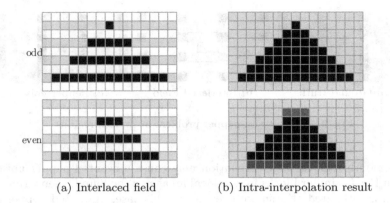

(a) Interlaced field   (b) Intra-interpolation result

Fig. 6. Edge flicker in texture based intra-interpolation

In the proposed algorithm, four neighboring fields are used as reference fields for both backward and forward motion estimations. And we choose full search method for the best results, and the optimal matched block (OMB) in the same parity reference field is selected by the smallest SAD.

As for compensation decision part, a check of whether the motion vector (MV) can be used for compensation is implement. [9,10] proposed a detail analysis of MC principle and we proposed a more effective version based on it, shown in Fig. 7. Figure 7(a) shows the original object.

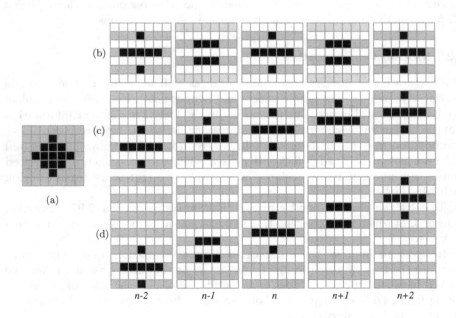

Fig. 7. A detail analysis of MC principle

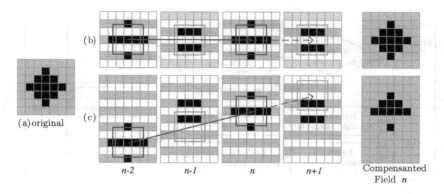

Fig. 8. Uniform motion and non-uniform motion (Color figure online)

We search the OMB for field n in the same parity field $n-2$ (and $n-2$), and calculate MV between field $n-1$ and n (field n and $n+1$). When the vertical motion is even, shown in Fig. 7(b) (vertical motion $= 0$) and Fig. 7(d) (vertical motion $= 2$), then the lost information of current field n can be found in opposite parity field $n-1$ (and $n+1$). This information may help in vertical resolution improvement.

When the vertical motion between field $n-1$ and n (field n and $n+1$) is odd, as shown in Fig. 7(c) (vertical motion $= 1$), then no compensated information can be found since the wanted information has been lost in every field.

For those blocks, which meet vertical motion conditions above, a reliability check of the estimated MV is still needed. The motion estimation and compensation based on a uniform motion is reliable. Figure 8 shows the different backward compensation performance for uniform and non-uniform motion. MV (the red vector) is estimated by the two red matching blocks, and the green block is the compensated information along the estimated MV. The compensation based on uniform motion improves vertical resolution in Fig. 8(b), but the compensation for non-uniform motion just bring artifacts in Fig. 8(c).

In order to check the reliability of the estimated MV, we evaluate the motion consistency by calculating SAD between blocks in field $n-1$ and $n+1$ (the green one and the blue one in Fig. 8) along the estimated MV. If the SAD is smaller than a threshold, the MV is considered to be uniform and thus reliable, and its compensated information can really help in vertical resolution improvement. Otherwise, which means non-uniform motion, the MV is considered to be unreliable and the compensation should be ignored. The threshold depends on a coefficient multiplied SAD between the current block and the OMB (the SAD between two red blocks in Fig. 8). The coefficient should between 1 and 2 [7].

3.3 Overall Algorithm

The flow chart of complete proposed method is shown in Fig. 9. First, the texture-based intra-interpolation is implemented. Then some reliable compensated

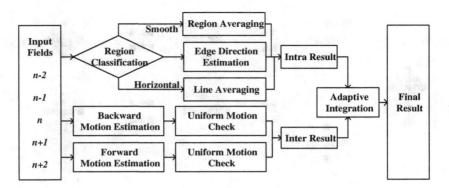

Fig. 9. Flow chart of the proposed method

information is provided via motion estimation and reliability check. Adaptive integration is finally constructed. In order to further reduce the artifacts introduced by motion compensation, we propose an adaptive integration for inter and intra results.

$$X = \omega_{intra}X_{intra} + \omega_{inter}X_{inter} \tag{4}$$

$$\omega_{intra} = \frac{1}{1 + e^{-(\frac{SAD_{OMB}-\mu}{\sigma})}} \tag{5}$$

$$\omega_{inter} = 1 - \omega_{intra} \tag{6}$$

The weights of intra and inter are calculated by the sigmoid function Eqs. 5 and 6. μ is the average SAD that can be accepted, σ controls the steepness of the sigmoid curve. ω_{intra} ranges from 0 to 1. If SAD between OMB and current block is small, which means the reliability of inter results is higher, then ω_{intra} can be set smaller and ω_{inter} can be set larger. Otherwise, ω_{intra} is smaller and ω_{inter} can be set larger. The SAD used here is allocated to every pixels in the block.

The adaptive integration in the proposed framework can not only reconstruct more real missing information, but also keep the robustness of texture-based intra-interpolation, which performs a convincing de-interlacing result.

4 Experimental Results

Several 1080P and 720P 4:2:0 YUV sequences are used to evaluate the performance of proposed method. The progressive sequences are first interlaced and then de-interlaced by six de-interlacing techniques: ELA [1], FuzzyELA [3], DOI [4], FFMC [9], FFMPEG and the proposed algorithm. Several local image details are provided to show subjective comparisons, and the peak signal-to-noise ratio (PSNR) of the major luminance channel Y are used to measure the objective performances.

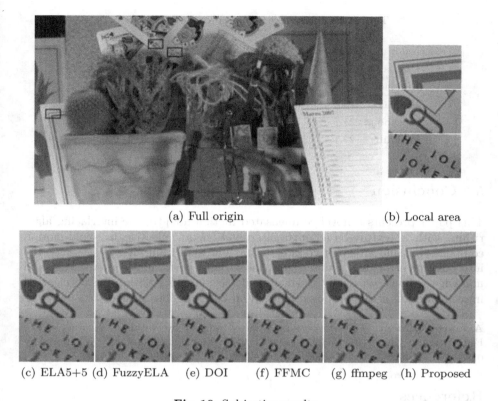

(a) Full origin   (b) Local area

(c) ELA5+5 (d) FuzzyELA   (e) DOI   (f) FFMC   (g) ffmpeg   (h) Proposed

Fig. 10. Subjective results

Figure 10 shows the subjective comparisons in sequence "Cactus". The ELA method has a poor performance even in some obvious edges. FuzzyELA cannot reconstruct the edges with small-angle. DOI performs well at obvious edges but provides poor quality in non-edge regions. FFMC provides a good performance in regions that satisfy motion compensation conditions. FFMPEG performs well in different regions, but jagged artifacts and errors still exists in some obvious edge regions. The proposed method offers the most robust quality in both non-edge and edge regions.

Table 1 shows the objective comparisons of PSNR in five sequences. We can see that the proposed method can achieve gain in PSNR with different level, which has 0 1.8 dB gain when compared with FFMPEG.

The parallelism nature of the proposed framework makes it easy to allow an accelerated implementation on GPU equipment. We have developed an accelerated implementation on GPU "GeForce GTX 750Ti". The experimental results show that at least 10 fields per second can be de-interlaced for 1080i video. Thus a real-time software de-interlacing system is expected on more powerful GPUs.

Table 1. Performance comparation in PSNR(dB)

Name	ELA5+5	FuzzyELA	DOI	FFMC	ffmpeg	Ours
Cactus	32.5	35.6	35.4	36.3	36.0	36.5
Kimono	37.5	42.3	41.9	41.1	41.1	42.4
Mobcal	26.3	33.4	32.4	30.5	31.9	33.7
Stockholm	25.7	30.1	27.9	29.6	30.1	29.9
Parkrun	22.1	25.9	24.2	26.5	26.9	26.9

5   Conclusion

This paper presents a novel compensated motion adaptive de-interlacing algorithm, with a texture-based intra-interpolation, an effective five-field-motion compensation and an adaptive integration. The algorithm further decreases the interpolation errors and artifacts, and has a robust performance in both edge and non-edge regions, especially in small-angle regions. In addition, an accelerated implementation of the proposed method on GPU are also provided.

Acknowledgment. This work was supported in part by National Natural Science Foundation of China (61133009, 61301116, 61221001), the Shanghai Key Laboratory of Digital Media Processing and Transmissions (STCSM 12DZ2272600).

References

1. Kuo, C.J., Liao, C., Lin, C.C.: Adaptive interpolation technique for scanning rate conversion. IEEE Trans. Circ. Syst. Video Technol. **6**(3), 317–321 (1996)
2. Jeon, G., Min, Y.J., Anisetti, M., Bellandi, V., Damiani, E., Jeong, J.: Specification of the geometric regularity model for fuzzy if-then rule-based deinterlacing. J. Disp. Technol. **6**(6), 235–243 (2010)
3. Brox, P., Baturone, I., Sanchez-Solano, S., Gutierrez-Rios, J.: Edge-adaptive spatial video de-interlacing algorithms based on fuzzy logic. IEEE Trans. Consum. Electron. **60**(3), 375–383 (2014)
4. Yoo, H., Jeong, J.: Direction-oriented interpolation and its application to de-interlacing. IEEE Trans. Consum. Electron. **48**(4), 954–962 (2002)
5. Lin, S.F., Chang, Y.L., Chen, L.G.: Motion adaptive de-interlacing by horizontal motion detection and enhanced ela processing. In: International Symposium on Circuits and Systems, pp. II-696–II-699 (2003)
6. Kim, W., Jin, S., Jeong, J.: Novel intra deinterlacing algorithm using content adaptive interpolation. IEEE Trans. Consum. Electron. **53**(3), 1036–1043 (2007)
7. Mohammadi, H.M., Langlois, P., Savaria, Y.: A five-field motion compensated deinterlacing method based on vertical motion. IEEE Trans. Consum. Electron. **53**(3), 1117–1124 (2007)
8. Ding, Y., Yan, X.: A robust motion estimation with center-biased diamond search and its parallel architecture for motion-compensated de-interlace. J. Supercomput. **58**(1), 68–83 (2011)

9. Mohammadi, H.M., Savaria, Y., Langlois, J.M.P.: Enhanced motion compensated deinterlacing algorithm. IET Image Process. **6**(8), 1041–1048 (2012)
10. Chang, Y.L., Chen, C.Y., Lin, S.F., Chen, L.G.: Four field variable block size motion compensated adaptive de-interlacing, vol. 2, pp. ii/913–ii/916 (2005)
11. Chang, Y.L., Lin, S.F., Chen, C.Y., Chen, L.G.: Video de-interlacing by adaptive 4-field global/local motion compensated approach. IEEE Trans. Circ. Syst. Video Technol. **15**(12), 1569–1582 (2006)
12. Sun, H., Liu, Y., Zheng, N., Zhang, T.: Motion compensation aided motion adaptive de-interlacing for real-time video processing applications. In: Conference on Circuits, pp. 1523–1527 (2008)
13. Trocan, M., Mikovicova, B., Zhanguzin, D.: An adaptive motion-compensated approach for video deinterlacing. Multimedia Tools Appl. **61**(3), 819–837 (2011)

Accelerating Digital Watermarking Algorithm Based on SOC

Jing Chen, Hong Fan[✉], Yanzi Sun, and Haiquan Ma

Engineering Research Center of Digitized Textile and Fashion Technology,
College of Information Science and Technology, Ministry of Education,
Donghua University, Shanghai 201620, China
dhfanhong@dhu.edu.cn

Abstract. This paper mainly researches the accelerating digital watermarking algorithm based on SOC. A digital watermarking system for software and hardware co-design is built by Xilinx high level synthesis tool HLS. DCT/IDCT algorithm is programmed by C++ language. After simulation and synthesis, HLS generates RTL code suitable for either ASIC or FPGA synthesis tools. 86.5% of the delay time is saved by optimizing the design. The hardware acceleration is realized by parallel processing, which is increasing the hardware design cost to improve the processing performance of time. The utilization of hardware system is improved by pipeline, the waiting time is reduced and each hardware module is in high efficiency. DCT-based invisible digital watermarking system IP core on SOC becomes the ideal choice for embedded real-time visual surveillance system for it can make use of existing manufacturing processes, and the hardware implementation of the system execution speed about 200 times higher than that of software.

Keywords: High-level synthesis · DCT/IDCT · Transformation matrix · Invisible watermarking · Hardware acceleration

1 Introduction

Digital watermarking is some special information, such as serial numbers, meaningful text, logos and so on, embedded in digital image, video and audio by some algorithm so as to identify the copyright. It does not affect the original information, also is not easy to be detected by others. As an effective means of digital copyright and data security protection, it has become a major branch in the field of Information hiding. Besides the software, large amount of data from the multimedia information intercommunion can also be processed by hardware. Real-time processing and high speed of processing makes hardware processing got attention. SOC is called system-on-a-chip, also known as the on-chip System. Parallel processing makes Field programmable gate array (FPGA) a huge advantage in speed. In order to implement an image processing algorithm on an FPGA, need to determine the underlying architecture of an algorithm, map the

© Springer Nature Singapore Pte Ltd. 2017
X. Yang and G. Zhai (Eds.): IFTC 2016, CCIS 685, pp. 24–33, 2017.
DOI: 10.1007/978-981-10-4211-9_3

architecture onto available resources within an FPGA and finally map the algorithm onto the hardware architecture [1]. Enough resources on FPGA ensure that the whole application can be implemented on SOC and the hardware/software co-design makes it become the ideal choice for embedded real-time vision system.

Vivado HLS (High-level synthesis) as a development tool which is launched by Xilinx is used in this paper, and the HLS tool can transfer the design written by C and C++ into RTL code directly. It can greatly accelerate development cycles on FPGA. DCT algorithm is used on digital watermarking system based on SOC. The DCT/IDCT IP core programmed by c++ language can help to embed invisible watermarking. The digital watermarking system runs on Zynq board xc7z010clg400-1, and compares the processing time with software implementation.

2   Digital Watermarking Technology

Digital watermark is a kind of information hiding, in order to identify the special information of the product. Under the environment of network, digital watermarking technology can be an effectual means about digital media copyright protection, data authentication and data hiding. According to the domain watermark embedded, watermarking can be divided into spatial domain algorithm and transform domain algorithm. Spatial domain techniques which implemented easier has fragile robustness in disadvantage, and it belongs to the visible watermark. Transform domain technology with better robustness has higher computational complexity, and it belongs to the invisible watermarking. A digital watermarking system usually consists of the watermark embedding system and watermark extraction system. Watermark embedding system is that the encrypted watermark information embeds into source data through embedding algorithm and generates the watermarked data. While, the watermark extraction system is that watermark is extracted from watermarked data by the watermark extraction algorithm. In this paper, both spatial domain and transform domain digital watermarking algorithm based on SOC are studied.

3   Theory of DCT Transformation

In this paper, discrete cosine transform, one of the most common linear transformation in the digital signal processing is used in digital watermarking system. It results in energy concentration after transformation, and has a good compression ability and reduce correlation [2]. The 8×8 two-dimensional DCT transform is often adopted in digital image processing.

3.1   Theory of 8×8 2-D DCT Transformation

Two dimensional DCT transform can be realized directly by the two-dimensional calculation formula, also can be realized by one-dimensional transformation in twice [3]. The IP core designed in this paper is realized by one-dimensional transformation in twice. It means a one-dimensional DCT transform for rows firstly, and then one-dimensional DCT transform for columns.

The one dimensional DCT is defined as:

$$X(t) = \sqrt{\frac{2}{N}} B(k) \sum_{n=0}^{N-1} x(n) \cos \frac{(2n+1)k\pi}{2N}, \ 0 \le k \le N-1 \tag{1}$$

And the one dimensional IDCT is defined as:

$$x(n) = \sqrt{\frac{2}{N}} \sum_{n=0}^{N-1} B(k)X(k) \cos \frac{(2n+1)k\pi}{2N}, \ 0 \le n \le N-1 \tag{2}$$

where, $B(k) = \frac{1}{\sqrt{2}}$, when $k = 0$, and $B(k) = 1$, when $k = others$.

For two dimensional DCT, the following calculation formulas are used:

$$X(u,v) = \frac{1}{N} C(u)C(v) \sum_{i=0}^{N-1} \sum_{j=0}^{N-1} x(i,j) \cos \frac{(2i+1)u\pi}{2N} \cos \frac{(2j+1)v\pi}{2N} \tag{3}$$

$$x(i,j) = \frac{1}{N} \sum_{u=0}^{N-1} \sum_{v=0}^{N-1} C(u)C(v)X(u,v) \cos \frac{(2i+1)u\pi}{2N} \cos \frac{(2j+1)v\pi}{2N} \tag{4}$$

where, $C(u), C(v) = \frac{1}{\sqrt{N}}$, when $u, v = 0$, and $C(u), C(v) = \frac{2}{\sqrt{N}}$, when $k = others$.

3.2 Matrix Implementation of DCT Transformation

In this paper, the design of the IP DCT/IDCT core is based on the matrix, the specific principles are as follows:

Positive transformation:

$$F = AfA^T \tag{5}$$

Because A is an orthogonal matrix, so $A^{-1} = A^T, f = A^{-1}F(A^T)^{-1}$ can be introduced.

Inverse transformation:

$$f = A^T FA \tag{6}$$

3.3 Invisible Watermarking Evaluation

The quality of the image which has been embedded watermarking image should evaluate from objective and subjective. Subjective evaluation mainly depends on the visual observation before and after the embedded images. Objective evaluation requires some objective data for analysis. We use PSNR (peak signal to noise ratio) indicates the effect of watermarking.

$$PSNR = 10 * log_{10} \frac{M * N * 255 * 255}{\sum_{i=0}^{M-1} \sum_{j=0}^{N-1} [f(x,y) - f'(x,y)]^2} \tag{7}$$

Where, $f(x, y)$ is the pixel value in location (x, y) in the original image, $f'(x, y)$ is the pixel value in location (x, y) in the embedded image. M and N means M rows and N columns. The value of PSNR is bigger, the better the embedding effect. Generally, values over 36 dB in PSNR are acceptable in terms of degradation, which means no significant degradation is observed by the human eye.

4   Introduction of Vivado HLS

Vivado suite design, a FPGA integration design environment, was launched by Xilinx company in 2012. The Xilinx Vivado High-Level Synthesis tool, one of the tool of Vivado, can transform a C specification into a register transfer level (RTL) implementation, then it can synthesize into a Xilinx FPGA. Programming with C, C++, SystemC greatly shorten the product development, can greatly improve the efficiency of using FPGA development [4].

For Vivado HLS tool development process, firstly using C or C++ language to design a specific function and a C test bench used to describe the expected design. Secondly to Run C Simulation to check whether the function meet the requirements. Then using Vivado HLS tool to generate corresponding functional RTL design, and the Verilog and VHDL code is under the syn folder. At last using Vivado simulation tool or the Modelsim to verify the architecture of the behavior and function design [5].

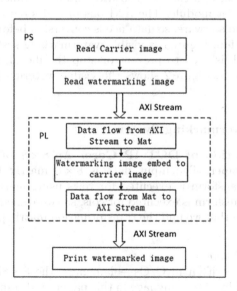

Fig. 1. Visible watermarking system

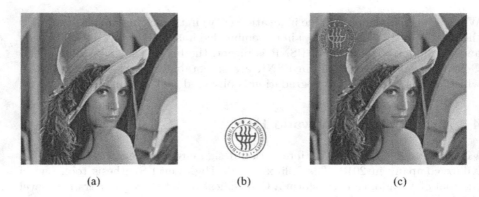

(a)   (b)   (c)

Fig. 2. Superimposition effect of visible watermark: (a) original image; (b) watermarking image; (c) watermarked image

5   Experiments and Analysis

5.1   Visible Watermarking System

To set up a visible watermarking system on the SOC, the watermarking image is embedded into the carrier image. The system mainly includes visible watermarking algorithm based on the superposition, input module, data flow conversion module and output module. The AXI bus provides data flow transmission between hardware and software, so data needs conversion before and after visible watermarking algorithm. Figure 1 is visible watermarking system.

Visible watermark is used to prevent or stop the illegal use of copyrighted image graphic products. Figure 2 shows the visible watermark superimposition effect.

5.2   Invisible Watermarking System

Design and Validation of DCT IP Core. An 8×8 DCT/IDCT IP core is realized in this paper. The input data is 8×8 matrix block, firstly one-dimensional DCT transform is executed for rows using matrix, and then one-dimensional DCT transform is executed for cols, so two-dimensional DCT transform is realized. From that we find the transformation matrix plays a very important role.

(1) HLS to design IP core

HLS can be directly written in C/C++ language, the 8×8DCT algorithm is directly programmed by C++ language in this paper, and commands (Directive) are added to optimize its performance. Create a new vivado HLS project and add the core module of the C++ code in the source column, the core module can realize that to (a) read a 8×8 matrix; (b) one-dimensional DCT transform for rows, input matrix is multiplied by the matrix transformation; (c) repeat step

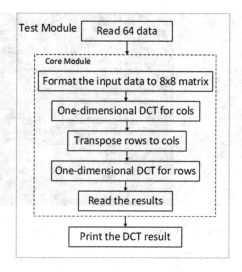

Fig. 3. Core algorithm flow chart

b for cols. Add the test module of the C++ code in the Bench Test. It is used to read the 64 data, and transfer it to the core module, the flow chart shows in Fig. 3:

(2) Design of Transform Matrix
Transformation matrix plays an important role in DCT transform. It is an 8×8 matrix which can be calculated by the following formula:

$$A = \sqrt{\frac{2}{N}} \begin{bmatrix} \sqrt{\frac{1}{2}} & \cdots & \sqrt{\frac{1}{2}} \\ \vdots & \ddots & \vdots \\ \cos\frac{(N-1)\pi}{2N} & \cdots & \cos\frac{(2N-1)(2N-1)\pi}{2N} \end{bmatrix} \tag{8}$$

From the formula, we can know that the range of matrix A depends on the range of cos. When the data are multiplied twice, the value of the data will be smaller because cos is range from $[-1, 1]$. The data transport from one part to another part, it will format the data via throw away some scattered numbers. So that the accuracy of the final processing results greatly reduced. In order to comply with the idea of hardware processing, improve the accuracy of data processing, reduce the data loss, we decide to enlarge transform matrix, and after the calculation reducing the final result to ensure correctness of results.

Implementation and Verification of IP Core. After C simulation and RTL synthesis, it can use Run C/RTL Consimulation to call Modelsim to generate waveform as shown Fig. 4: The results of DCT transform are shown in Fig. 5. From Fig. 5(a), value which locates in the upper left corner in the results of DCT

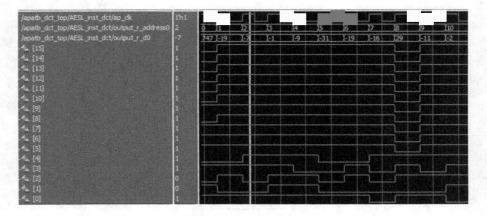

Fig. 4. Waveform display in decimal

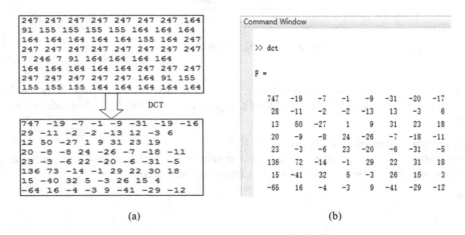

(a)   (b)

Fig. 5. Results of data transformation

transformation is bigger and it means more energy there. The results executes in Matlab with the same input data is similar with results from HLS, Fig. 5(b) is the calculation result of the Matlab.

Optimization for IP Core. Add the PIPELINE command to the outer loop in DCT algorithm, which can transfer the serial execution into parallel execution in each unit of time to increase the flow of data and then affect the running time. Then add ARRAY optimization command to array, the array is realized in RAM. The array is divided into single component, the dual port RAM can provide better traffic. Pipelining can improve the utilization rate of the hardware system and also reduce the waiting time, so it ensures that each hardware module in the high efficiency [6].

Table 1. Contrast of latency

	Before optimization	After optimization
Latency	3959	535

Table 2. Contrast of resources occupancy

	Before optimization	After optimization
BRAM-18K	5	22
DSP48E	1	16
FF	272	2179
LUT	354	5200

Table 1 shows the contrast of latency before and after optimization, Table 2 lists the resource occupancy before and after optimization. BRAM-18K is embedded block RAM, it is often configured as single port RAM, dual port RAM, content address memory (CAM) and FIFO storage structure, and dual port RAM is used in this paper; DSP48E is mainly used as multiplier and divider; FF is trigger; LUT is a lookup table, which is used as the trigger and the latch to execute addition and subtraction. After optimization delay greatly reduced, and saved nearly 86.5%, while resources occupancy rate become higher. The resources are used to save time.

Invisible Watermarking System. An invisible digital watermarking system is set up on the SOC with DCT transform. Firstly divided carrier image into 8×8 pixels block, secondly the DCT IP core is used to convert the image to the frequency domain, then embed watermarking image to carrier image, next IDCT IP core is used to convert image back to the time domain. The result of watermark embedding is shown in Fig. 6.

PSNR between carrier image and the watermarked image is 40.4893, as generally, values over 36 dB in PSNR are acceptable in terms of degradation, which means no significant degradation is observed by the human eye. And C and RTL Consimulation costs 5505400 ps, while time of executing dct in the Matlab is 1.155694 s. Obviously the digital watermarking system based on SOC runs 200 times faster than software. The DCT based on SOC IP core design can use the existing manufacturing process to get the optimal solution to satisfy all constraint.

5.3 Comparison and Analysis

The resources occupancy about visible watermarking system and invisible watermarking system are shown in Table 3.

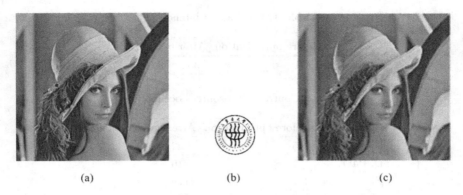

(a)   (b)   (c)

Fig. 6. Superimposition effect of invisible watermark: (a) original image; (b) watermarking image; (c) watermarked image

Table 3. Resources occupancy about visible and invisible watermarking system

	Visible	Invisible
BRAM-18K	0	22
DSP48E	3	16
FF	691	2179
LUT	922	5200

The resources costs in visible watermark is the processing of embed, while DCT transform needs more resources besides embedding in invisible watermarking system. Computation of matrix multiplication is the main part of the consumption of resources, so the invisible watermarking system consume more resources.

6   Conclusion

Digital watermarking accelerated algorithm based on SOC implemented by Vivado HLS tool. DCT and IDCT algorithm programmed by C/C++ language is converted to the RTL code. The RTL code is encapsulated into the IP core after simulation and optimization. HLS plays an important role to shorten the design cycle. Digital watermarking system based on SOC runs faster than the software implementation as well as its better real-time performance. Parallel processing speeds up the system and also causes the cost of hardware resource. The method of hardware and software co-design fully embodies the advantages of SOC.

References

1. Zhao, W., He, H.: FPGA-based video image processing system research. In: IEEE International Conference on Computer Science and Information Technology, vol. 147, pp. 680–682 (2010)
2. Baba, S.E.I., Krikor, L.Z., Arif, T., et al.: Watermarking of digital images in frequency domain. Int. J. Autom. Comput. **7**(1), 17–22 (2010)
3. Dexue, Z., Tao, F.: Design of 2-D DCT IP core based on FPGA. Microcomput. Inf. **26**(14), 23–25 (2015)
4. Juntao, Z., Yuanwei, W., Duo, P.: A method to accelerate the OpenCV program in image processing. Microcomput. Its Appl. **34**(22), 41–43 (2015)
5. ug902-vivado-high-level-synthesis. www.xilinx.com
6. ug871-vivado-high-level-synthesis-tutorial. www.xilinx.com

Scrolling Subtitle Processing of Frame Rate Up-Conversion Based on Global Text Motion Estimation

Guirui Li$^{(\boxtimes)}$, Xiaoyun Zhang, and Zhiyong Gao

Institute of Image Communication and Network Engineering,
Shanghai Jiao Tong University, Shanghai 200240, China
{lgrsjtu,xiaoyun.zhang,zhiyong.gao}@sjtu.edu.cn

Abstract. Motion compensated frame rate up-conversion (MC-FRUC) is a popular practical video processing technique to increase frame rate, which mainly composes of motion estimation (ME) and motion compensated frame interpolation (MCFI). However, for scrolling text embedded in videos, such as subtitle or scrolling TV news, ME usually fails to produce true trajectory when the scrolling motion of subtitle is irrelevance with background's movements. In this paper, we propose an effective scrolling subtitle post-processing technique to reduce artifacts such as text broken and motion blur around subtitle regions. True global text motion estimation is put forward to predict the motion vector of subtitle after detecting the text area in the intermediate frame. Finally, a fusion of subtitle and background method is proposed to obtain a correct intermediate frame. Experimental results show that the proposed algorithm can significantly reduce the broken artifact with low complexity.

Keywords: Frame rate up-conversion (FRUC) · Scrolling subtitle · Global text motion estimation · Motion compensation

1 Introduction

With the development of high definition (HD) video service and the progress in display technologies, high frame rate becomes a key element for high quality displaying. However, videos may be encoded at a low frame rate because of the limited transmission bandwidth, and are needed to be converted to a higher frame rate before displaying. Frame rate up-conversion (FRUC) is widely used for increasing frame rate by inserting new frames into the original moving sequence.

There are some simple approaches to achieve FRUC, such as frame repetition (FR) and frame linear interpolation (FA), but they do not utilize the motion of objects and cause artifacts like motion blur. Motion compensated frame rate up conversion (MC-FRUC) exploits the motion information between the previous and next reference frames to improve the accuracy of motion trajectories and achieve a higher video quality. A typical MC-FRUC algorithm generally consists of two stages: Motion estimation (ME) and Motion interpolation (MCFI). In the

© Springer Nature Singapore Pte Ltd. 2017
X. Yang and G. Zhai (Eds.): IFTC 2016, CCIS 685, pp. 34–43, 2017.
DOI: 10.1007/978-981-10-4211-9_4

ME process, the motion vectors (MV) are determined by using the unilateral or bilateral block matching (BM) methods. Then MCFI uses the estimated MVs to construct a new intermediate frame. Nowadays, many algorithms based on MC-FRUC [1–5] have been proposed. For example, Haan et al. [1] addressed to improve the accuracy of MV, blocking artifact has been reduced in [2,3], and halo effect at occlusion areas has been studied in [4,5]. Besides the problems mentioned above, scrolling subtitle is also a critical issue for high subjective quality.

In practical applications, subtitle is the text added to the videos or TV programs in post-production to display the content of the voice messages in caption format. These text information aims at helping the viewers understand the messages delivered by the video scenarios. For example, foreign language can be displayed in subtitle form after being transmitted. However, from the perspective of FRUC, there is little motion correlation between the subtitle and the original video content because the subtitle is added by post-production. So the text blocks's MVs obtained by ME based on spatial and temporal correlation are likely to be incorrect. And the intermediate frames will be interpolated with subtitle broken or motion blur.

Several subtitle processing methods for FRUC have been proposed to improve visual quality in text areas. In [6,7], stationary subtitle correction algorithms are proposed. In [6], the motion vectors of the text blocks are changed to be zero. Although it fixes motion vectors of the blocks with stationary text, severe artifacts may occur in moving background. A pre-post processing algorithm with stationary subtitle detection and in-painting is proposed in [7], which erases the stationary subtitle to do ME and MCFI. Then the intermediate frame is overlaid with subtitle at last. A horizontal scrolling text processing method proposed in [8] utilized the text detection method but it neglected the complex moving background.

In this paper, a low complexity post-processing algorithm is proposed to deal with the scrolling subtitle problem with complex motion background. Firstly, the scrolling text location in the intermediate frame will be detected. After that, true global text motion estimation will be proposed to predict subtitle's motion trajectory. Finally, the final intermediate frames are obtained by combining the initial interpolated background with the complete subtitle.

This paper is organized as follows. In Sect. 2, the motion estimation in the subtitle area is investigated and analyzed. And the proposed algorithm for FRUC with subtitle processing is presented in Sect. 3. Then Sect. 4 shows the experimental results and assesses the performance of the proposed algorithm using subjective and objective evaluations. Finally, the conclusion is drawn in Sect. 5.

2   Analysis of the Motion Estimation

Motion estimation (ME) is an extremely important process to approximate the true motions between consecutive frames. Bilateral or unilateral block matching methods are always conducted in ME stage because of the low computational complexity.

In our ME process, motion vectors for intermediate frames are predicted through bilateral motion estimation (BME) [9] which utilizes the spatial and temporal information. Specifically, the motion vector is obtained by comparing the matching blocks in previous and next reference frames. And it is important to note that a block's MV is initially estimated by searching for neighboring blocks' MV as its candidates. We compute the sum of bilateral absolute differences (SBAD) to measure the reliability of the motion vectors. The candidate that is closer to the true MV usually have smaller SBAD in probability.

Let $B_{i,j}$ denote a block in the intermediate frame and m is a pixel in that block, f_n and f_{n+1} are the two reference frames. For the candidate motion vector v, SBAD is calculated as:

$$SBAD(B_{i,j}, v) = \sum_{m \in B_{i,j}} |f_n(m - v) - f_{n+1}(m + v)| \tag{1}$$

BME can provide acceptable motion vectors when the video sequence contain simple motions. However, it does not trace reliable motion trajectories in the scrolling subtitle areas where blocks with text or without text both exist. Generally, subtitle's scrolling orientation is little correlated with background's moving direction as the subtitle is added by post-production. The candidate MV set for a text block usually contains background's MV. And the BME process usually results in incorrect MVs which do not track the true scrolling trajectory for subtitle.

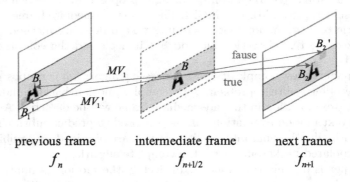

previous frame　　　intermediate frame　　　next frame
f_n　　　　　　　$f_{n+1/2}$　　　　　　　f_{n+1}

Fig. 1. Bilateral motion estimation for a subtitle block

As illustrated in Fig. 1, B is a text block in intermediate frame, MV_1' and MV_1 are the candidate MVs, $B_1'(B_1)$ and $B_2'(B_2)$ are the corresponding matching blocks in previous frame and next frame respectively. MV_1' will be determined as the optimal MV for block B when the SBAD value of MV_1' is the smallest. In that case, the true MV_1 will not be chosen. So it is difficult to track the true scrolling trajectory of subtitle even if the correct MV is included in the candidate set. Consequently, the subtitle will be interpolated broken. For

Fig. 2. Subtitle interpolation with traditional FRUC algorithm

example, a portion of the letter "A" was interpolated with background's pixels and resulting in text broken.

An interpolation result for subtitle areas with the estimated MVs is presented in Fig. 2. In this video, the background is moving right and the subtitle is scrolling horizontally from right to left. So the scrolling motion of subtitle is weakly correlated with the movement of background. The broken text is interpolated with bilateral ME and MCFI which did not consider the problem of scrolling subtitle. The MVs in "area 1" denote the background's motion. Text in "area 2" is complete with correct MVs and is broken in "area 3" with inaccurate motions. It is pretty clear from the vector plots in "area 3" that the motion vectors estimated for these text blocks are misled by background's MVs in "area 1". In summary, motion vectors estimated with traditional BME methods could not correctly approximate the true motions of the text.

3   The Proposed Algorithm

The proposed FRUC algorithm is dedicated to improve the performance of the motion estimation and the interpolation in the subtitle areas. Figure 3 shows the proposed FRUC system. Firstly, using the information in previous and next reference frame, the bilateral motion estimation method is performed to predict the motion vectors for the intermediate frame. In this process, the MVs for text blocks may be wrongly estimated. So the true global text motion estimation is proposed to predict the motion trajectory of the text after detecting the subtitle in the intermediate frame. Finally, the proposed motion compensation is executed by a two-stage interpolation in the subtitle area. The subtitle and background are interpolated respectively to minimize the interference with each other. And the final intermediate frames are the background interpolation results overlaid with the complete subtitle.

Compared with the traditional FRUC algorithms, the proposed algorithm employs the global text motion estimation and two-pass compensation techniques. The global text motion vector extracted for the moving subtitle improves the reliability of the BME method. And thus leads to better subtitle interpolation.

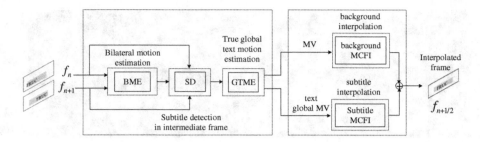

Fig. 3. The proposed FRUC system

3.1   Subtitle area detection

For videos with scrolling subtitle, we could not locate the text blocks directly within the intermediate frame since this frame does not exist originally. So the traditional text detection techniques, such as texture-based and edge-based techniques, could not be applied to identify text blocks. In our algorithm, motion irrelevance and subtitle's features are combined to locate subtitle area in the intermediate frame.

Text blocks and background blocks are likely spatial neighborhood. So the candidate MV set initialized for a text block usually contains the background's MV. But the motion of the text is irrelevance with background's movement. Besides, text blocks probably contain more complex texture than background blocks. Thus larger SBAD values are produced in these areas. And it is easy to mark some text blocks whose spatial candidate MVs and the final determined MV have larger SBAD values than a threshold. Therefore, we can obtain the initial marking area which contains the incorrect text blocks in intermediate frames.

In addition, scrolling features of subtitle can be adopted to obtain a more accurate location. First of all, it is assumed that the luminance value of subtitle is unified and visually recognizable from the background. Moreover, the scrolling subtitle generally appears in consecutive frames with the location area remaining unchanged. If a block is marked in the intermediate frame in a block row X, we will check the blocks of the same row in previous and next reference frames. The row X will be identified as the subtitle area when it contains text blocks in both two reference frames. And this block row X is detected as subtitle area in the intermediate frame.

3.2   True global text motion estimation

As shown in Fig. 2, the pixels of the text area may be well interpolated or badly interpolated by traditional BME algorithm. Although not all the motion vectors for text area are correct, there still exist true motion vectors among them. So it is feasible to extract the true MVs for text blocks in the text area.

Moreover, subtitle generally appears in consecutive frames with scrolling. It should also be noted that the scrolling motion of subtitle is global. So a global motion vector could be estimated for all of the text blocks. And there is only one global motion which can represent the true scrolling movement. We refer to this global motion as GTMV (global text motion vector) in our algorithm.

ME results for text blocks in Fig. 2 are exploited to conduct a statistical analysis shown in Fig. 4. In the horizontal scrolling subtitle applications, the vertical component of MVs for text blocks approximate zero. So we performed the statistics with horizontal component of MVs.

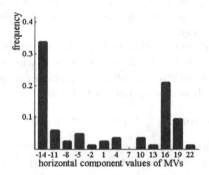

Fig. 4. Frequency statistics of text blocks MVs

In Fig. 4, the x-coordinate describes the horizontal component of MVs while the y-coordinate is the corresponding frequency for each MV. After the statistics, the top n MVs with highest frequency are obtained. And these MVs can constitute a candidate set for GTMV, denoted as $GMV_i (i = 1, 2, ...n)$. For a text block in the intermediate frame, its matched blocks in previous and next frames should also be text blocks. Besides, the SBAD can be calculated to measure the reliability of the motion vectors. If MV is closer to the true motion, the SBAD will have smaller value. Therefore, for each candidate GMV_i, the reliability $R(i)$ is calculated to measure which candidate is the global motion of text. And the GTMV is determined by minimizing $R(i)$.

$$R(i) = \frac{SBAD(i)}{C(i) + \varepsilon} \ (i = 1, 2, ...n) \tag{2}$$

$$C(i) = \frac{M_{i,p} + M_{i,n}}{2 * N * N} \ (i = 1, 2, ...n) \tag{3}$$

where $i = 1, 2, ...n$ represents that there are n candidates for GTMV. $N*N$ is the total text pixel number in a block. $M_{i,p}$ and $M_{i,n}$ are the text pixel number in the block of previous frame and next frame respectively with candidate GMV_i. $C(i)$ is computed to illustrate the confidence of whether the matching block is text or not. $SBAD(i)$ denotes the SBAD value for the candidate GMV_i. And ε is a smoothing parameter to avoid singular value of $C(i)$.

3.3 MCFI in Subtitle Area

In subtitle area, there is no guarantee whether a block-based FRUC algorithm could perfectly divides the text and background pixels into different blocks. For a text block in which the non-text pixels account for a large proportion, the movement of the non-text part is inconsistent with the motion of scrolling text. Hence, the text block may be interpolated partly broken because the GTMV is accepted as its optimal MV. Therefore the incomplete separation decreases the visual quality of interpolated frames.

As we mentioned above, it is difficult to construct complete subtitle and background in a single-pass MCFI with block-based ME and MC. In our proposed system, we conduct a two-pass compensation for the subtitle pixels and the background respectively.

The proposed global text motion estimation has improved the accuracy of the motion vectors for text blocks. So complete subtitle pixels should be interpolated with GTMV. We utilize the bilateral motion compensation to generate intermediate frame which is determined as follows:

$$f_{n+1/2}(m) = \frac{1}{2}[f_n(m - v) + f_{n+1}(m + v)] \qquad (4)$$

where f_n and f_{n+1} are the previous and next reference frames, $f_{n+1/2}$ is the intermediate frame, v represent the MV used to interpolate new frames.

Using the previous and next reference frames, the motion compensation for subtitle pixels can be conducted subsequently with the true global text motion vectors. And the integrity of subtitle can be well guaranteed.

The incomplete separation between the text and the background may lead to broken background even if text pixels have been well interpolated with GTMV. So a special motion compensation for the background around subtitle is particularly essential. Because the background is covered by text pixels, it should be reconstructed with reference frames whose subtitle is removed. The holes left by removed text can be replaced with the spatial information provided by pixels around subtitle. In order to avoid a blurry in-painting result, we utilize the directional interpolation method proposed in [10]. The information on local edges and textures will be extracted within blocks and then used for filling the text pixels.

After subtitle removing and in-painting, the subtitle pixels' damage on background can be effectively eliminated. Then the background can be interpolated with the regular MCFI as shown in (4).

The final intermediate frames are the background interpolation results overlaid with the complete subtitle. Therefore, the proposed interpolation method has two advantages which come from its complete background and the appropriate subtitle attributes.

4 Experiment

In order to demonstrate the performance of our method, we use the HD(1920 * 1080) test sequences with scrolling subtitle and moving background.

The experiment results are examined in comparison with the traditional FRUC method which does not consider the scrolling subtitle problem.

One of the compared results with and without scrolling subtitle processing algorithm is depicted in Fig. 5. The sequence "CMO" contains scrolling subtitle and moving background. The two motions are inconsistent with each other.

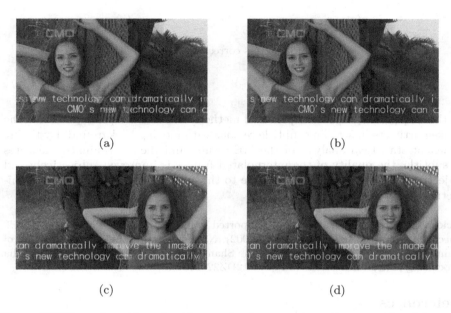

(a)   (b)

(c)   (d)

Fig. 5. FRUC results with and without subtitle processing. The interpolated frames with traditional FRUC method are shown in left column and improved ones using the proposed algorithm are shown in the right. (a) (PSNR = 27.94) and (b) (PSNR = 28.75) are reconstructed frames of 28th. (c) (PSNR = 27.65) and (d) (PSNR = 28.93) are reconstructed frames of 58th.

As shown in Fig. 5(a) and (c), the interpolated subtitle has a poor visual quality. Some of the texts, such as "technology" and "can", are broken since they are interpolated with background's pixels rather than the text pixels. The subtitle information has been damaged severely which affects the visual experience. In Fig. 5(b) and (d), the proposed algorithm achieves considerable improvement on the completeness of subtitle. Besides, it also demonstrates that the proposed algorithm provides a better quality objectively by an average 1 dB gain in PSNR.

Figure 6 presents the text processing results for some letters. Letters "improve" and "technology" are partly broken or fuzzy when using traditional FRUC. With the proposed subtitle processing method, letters are interpolated completely and clearly.

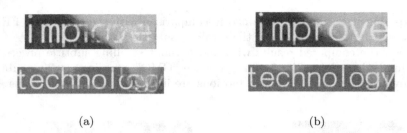

(a)   (b)

Fig. 6. Letters correction results

5   Conclusion

In this paper, we proposed a practical method with low complexity to solve the broken artifacts in scrolling subtitle regions with moving background. By taking sufficient statistical analysis of the ME results and the discriminative features of subtitle, the quality of the interpolated frames is improved subjectively and objectively. Moreover, it is compatible to the current block-based FRUC architecture.

Acknowledgment. This work was supported in part by Chinese National Key S&T Special Program (2013ZX01033001-002-002), National Natural Science Foundation of China (6113300961221001, 61301116), the Shanghai Key Laboratory of Digital Media Processing and Transmissions (STCSM 12DZ2272600).

References

1. de Haan, P.W.G., Biezen, H.H., Ojo, O.A.: True-motion estimation with 3-D recursive search block matching. IEEE Trans. Circ. Syst. Video Technol. **3**(5), 368–379 (1993)
2. Choi, B.D., Han, J.W., Kim, C.S.K., Ko, S.J.: Overlapped block motion compensation: an estimation-theoretic approach. IEEE Trans. Image Process. **3**(9), 693–699 (1994)
3. Choi, B.D., Han, J.W., Kim, C.S., Ko, S.J.: Motion compensated frame interpolation using bilateral motion estimation and adaptive overlapped block motion compensation. IEEE Trans. Circ. Syst. Video Technol. **17**(4), 407–416 (2007)
4. Bellers, E.B., van Gurp, J.W., Janssen, J.G.W.M., Braspenning, J.R., Wittebrood, R.: Solving occlusion in frame-rate up-conversion. In: Proceedings of IEEE International Conference on Consumer Electronics, pp. 1–2 (2007)
5. Hong, W.: Low-complexity occlusion handling for motion-compensated frame rate up-conversion. In: Proceedings of IEEE International Conference on Consumer Electronics, pp. 1–2 (2009)
6. Kang, S.J., Yoo, D.G., Lee, S.K., Kim, Y.H.: Multiframe-based bilateral motion estimation with emphasis on stationary caption processing for frame rate up-conversion. IEEE Trans. Consum. Electron. **54**(4), 1830–1838 (2008)
7. Guo, Z.Y., Gao, L.C.: Stationary subtitle processing for real-time frame rate up-conversion. In: Proceedings of IEEE International Symposium on Broadband Multimedia Systems and Broadcasting, pp. 1–4 (2013)

8. Gim, G.Y., Kim, Y.J., Ahn, T.G., Park, S.H.: Horizontal scrolling text processing for frame rate conversion. In: Proceedings of IEEE International Conference on Consumer Electronics-Berlin (2012)
9. Choi, B.T., Le, S.H., Ko, S.J.: New frame rate up-conversion using bi-directional motion estimation. IEEE Trans. Consum. Electron. **46**(3), 603–609 (2000)
10. Wang, A.D., Vincent, P.B., Klepko, R.: Motion-compensated frame rate conversionpart II: new algorithms for frame interpolation. IEEE Trans. Broadcast. **56**, 142–149 (2010)

Liver Segmentation in Ultrasound Images by Using FCM and Mean Shift

Hong Ding[1,4], Huiqun Wu[2,4], Nianmei Gong[3,4], Jun Wang[3,4], Shi Chen[1,4], and Xiaofeng Zhang[1,4(✉)]

[1] School of Computer Science and Technology, Nantong University, Nantong, China
dinghong@ntu.edu.cn, ntuzxf@163.com
[2] Department of Medical Informatics, Medical School of Nantong University, Nantong, China
[3] The Third People's Hospital of Nantong, Nantong, China
[4] Jiangsu College of Engineering and Technology, Nantong, China

Abstract. Ultrasonic examination is widely used in physical examination and various types of organ inspections because of its merits, such as no harm to human body, cheap and relative high precision. In this paper, a method is proposed to extract liver region in ultrasound images for better liver disease detection. The proposed method firstly smoothes the images by using mean shift, which makes the brightness of the whole liver region to be consistent. Then, the Fuzzy C Mean (FCM) method is used for obtaining the main part of liver region and brightness compensation is applied around the main part. Finally, image segmentation is realized by FCM and the largest foreground area in the image is segmented as the result according to the distribution and shape of the liver. The proposed method has satisfactory results in the experiment of the abdominal ultrasound image segmentation.

Keywords: Ultrasonic examination · Fuzzy C Mean · Mean shift · Liver segmentation

1 Introduction

Ultrasound is a technology that can be applied to physical examination. It uses the reflection feature of human body among ultrasound to construct images. Then, shape and density data of organizational structure are measured in these images and disease symptoms may be found. As a conventional means of physical examination, ultrasound has many advantages. First of all, it uses ultrasonic waves, which is a safe means of inspection and is harmless to humans. In contrast, if using variety of X-rays in inspection, the human body will be suffered a lot. Secondly, the price of ultrasonic examination is cheap and most persons can afford it. But fees of Computed Tomography (CT) and Magnetic Resonance Imaging (MRI) are much more expensive. In addition, the detection accuracy of ultrasound in recent years has been greatly improved. For example, in abdominal

© Springer Nature Singapore Pte Ltd. 2017
X. Yang and G. Zhai (Eds.): IFTC 2016, CCIS 685, pp. 44–52, 2017.
DOI: 10.1007/978-981-10-4211-9_5

examination, small liver cancer can be checked out by using ultrasound. However, ultrasound also has its own defects, such as easy to be affected by noise. These defects make it difficult in acquiring localizations of lesions. Therefore, ultrasound is often used for physical examination and screening, while CT and MRI are used for confirming the condition.

In recent years, there are two ways to improve the accuracy of ultrasound examination. One is directly improving the ultrasound image quality by denoising methods and the other is to limit the judgment region of the lesion. Direct denoising, which can improve the visual effect of the image, reduces the errors caused by the poor quality of the image. Wang et al. [1] used Gauss pyramid to construct multi-resolution images and smoothed out the speckle noise at high levels of the pyramid. Deshpande et al. [2] used anisotropic diffusion filter to improve the quality of ultrasound images. Then Chan-Vese active contour method was used for segmentation. Rahman et al. [3] developed and implemented a system to segment human kidney from ultrasound images. They reduced speckle noise and smoothed resultant image using Gabor filter, and enhanced the image quality by using histogram equalization. The main reason for limiting the judgement area is to reduce the impacts of background environment. Xian et al. [4] proposed two new concepts of neutrosophic subset and neutrosophic connectedness to generalize the fuzzy subset and fuzzy connectedness for breast tumor segmentation. The proposed neutrosophic connectedness modeled the inherent uncertainty and indeterminacy of the spatial topological properties of the image. Zhang et al. [5] continued the work of a parameter-automatically-optimized robust graph-based segmentation method and proposed a multi-objectively-optimized robust graph-based segmentation method. Then, they applied the method on breast ultrasound images and get better segmentation results. Namburete et al. [6] used shape information to extract fetal head in ultrasound images. Chuang et al. [7] used the shape and edge information of the finger tendon in ultrasound image and proposed an active contour model based on adaptive texture to extract the finger tendon.

In this paper, a method for liver extraction in ultrasound images is proposed. The liver image in ultrasound has the following characteristics. The region of liver is not uniform, which leads it difficult to be extracted perfectly. It is connected with other organ areas, which leads the extraction results wrongly contain other organs. In order to extract the whole liver region, Fuzzy C Means (FCM) and mean shift are combined in our method. Firstly, our proposed algorithm makes the images more uniform by using mean shift filtering. Then, FCM is used to segment the image and the approximate region of liver is abstracted. In the edge region, background may be wrongly segmented into foreground. So, brightness compensation is applied in these regions. Finally the image is segmented by FCM again and the liver region is obtained. The proposed algorithm uses mean shift to filter the noise area, FCM to reduce the chances of the false positives and brightness compensation to reduce the problem of uneven brightness. The proposed algorithm obtained a better segmentation results in the liver ultrasound images provided by the hospital.

2   FCM Introduction

FCM is a classical clustering algorithm among image processing algorithm [8]. It minimizes the objective function by an iteration procedure. Then, each pixel in the image gets its membership value and is divided according to the principle of maximum membership. FCM has many merits. It needs less iteration and its calculation speed is fast. It has a strong resist noise ability by using the related information.

Given image I, the objective function of FCM is

$$E^{FCM} = \sum_{i=1}^{C} \sum_{j=1}^{N} u_{ij}^m d_{ij}^2, \tag{1}$$

where i is the subscripts of category (There are C categories.), j is the subscripts of pixel (There are   pixels.). m is the fuzzification factor and is used to adjust the fuzzy membership. $m = 2$ in our experiment. $d_{ij} = ||x_j - v_i||$ is the difference between pixel x_j and the center of category i. u_{ij} is the fuzzy membership of x_j belonging to v_i. Fuzzy membership is the probability of a pixel belonging to a category, its value is in $[0, 1]$. For each pixel, the sum of its all fuzzy memberships is 1, that is

$$\sum_{i=1}^{C} u_{ij} = 1. \tag{2}$$

Lagrange multiplier method can acquire the extreme value of Eq. (2) in restricted condition Eq. (1). To take the derivative of each variable, the fuzzy membership u_{ij} and category center v_i can be calculated as

$$u_{ij} = \frac{1}{\sum_{k=1}^{C} (d_{ij}/d_{kj})^{2/(m-1)}}, \tag{3}$$

$$v_i = \frac{\sum_{j=1}^{n} u_{ij}^m x_j}{\sum_{j=1}^{n} u_{ij}^m}. \tag{4}$$

By the iteration of Eqs. (3) and (4), the objective function (1) will be minimized. Then each pixel get its fuzzy membership and the segmentation is realized.

The main shortcoming of the original FCM algorithm is that the objective function does not contain any spatial information. So, its anti noise ability is poor. In general, noise is independent and distinct from its surrounding pixels. So the algorithm is easy to separate noise alone form a region, which makes an integrity region full of holes. Another shortcoming is that the original FCM is easy to divide images into too many parts when the color is not uniform, which increases the difficulty of post processing. Thus the use of neighborhood information FCM (FCM_S) algorithm is proposed in [9]. Its objective function is

$$E^{FCM\_S} = \sum_{i=1}^{C} \sum_{j=1}^{N} u_{ij}^m d_{ij}^2 + \frac{\alpha}{N_r} \sum_{i=1}^{C} \sum_{j=1}^{N} u_{ij}^m \sum_{x_r \in N_j} d_{ij}^2, \tag{5}$$

where N_j is the neighbourhood of pixel j, N_r is the number of pixels in the neighbourhood. The calculation method of Eq. (5) is similar to Eq. (1), which follows next iteration of equations,

$$u_{ij} = \frac{(d_{ij}^2 + \frac{\alpha}{N_r}\sum_{x_r \in N_j} d_{ir}^2)^{1/(m-1)}}{\sum_{k=1}^{C}(d_{kj}^2 + \frac{\alpha}{N_r}\sum_{x_r \in N_j} d_{kr}^2)^{1/(m-1)}}, \tag{6}$$

$$v_i = \frac{\sum_{j=1}^{n} u_{ij}^m (x_j + \frac{\alpha}{N_r}\sum_{x_r \in N_j} x_r)}{\sum_{j=1}^{n}(1+\alpha)u_{ij}^m}. \tag{7}$$

Even FCM_S only uses the information in the neighborhood. So FCM segmentation will not have perfect results when heavy noisy images are processed. If light is not uniform or color is distorted, it will lead to a failure by using the FCM algorithm.

3 Liver Segmentation Based on FCM and Mean Shift

3.1 Preprocessing Based on Mean Shift

The mean shift method is an iterative clustering algorithm which could be applied to related fields of various characteristic space analyses, including the image segmentation.

According to literature [10], the steps of mean shift filter is as following.

1. Initialize $j = 1$ and $y_{i,1} = x_i$, where y is the feature of pixel x.
2. Compute $y_{i,j+1}$ according to Eq. (8) until convergence.

$$y_{i+1} = \frac{\sum_{i=1}^{n} x_i g(||\frac{x-x_i}{h}||^2)}{\sum_{i=1}^{n} g(||\frac{x-x_i}{h}||^2)}. \tag{8}$$

3. Assign $z_i = (x_i^s, y_{i,c}^r)$, where z_i is the filtered image pixel, s and r denote the spatial and range components of a vector, respectively.

Sun et al. [11] modified the mean shift in handling the pixels of image in batches. The modified method is 100 times faster than the traditional mean shift method. In our experiments, the modified mean shift method is applied.

3.2 Brightness Compensation

Due to the FCM only using color information for classification, there are many pixels wrongly classified in the result. If the colors of these misclassification regions are corrected, better segmentation results can be obtained.

The region that needs to be compensated brightness is at the edge region of the liver. In order to determine the approximate location of the liver, the original FCM is used. Then brightness compensation is applied in the edge region of liver.

The brightness compensation has two different plans. In bright part, the dark regions grow. While in dark part, the bright regions grow.

3.3   Liver Segmentation Method

Our method uses FCM and mean shift to segment livers from ultrasound images with heavy noise. The whole procedure is described in the following.

1. Preprocessing
   The input image is filtered by mean shift. In order to get a more uniform image, the regions with little difference are further merged. Figure 1 shows the result of our preprocessing. The preprocessing of mean shift makes image more uniform for the next step of segmentation.

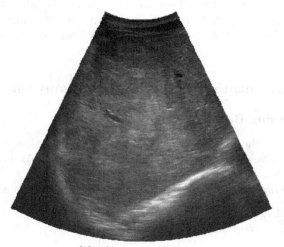

(a) The original image.

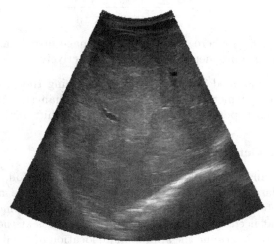

(b) The result after preprocessing.

Fig. 1. Result of the preprocessing.

2. Rough segmentation

   In this step, FCM is used to segment the images. Because of non-uniform illumination of ultrasound image, this segmentation can not obtain satisfied results. The rough liver region is abstracted for next step.

3. Brightness compensation

   Brightness compensation only applied at the region edge of the liver. As shown in Fig. 2, the brightness compensation adjusts the brightness of the edge regions.

4. Liver segmentation

   FCM is used to segment the image once more. Because the input image has been applied brightness compensation, the result is better than last time. The liver is usually the largest organ in the abdominal ultrasound image. Using this prior knowledge can obtain the largest area in the foreground as the liver.

4   Experiments

The proposed method has been tested on ultrasound images, which are provided by the Third People's Hospital of Nantong. The equipment and inspector information of these images has been removed. As shown in Fig. 1(a), the image has a lot of noise and its brightness is uneven. The proposed algorithm is compared with the original FCM and FCM_S. In experiments, the cluster number of FCM is 3. Figure 3 shows examples of the clustering results of the three algorithms. The result of proposed method is more complete than original FCM and FCM_S. It is obvious that the proposed method can combine the advantages of FCM and Mean shift to improve the classification performance.

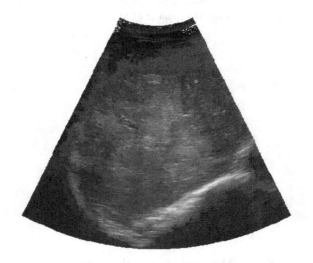

Fig. 2. The result of brightness compensation.

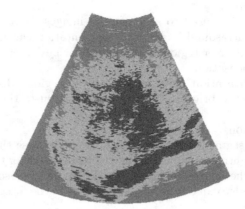

(a) The result of original FCM.

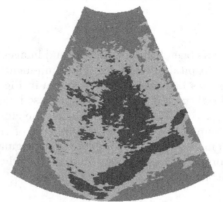

(b) The result of FCM_S.

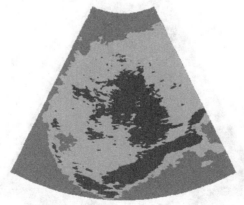

(c) The result of the proposed method.

Fig. 3. The comparison of three methods.

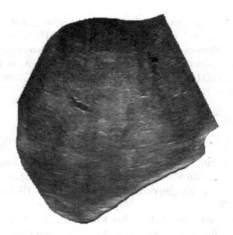

Fig. 4. The example of reference images.

Table 1. The comparison of three methods.

Method	Performance	
	Precision P	Recall R
FCM	78.83%	82.29%
FCM_S	79.00%	83.3%
The proposed method	83.85%	92.50%

In order to obtain a more accurate comparison of these methods, correct parts of livers are extracted by doctors and used as references in the experiments. Figure 4 shows the reference image. The results of three algorithms are compared with these references by following performance measures: Precision $P = TP/(TP + FP)$ and Recall $R = TP/AP$, where TP is the number of pixels correctly classified, FP is the number of pixels wrongly classified and AP is the total number of pixels in liver region. Table 1 shows that the Precision and Recall of the proposed method are better than FCM and FCM_S.

5   Conclusion

In this paper, a method of using FCM and mean shift is presented to extract liver regions in ultrasound images. The proposed method uses mean shift and FCM to improve its ability of resisting noise. In addition, the algorithm combined with a brightness compensation procedure in the edge region and a relatively complete liver region is obtained. In the further research, it will consider how to integrate a priori information directly into the FCM and active contour algorithm will be used to further optimize the segmentation of the liver region.

Acknowledgments. This project is supported by the grant of National Natural Science Foundation of China (No. 81271668, No. 81501559, No. 61300167 and No. 61671255), the Natural Science Foundation of Jiangsu Province (No. BK20151274), the Natural Science Foundation of the Jiangsu Higher Education Institutions of China (No. 14KJB510031, 14KJB310014, 15KJB310015, and 15KJB520029) and Science and the Technology Project of Nantong (MS12015105).

References

1. Wang, W., Qin, J., Chui, Y.-P., et al.: A multiresolution framework for ultrasound image segmentation by combinative active contours. In: 35th Annual International Conference of the IEEE Engineering in Medicine and Biology Society (EMBC), pp. 1144–1147 (2013)
2. Deshpande, R., Ramalingam, R.E., Chockalingam, N., et al.: An automated segmentation technique for the processing of foot ultrasound images. In: IEEE Eighth International Conference on Intelligent Sensors, Sensor Networks and Information Processing, pp. 380–383 (2013)
3. Rahman, T., Uddin, M.S.: Speckle noise reduction and segmentation of kidney regions from ultrasound image. In: International Conference on Informatics, Electronics and Vision (ICIEV), pp. 1–5 (2013)
4. Xian, M., Cheng, H.D., Zhang, Y.: A fully automatic breast ultrasound image segmentation approach based on neutro-connectedness. In: 2014 22nd International Conference on Pattern Recognition (ICPR), pp. 2495–2500 (2014)
5. Zhang, Q., Zhao, X., Huang, Q.: A multi-objectively-optimized graph-based segmentation method for breast ultrasound image. In: The 7th International Conference on Biomedical Engineering and Informatics, pp. 116–120 (2014)
6. Namburete, A.I.L., Noble, J.A.: Fetal cranial segmentation in 2D ultrasound images using shape properties of pixel clusters. In: IEEE 10th International Symposium on Biomedical Imaging, pp. 720–723 (2013)
7. Chuang, B.-I., Sun, Y.-N., Yang, T.-H., et al.: Model-based tendon segmentation from ultrasound images. In: 40th Annual Northeast Bioengineering Conference (NEBEC), pp. 1–2 (2014)
8. Bezdek, J.C., Pal, S.K.: Fuzzy Models for Pattern Recognition. IEEE Press, Piscataway (1991)
9. Ahmed, M.N., Yamany, S.M., Mohamed, N., et al.: A modified Fuzzy C-Mean algorithm for bias field estimation and segmentation of MRI data. IEEE Trans. Med. Imaging **21**(3), 193–199 (2002)
10. Comaniciu, D., Meer, P.: Mean shift: a robust approach toward feature space analysis. IEEE Trans. Pattern Anal. Mach. Intell. **24**(5), 603–619 (2002)
11. Sun, Q., Lu, Y.: Text location in camera-captured guidepost images. In: 2010 Chinese Conference on Pattern Recognition (CCPR), pp. 1–4 (2010)

A Modified Joint Trilateral Filter for Depth Image Super Resolution

Shengqian Zhang, Wei Zhong$^{(\boxtimes)}$, Long Ye, and Qin Zhang

Key Laboratory of Media Audio and Video, Communication University of China,
Ministry of Education, Beijing 100024, China
{zhangsq,wzhong,yelong,zhangqin}@cuc.edu.cn

Abstract. Depth image can be easily obtained by RGB-D sensors such as Microsoft Kinect, but the low resolution and poor quality of the obtained results pose a notable challenge on practical applications. To solve this problem, this paper proposes an algorithm of modified joint trilateral filter for depth image super resolution. In the proposed method, considering less texture contained in depth image, the high resolution (HR) edge is first extracted from its corresponding HR color image and then introduced to guide the modified joint trilateral filter primarily. Meanwhile, the intensity information is taken into account to avoid the fake edges in the HR edge map. With the guidance of HR edge and intensity information, the HR depth image could be simply interpolated via the modified joint trilateral filter. The experimental results manifest that our approach could not only save the running time but also obtain better performance compared with the state-of-the-art methods.

Keywords: Depth image · Super resolution · Joint trilateral filter · Edge map · Intensity information

1 Introduction

Recently the virtual reality and augmented reality technologies have made great progress, especially in the fields of game and entertainment. However, the authentic immersive experience poses severe requirements on geometric consistency, which means that the virtual objects have to be consistent with the real world on geometry including location, perspective and occlusion relations. The depth value of each object is the critical factor to guarantee geometric consistency. Depth image can be simply obtained with depth sensors at present such as Kinect, but the obtained result does have a series of problems caused by the limitation of hardware, such as low resolution (LR), blurred edge and lost local depth information. To be exact, we could utilize Kinect to get the depth image, whose resolution is only 512×424 for Kinect V2. Obviously, it is

This work is supported by the National Natural Science Foundation of China under Grant Nos. 61201236 and 61371191, and the Project of State Administration of Press, Publication, Radio, Film and Television under Grant No. 2015-53.

© Springer Nature Singapore Pte Ltd. 2017
X. Yang and G. Zhai (Eds.): IFTC 2016, CCIS 685, pp. 53–62, 2017.
DOI: 10.1007/978-981-10-4211-9_6

much lower than that of the corresponding color image (1920 × 1080) Moreover, the performance of 3D applications utilizing depth image greatly depends on the accuracy of depth value. Therefore, super resolution (SR) is urged to be done with depth image both effectively and efficiently. This work can be achieved by improving the hardware performance, but the software-based algorithms take the priority in terms of cost, complexity and stability.

Generally speaking, the traditional methods of depth image SR can be classified into two categories according to the number of inputs, which refer to depth image SR with single depth image or multiple images. The single depth image SR refers to reconstruct a high resolution (HR) depth image using a single depth image as input without any other prior information. Hornacek et al. [1] proposed a method by identifying and merging patch correspondences to exploit the patchwise self-similarity such as repetition of geometric primitives or object symmetry. In [2], HR candidate patches are searched for each LR input depth patch using only a generic database. In [3], the patch-based approach [2] was improved with the additional geometric constraints from self-similar structures. However, the above methods may fail to establish patch correspondences due to their patch-based principle. To solve this problem, Refs. [4, 5] imposed the locality constraint on the sparse representation of depth image patches in case of over-fitting of the learning based methods. Still, there are also similar but less artifacts involved as other learning based methods. In [6], the SR problem was converted from HR texture prediction to HR edge map prediction and then the HR depth image was interpolated via modified joint bilateral filter with the reference of HR edge map. Although the methods of single depth image SR can help avoid negative effects with texture interference and get good performance with complete dictionary, the matching process may fail due to the limitation of external training dataset or self-similarity, which will lead to edge effects between patches or inaccurate depth values. Moreover, their improvements would be restricted by the insufficient prior information with single depth image as input. And thus we turn our attention to the methods with multiple images as input.

Depth image SR with multiple images always means the process is achieved with the guidance of its corresponding HR color image. Kopf et al. [7] proposed a method of joint bilateral filter (JBF) in which the weight of the kernel was calculated with the guidance of RGB image. Considering the smoothness caused by bilateral filter, Yang et al. [8] took the HR color image and interpolated HR depth image as input to establish various depth layers and their corresponding energy, and then the JBF was applied with energy items. But it does need enough time for the iteration of the algorithm. For high efficiency on calculation, Diebel et al. [9] first proposed the Markov random field (MFR) method, converting the SR problem to the calculation of optimal energy solution. Park et al. [10] introduced the nonlocal means regularization to keep the detailed structure based on the work of [9], which reduces edge smoothness caused by original MRF model. Lu et al. [11] modified the energy items in MRF model according to the depth image features to guarantee the discontinuity of different objects. In [12], the weight item of bidirectional gradient was put forward to reduce the depth noise on the edge. However, the MRF based methods always involve complex algorithm framework and optimizing measures and may lead to the edge artifacts in spite of the improvements of [11, 12]. In addition, the general color image SR approaches can also be applied to depth image SR. Yang et al. [13] proposed a method of sparse representation which means the reconstruction of HR image can be achieved via sparse linear combinations of learned coupled dictionary atoms. In [14], Dong et al. introduced the deep learning method for image SR based on the convolution network. Also in [15], the self-similarity was utilized to expand the internal patch search space. These learning based methods depend on the quality of training data and fractal nature of images, resulting in the uncertainty. Therefore, it is still valuable to exploit the efficient way to depth image SR, which can obtain accurate edges with high time efficiency.

As our contribution, we come up with a modified joint trilateral filter for depth image SR using the HR color image and intensity information as reference. Different from the existing joint filter methods, we propose to merge the edge map extracted from HR color image and that from LR depth image so as to construct an HR edge map without useless texture information. And then the HR depth image can be interpolated via our modified trilateral filter with the guidance of HR edge map and HR intensity information. The process of interpolation is conducted with consideration of the relative position between each pixel and edges, which use the real edge map to preserve edges in depth image virtually. Since the Kinect can produce HR color image and LR depth image almost simultaneously, we could save time using the HR RGB image as guidance instead of external dataset or dictionary and improve the quality of the reconstructed image. The experimental results demonstrate that our approach could generate HR depth images with high quality and short running time efficiently.

The rest of the paper is organized as follows. Section 2 presents the framework of our proposed method and the detailed operations involved. The experimental results are illustrated and the comparisons are made with the existing typical methods in Sect. 3. Finally some conclusions are drawn in Sect. 4.

2 The Proposed Method

The proposed method is inspired by the fact that the HR RGB image can provide prior information which can be utilized in the process of SR. In the consideration of less texture contained in depth image, we first extract edges from the interpolated depth image, which is the bicubic interpolation result of LR depth image. But the obtained edges are jagged due to the direct interpolation. And thus we operate the HR color image at the same time in order to get the HR edge map, which contains noisy texture information. Then we use the edge map extracted from interpolated depth image to help remove the texture interference in the HR edge map with Gaussian mask. As a result, the HR depth image is reconstructed with the guidance of the HR edge map and intensity information by the modified joint trilateral filter based on the location of pixel. The framework of our proposed algorithm is illustrated in Fig. 1.

In the next subsections, the concrete procedures involved in the proposed framework are described in detail from the three operations of HR edge extraction, depth interpolation with edge and intensity and edge preservation based on pixel location.

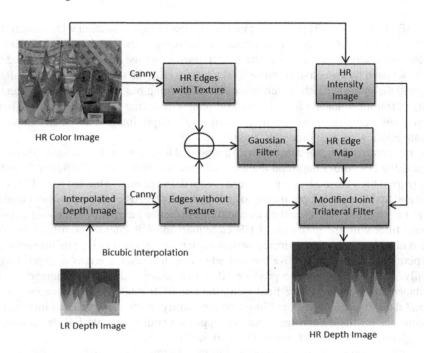

Fig. 1. The framework of our proposed method.

2.1 HR Edge Extraction

In this subsection, the HR edge map is constructed for guiding the joint trilateral filter thereafter. Given the HR RGB image I^h, we extract the edges from it directly with edge detector to get the HR edge map E. In our work, the edges are extracted by using the Canny operator to guarantee the quality of the edge map. And then we select the threshold value being 0.08 for the detector to obtain enough edges. Some of the textures in color image will also be detected as a consequence. In order to reduce the useless texture information, we merge the edge map extracted from HR color image with the edges from interpolated depth image, which refers to the bicubic interpolation result of LR depth image. Here the Gaussian mask is applied to disperse the pixel energy for the subsequent threshold classification. The process of generating HR edge map is illustrated in Fig. 2, which could remove those useless textures effectively. Finally, we can get a clean HR edge map denoted as E^h.

Figure 3 illustrates the results of HR edge map obtained via learning based method [6] and the proposed approach. Here we select the image cones from Middlebury dataset as input to perform the comparison. It can be seen from Fig. 3 that, the HR edge map obtained by our method presents uneven thickness and that by [6] is slightly smoother. This is because the learning based method [6] uses the external HR dataset for reference, spending more time in approximate nearest neighbor searching. While our approach can achieve comparable result without the reference of external dataset, saving at least one minute of running time than [6].

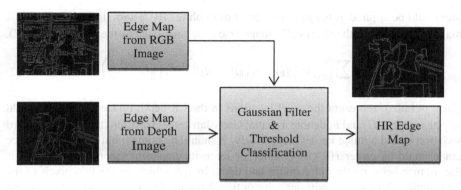

Fig. 2. The process of generating HR edge map.

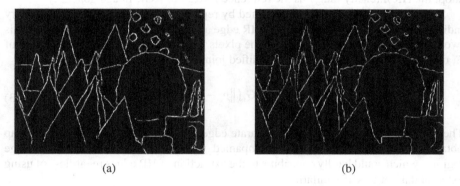

(a)   (b)

Fig. 3. Edges constructed from (a) external dataset in [6], (b) HR color image with our method.

2.2 Depth Interpolation with Edge and Intensity

With the HR edge map constructed, in this section we will discuss the formulation of the modified joint trilateral filter.

In the previous work of joint bilateral filter, both the spatial and guided information are considered to calculate the depth value. Given an input image I, we denote the value of pixel p within the reconstructed image I' as I'_p. And $\tilde{I}_p$ and $\tilde{I}_q$ respectively denote the intensity values of pixels p and q in the intensity image $\tilde{I}$, which is the reference or guidance. Then the formulation of joint bilateral filter can be defined as follows:

$$I'_p = \frac{1}{k_p} \sum_{q \subseteq \Omega} I_q \cdot G_s(\|p - q\|) \cdot F_r\left(\left\|\tilde{I}_p - \tilde{I}_q\right\|\right), \tag{1}$$

where G_s is the spatial Gaussian kernel and F_r is the range kernel with Gaussian distribution, k_p is a normalization factor and Ω is a w by w spatial pixel block centered at pixel p.

Under the definition of LR and its corresponding HR depth images as D^l and D^h respectively, if we replace I and I' with D^l and D^h, it can be derived that the joint bilateral filter could be applied as the joint bilateral upsampling (JBU) with the guidance of HR image $\tilde{I}$. Then the depth value of HR image D^h can be calculated by the following Eq. (2),

$$D^h(p) = \frac{1}{k_p} \sum_{q_\downarrow \subseteq \Omega} D^l(q_\downarrow) \cdot G_s(\|p_\downarrow - q_\downarrow\|) \cdot F_r\left(\left\|\tilde{I}_p - \tilde{I}_q\right\|\right), \tag{2}$$

where $p_\downarrow$ and $q_\downarrow$ represent the pixel locations in the LR depth image D^l, which should only be integers. G_s and F_r denote a spatial Gaussian kernel with zero mean and standard deviation σ_s and a range kernel respectively. It should be pointed out that the reference image could be either HR color image or intensity image in theory. But if there is discordance between the color image and depth image, which means two pixels of the same depth values have dissimilar color or they have similar color but are not consistent in depth value, the accuracy of SR will decrease markedly. Therefore, in this case we adopt the HR intensity image as the reference instead of RGB image generally.

In the work of [1], the JBF is modified by replacing the range kernel with a binary indicator F_r, which considers both the HR edge and the location of pixels p and q. This two-valued function equals to 1 when the pixels p and q are located at the same side of E, otherwise it is 0. And in [6], the modified joint bilateral filter is defined as:

$$D^h(p) = \frac{1}{k_p} \sum_{q_\downarrow \subseteq \Omega} D^l(q_\downarrow) \cdot G_s(\|p_\downarrow - q_\downarrow\|) \cdot F_r(E^h, p, q). \tag{3}$$

The above process is based on the accurate edge prediction, but the initial depth map obtained from Kinect is always accompanied with holes in both smooth and edge regions, which could hardly contribute to the extraction of HR edges regardless of using external dataset or self-similarity.

Therefore, as is illustrated in Eq. (4), we propose that the interpolation process is guided with the HR edge map E^h and the intensity information using the modified joint trilateral filter, from which we can get the depth value for each pixel in the desired HR depth image D^h,

$$D^h(p) = \frac{1}{k_p} \sum_{q_\downarrow \subseteq \Omega} D^l(q_\downarrow) \cdot G_s(\|p_\downarrow - q_\downarrow\|) \cdot F_r\left(\left\|\tilde{I}_p - \tilde{I}_q\right\|\right) \cdot B(E^h, p, q), \tag{4}$$

where $B(E, p, q)$ works as the binary indicator, which is the same as F_r in (3). In this way, the Gaussian kernel can improve the depth image quality within the interpolation process. The intensity information will improve the confidence of the edge map extracted from color image. And the HR edges could be really preserved using the binary function, which could tell whether the two pixels are at the same side of the edge or not.

2.3 Edge Preservation Based on Pixel Location

In this subsection, we consider the problem of edge preservation based on pixel location. First, we obtain T by dilating the pixel to its four conjunctive neighbors. And then we define that $T(p_i)$ equals to 1 if the pixel i is exactly on or connected with the edge, otherwise it equals to 0. Now we use the function $w(i,j)$ to calculate the weight of path between pixels p_i and p_j,

$$w(i,j) = \left\| p_i - p_j \right\| \cdot \left(T(p_i) + T(p_j) + 1 \right).\tag{5}$$

Then we could analyze the shortest path in terms of the weight. At the same time, the pixels adjacent to edge will be added more weights so that the path will avoid touching the edge to the greatest extent. The shortest path is denoted as S, and it is shown with 4-conntected neighbors as S'.

To be specific, we discuss the edge preservation process under the following two cases:

(1) Case when the pixel p is not on the edge. The pixels p and q would be identified as at different side of edge if S' overlaps with edge, otherwise they are at the same side. Since S' is definitely wider than S, the location will be classified incorrectly without adding additional weights on pixels near the edge.

(2) Case when the pixel p is exactly on the edge. If the number of overlapping pixels between S' and the edge exceeds one, the two pixels should be identified as at the two sides of the edge. If not, they are at the same side. However, the coordinates of p should change a unit both horizontally and vertically until S' does not overlap with the edge.

As the relation between the two pixels and edge is identified correctly, which also means the function $B(E,p,q)$ is determined, we can get the HR depth image via the modified joint trilateral filter given in Eq. (4). In some cases when the pixel p does not have any conjunctive neighbors at the same side, the corresponding bicubic interpolation result will be used for p.

3   Experimental Results

In this section, we conduct the experiments on depth images from Middlebury Stereo dataset. As for the LR depth images, we get them by down-sampling their HR counterparts. And then the comparisons are made between the proposed approach and other state-of-the-art methods on depth image SR both quantitatively and qualitatively.

For the first example, we take the image cones as input and choose the typical methods for depth image SR [2] and general color image SR [13] to perform the comparison. Figure 4 shows the obtained depth image SR results of the proposed approach and methods of Aodha [2] and Yang [13]. It can be seen from Fig. 4 that, compared with Aodha [2] and Yang [13], our method can achieve more smooth result generally without loss of local depth information. While for the patch based method [2], the patches are substituted with their HR counterparts, contributing to artifacts in the region with special pattern such as those in the bottom right corner of Fig. 4(a). And for the basis learning approach [13], as it does not remove the texture artifacts around edges, the reconstructed HR depth image contains jagged edges. It should be noticed that, as

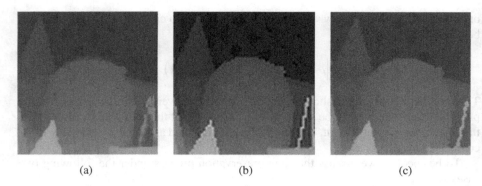

(a)   (b)   (c)

Fig. 4. The depth image SR results of (a) Aodha [2], (b) Yang [13], (c) our proposed method.

for the wavy region in the lower right part of Fig. 4(c), it is because the distance between two edges of the thin stick is too close, which is not solved well so far.

For the second example, we take the image teddy as input and compare the proposed method with Xie [6]. The reconstructed HR depth images of our method and Xie [6] are shown in Fig. 5. It can be seen from Fig. 5 that, the proposed method can achieve comparable reconstruction results as Xie [6], except several details circled with red lines in Fig. 5(b). It is the external dataset used in Xie [6] that contributes to the slightly better reconstruction result of Xie [6]. However, the use of external dataset is time consuming and the reconstruction result also largely depends on the performance of external dataset or dictionary. In contrast, our proposed method can achieve comparable reconstruction results without external dataset or dictionary, saving almost one minute of running time than Xie [6].

Further in order to describe the performance in quantitative sense, we choose the root mean square error (RMSE) and percent error score (PE) as the assessment measures to compare our approach with the existing typical methods. The PE is generally identified as a much fairer metric for depth image. Here four methods for depth image SR and

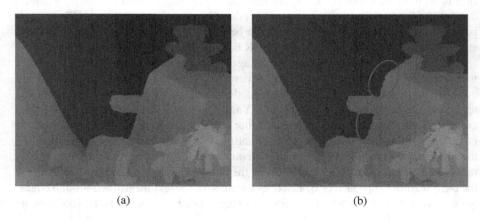

(a)   (b)

Fig. 5. The HR depth images reconstructed via (a) Xie [6] and (b) our proposed approach.

three ones for general color image SR are selected to perform the comparison. The comparison results are shown in Table 1.

Table 1. RMSE & PE comparison results

Input	The depth image SR methods				The general color image SR methods			
RMSE x4	Park [10]	Aodha [2]	Xie [4]	Xie [6]	Yang [13]	Dong [14]	Huang [15]	Ours
Cones	1.52	1.56	1.07	1.16	1.45	1.41	1.48	1.18
Teddy	1.08	1.26	0.85	0.95	1.18	1.10	1.23	0.93
PE x4	Park [10]	Aodha [2]	Xie [4]	Xie [6]	Yang [13]	Dong [14]	Huang [15]	Ours
Cones	7.18	9.73	5.79	3.09	9.33	8.64	8.44	4.56
Teddy	6.27	8.03	4.72	3.11	7.79	6.92	7.37	4.12

It can be seen from Table 1 that, the PEs of our method are better than other state-of-art approaches except Xie [6]. The work of [6] adopts an external dataset as dictionary for HR matching, which is limited to the quality of external factors. In contrast, our method only needs a LR depth image and an HR color image as inputs instead of any external dataset. In the experiments, we carry out the simulations with MATLAB on a computer with a quad-core 1.7 GHz Intel i5-4210 CPU and 8.0 GB RAM. As is illustrated in Table 2, on account of extracting edges directly from HR color image, we save almost one minute in the whole process, which almost equals to the half of the running time of [6]. Meanwhile, the RMSE of our approach is lower than most of the listed methods and close to [4, 6]. The reason for slightly better result of [4] lies in the use of shock filter [16], which does work in removing jagged artifacts.

Table 2. Comparisons of running time

Running time	Method	Edge reconstruction	Super resolution	Total
Cones	Ours	3.1 s	41.3 s	44.4 s
	Xie [6]	55.7 s	48.1 s	103.8 s
Teddy	Ours	3.3 s	34.6 s	37.9 s
	Xie [6]	49.8 s	43.1 s	92.9 s

4   Conclusion

In this paper, we present a modified trilateral filter for depth image SR. Inspired by the features of both color and depth images, the edges extracted from less-textured LR depth image are used to remove the useless texture information involved in the HR edges from color image. Then we construct an HR edge map with Gaussian filter and threshold filtration. And thus the HR depth image can be interpolated via the modified trilateral filter with the guidance of HR edges and intensity information. Different from learning based methods, the proposed method does not need any external dataset, helping to shorten the running time and improve the efficiency. Moreover, our algorithm fulfills the real-time requirement for the practical applications such as the interaction in the immersive virtual environment.

References

1. Hornacek, M., Rhemann, C., Gelautz, M., Rother, C.: Depth super resolution by rigid body self-similarity in 3D. In: Proceedings of IEEE Conference on Computer Vision and Pattern Recognition, pp. 1123–1130 (2013)
2. Mac Aodha, O., Campbell, Neill, D.,F., Nair, A., Brostow, Gabriel, J.: Patch based synthesis for single depth image super-resolution. In: Fitzgibbon, A., Lazebnik, S., Perona, P., Sato, Y., Schmid, C. (eds.) ECCV 2012. LNCS, vol. 7574, pp. 71–84. Springer, Heidelberg (2012). doi:10.1007/978-3-642-33712-3_6
3. Li, J., Lu, Z.C., Zeng, G., Gan, R., Zha, H.B.: Similarity-aware patchwork assembly for depth image super-resolution. In: Proceedings of IEEE Conference on Computer Vision and Pattern Recognition, pp. 3374–3381 (2014)
4. Xie, J., Chou, C.C., Feris, R., Sun, M.T.: Single depth image super resolution and denoising via coupled dictionary learning with local constraints and shock filtering. In: Proceedings of IEEE International Conference on Multimedia and Expo, pp. 1–6 (2014)
5. Xie, J., Feris, R.S., Yu, S.S., Sun, M.T.: Joint super resolution and denoising from a single depth image. IEEE Trans. Multimedia 17(9), 1525–1537 (2015)
6. Xie, J., Ferisand, R.S., Sun, M.T.: Edge-guided single depth image super resolution. IEEE Trans. Image Process. 25(1), 428–438 (2016)
7. Kopf, J., Cohen, M.F., Lischinski, D.: Joint bilateral upsampling. ACM Trans. Graph. 26(3), 96 (2007)
8. Yang, Q., Yang, R., Davis, J.: Spatial-depth super resolution for range images. In: Proceedings of IEEE Conference on Computer Vision and Pattern Recognition, pp. 1–8 (2007)
9. Diebel, J., Thrun, S.: An application of Markov random fields to range sensing. In: Proceedings of Conference on Neural Information Processing Systems, pp. 291–298 (2005)
10. Park, J., Kim, H., Tai, Y.W., Brown, M.S., Kweon, I.: High quality depth map upsampling for 3D-TOF cameras. In: Proceedings of IEEE International Conference on Computer Vision, pp. 1623–1630 (2011)
11. Lu, J., Min, D., Pahwa, R.S.: A revisit to MRF-based depth map super-resolution and enhancement. In: Proceedings of IEEE International Conference on Acoustics, Speech and Signal Processing, pp. 985–988 (2011)
12. Daeyoung, K., Kuk-jin, Y.: High-quality depth map upsampling robust to edge of range sensors. In: Proceedings of IEEE International Conference on Image Processing, pp. 553–556 (2012)
13. Yang, J., Wright, J., Huang, T.S., Ma, Y.: Image super-resolution via sparse representation. IEEE Trans. Image Process. 19(11), 2861–2873 (2010)
14. Dong, C., Loy, C.C., He, K., Tang, X.: Learning a deep convolutional network for image super-resolution. In: Fleet, D., Pajdla, T., Schiele, B., Tuytelaars, T. (eds.) ECCV 2014. LNCS, vol. 8692, pp. 184–199. Springer, Heidelberg (2014). doi:10.1007/978-3-319-10593-2_13
15. Huang, J.B., Singh, A., Ahuja, N.: Single image super-resolution from transformed self-exemplars. In: Proceedings of IEEE Conference on Computer Vision and Pattern Recognition, pp. 5197–5206 (2015)
16. Gilboa, G., Sochen, N., Zeevi, Y.Y.: Image enhancement and denoising by complex diffusion processes. IEEE Trans. Pattern Anal. Mach. Intell. 26(8), 1020–1036 (2004)

A Modified Just Noticeable Depth Difference Model for 3D Displays

Chunhua Li[1,2], Ping An[1(✉)], Liquan Shen[1], Kai Li[1], and Jian Ma[1]

[1] School of Communication and Information Engineering, Shanghai University,
Shanghai 200072, China
{jinhao,anping,jsslq,kailee,13820251}@shu.edu.cn
[2] School of Information Science and Engineering,
Hebei University of Science and Technology, Shijiazhuang 050018, China

Abstract. With the flourishment of 3D content, more and more 3D videos need to be transmitted and stored. The contradiction between the bitrate and the quality loss of stereoscopic images becomes a bottleneck problem. To tackle the problem, the perception characteristics of human visual system (HVS) should be exploited. In this paper, we modify the just noticeable depth difference model (JNDD) and verify its effectiveness using subjective experimental results. The modified JNDD model (MJNDD) consists of a three-piecewise linear function, which is consistent with the characteristics of the physiological structure of HVS. Each segment of the three-piecewise linear function depicts the unique depth perception characteristics in the corresponding depth range. Since MJNDD obtains the support of the physiological experimental results, it fits the subjective experimental data more accurate than the state of the art JNDD models.

Keywords: Just noticeable depth difference · Depth perception characteristics · Depth map · 3D displays

1 Introduction

Benefit from the large amount of the infrastructure construction of the information transmission as well as the progress of the imaging devices in the past decades, a rapid growth of 3D video application has been emerging. However, when transmitting or storing 3D videos, noisy is introduced by the compressing algorithm and 3D videos are polluted by some level of distortions. For 3D videos in depth enhanced format, depth map also needs to be compressed. Depth map distortion will make the audience feeling discomfortable. In order to control the depth map distortion not to be perceptible, depth perception characteristics of human visual system (HVS) should be explored.

Just noticeable depth difference (JNDD) is one of the most important perception characteristics of HVS, which describes the thresholds of just noticeable depth variation. Researches on depth perceptual ability of HVS for natural scenarios had been carried out since long before [1]. J. Cutting et al. provided a framework theory of JNDD thresholds for natural scenarios based on previous research achievements [2]. However, it

© Springer Nature Singapore Pte Ltd. 2017
X. Yang and G. Zhai (Eds.): IFTC 2016, CCIS 685, pp. 63–71, 2017.
DOI: 10.1007/978-981-10-4211-9_7

couldn't be directly applied to guide 3D video processing because convergence-accommodation conflict occurs when watching 3D displays. D.V.S.X. De Silva et al. proposed a two-piecewise JNDD model for displays [3], which was simplified into a four-phase constant function later [4]. The simplified JNDD model had been widely used to prefilter depth maps for coding [4] or enhance depth maps for improving depth sensation [5]. Jung further eliminated the size constancy conflict effect in testing videos, which refines the JNDD model's thresholds [6]. However, the accuracy of the refined thresholds wasn't satisfied yet, for the model is lack of the physiological research basis. In order to further improve the JNDD models, the related physiological experimental results should be paid attention to when building a precise JNDD model.

These existing JNDD modes build the JNDD thresholds function of the depth stimulus, and classify the depth stimulus into two or four ranges symmetrically. However, the physiological structure of HVS prompts that the depth perception ability should distribute in three depth ranges and it isn't symmetrical in the middle depth range. In this paper, we proposed a modified JNDD (MJNDD) model of a three-piecewise linear function, which is consistent with the depth perception characteristics of HVS. Supported by the related physiological basis, it improves the accurate of the estimated JNDD thresholds.

The rest of this paper is organized as follows: Sect. 2 briefly describes the related physiological structure of HVS. Section 3 presents the proposed MJNDD model based on the characteristics of physiological structure of HVS. Section 4 verifies the MJNDD model with the subjective experimental results and conclusions are given in Sect. 5.

2 Depth Perception Related Physiological Structure of HVS

Physiological experiment results discover that depth perception of HVS depends on disparity-sensitive neurons and relevant regions in the brain. Disparity-sensitive neurons have been found in the visual cortex of cats and in striate and in the prestriate cortex of monkeys [7, 8]. These disparity sensitive neurons participate in depth perception and play a crucial role. Four types of depth-sensitive neurons are recognized in [8]: the tuned excitatory neuron, the tuned inhibitory neuron, the near neuron and the far neuron, which selectively respond to the stimuli of binocular disparity from two retinas. According to the characteristics of the depth-sensitive neurons responding to the binocular stimuli, depth space is classified in to three regions: the fixation region, the nearer region and the father region. The fixation region is a narrow region around the fixation point, and other regions beyond the fixation region are divided into the nearer region and the father region respectively. The former is near to the observer, and the latter is far away the observer.

The tuned excitatory cells are activated by the stimuli in the fixation region, giving dramatic change in the cell response to the binocular interaction. However, they present inhibitory response along the flanks of the fixation region. The maximal binocular effects of the depth tuned cells are termed as the preferred disparities. For either of the two types depth tuned cells, its preferred disparities are distributed from zero to at least 0.1 degree of disparities relative to the fixation point [8]. Two types of the depth tuned cells collaboratively provide the fine depth perception for the objects within the fixation region.

The near cells and far cells respond well to the stimuli in the nearer and father regions respectively. Cell responses of them are steady and a slight decrease with the increasing viewing distance. Therefore, they only produce coarse depth perception in the two depth regions.

Recently, three regions showing preferential functional magnetic resonance imaging (fMRI) responses to stimuli appearing in the three depth regions in the brain of Alert monkeys are reported in [9]. This further confirms that the depth perception of HVS to objects in three depth regions is differently.

3 Proposed MJNDD Model

Based on the analysis of the physiological structure of HVS depth perception, we propose an MJNDD model, which is built by a three-phase linear function. The details are described as follows.

3.1 Depth Space Partition

We assume that eyes always keep on the screen when watching 3D displays, so that clear images appear on the retinas. In this case, depth perception ability is only up to the response of the depth sensitive cells. According to the response characteristics of the depth sensitive cells as discussed in Sect. 2, we divide the depth space into three sections from the observer to the distance: the nearer region, the center region, and the farther region.

The center region is around the screen. As illustrated in Fig. 1, d_n and d_f are the near bound and the far bound of the fixation region respectively. If the object appears at the far bound, the binocular disparity is 2 times of $\angle 1$. And $\angle 1 = \angle 2 = \angle 3 - \angle 4$ is met. Thus, the far bound of the center region d_f can be ascertained as:

$$arctg\frac{e}{2 \cdot v} - arctg\frac{e}{2 \cdot d_f} = \frac{\eta^*}{2} \tag{1}$$

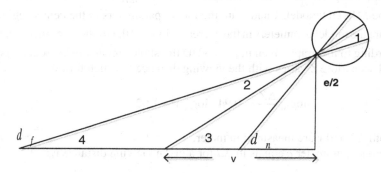

Fig. 1. Calculation of d_n and d_f

Similarly, the near bound of the center region d_n is solved as:

$$arctg\frac{e}{2 \cdot d_n} - arctg\frac{e}{2 \cdot v} = \frac{\eta^*}{2} \tag{2}$$

where η^* is the distribution scope of the depth tuned cells, and e is the inter-pupillary distance. v is the viewing distance, i.e. the perpendicular distance from the eyes to the location where the virtual target is presented. Since the preferred disparities of the depth tuned cells cover $0.1°$ at the two sides of the screen respectively, η^* is set as $0.1°$ in the MJNDD model.

In the center region, the tuned excitatory cells and the tuned inhibitory cells ensure the depth difference of objects to be perceived finely. In other regions, the near cells and far cells only provide coarse depth perception. Obviously, such a depth space partition is supported by the response characteristics of the depth sensitive cells.

3.2 MJNDD Model

To reflect the depth perception characteristics of HVS in the three different depth ranges, we build a MJNDD model using a three-piecewise linear function. In the central region, both clear retina images and the fine depth measurement are satisfied, which lead to the same depth discernment as that in natural scenario. Therefore, the MJNDD thresholds in the central region is the same as those in the JNDD model for natural scenario. In the nearer region and the farther region, coarse depth measurement makes the depth discernment declined. In other words, JNDD thresholds are enlarged in the two depth regions. Therefore, the MJNDD model can be expressed as:

$$\Delta d_{MJNDD}(d_s) = \begin{cases} k \cdot d_n + c + k_n \cdot (d_s - d_n) & d_s < d_n \\ k \cdot (d_s - v) + c & d_n \leq d_s \leq d_f \\ k \cdot d_f + c + k_f \cdot (d_s - d_f) & d_s > d_f \end{cases} \tag{3}$$

where d_s is the depth level in the virtual space, and $\Delta d_{MJNDD}(d_s)$ refers to JNDD threshold at d_s in the MJNDD model. k and c are the model parameters in the center region, and k_n and k_f are the model parameters in the nearer region and the farther region respectively.

According to the graph given in [2], JNDD thresholds related to binocular disparity in natural scenario ΔZ varies with the viewing distance v, which follow:

$$\log_{10} \frac{\Delta Z}{v} = 0.94 \cdot \log_{10} v - 1.92, \tag{4}$$

where both ΔZ and v are measured in meter.

The model parameter c equals to Δd for a given viewing distance v_0:

$$c = \Delta Z\big|_{v=v_0} = v_0^{1.94} \cdot 10^{-1.92} \tag{5}$$

To obtain the model parameter k, we compute the derivative of the JNDD threshold in natural scenario ΔZ relative to the viewing distance v:

$$\frac{\partial(\Delta Z)}{\partial v} = 0.023 \cdot v^{0.94} \tag{6}$$

The model parameter k equals to the derivative at the viewing distance v_0:

$$k = \left.\frac{\partial(\Delta Z)}{\partial v}\right|_{v=v_0} = 0.023 \cdot v_0^{0.94} \tag{7}$$

The model parameters k_n and k_f are fitted according to the subjective experiment results, which will be discussed in the next section.

4 Experimental Results

4.1 Experiments Design

We have performed subjective test experiments in this section to fit and verify the effectiveness of the proposed MJNDD model. The subjective test experiments are performed on a stereoscopic display with active shutter glasses (Panasonic TH-P50ST30C). The resolution is 1920 × 1080 with the aspect ratio 16:9. The peak luminance is 200 cd/m^2 and the contrast ratio is 2000:1. The viewing distance is 2.5 m.

To avoid the conflictions between monocular depth cues and binocular disparity, we shoot the testing videos, as shown in Fig. 2. At the beginning of each testing video, two boxes lie on the same depth, as shown in Fig. 2(a). Then the left box keeps unchanged, whereas the right box is moved gradually till the two boxes are separated apparently as shown in Fig. 2(b). The testing depth levels are limited within the comfortable range, covering from 1.5 m to 4 m with the interval of 0.5 m. Extrainterval of 0.1 m is set from 2 m to 3 m to explore the fine depth perception ability in the central region. The zero parallax planes are set in 2.5 m for all the testing depth levels, while the focusing planes are varied with the testing depth levels to keep the clear imagines on the retinas.

A total of 19 subjects (10 male and 9 female) take part in the subjective experiments, whose ages range from 21 to 28 with the average age of 24.3. All of them are with normal vision or corrected normal vision, and with good stereo vision and color vision, as required by [10]. The subjects are required to keep their eyes on the screen. When they notice the difference of the depth position between the left and right boxes, they should inform the coordinator at once. To ensure the reliability of the experimental results, the participants need to identify the moving direction of the right box also.

4.2 Experimental Results

The results of the subjective experimental results are shown in Fig. 3. The horizontal axis represents the testing depth levels, and the vertical axis represents the JNDD thresholds. Obviously, the three piecewise segments with linear trend is presented by the tested JNDD

a) Two boxes at the same depth level

b) The right box has been moved backward

Fig. 2. The shot of the testing videos.

thresholds. In Fig. 3, both the testing depth levels and the JNDD thresholds are presented in the virtual depth space in which it is easy to fit the MJNDD model parameters.

Since the original experimental results are obtained in the shooting space, it is necessary to transform them into virtual depth space. In the virtual depth space, the origin of coordinates is set at the midpoint of two eyes, corresponding to the origin of the shooting space. The difference between the two spaces is that the testing depth levels are scaled according to shooting parameters and displaying condition. To transform the data from the shooting space to the virtual depth space, three steps are carried out. At first, the depth level Z in shooting space is transformed to screen disparities d_l measured in pixels as:

$$d_l = \frac{Bf}{Z} \tag{8}$$

where B is the baseline. And f is focal length, which is obtained via the camera calibration. Then the screen disparity d_l is transformed to the perceived depth d_p, i.e. the distance from the screen to the virtual objects, as follows [11]:

$$d_p = \frac{v \cdot d}{e} = \frac{v \cdot d_l \cdot p_x}{e} \tag{9}$$

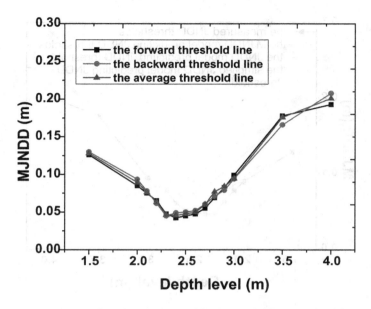

Fig. 3. The subjective experimental results.

where e is the inter-pupillary distance, 6.5 cm for adults on average. v is the viewing distance. d is the screen disparity in unit of cm, which can be transformed from screen disparity in unit of pixel d_l by multiplying the horizontal pixel size p_x. At last, the perceived depth d_p is transformed to the depth level d_s in virtual space as:

$$d_s = v - d_p \qquad (10)$$

For the given displaying condition, the near bound and the far bound of the fixation region d_n and d_f are 2.34 m and 2.67 m respectively. And the model parameters k_n and k_f are fitted as -0.098 and 0.117 respectively, according to the subjective experimental results. Therefore, the MJNDD model can be expressed in the given displaying condition as:

$$\Delta d_{MJNDD}(d_s) = \begin{cases} 0.061 - 0.098 \cdot (d_s - 2.34) & d_s < 2.34 \\ 0.054 \cdot (d_s - 2.5) + 0.07 & 2.34 \le d_s \le 2.67 \\ 0.083 + 0.117 \cdot (d_s - 2.67) & d_s > 2.67 \end{cases} \qquad (11)$$

4.3   Predicting Performance Evaluation

We compare the predicting performance of the MJNDD model with the JNDD model [3] and the simplified JNDD model [4]. As illustrated in Fig. 4, the black curve is the subjective experimental results. The red curve represents the JNDD thresholds predicted by the MJNDD model, which matches with the subject experimental data better than the other two models. It confirms that the MJNDD model is effective. The blue curve and

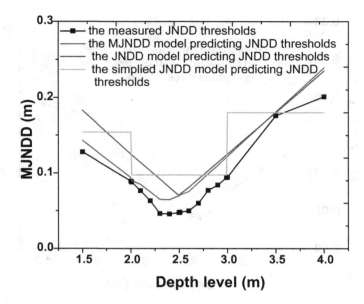

Fig. 4. The subjective experiment results. (Color figure online)

Table 1. Comparison of the PLCC of the three models

Model	Average fitting error	PLCC
JNDD	0.14	0.971
Simplified JNDD	0.17	0.808
MJNDD	0.09	0.977

the green curve represent the JNDD model [3] and the simplified JNDD model [4] respectively. The predicting performances of them are less than that of the MJNDD model. Especially, the lowest threshold point in either JNDD model or simplified JNDD model is at the zero parallax planes. However, the lowest threshold point in the subjective experimental data is a little in front of the screen. Only the MJNDD model reflects the phenomenon rightly.

To further compare the prediction performances of the three models quantitatively, we computer the fitting error and Pearson linear correlation coefficient (PLCC). The fitting degrees of the three models are listed in Table 1. We can see from Table 1, the performance of the MJNDD model is better than the other two models, which demonstrates the MJNDD model is more accurate.

5 Conclusion

In this paper, we present a MJNDD model of a three-piecewise linear function. Since the MJNDD model is built on the base of the related physiological structure of HVS, it predicted the JNDD thresholds more accurate than the state of the art JNDD model.

Besides, the MJNDD model is built in the virtual space, so that it is general. When the viewing condition varies, the relative parameters can be computed according to the displaying parameters.

Acknowledgment. This work was supported in part by the National Natural Science Foundation of China, under Grants 61571285, U1301257, and 61422111.

References

1. Carr, H.: A Introduction to Space Perception. Longmans, Green and Co., New York (1935)
2. Cutting, J., Vishton, P.: Perceiving layout and knowing distances: the interaction, relative potency, and contextual use of different information about depth. In: Handbook of Perceive and Cognition, vol. 5. Academic Press (1995)
3. De Silva, D.V.S.X., Fernando, W.A.C., Worrall, S.T., Kodikara Arachchi, H., Kondoz, A.: Sensitivity analysis of humans for depth cues in stereoscopic 3D displays. IEEE Trans. Multimedia **13**(3), 498–506 (2011)
4. De Silva, D.V.S.X., Ekmekcioglu, E., Fernando, W.A.C., Worrall, S.T.: Display dependent preprocessing of depth maps based on just noticeable depth difference modeling. IEEE J. Sel. Top. Sign. Process. **5**(2), 335–351 (2011)
5. Jung, S.-W., Ko, S.-J.: Depth sensation enhancement using the just noticeable depth difference. IEEE Trans. Image Process. **21**(8), 3624–3637 (2012)
6. Jung, S.-W.: A modified model of the just noticeable depth difference and its application to depth sensation enhancement. IEEE Trans. Image Process. **22**(10), 3892–3903 (2013)
7. Pettigrew, J.D., Nikara, T., Bishop, P.O.: Binocular interaction on single units in cat striate cortex: simultaneous stimulation by single moving slit with receptive fields in correspondence. Exp. Brain Res. **6**, 391–410 (1968)
8. Poggio, G.F., Fisher, B.: Binocular interaction and depth sensitivity in striate and prostrate cortex of behaving rhesus monkey. J. Neurophysiol. **40**(6), 1392–1405 (1977)
9. Verhoef, B.E., Bohon, K.S., Conway, B.R.: Functional architecture for disparity in macaque inferior temporal cortex and its relationship to the architecture for faces, color, scenarios, and visual field. J. Neurosci. **35**(17), 6952–6968 (2015)
10. Foley, J.M.: Perception. Handbook of Sensory Physiology, vol. VIII. Springer, Heidelberg (1978)
11. Committee Draft of ISO/IEC 23002-3 Auxiliary Video Data Representations, ISO/IEC JTC 1/SC 29/WG 11, WG 11 Doc. N8038 (2006)

A Joint Spatial-Temporal 3D Video Stabilization Algorithm

Jie Zhou[1], Zhixiang You[1], Ping An[1(✉)], Xinliang Wu[2], and Tengyue Du[1]

[1] School of Communication and Information Engineering,
Shanghai University, Shanghai 200072, China
`anping@shu.edu.cn`
[2] China Aeronautical Radio Electronics Research Institute,
Shanghai 200233, China

Abstract. This paper presents a 3D (Three dimensional) video stabilization algorithm combined with a joint spatial and temporal strategy. On the temporal axis, SURF (Speeded-Up Robust Features) are extracted from the consecutive frames and then motion parameters are estimated, with which we calibrate and compensate the video frames after smoothing the motion parameters using Kalman filtering. Then, on the spatial axis, a histogram statistics method based on the extracted features is applied to detect the vertical parallax between the two views. Adjustments are implemented only when the parallax is larger than the safety threshold, which is conducted through subjective assessment, to maintain the consistency of 3D videos. The experimental results have shown that the proposed method is effective to reduce the vertical instability and inconsistency between binocular views and improve the quality and comfortableness of 3D videos.

Keywords: 3d video stabilization · SURF feature · Motion parameters · Kalman filter

1 Introduction

With the development of image sensing technology and mobile computing power in last years, the video acquisition is gradually shifting to hand-held devices, which allow many amateurs to capture personal videos easily despite that a considerable number of these videos are affected by unwanted camera shakes and jitters, leading to low quality video and visual uncomfortableness. The hardware methods make use of mechanical principle such as fixing the cameras on the Steadicam, which are too expensive or inconvenient for amateurs.

On the other hand, digital video stabilization is the process of removing undesirable shakes and jitters and compensating the video sequences, which only takes advantage of the information of video frames and does not need camera motion information additionally. So that it is not expensive and has high stability precision. Furthermore, this technology can be implemented in real-time. In recent years, digital video stabilization is widely applied to improve the quality of videos captured by hand-held cameras, video

© Springer Nature Singapore Pte Ltd. 2017
X. Yang and G. Zhai (Eds.): IFTC 2016, CCIS 685, pp. 72–82, 2017.
DOI: 10.1007/978-981-10-4211-9_8

monitoring based on the motion platform, vehicle-mounted mobile video stabilization and robot navigation.

Video stabilization system is generally divided into two basic parts: motion estimation and motion smoothing. The motion estimation system generally makes an attempt to establish the global motion between nearby frames in a video. To reach this goal, there are two main current strategies: optical flow estimation and feature matching methods. In [1], the motion between successive frames was estimated by optical flow. In [2], a special optical flow called SteadyFlow was proposed. Different from the optical flow, the SteadyFlow has strong spatial smoothness, so that the pixel profiles from the SteadyFlow can be smoothed to stabilize the video. On the contrary, the latter method makes use of the features between successive frames to track the motion. In [3], the video stabilization algorithm tracked the Scale Invariant Feature Transform features to estimate the interframe motion. Then a modified Iterative Least Squares method reduced the estimation errors in order to improve video stability. In [4], a full-frame video stabilization algorithm based on SIFT feature matching was presented. Firstly, SIFT features were extracted to define the affine of 2D perspective warp between nearby frames. Finally, a temporal domain filter was applied to every frame to remove the high frequency components that are thought as noise or undesired camera jitters. The algorithm in [5] also extracted the SIFT features to track the video motion. With the regard to motion smoothing, a considerable number of methods have been proposed. In [6], Matsushita et al. averaged some affine matrices of neighboring frames as new transformation. In [5], Mengsi et al. firstly filtered the global motion by means of Kalman filter and an ideal low-pass filter with the Hanning window. The drawback of [5] is that the filter was not adaptive and the cutoff frequency should be set before filter processing. In [7], it compared Kalman filter and least square fitting in respect of motion smoothing and drew a conclusion that the fitting method performs better than Kalman filter, while Kalman filtering is more suitable for real-time environments because it needs only one observation data from the previous state. Liu et al. presented a joint subspace stabilization method for 3D video in [11], they jointly constructed a common subspace from the left and right video and it was used to stabilize the two videos simultaneously. The method achieved high-quality stabilization for 3D video. But it had difficulties to handle dominating scene motion, excessive shake and strong motion blur. In [12], feature points were tracked to model stabilized camera motion, and then projected the tracked points onto the stabilized frames using epipolar point transfer technology and image-based frame warping. The algorithm was robust to ambiguities and degenerate camera motion, but it could not deal with strong camera jitters and scene where only little features could be detected.

This paper presents a stabilization method for binocular 3D video combined with both spatial domain and temporal domain. In the temporal domain, for each 2D video, the interframe motion is estimated by tracking the SURF features through successive frames and Kalman filtering is applied to remove the high frequency components (impulsive jitters). Finally, we use a low-pass filter to improve the stabilization performance and fill the miss pixel in order to protect the original resolution. On the other hand, we adjust the vertical disparity between two views in the spatial domain. To speed up the algorithm, we establish a vertical parallax histogram for the extracted features and adjust the vertical parallax according to the histogram.

The rest of this paper is organized as follows: In Sect. 2, the temporal method for video stabilization based on SURF feature matching is presented. In Sect. 3, the spatial method is described in detail. And the whole algorithm combined with Sects. 2 and 3 is proposed in Sect. 4. Experimental results are given in Sect. 5. Finally, the paper draws the conclusions in Sect. 6.

2 Video Stabilization

This section introduces the video stabilization via feature tracking and hybrid filtering. Our approach uses SURF keypoints as features for tracking interframe motion of each 2D view respectively. SURF features are extracted from two consecutive frames and then these features are required to be matched correctly so as to estimate the motion. However the initial matching cannot give correct information how the current frame moves relatively to the previous. Effective verification procedure should be applied to discard wrong matches.

This scheme assumes that the first frame is stable and take the previous frame as the reference frame to stabilize the current frame. The process doesn't terminate until the last frame is stable.

2.1 Motion Estimation

Paper [3] used Euclidean distance between descriptors' vectors and a distance ratio to refine the feature matches. For every keypoint in the previous frame, there are two candidate matching points in the current frame, which are the closest and the second closest points. The distance ratio means the ratio of closest distance to the second closest one. The reliable match is that the closest distance is small when the second closest distance is larger. As a result, the ratio should be small. On the other hand, when these two distances are close to each other and the ratio is close to one, we can't determine which match is more reliable. We check the ratio against the predefined threshold. If the ratio is smaller than the threshold, the match is reliable. On the contrary, if the ratio is larger, the match should be discarded.

Although the distance ratio can improve the reliability of matches, there is a problem that a point A from the previous frame can match a point B well, but any matching point can not be found in the previous frame for the point B. To solve this problem, we use a symmetrical strategy and two sets of features are verified whether they are matched each other. Finally the RANSAC algorithm [17] is applied to further verify the reliability of feature matches. After the above processing, matches are reliable enough. According to these reliable matches, the video motion can be tracked. However, the video motion should also be smoothed because of the noise in the video.

2.2 Motion Smoothing

As described in the previous section, the motion can be described by homography of 2D perspective transformation. The transformation matrix T can be computed by reliable matches. To smooth the noise in the video, motion filtering are necessary.

First, neighboring frames should be taken into consideration to smooth the series of transformation in the video. Let T_i^j denote the transformation from frame i to j. Here, the index of current frame is assumed as t, and the indices of its 2k+1 neighboring frames can be denoted by $N_t = \{w|t - k \leq w \leq t + k\}$. The final transformation T_{final} for smoothing can be denoted as following:

$$T_{final} = \sum_{i \in N_t} T_i^t * G(||t - i||, \sigma) \tag{1}$$

Where $G(u, \sigma) = \dfrac{1}{\sqrt{2\pi}\sigma} e^{-\dfrac{u^2}{2\sigma^2}}$ and $\sigma = \sqrt{k}$. Then the transformation T_{final} is performed on the current frame in order to smooth the motion.

After the perspective transformation, the Kalman filtering algorithm is adopted to remove the camera jitter further. The Kalman filter is known as a recursive filter, which uses a series of measurements over time and produces estimates. Figure 1 shows the structure of Kalman filter.

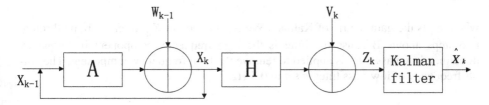

Fig. 1. Kalman filter structure

In Fig. 1, matrix A is the state transformation model between time $k - 1$ to k, and W_{k-1} is the system noise obeying Gaussian distribution and its covariance matrix is Q. The current state of the system can be described as follows:

$$X_K = AX_{k-1} + W_{k-1} \tag{2}$$

Z_k is the measurement of state X_k at time k, and matrix H is the measurement matrix. V_k is the measurement of noise and it also obeys Gaussian distribution, whose mean is zero and covariance matrix is R. The measurement state Z_k is:

$$Z_K = HX_k + V_k \tag{3}$$

The relevant matrix of Kalman filter is set up as follows:

$$A = \begin{bmatrix} 1 & 0 & 1 & 0 \\ 0 & 1 & 0 & 1 \\ 0 & 0 & 1 & 0 \\ 0 & 0 & 0 & 1 \end{bmatrix} \quad H = \begin{bmatrix} 1 & 0 & 0 & 0 \\ 0 & 1 & 0 & 0 \\ 0 & 0 & 1 & 0 \\ 0 & 0 & 0 & 1 \end{bmatrix} \tag{4}$$

The covariance matrix of the system noise Q and the covariance matrix of the measurement noise R are predefined, and we choose the diagonal matrix of 0.01 in this paper. We assume that $\hat{X}_k$ is the estimated value of X_k, and P_k is the posteriori error estimate covariance matrix of X_k. The initial value of $\hat{X}_k$ and P_k can be set as any value.

The operation of Kalman is mainly divided into two parts: prediction and correction.

(1) prediction:

$$\hat{X}_{k|k-1} = A\hat{X}_{k-1|k-1}$$
$$P_{k|k-1} = AP_{k-1|k-1}A^T + Q_k \tag{5}$$

(2) correction:

$$K_k = P_{k|k-1}H^T\left(HP_{k|k-1}H^T + R_k\right)^{-1}$$
$$\hat{X}_{k|k} = \hat{X}_{k|k-1} + K_k\left(Z_k - H\hat{X}_{k|k-1}\right) \tag{6}$$
$$P_{k|k} = (I - K_kH)P_{k|k-1}$$

where K_k is the gain matrix of Kalman. We can get output $\hat{X}_{k|k}$ of each frame through two steps above. Because the jitter is the high frequency component in frequency domain, a low-pass filter is applied to remove the high frequency component. The cut-off frequency of low-pass filter is set to 0.5 Hz.

2.3   Video Completion

Since the process of motion smoothing and low-pass filtering results for the missing pixels, a video completion is required to fill the missing pixels so that the original resolution can be protected. This paper uses an average method and a missing pixel is described as follows:

$$I_t(m, n) = \frac{1}{N_t} \sum_{i \in N_t} I'_i(m, n) \tag{7}$$

Where I_t is the current frame which is needed to be stabilized and I'_i is the frame that has been stabilized.

3   Parallax Adjustment

In [8], Kooi et al. found that vertical parallax, crosstalk and blur could determine the comfort of viewing 3D video through subjective experiments. The definition of vertical parallax is the vertical distances between the same points from different viewpoints. In this paper, pixels in the left view are taken as the baseline and thus the vertical parallax is computed from pixels in the right view to their counterparts in the left view. In addition to horizontal parallax, vertical disparity should be controlled in a certain range. Large vertical parallax in parallax images should be avoided because it is disadvantageous to stereo vision due to the presence of visual fatigue. The larger vertical parallax is, the deeper the level of visual fatigue will be. From the above, we must remove the jitter or parallax in the vertical direction for better 3D vision effect.

First, we extract the SURF features instead of every pixels in the left and right views. This strategy can reduce the complexity greatly. Compared with commonly used SIFT features, SURF features can be extracted faster. To be precise, extracting SIFT features is three times as fast as SURF, but SURF performs worse than SIFT in terms of scale and rotation transformation. Second, we use FLANN (Fast Library for Approximate Nearest Neighbors) for matching extracted features in two views. To ensure the feature point matching is robust and reliable, RANSAC algorithm is implemented to reject outliers and wrong matches. Not many correct feature matches are needed to represent whole pixels in order to compute the vertical parallax. Third, we compute the vertical parallax of matched feature points respectively and average them to obtain the statistical vertical parallax. Finally, we rectify the vertical parallax according to the third step. The experiments in Sect. 4 show that the vertical parallax of the two viewpoints is almost zero in most frames.

4   Overall Framework

Figure 2 shows the framework of this paper. Disparity rectification and video stabilization are put into a framework. The statistics vertical parallax is computed for each frame and it will be compared with a threshold. If it is less than the predefined threshold, we think the parallax is caused by difference of CMOS or CCD in cameras and we will apply parallax rectification to rectify the parallax. On the other hand, if the vertical parallax is larger than the threshold, which maybe created by camera jitter, so that the video stabilization is performed.

5   Experimental Results

The experimental system is implemented in Visual C++ 2013, and the resolution of the experimental video is 1920 × 1080. Because of the deformation of the holder, the inconsistency of CCD or CMOS or inaccuracy crafts, these factors will bring vertical disparity of different level. Vertical disparity will influence the quality of 3D images and large disparity will produce ghosting. In addition, vertical parallax can lead to keystone distortion or other geometric distortion, which will affect the comfort of 3D images. In

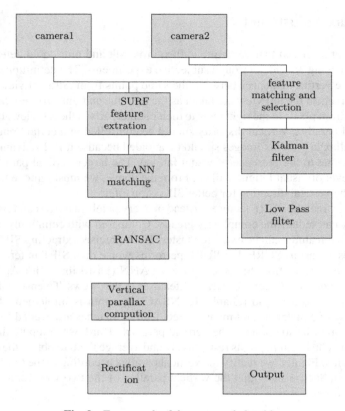

Fig. 2. Framework of the proposed algorithm

view of the disparity, we have done sixteen groups of subjective experiments. Figure 3 is two groups. The horizontal ordinate represents the pixels difference between two views and the vertical ordinate is the subjective scores from fifteen experimenters. The higher scores are, the better comfort viewers can get. In these subjective experiments, we conclude that vertical disparity of more than forty pixels will bring uncomfortable-ness and the scores drop sharply. The aim of our method is to reduce vertical disparity which caused by jitter motion or any other cue.

Figure 4(a) shows the SURF feature matching and Fig. 4(b) presents the matching result refined by RANSAC. Comparing the two figures, some wrong matches in Fig. 4(a) have been discarded and remain the reliable ones. Correct feature matches can track camera motion more robust.

After the reliable features matches are captured, a hybrid filtering method (Kalman and low-pass filter) is applied to the jitter video. Figure 5 shows the vertical parallax after the video stabilization algorithm is performed, where x-axis is the number of frames and y-axis means the video motion in the vertical direction. The red curve shows the original parallax between the successive frames, while the blue curve is the result after stabilizing the video. The parallax of most frames in blue curve are close to zero.

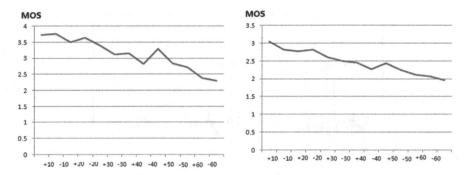

Fig. 3. Subjective experiments of vertical disparity

Figure 6 shows the vertical parallax between original left and right video after corrected feature matching and parallax adjustment, where x-axis represents the number of frames and y-axis means the vertical disparity. The red curve is original parallax between two views and the blue curve is the result of parallax rectification. In this figure, we can see that the rectification process can't deal with large and impulsive vertical parallax.

(a) Initial matching

(b) Refined matching

Fig. 4. Initial and refined SURF feature matching

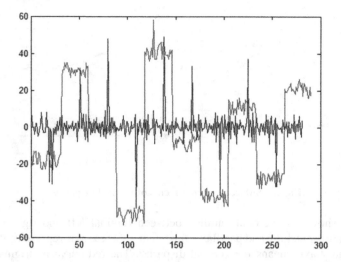

Fig. 5. Vertical parallax curves of video stabilization; the red curve indicates the original parallax and the blue curve is the result after stabilization. (Color figure online)

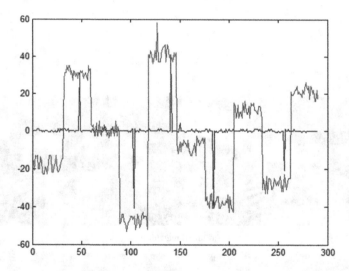

Fig. 6. Vertical parallax curves of parallax rectification; the red curve indicates the original parallax and the blue curve is the result after the parallax adjustment. (Color figure online)

To remove such large and impulsive vertical parallax, the strategy is that the video should be stabilized first and parallax adjustment can be operated on the stabilized video. Because the jitters in the vertical direction can also bring vertical parallax. The vertical parallax from jitter motion should be processed first and then the parallax adjustment algorithm is applied to reduce the vertical parallax further.

In Fig. 7, the blue curve is the original vertical parallax and the red curve is the final result of this paper. It shows that our approach can remove the vertical parallax in most frames and smooth the camera motion at the same time.

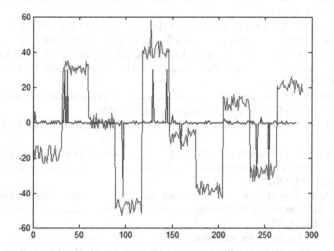

Fig. 7. Vertical parallax curve of final result; the red curve indicates the original parallax and the blue curve is the final result of our algorithm. (Color figure online)

6 Conclusion

In this paper, we present a video stabilization algorithm combined with parallax rectification and feature-based stabilization technology. For smaller parallax, we rectify it directly based on parallax of the feature points. For larger parallax, we take advantage of temporal stabilization strategy for 2D video to smooth the inter-frame motion. Our method has difficulty to handle the strong camera motion and large vertical disparity in few frames, while the algorithm gets good performance in most video frames.

However our temporal method is not a 3D video stabilization, and the next work is to stabilize the video based on the video of the other view. In future work, our algorithm will be speeded up and the stabilized 3D video can be displayed in real time.

Acknowledgment. This work was supported in part by the National Natural Science Foundation of China, under Grants 61571285, and U1301257. The work is also supported by the 2016 peak discipline of filmology of Shanghai University.

References

1. Gleicher, M.L., Liu, F.: Re-cinematography: improving the camera dynamics of casual video. In: International Conference on Multimedia, pp. 27–36. ACM (2007)
2. Liu, S., Yuan, L., Tan, P., et al.: SteadyFlow: spatially smooth optical flow for video stabilization. In: Computer Vision and Pattern Recognition, pp. 4209–4216. IEEE (2014)

3. Battiato, S., Gallo, G., Puglisi, G., et al.: SIFT features tracking for video stabilization. In: International Conference on Image Analysis and Processing, pp. 825–830 (2007)
4. Chen, Y.H., Lin, H.Y.S., Su, C.W.: Full-frame video stabilization via sift feature matching. In: Tenth International Conference on Intelligent Information Hiding and Multimedia Signal Processing. IEEE (2014)
5. He, M., Huang, C., Xiao, C., et al.: Digital video stabilization based on hybrid filtering. In: International Congress on Image and Signal Processing, pp. 94–98. IEEE (2014)
6. Matsushita, Y., Ofek, E., Tang, X., et al.: Full-frame video stabilization. In: IEEE Computer Society Conference on Computer Vision and Pattern Recognition 2005, CVPR 2005, vol. 1, pp. 50–57 (2005)
7. Yu, H., Zhang, W.: Moving camera video stabilization based on Kalman filter and least squares fitting. In: Intelligent Control and Automation. IEEE (2015)
8. Kooi, F.L., Toet, A.: Visual comfort of binocular and 3D displays. Displays 25(2–3), 99–108 (2004)
9. Liu, W.X., Chin, T.J.: Smooth globally warp locally: video stabilization using homography fields. In: International Conference on Digital Image Computing: Techniques and Applications. IEEE (2015)
10. Salunkhe, A.U., Jagtap, S.K.: A survey on an adaptive video stabilization with tone adjustment. In: International Conference on Computing Communication Control and Automation. IEEE (2015)
11. Liu, F., Niu, Y., Jin, H.: Joint subspace stabilization for stereoscopic video. In: 2013 IEEE International Conference on Computer Vision (ICCV), pp. 73–80. IEEE (2013)
12. Goldstein, A., Fattal, R.: Video stabilization using epipolar geometry. ACM Trans. Graph. 32(5), 573–587 (2012)
13. Liu, S., Yuan, L., Tan, P., et al.: Bundled camera paths for video stabilization. ACM Trans. Graph. 32(4), 96 (2013)
14. Song, J., Ma, X.: A novel real-time digital video stabilization algorithm based on the improved diamond search and modified Kalman filter 91–95 (2015)
15. Pinto, B., Anurenjan, P.R.: Video stabilization using speeded up robust features. In: 2011 International Conference on Communications and Signal Processing (ICCSP), pp. 527–531. IEEE (2011)
16. Mayen, K., Espinoza, C., Romero, H., et al.: Real-time video stabilization algorithm based on efficient block matching for UAVs. In: The Workshop on Research, Education and Development of Unmanned Aerial Systems. IEEE (2015)
17. Fischler, M.A., Bolles, R.C.: Random sample consensus: a paradigm for model fitting with applications to image analysis and automated cartography. Commun. ACM 24(6), 381–395 (1981)

Enhanced SURF-Based Image Matching Using Pre- and Post-processing

Chenfei Zhang, Yaozu Wu, Ning Liu$^{(\boxtimes)}$, and Chongyang Zhang

Institute of Image Communication and Network Engineering,
Shanghai Jiao Tong University, Shanghai 200240, China
ningliu@sjtu.edu.cn

Abstract. SURF-based algorithms have been proved to be one of the most effective image matching methods. Considering the challenges induced by the poor illumination conditions or local-feature-similar noises, one enhanced SURF-based image matching method(E-SURF) using pre- and post-processing is developed in this work: pre- and post-processing is adopted to enhance the image matching performance in some challenging cases: Median filtering and Histogram linear transformation is adopted as the preprocessing to remove the isolated noises and amplify the illumination contrast, so that more SURF points can be found; After SURF matching, one LBP-based filtering is used to filter the possible false matching points using local texture features. Experimental results on some complicated images show that the proposed method can outperform the existing SIFT and SURF schemes.

Keywords: Image matching · SURF (Speeded Up Robust Features) · Local Binary Patterns (LBP) · Median filter

1 Introduction

With the development of automation technology, the object recognition application is widely used in the automatic production lines. To ensure the accuracy of object recognition, image matching algorithms stand on a vital position. One of the most effective algorithms for identifying several images with similar feature is SURF (Speeded Up Robust Features) [1]. Based on SIFT(Scale Invariant Feature Transform) method [2], SURF algorithm inherits the advantages of rotation invariant, scale invariant and affine invariant. In addition, it requires shorter running time and has better robustness for multiple images.

The traditional SURF algorithm is divided in three main steps, which can be sketched as finding interest point, forming descriptor and matching. There have been a large number of improved algorithms based on SURF algorithm proposed in the literatures(e.g. [6–12]). For example, an improved algorithm based on SURF uses a matching method of subset of features to improve the speed of registration [6]. Another example is that an improved SURF algorithm based on distance constraint improves the accuracy of matching [7]. When the

© Springer Nature Singapore Pte Ltd. 2017
X. Yang and G. Zhai (Eds.): IFTC 2016, CCIS 685, pp. 83–92, 2017.
DOI: 10.1007/978-981-10-4211-9_9

image is formed with some rigid bodies, interest points can be detected easily, the matching time can be much shorter and the accuracy can be high enough. However, in some complicated cases, such as the images brightness is too low or too high to find enough interest points, the SURF-based matching methods may not perform very well. Another challenge is the noise, especially the noise that has similar local features with the interest points, which will cause the false matching [13,14].

Considering the above challenges, especially the poor illumination conditions and local-feature-similar noises, one enhanced SURF-based image matching method(E-SURF as short) using pre- and post-processing is developed to promote the robustness in these challenging cases: Median filtering and Histogram linear transformation is adopted as the preprocessing to remove the isolated noises and amplify the illumination contrast, so that more SURF points can be found. After SURF matching, one LBP (Local Binary Patterns) [4] based filtering is used to filter the possible false matching points using local texture features.

The paper is organized as follows. Section 2 describes the principle of E-SURF method, including the histogram linear transformation, LBP feature based filtering and median filtering. In Sect. 3, results are given and analyzed. Section 4 concludes the whole work.

2   Enhanced SURF-Based Image Matching Using Pre- and Post-processing (E-SURF)

The proposed E-SURF algorithm is divided in four main steps, which can be sketched as Median filtering, Histogram linear transformation, SURF-based matching, and LBP-based filtering (Fig. 1). The details of the three components (except the well-known SURF-based matching) are shown in the following subsections.

2.1   Histogram Linear Transformation and Median Filtering

The detector of SURF algorithm is based on the Hessian matrix, as well as the non-maximum suppression and scale space interpolation. In some extreme

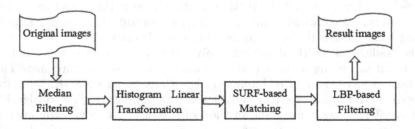

Fig. 1. The flow chart of the proposed E-SURF algorithm

conditions like the left image in Fig. 2(Left), the contrast of the image is too low to detect enough interest points(For the image in Fig. 2(Left), no interest points can be detected) [15]. Given an image with low contrast like that, the gray values of that images histogram are within a very small range, which causes the failure of interest point detection. FOR those extreme conditions, we use Histogram linear transformation to enhance the contrast of images. Since the maximum range of gray value is [0,255], we enhance the contrast of the image by widening the gray value range. This is achieved by using Histogram linear transformation [3]. Before matching, images are processed with Histogram linear transformation. That is defined as follows

$$r' = \frac{r'_b - r'_a}{r_b - r_a}(r - r_a) + r'_a, \quad r \in [r_a, r_b]$$

$$r' = r'_a, \qquad\qquad\qquad r \in [r_{min}, r_a] \qquad\qquad (1)$$

$$r' = r'_b, \qquad\qquad\qquad r \in [r_b, r_{max}]$$

where $r \in [r_a, r_b]$ is the gray value range of the original image, $r \in [r'_a, r'_b]$ is the gray value range of the transformed image, r is the original gray value, and r' is the transformed gray value.

After a series of experiments, [0,110] is chosen for the empirical value of $r \in [r'_a, r'_b]$. The contrast of the image becomes strong enough for the interest point detection after Histogram linear transformation (Fig. 2(Right)): For the image in Fig. 2(Left), no interest points can be detected due to the low illumination; while all the center points of the circle objects can be detected as SURF points when histogram linear transformation is applied (Fig. 2(Right)).

(a)   (b)

Fig. 2. Illustration of SURF detection without (Left) or with histogram linear transformation (Right)

In the SURF algorithm, a matching pair is detected if its Euclidean distance is closer than 0.7 times the distance of the second nearest neighbor. Inevitably, some similar but different interest points are matched because they meet the threshold. Histogram linear transformation is used to reduce those false positive matches. Consider the threshold, Histogram linear transformation can enhance the contrast and enlarge the discrepancy in gray value between pixels, which can make most of the false positive matches do not meet the threshold. Hence,

Table 1. Comparison of correct matching rate for different filters

	Median filter	Bilateral filter	Mean filter	Gaussian filter
Figure 4(a)	87.50%	54.35%	75.00%	75.00%
Figure 4(b)	96.15%	90.00%	90.32%	93.33%
Figure 4(c)	79.49%	45.76%	46.77%	40%

Histogram linear transformation allows for more detected interest points and gives a significantly increase in correct matching rate.

In many times, there is much noise in the original images which make the matching interfered. The isolated noises, such as salt-and-pepper noises, will make up as corner points and result in false matching easily. Because we focus on the interest points, the impulse noises are most likely to cause the mismatches. Comparing to other useful filters, the median filter has better performance in our experiments. The comparison is shown in Table 1. Thus, median filter algorithm can be a proper method of removing those noises before the Histogram linear transformation [5].

The median filter algorithm can be divided into two steps. Firstly of all, put the gray-level value of a pixel and its eight adjacent pixels in numerical order. Then, obtain the mid-value and assign these nine pixels the mid-value [19,20]. The formula of median filter is shown as follows

$$g(m,n) = \underset{i,j \in S}{Median}[f(i,j)] \tag{2}$$

where S corresponds to a 3×3 block revolved around the center pixel.

2.2 LBP-Based Filtering

Another problem in traditional SURF algorithm is incorrect estimation for matching interest points [16]. In a realistic scenario, there will be many similar corner points and noise in an image. For better object description, extracted features should have distinctiveness, which means a special value to distinguish the detected interest points and any other points [21]. With the traditional SURF description based on the Haar wavelet feature, which has good robustness to region directionality, the features of interest points are defined as the sum of Haar response values in a small region. The description described by a sum means that it focuses on the directionality but has less rotation variant. So when meeting some interest points having similar feature, those points will be matched each other directly and there is no method to filter disturbance points. To overcome this problem, mismatches should be corrected and interest points should have not only directional feature, but also texture feature. Therefore, local Binary Patterns, referred to simply as LBP is taken into consideration [4]. LBP can extract feature from a 3×3 block to make interest points have their own region texture feature, as well as ignore the scaling of gray level. The region texture feature is closely related to better rotation invariant. So LBP-based filtering can be used as one post-processing to remove the error matching points which have similar Haar wavelet feature but different LBP feature. In the procedure of matching, most of similar corner points and noises will be distinguished for different LBP feature. The formula of LBP-based filter is shown as follows

$$LBP_9value = \sum_{i=0}^{8} f(g_i - g_c) \times 2^i, f(x) = \begin{cases} 1 & x \geqslant 0 \\ 0 & \text{otherwise} \end{cases} \tag{3}$$

where g_c corresponds to the gray-level value of the chosen interest point and g_i to the gray-level value of the adjacent eight pixels revolved around the interest point.

An example chart of LBP feature extraction is shown in Fig. 3. There is a 3×3 block revolved around the template interest point in the top left hand corner in figure (b). In figure (a), one block is similar to the template block and another one is acquired by 180° rotation from the former block. For traditional matching method, it is obvious that both of the interest points in figure (a) are matched to the template interest point in figure (b) because their Haar wavelet feature is almost the same. However, only one matching is correct. Then for LBP feature filtering, the LBP values of those two interest points in figure (a) are different. [17]. Just obtain the difference of two digital numbers extracted from two images. '5' is the chosen threshold for the difference. Only one difference is less than the pre-set threshold. Therefore, only one pair of interest points is matched. So the LBP feature can be used to filter the mismatched points.

3 Experimental Results

In this section, the results of the experiment as well as the comparison are presented and illustrated using a standard evaluation set and an industrial object recognition application. In this paper, all the experimentations are conducted using Opencv2.4.9 with a 2.8 GHz Core i5 processor and a 4 GB of memory.

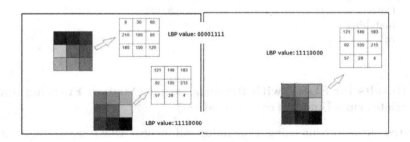

Fig. 3. The flow chart of the proposed E-SURF algorithm

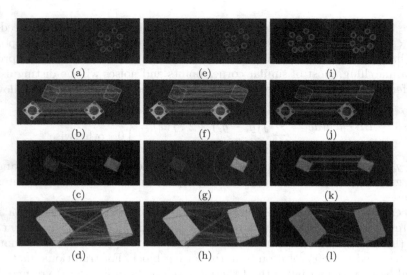

Fig. 4. Images from top to bottom: (a) (b) (c) (d) are matching results using original SIFT algorithm; (e) (f) (g) (h) are matching results using SURF algorithm; (i) (j) (k) (l) are results using SURF with pre-processing (Median Filtering and Histogram Linear Transformation)

Table 2. Comparison of detected points number, correct matching pairs number, and correct matching rate for the first group of test images (First line in Fig. 4)

First test group (First line in Fig. 4)	SIFT (Fig. 4(a))	SURF (Fig. 4(e))	SURF with pre-processing (Fig. 4(i))	Proposed E-SURF (Fig. 5(a))
Detected points	0	0	9	8
Correct matching pairs	0	0	8	8
Correct matching rate	0	0	88.90%	100%

3.1   Results for SURF with Pre-processing (Median Filtering and Histogram Linear Transformation)

We tested our algorithm using some industrial images. Due to space limitations, we selected four groups of typical images. For Histogram linear transformation (HLT), it is compared to the difference of SURF [1], and SIFT propose by Lowe [2]. The comparison results are shown in Fig. 4, Tables 2, 3, 4 and 5.

Table 3. Comparison of detected points number, correct matching pairs number, and correct matching rate for the second group of test images (Second line in Fig. 4)

Second test group (Second line in Fig. 4)	SIFT (Fig. 4(b))	SURF (Fig. 4(f))	SURF with pre-processing (Fig. 4(j))	Proposed E-SURF (Fig. 5(b))
Detected points	255	197	78	33
Correct matching pairs	221	170	75	33
Correct matching rate	86.67%	86.29%	96.20%	100%

Table 4. Comparison of detected points number, correct matching pairs number, and correct matching rate for the third group of test images (Third line in Fig. 4)

Third test group (Third line in Fig. 4)	SIFT (Fig. 4(c))	SURF (Fig. 4(g))	SURF with pre-processing (Fig. 4(k))	Proposed E-SURF (Fig. 5(c))
Detected points	5	0	12	6
Correct matching pairs	2	0	12	12
Correct matching rate	40.00%	default	100%	100%

Table 2 gives the comparison for the first test group (Fig. 4(a), (e), (i)). As can be seen, when the images have very low contrast (the case of first group), the original SIFT and SURF algorithm cannot detect any interest points but the E-SURF method can detect enough interest points due to the enhanced pre-processing using Histogram linear transformation.

Table 3 gives the comparison for the second test group (Fig. 4(b), (f), (j)). In this case, the correct matching rate of proposed algorithm is about ten percent higher than that of SURF or SIFT, and the most important correct matching pairs can also be retained.

Table 4 gives the comparison for the third test group (Fig. 4(c), (g), (k)). As we can see, SIFT and SURF do not work well in this case. But the E-surf method can detect enough interest points and improve the correct matching rate to 100%.

Table 5. Comparison of detected points number, correct matching pairs number, and correct matching rate for the fourth group of test images (Fourth line in Fig. 4)

Fourth test group (Fourth line in Fig. 4)	SIFT (Fig. 4(d))	SURF (Fig. 4(h))	SURF with pre-processing (Fig. 4(l))	Proposed E-SURF (Fig. 5(d))
Detected points	224	83	38	4
Correct matching pairs	31	14	11	3
Correct matching rate	13.84%	16.00%	28.95%	75.00%

In most conditions, our algorithm performs well in the interest point detection and matching. But in some extreme conditions like the group in Fig. 4(d), (h), (l), the proposed algorithm improves the correct matching rate but also has some problems in the interest point matching (Table 5). In some conditions like Table 3, the number of the matching pairs decreases a bit after our algorithm. But there are still remaining enough correct matching pairs to achieve the image matching [2].

3.2   Results for E-SURF (Pre-processing + SURF + Post-processing (LBP Filtering))

After the gray scale linear transformation, the accuracy of circular matching and the rectangle matching has been improved apparently, and the number of points of incorrect estimation has reduced slightly. In order to remove the error matching points which have similar Haar wavelet feature but different texture features, LBP-based filtering can be used as one effective post-processing.

Figure 5 gives the matching result using proposed E-SURF (Pre-processing + SURF + Post-processing). See Fig. 5(a), the mismatched point has been removed and the accuracy is up to 100% (last column in Table 2). In Fig. 5(b), it is obvious that all the remained match-lines are correct and the accuracy is also up to 100% (last column in Table 3). In Fig. 5(c), as can be seen, all the matching pairs are correct and some redundant matching pairs are suppressed (last column in Table 4). In the case of the fourth test images (Fig. 5(d)), the matching accuracy of the rectangle objects has achieved 75% with the proposed E-SURF, compared with the accuracy of less than 30% with the traditional SIFT and SURF methods (Table 5).

One of the disadvantages of the proposed E-SURF is that the matched SURF points will reduced greatly due to the filtering in pre and post processing,

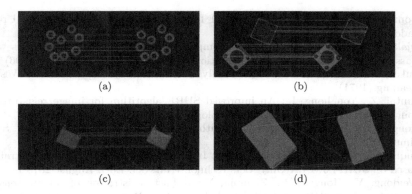

(a)   (b)

(c)   (d)

Fig. 5. Image matching result using the proposed E-SURF (Pre-processing + SURF + Post-processing).

especially for the case of fourth test group (only four pairs are left, Fig. 5(d)). But as the conclusion pointed out in [2], the ability to detect small objects in cluttered backgrounds requires that at least 3 features be correctly matched from each object for reliable identification. In all the cases, more than 3 pairs of points can be detected. So the image objects can be matched correctly.

4   Conclusion

We have presented a more accurate and robust algorithm based on SURF. With median filtering and histogram linear transformation as preprocessing, and LBP feature based filtering as post-processing, the proposed E-SURF algorithm is suitable to detect interest points with the image for very low contrast or very low brightness, and it can improve the correct matching rate at the same time. Future work will concentrate on eliminating the effect of fuzzy edge, increasing interest points in multiple rectangle matching, and reducing the time complexity by graph model.

Acknowledgements. This work was partly funded by NSFC (No. 61571297, No. 61371146, No. 61527804, and No. 61521062), 111 Project (B07022), and China National Key Technology R&D Program (No. 2012BAH07B01). We also thank GFocus Technologies Co. Ltd. for their test images supporting.

References

1. Bay, H., Tuytelaars, T., Gool, L.: SURF: speeded up robust features. In: Leonardis, A., Bischof, H., Pinz, A. (eds.) ECCV 2006. LNCS, vol. 3951, pp. 404–417. Springer, Heidelberg (2006). doi:10.1007/11744023_32
2. David, G.: Lowe: distinctive image features from scale-invariant keypoints. IJCV **60**(2), 91–110 (2004)

3. Gonzalez, R.C., Woods, R.E.: Digital Image Processing. Prentice Hall, Upper Saddle River (2007)
4. Ojala, T., Pietikinen, M., et al.: A comparative study of texture measures with classification based on feature distribution. Pattern Recogn. **29**, 51–59 (1996)
5. Tukey, J.W.: Exploratory Data Analysis (Preliminary Ed.). Addison-Wesley, Reading (1971)
6. Juntai, Z., Yonghong, L.: An improved SURF algorithm for image registration. Journal of Hunan University of Technology, March 2011
7. Hongbo, L.: An improved SURF algorithm based on distance constraint. J. Syst. Simul. **16**(12) (2014)
8. Suqing, G., Xunjun, T., Chengxia, H.: Improved algorithm of image registration based on SURF. J. PLA Univ. Sci. Technol. (Nat. Sci. Ed.), August 2013
9. Weidong, Y., Hongwei, S., Zhanbin, Y.: Robust registration of remote sensing image based on SURF and KCCA. J. Indian Soc. Remote Sens. **42**(2), 291–299 (2014)
10. Seung Hyeon Cheon, I.K., Ha, S., Moon, Y.H.: An enhanced SURF algorithm based on new interest point detection procedure and fast computation technique. J. Real-Time Image Proc., 1–11 (2016)
11. Lukashevich, P.V., Zalesky, B.A., Ablameyko, S.V.: Medical image registration based on SURF detector. Pattern Recogn. Image Anal. **21**(3), 519–521 (2011)
12. Sun, W., Shen, Q., Liu, C.: SURF feature description of color image based on gaussian model. In: Li, K., Li, J., Liu, Y., Castiglione, A. (eds.) ISICA 2015. CCIS, vol. 575, pp. 275–283. Springer, Singapore (2016). doi:10.1007/978-981-10-0356-1_28
13. Wu, Z., Xu, P.: A fast gradual shot boundary detection method based on SURF. In: Wen, Z., Li, T. (eds.) Practical Applications of Intelligent Systems. AISC, vol. 279, pp. 699–706. Springer, Heidelberg (2014). doi:10.1007/978-3-642-54927-4_66
14. Abeles, P.: Speeding up SURF. In: Bebis, G., et al. (eds.) ISVC 2013. LNCS, vol. 8034, pp. 454–464. Springer, Heidelberg (2013). doi:10.1007/978-3-642-41939-3_44
15. Mok, S.J., Jung, K., Ko, D.W., Lee, S.H., Choi, B.-U.: SERP: SURF enhancer for repeated pattern. In: Bebis, G., et al. (eds.) ISVC 2011. LNCS, vol. 6939, pp. 578–587. Springer, Heidelberg (2011). doi:10.1007/978-3-642-24031-7_58
16. McGuinness, K., McCusker, K., O'Hare, N., O'Connor, N.E.: Efficient storage and decoding of SURF feature points. In: Schoeffmann, K., Merialdo, B., Hauptmann, A.G., Ngo, C.-W., Andreopoulos, Y., Breiteneder, C. (eds.) MMM 2012. LNCS, vol. 7131, pp. 440–451. Springer, Heidelberg (2012). doi:10.1007/978-3-642-27355-1_41
17. Janusch, I., Kropatsch, W.G.: Persistence based on LBP scale space. In: Bac, A., Mari, J.-L. (eds.) CTIC 2016. LNCS, vol. 9667, pp. 240–252. Springer, Cham (2016). doi:10.1007/978-3-319-39441-1_22
18. Wei, Y., Lin, G., Sha, Y., Yonggang, D., Pan, J., Jun, W., Shijun, L.: An improved LBP algorithm for texture and face classification. SIViP **8**(Suppl. 1), 155–161 (2014)
19. Pitas, I., Venetsanopoulos, A.N.: Median filters. In: Nonlinear Digital Filters. The Springer International Series in Engineering and Computer Science, vol. 84, pp. 63–116. Springer, New York (1990)
20. Smolka, B., Szczepanski, M., Plataniotis, K.N., Venetsanopoulos, A.N.: Fast modified vector median filter. In: Skarbek, W. (ed.) CAIP 2001. LNCS, vol. 2124, pp. 570–580. Springer, Heidelberg (2001). doi:10.1007/3-540-44692-3_69
21. Abdel-Hakim, A.E., Farag, A.A.: CSIFT: a SIFT descriptor with color invariant characteristics. Proc. IEEE Comput. Soc. Conf. Comput. Vis. Pattern Recogn. **2**, 1978–1983 (2006)

Stereoscopic Image Quality Assessment Using Wavelet Decomposition and Natural Scene Statistics

Xianqiu Geng[✉], Liquan Shen, Yang Yao, and Ping An

School of Communication and Information Engineering,
Shanghai University, Shanghai 200072, China
jsslq@163.com

Abstract. Recently, stereoscopic image quality assessment (SIQA) has been attracted more attention in academia and industry nowadays. In this paper, a wavelet decomposition and natural scene statistics based no reference stereoscopic image quality assessment algorithm is proposed. Our motivation is based on the observation that the statistics of the wavelet coefficients can be effectively captured by a generalized Gaussian distribution (GGD), and the distributions of image with different distortion have different shape and spread. The fitting parameters of GGD are extracted as the features. In this paper, stereoscopic image relevant information including stereo pairs, cyclopean image and binocular disparity are regarded as the factors that affecting stereoscopic image quality, and they are involved in the process of feature extraction. Support vector regression (SVR) is utilized to learn a regression model to predict the quality of stereoscopic image. Experimental results demonstrate that the proposed algorithm achieves high consistency with subjective assessment on two public available 3D image quality assessment databases.

Keywords: Wavelet decomposition · Natural scene statistics · Generalized Gaussian distribution · Feature extraction · Support vector regression

1 Introduction

Recently, many researches have focused on the development of image quality assessment (IQA), and stereoscopic/3D-IQA has becoming a super-hot.

The existing stereoscopic image quality assessment (SIQA) methods can be classified into full-reference (FR) [1–3], reduced-reference (RR) [4], and no-reference (NR) methods [5–9]. Our work aims emphasis on no-reference stereoscopic image quality assessment (NR-SIQA), in which no reference image information is available. Akhter et al. [5] propose a NR-SIQA algorithm by extracting segmented local features of artifacts from stereo pairs and the estimated disparity map. Chen et al. [6] first use the binocular fusion model to compute cyclopean image from left and right images of stereo pairs. Features including 2D features and 3D features are extracted in spatial domain by natural scene statistics (NSS). In [7], Su et al. also consider the binocular combination model to generate a convergent cyclopean image from left and right images of stereo pairs. Spatial domain univariate NSS features, wavelet domain univariate NSS features,

© Springer Nature Singapore Pte Ltd. 2017
X. Yang and G. Zhai (Eds.): IFTC 2016, CCIS 685, pp. 93–103, 2017.
DOI: 10.1007/978-981-10-4211-9_10

and bivariate density and correlation NSS features are extracted from the convergent cyclopean image. Zhou et al. [8] utilize the complementary local patterns of binocular energy response and binocular rivalry response to simulate the binocular visual perception. The local patterns of the binocular responses' encoding maps are used to form various binocular quality-predictive features. In [9], Wang et al. construct feature vectors from binocular energy response and then use the machine learning method to learn a visual quality prediction model. However, the problem is that all these existing methods do not simultaneously take perceptual factors affecting 2D image quality and 3D stereo perception into consideration. Furthermore, 3D visual characteristics are partial simulated. In order to design a well-defined NR-SIQA method, quality relevant features from the independent left and right images could be useful. Moreover, features from transformed domain of cyclopean images are supplements. Others 3D visual perception information should be involved.

In this paper, we propose a perceptual NR-SIQA algorithm, in which quality relevant information including stereo pairs, cyclopean image and binocular disparity are considered. Features are extracted from the wavelet coefficients using natural scene statistics in the wavelet domain when stereo pairs, cyclopean image and binocular disparity map are transformed by the steerable pyramid decomposition. Support vector regression (SVR) is utilized to learn a regression model to predict the quality of stereoscopic image.

The remainder of this paper is organized as follows. The proposed algorithm is described in detail in Sect. 2. Experimental results are analyzed in Sect. 3, and finally conclusions are drawn in Sect. 4.

2   Proposed Algorithm

The flowchart of the proposed NR-SIQA algorithm is shown in Fig. 1.

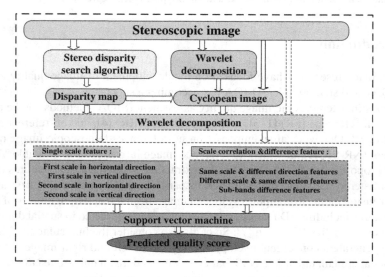

Fig. 1. Flowchart of the proposed algorithm

2.1   Binocular Disparity Search

The binocular disparity of one point in 3D image is the distance between two projected points in the left image and the right image, and the estimate of disparity for any point in left image is to find the same point in the right image.

In this paper, a Gaussian average SSIM based disparity search algorithm is proposed. SSIM index [10] measures the similarity between two image patch by

$$\text{SSIM}(1,r) = \frac{\left(2\mu_l\mu_r + c_1\right)\left(2\sigma_{lr} + c_2\right)}{\left(\mu_l^2 + \mu_r^2 + c_1\right)\left(\sigma_l^2 + \sigma_r^2 + c_2\right)} \tag{1}$$

where μ_l and μ_r are the average of left image patch and the right mage patch. σ_l^2 and σ_r^2 are the variance of left image and right image. σ_{lr} is the covariance of l and r. c_1 and c_2 are two parameters avoiding meaningless of the equation

In the process of disparity search, the leftmost part of the left image and the rightmost part of the right image should be discarded, since they cannot be captured by both cameras. For any point in left image with coordinate $[x_l, y_l]$, its related point in the right image is search from $[x_l - \text{range}, y_l]$ to $[x_l + \text{range}, y_l]$. In our experiment, the range is 32. The matched point in the right image has the largest similarity between the current point in the left image and the matched point in the search range of right image. The SSIM value between point in the left block and related point in the right image is calculated, and all the SSIM values are merged together with a Gaussian weighted sum. Figure 2 shows the stereo pairs and disparity image. Figures 2(a) and (b) denote the right view and left view of stereo pairs with high quality, respectively. The estimated disparity image of the stereo pairs is shown in Fig. 2(c). Figures 2(d) and (e) denote stereo pairs with gauss noise distortion, and the estimated disparity is shown in Fig. 2(f).

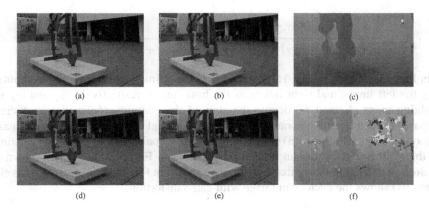

Fig. 2. Stereo pairs and disparity image

2.2   Cyclopean Image Generation

Cyclopean image is a single metal image of a scene created by the brain when combining two images from the two eyes. This process can be explained by binocular vision combination characteristic.

In this paper, the latest biological model, Gain-Control Theory model is utilized to simulate binocular fusion and explain cyclopean perception. The first step of cyclopean image generation is to decide the base image between the left image and the right image. In our implement, the image with better quality is selected as the base image, while the other one image is the aid image.

If the left image is selected as base image, the synthesized cyclopean image I(x, y) is calculated as follows,

$$I(x, y) = \omega_L(x, y) \cdot I_L(x, y) \\ + \omega_R(x - D_L(x, y), y) \cdot I_R(x - D_L(x, y), y) \tag{2}$$

where

$$\omega_L = \frac{E_L(x, y)}{E_L(x, y) + E_R(x - D_L(x, y), y)}; \omega_R = \frac{E_R(x - D_L(x, y), y)}{E_L(x, y) + E_R(x - D_L(x, y), y)}$$

While if the right image is selected as base image, the synthesized cyclopean image I(x, y) can be calculated as,

$$I(x, y) = \omega_L(x + D_R(x, y), y) \cdot I_L(x + D_R(x, y), y) \\ + \omega_R(x, y) \cdot I_R(x, y) \tag{3}$$

where

$$\omega_L = \frac{E_L(x + D_R(x, y), y)}{E_L(x + D_R(x, y), y) + E_R(x, y)}; \omega_R = \frac{E_R(x, y)}{E_L(x + D_R(x, y), y) + E_R(x, y)}$$

In Eqs. (2) and (3), $D_L(x, y)$ and $D_R(x, y)$ are the estimated disparity map computed using the left image and right image as the base image, respectively. ω_L and ω_R are weighting maps. E_L and E_R denote the sum of the energies of wavelet coefficient computed using a steerable pyramid. The stereo pairs and synthesized cyclopean image are shown in Fig. 3. Figures 3(a) and (b) show the stereo pairs with no distortion existing, and the synthesized cyclopean image computed from Fig. 3(a) and (b) is shown in Fig. 3(c). Stereo pairs with gauss distortion are shown in Fig. 3(d) and (e), respectively. Figure 3(f) shows the cyclopean image with gauss distortion.

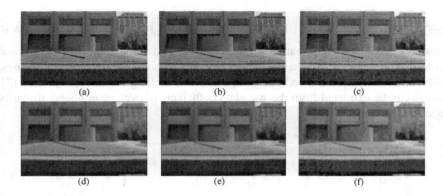

Fig. 3. Stereo pairs and cyclopean image

2.3 Features Extraction

The strategy that adopted for feature extraction is based on natural scene statistics (NSS), which has been proved to be effective in image quality assessment [11].

To extract features, the estimated disparity image, synthesized cyclopean image and image with better quality from the stereo pairs are processed by wavelet decomposition to form oriented band-pass responses. The motivation is based on the fact that the scale-space-orientation decomposition achieves a high performance in modeling the visual signal processing mechanism, which occurs in the primary visual cortex of human visual system (HVS).

In our implement, we perform wavelet decomposition over 2 scales and 6 orientations. Thus, 12 sub-bands across scales and orientations labeled $S_\beta^\theta (\beta \in \{1, 2\}$ and $\theta \in \{0°, 30°, 60°, 90°, 120°, 150°\})$ are obtained for each image. Then, a series of statistics features will be extracted from the obtained sub-band coefficients as follow.

2.3.1 Single Sub-band-Based NSS Feature

To extract single scale feature, it is not necessary to use all the sub-bands, since some of the sub-bands may be correlated with others. In this paper, four sub-bands (i.e., $S_1^{0°}, S_1^{90°}, S_2^{0°}$ and $S_2^{90°}$) are chosen to extract single sub-band based feature.

The single sub-band coefficients statistics of the cyclopean image in Fig. 3(c) for various distortions are shown in Fig. 4. It demonstrates that the probability density distribution of the sub-band coefficients exhibits a Gaussian-like appearance, which can be effectively captured by a generalized Gaussian distribution (GGD). The density function of GGD with zero mean is given by,

$$f(x; \alpha, \sigma^2) = \frac{\alpha}{2\beta\Gamma(1/\alpha)} \exp\left(-\left(\frac{|x|}{\beta}\right)^\alpha\right) \tag{4}$$

where $\beta = \sigma\sqrt{\dfrac{\Gamma(1/\alpha)}{\Gamma(3/\alpha)}}$, and $\Gamma(.)$ is the gamma function: $\Gamma(\alpha) = \int_0^\infty t^{a-1}e^{-t}dt$ a > 0. In the model of GGD, the shape parameter α controls the real shape of the distribution, and σ^2 controls the variance. We use the parameter α and σ^2 as the quality relevant features, which can be reliably estimated using the moment-matching based approach in [12]. Features can be extracted from the wavelet coefficients of cyclopean image, disparity image and stereo pairs.

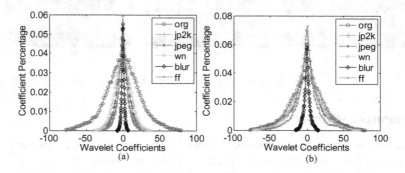

Fig. 4. Single sub-band statistics of the cyclopean image

2.3.2   Spatial Correlation-Based NSS Feature

There is a high correlation between sub-bands over the same scale and different orientation, as well as sub-bands over different scale and same orientation.

In Fig. 5(a), we plot the probability density distribution of coefficients formed by $[S_1^{0^\circ} : S_1^{90^\circ}]$ to demonstrate the sub-bands correlation over the same scale and different orientation. To show the correlation over different scale and same orientation, the probability density distribution of coefficients formed by $[S_1^{0^\circ} : S_2^{0^\circ}]$ is shown in Fig. 5(b).

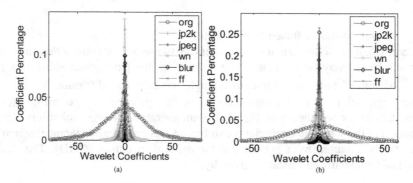

Fig. 5. Sub-bands statistics of spatial correlation

To extract features, the GGD model can also be utilized to fit the Gaussian-like distortion. The parameter (α, σ^2) of GGD is extracted as features from the wavelet coefficients of cyclopean image, disparity image and stereo pairs.

2.3.3 Spatial Difference-Based NSS Feature

In our work, we calculate the difference between two sub-bands coefficient at the same scale across different orientation as,

$$D_1^{(\theta_i - \theta_j)} = S_1^{\theta_i} - S_1^{\theta_j}; D_2^{(\theta_i - \theta_j)} = S_2^{\theta_i} - S_2^{\theta_j} \tag{5}$$

where $\theta_i \in \{0^\circ\}$ and $\theta_j \in \{0^\circ, 30^\circ, 60^\circ, 90^\circ, 120^\circ, 150^\circ\}$.

The probability density distribution of $D_1^{(0^\circ - 90^\circ)}$ and $D_2^{(0^\circ - 90^\circ)}$ computed from the cyclopean image are shown in Fig. 6(a) and (b). Similarly, to extract features from spatial difference, the GGD model is used to fit the distributions of the difference. Thus, the parameter (α, σ^2) of GGD computed from cyclopean image, disparity image and stereo pairs are extracted as features.

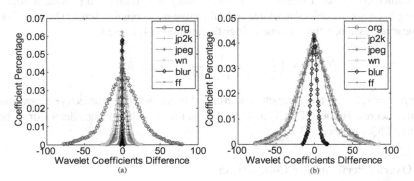

Fig. 6. Sub-band statistics of spatial difference

2.4 Quality Prediction

Machine learning is applied to map these features to quality score. Specifically, in the train phase, the best map between features and subjective quality scores (MOSs) included in the 3D image databases is obtained by the regression module. In the test phase, correlation between predicted objective scores obtained by SIQA algorithm and subjective scores is received. Multiple iterations of the above training and testing procedure are performed by varying the splitting of data over the training and test sets.

3   Experimental Results and Analysis

3.1   Databases and Evaluation Criteria

The proposed 3D-IQA method is evaluated on two publicly available subject-rated image quality databases: LIVE 3D IQA Database Phase I [13] and LIVE 3D IQA Database Phase II [6]. The LIVE 3D IQA Database Phase I consists of 20 reference images and 365 distorted images. Five types of distortions: JPEG and JPEG2000 (JP2K) compression, Gaussian blur (GB), White noise (WN) and a Rayleigh fast-fading (FF) are symmetrically applied to the left and right reference images at various levels. The LIVE 3D IQA Database Phase II consists of 120 symmetrically and 240 asymmetrically distorted images generated from 8 reference images, with the same distortions as Database Phase I.

Three criterions including Pearson linear correlation coefficient (PLCC), Spearman rank order correlation coefficient (SROCC) and root mean squared error (RMSE) are used to evaluate the SIQA metrics. PLCC and RMSE are used to evaluate prediction accuracy of SIQA metrics, and SROCC is used for prediction monotonicity. Before computing these performance criterions, a nonlinear regression analysis is utilized to provide a nonlinear mapping between the objective scores and subjective mean opinion scores (MOSs). For the nonlinear regression, a five-parameter logistic function [14] is used,

$$f(x) = \beta_1 \cdot \left(\frac{1}{2} - \frac{1}{1 + e^{\beta_2 (x - \beta_3)}} \right) + \beta_4 x + \beta_5 \tag{6}$$

where $\beta_i, i = 1, 2 \ldots 5$, are parameters determined by the best fit of subjective scores and the objective scores. Higher SROCC and PLCC and lower RMSE values demonstrate better objective SIQA metrics.

3.2   Overall Performance Comparison

The overall performance comparison of proposed algorithm and other NR-SIQA methods on both LIVE 3D image database Phase I and Phase II is shown in Table 1. The top metric has been highlighted in boldface. It can be seen from Table 1 that the proposed algorithm significantly outperforms (i.e., PLCC and SROCC are highest, while RMSE is lowest) all the considered other metrics on both the two databases. Meanwhile, the proposed metric and other NR-SIQA metrics achieve a better performance on LIVE 3D image quality database phase I than those on database phase II. The reason is that LIVE 3D image quality database phase I contains only symmetric distortions, while phase II contains both symmetric and asymmetric distortions. It is much more difficult to assess the stereoscopic images with asymmetric distortions. That is because of the limited understanding of human visual system when human eyes watching asymmetric stereoscopic images.

Table 1. Overall performance on LIVE Phase I and Phase II

Database	Live Phase I			Live Phase II		
Criteria	SROCC	PLCC	RMSE	SROCC	PLCC	RMSE
Akhter [5]	0.383	0.626	14.827	0.543	0.568	9.249
Chen [6]	0.891	0.895	7.247	0.880	0.895	5.102
Su [7]	–	–	–	0.905	0.913	4.657
Zhou [8]	0.887	0.928	6.025	0.823	0.861	5.779
Wang [9]	0.828	0.885	7.238	0.794	0.784	7.236
Proposed	**0.934**	**0.945**	**5.433**	**0.915**	**0.928**	**4.215**

We also evaluate our proposed algorithm on each type of distortion. To make a comprehensive comparison, several state-of-the-art FR-SIQA metrics (i.e., Benoit [1], You [2], and Chen [3]) are also considered. Performances on LIVE 3D image database Phase I and Phase II are listed in Tables 2 and 3, respectively. The top two metrics are highlighted in bold-face, and italicized algorithms are FR-SIQA algorithms. It can be seen that the proposed metric belongs to the top two metrics, which mean that the proposed method can predict the stereoscopic image quality consistently across different types of distortions. For FR-SIQA metrics, Benoit's and You's methods are based on 2D-IQA algorithms and simultaneously consider disparity information. Chen's algorithm in [3] uses the SSIM index to assess the quality of cyclopean image. Even though the reference information is available in these FR-SIQA metrics, the performance is not better than our method. For NR-SIQA metrics, the scheme in [6] extracts NSS-model-based features of cyclopean in spatial domain, but others 3D visual perception are not considered adequately. Therefore, the performance is worse than our proposed algorithm.

Table 2. Performance on each type of distortion on LIVE Phase I

		FR-SIQA			NR-SIQA			
		Benoit [1]	You [2]	Chen [3]	Akhter [5]	Chen [6]	Su [7]	**Proposed**
PLCC	JPEG	*0.640*	*0.487*	*0.603*	**0.905**	**0.907**	–	0.861
	JP2K	*0.939*	*0.939*	*0.912*	0.904	0.917	–	**0.946**
	WN	*0.925*	*0.925*	*0.942*	0.729	0.695	–	**0.975**
	GB	*0.948*	*0.948*	*0.942*	0.617	0.917	–	**0.980**
	FF	*0.747*	*0.747*	*0.776*	0.503	0.735	–	**0.856**
SROCC	JPEG	*0.603*	*0.439*	*0.530*	**0.866**	**0.863**	–	0.846
	JP2K	*0.910*	*0.860*	*0.888*	0.914	**0.919**	–	**0.942**
	WN	*0.930*	*0.940*	*0.948*	0.675	0.617	–	**0.960**
	GB	*0.931*	*0.882*	*0.925*	0.555	0.878	–	0.910
	FF	*0.699*	*0.588*	*0.707*	0.640	0.652	–	**0.747**
RMSE	JPEG	*5.022*	*5.709*	*5.216*	5.438	5.402	–	**3.076**
	JP2K	*4.426*	*6.206*	*5.320*	7.092	6.433	–	**3.378**
	WN	*6.307*	*5.621*	*5.581*	**4.273**	4.532	–	**3.601**
	GB	*4.571*	*5.679*	*4.822*	11.387	5.898	–	**2.786**
	FF	*8.257*	*8.429*	*7.837*	9.332	8.322	–	**6.255**

Table 3. Performance on each type of distortion on LIVE Phase II

		FR-SIQA			NR-SIQA			
		Benoit [1]	You [2]	Chen [3]	Akhter [5]	Chen [6]	Su [7]	**Proposed**
PLCC	JPEG	0.853	0.830	0.862	0.776	**0.899**	**0.888**	0.854
	JP2K	0.784	0.905	0.834	0.722	**0.947**	0.847	**0.933**
	WN	0.926	0.912	**0.957**	0.786	0.901	**0.953**	0.941
	GB	0.535	0.784	0.963	0.795	0.941	**0.968**	**0.966**
	FF	0.807	0.915	0.901	0.674	0.932	**0.944**	0.923
SROCC	JPEG	**0.867**	0.795	0.843	0.724	**0.867**	0.818	0.786
	JP2K	0.751	0.894	0.814	0.714	**0.950**	0.845	**0.907**
	WN	0.923	0.909	**0.940**	0.649	0.867	**0.946**	0.902
	GB	0.455	0.813	0.905	0.682	0.900	0.903	**0.906**
	FF	0.773	0.891	0.884	0.559	**0.933**	0.899	0.923
RMSE	JPEG	**3.787**	4.086	3.865	6.189	4.298	4.169	**3.337**
	JP2K	6.096	4.186	5.562	7.416	**3.513**	5.482	**3.224**
	WN	4.028	4.396	3.368	4.535	**3.342**	3.547	**3.289**
	GB	11.763	8.649	**3.747**	8.450	4.725	4.453	**3.177**
	FF	6.894	4.649	4.966	8.505	**4.180**	4.199	**4.120**

4   Conclusion

In this paper, we propose a novel no-reference quality assessment for stereoscopic image using wavelet decomposition and natural scene statistics. We find that the statistics of the wavelet coefficients can be effectively captured by a generalized Gaussian distribution (GGD). Therefore, the parameters of GGD are extracted as the quality relevant features. To extract feature, stereo pairs, cyclopean image and binocular disparity image are considered. Finally, machine learning is applied to map these features to quality score. Experimental results demonstrate that the proposed algorithm achieves high consistency with subjective assessment on two public available 3D image quality assessment databases.

Acknowledgment.   This work is sponsored by Shanghai Pujiang Program (15pjd015) and Innovation Program of Shanghai Municipal Education Commission (13ZZ069), and is supported by the National Natural Science Foundation of China under grant No. 61171084, 61172096, 61422111 and U1301257.

References

1. Benoit, A., Le Callet, P., Campisi, P., Cousseau, R.: Quality assessment of stereoscopic images. EURASIP J. Image Video Process. (2008)
2. You, J., Xing, L., Perkis, A., Wang, X.: Perceptual quality assessment for stereoscopic images based on 2D image quality metrics and disparity analysis. In: VPQM, Scottsdale, Arizona, USA (2010)

3. Chen, M.J., Su, C.C., Kwon, D.K., et al.: Full-reference quality assessment of stereo pairs accounting for rivalry. Sign. Process. Image Commun. **28**(9), 1143–1155 (2013)
4. Qi, F., Zhao, D., Gao, W.: Reduced reference stereoscopic image quality assessment based on binocular perceptual information. IEEE Trans. Multimedia **17**(12), 2338–2344 (2015)
5. Akhter, R., Baltes, J., Parvez Sazzad, Z.M., Horita, Y.: No reference stereoscopic image quality assessment. In: Proceedings of SPIE, vol. 7524, p. 75240T, February 2010
6. Chen, M.J., Cormack, L.K., Bovik, A.C.: No-reference quality assessment of natural stereopairs. IEEE Trans. Image Process. **22**(9), 3379–3391 (2013)
7. Su, C.C., Cormack, L.K., Bovik, A.C.: Oriented correlation models of distorted natural images with application to natural stereopair quality evaluation. IEEE Trans. Image Process. **24**(5), 1685–1699 (2015)
8. Zhou, W., Yu, L.: Binocular responses for no-reference 3D Image quality assessment. IEEE Trans. Multimedia **18**(6), 1077–1084 (2016)
9. Wang, S., Shao, F., Jiang, G.: Supporting binocular visual quality prediction using machine learning. In: IEEE International Conference on Multimedia and Expo Workshops (ICMEW 2014), Chengdu, pp. 1–6 (2014)
10. Wang, Z., Bovik, A.C., Sheikh, H.R., Simoncelli, E.P.: Image quality assessment: from error visibility to structural similarity. IEEE Trans. Image Process. **13**(4), 600–612 (2004)
11. Mittal, A., Moorthy, A.K., Bovik, A.C.: No-reference image quality assessment in the spatial domain. IEEE Trans. Image Process. **21**(12), 4695–4708 (2012)
12. Sharifi, K., Leon-Garcia, A.: Estimation of shape parameter for generalized Gaussian distributions in subband decompositions of video. IEEE Trans. Circuits Syst. Video Technol. **5**(1), 52–56 (1995)
13. Moorthy, A.K., et al.: Subjective evaluation of stereoscopic image quality. Sign. Process. Image Commun. **28**(8), 870–883 (2013)
14. Sheikh, H.R., Sabir, M.F., Bovik, A.C.: A statistical evaluation of recent full reference image quality assessment algorithms. IEEE Trans. Image Process. **15**(11), 3440–3451 (2006)

Combining Visual Saliency and Binocular Energy for Stereoscopic Image Quality Assessment

Yang Yao, Liquan Shen[✉], Xianqiu Geng, and Ping An

School of Communication and Information Engineering,
Shanghai University, Shanghai 200072, China
jsslq@163.com

Abstract. With the flourishment of 3D content, the loss of quality of the stereoscopic images has been a large problem while being received by human beings. We develop a new metric in this paper to automatically assess the quality of stereoscopic images with the guidance of reference images. Visual saliency (VS) has been largely explored by researchers in the past decade to find out which areas of an image attract most attention of the viewers. We use the similarity of the VS map between original and distorted images as one of the quality-aware features since the degradation of VS map of the images can depict the quality loss in a certain degree. Meanwhile, gradient magnitude (GM) is enriched with image information, and GM similarity is exploited as another feature. While the difference of binocular energy between original and distorted versions reflects the severities of distortion, it can also act as weights between stereo pairs to simulate the binocular perception properties. Therefore, we introduce the difference of binocular energy as part of the features. The depth/disparity information between stereo pairs contains much properties of stereoscopic vision, and we extract features from disparity map. Finally, in order to take advantage of all the features, we utilize support vector machine based regression module to derive the overall quality score. Experimental results show that the proposed algorithm can assess the image quality in a manner of high consistency with human judgments.

Keywords: Visual saliency · Gradient magnitude · Binocular disparity · Binocular energy

1 Introduction

Benefit from the large amount of the infrastructure construction of the Internet as well as the progress of the photography in the past decades, there is a rapid growth of the digital images. However, when processed by some compression algorithms or transmitted in the noisy channel, digital images will be polluted by some level of distortions which will cause loss of information and discomfort of people who watch the pictures.

In order to assess the image quality objectively and consistently with human judgments, tremendous researches has been done to the 2D image quality assessment (IQA). The structural similarity index (SSIM) [1] first takes the structural information into consideration based on the theory that human visual system (HVS) is sensitive to the

© Springer Nature Singapore Pte Ltd. 2017
X. Yang and G. Zhai (Eds.): IFTC 2016, CCIS 685, pp. 104–114, 2017.
DOI: 10.1007/978-981-10-4211-9_11

structural information. The metrics [2, 3] proposed by the Laboratory for Image & Video Engineering (LIVE) extract quality-aware features in the DCT and DWT domains respectively using natural scene statistics (NSS).

Unlike the prosperity of the field of the 2D IQA, stereoscopic IQA (SIQA) has been less explored due to the fact that the 3D vision properties contained by stereo pairs cannot be exactly encoded by algorithms. A stereoscopic image contains two slightly different images, and points in one of images can be found in another image in different place. When the two views are projected separately onto human eyes, it is the difference between two views brings about the depth perception. The difference of each points in the view forms the disparity map.

In the early years, researchers apply 2D IQA directly to the left and right views of the stereo pairs, and then simply combine the two scores to an overall quality score (e.g., [4, 5]). This kind of metrics only works when the two views are equally polluted by distortion, and the performance will deteriorate on estimating the asymmetric distorted pairs. Later, the disparity information is utilized to model the 3D perceptual geometric properties [6]. Since the ground truth depth/disparity is usually not accessible, such models can only use the estimated disparity map. Hence this kind of SIQA performance may depend on the accuracy of the disparity estimation algorithm. When the left and right stimuli get into human retina, the brain will form a 3D merged mental view. Based on this observation, researchers try to use some delicate models to mimic the internal image inside human brain [7–9]. Chen et al. use binocular perceptual characteristics such as binocular rivalry and binocular suppression to synthesize a cyclopean image to simulate the merged mental view [7]. During the generation, the disparity map is used for shifting the views so that the same points in both views are at the corresponding positions. Inspired by this idea, the MAD algorithm [10] is extended to SIQA metric by incorporating with the information of cyclopean image [8]. However, all the literature based on the cyclopean image utilize the estimated disparity map. Meanwhile, the disparity estimation algorithm cannot obtain a disparity map as precise as the ground truth disparity especially the distortion in the stereo pairs will cause much mismatch while estimating the disparity. This makes the cyclopean method less persuasive.

In this paper, we propose a new metric by exploiting the VS, the 3D properties and the binocular energy. The rest of the paper is organized as follows. Section 2 analyzes the relevant perceptual characteristics which are used to construct the proposed framework. Section 3 presents the full reference stereoscopic image quality assessment (FR-IQA) index in detail. Experimental results are given in Sects. 4, and 5 concludes the paper.

2 Relevant Perceptual Characteristics

2.1 Visual Saliency

Image salient region detection has been largely explored in neuroscience and psychology during the last decade. The VS map of a given image computed by a well-designed VS model can indicate the local areas that attract the most attention of the HVS. The distortion in the salient region will cause more quality loss compared to the distortion in the less salient region which can even be ignored. Besides, the distortion region can be a salient area due to its disturbance to the naturalness of images. Based on the above considerations, the visual saliency data which is obtained by eye tracking is adopted as spatially varying weights for pooling to enhance the common IQA indices [11], and experimental results have confirmed the promotion of the performance. The VS model is exploited to automatically compute the VS information instead of using the subjective data to enhance the IQA metrics [12].

Therefore, we can conclude that the VS can act as an indicator of the fluctuation of the image quality. The experiments conducted in [13] show that the difference between VS map of the reference and distorted images changes consistently with the level of the distortion introduced to the image. In this paper, we exploit the VS to predict the image quality. The saliency region detection model used in our method is SDSP proposed by Zhang et al. [14]. Figure 1 shows the reference image and its VS map. The VS model is built on three simple priors. Firstly, the HVS detects salient objects in a manner of band-pass filtering. Secondly, the center of an image will attract more attention than the marginal areas. Thirdly, warm colors are more attractive to people than cold colors.

(a) reference map   (b) VS map

Fig. 1. Visual saliency (VS) map of reference image.

2.2 Gradient Magnitude

The visual saliency map is lack of contrast and edge information of the images. Hence the gradient magnitude map is used as the complementarity of the VS map to evaluate the quality of 2D content of the stereo pairs. There are several different operators to derive the gradient component. Here we adopt the Scharr gradient operator which is proved useful in [9, 13]. The Scharr operator is a 3×3 template gradient filter with horizontal and vertical directions which is defined as,

$$h_x = \frac{1}{16}\begin{bmatrix} 3 & 0 & -3 \\ 10 & 0 & -10 \\ 3 & 0 & -3 \end{bmatrix} \quad h_y = \frac{1}{16}\begin{bmatrix} 3 & 10 & 3 \\ 0 & 0 & 0 \\ -3 & -10 & -3 \end{bmatrix} \tag{1}$$

The image horizontal and vertical gradient components (first derivative of the intensity function) $GM_x(x)$ and $GM_y(x)$ are produced by convolving h_x and h_y with image $f(x)$. The gradient magnitude of image is defined as,

$$GM(\mathrm{x}) = \sqrt{\left(f(x) \otimes h_x\right)^2 + \left(f(x) \otimes h_y\right)^2}$$
$$= \sqrt{GM_x(\mathrm{x})^2 + GM_y(\mathrm{x})^2} \tag{2}$$

where symbol "$\otimes$" represents the convolution operation.

Since the second derivative can also describe the quality degradation, we employ the second gradient magnitude as well. Figure 2 demonstrates the original image and its corresponding GM map and the second GM map. The second gradient magnitude is defined as,

$$GMM(\mathrm{x}) = \sqrt{\left(f(x) \otimes h_x \otimes h_x\right)^2 + \left(f(x) \otimes h_y \otimes h_y\right)^2}$$
$$= \sqrt{GMM_x(\mathrm{x})^2 + GMM_y(\mathrm{x})^2} \tag{3}$$

(a) original image   (b) GM map   (c) second GM map

Fig. 2. Binocular disparity map of reference stereo pair.

2.3   Binocular Disparity

The main difference between 2D image and 3D image is that 3D contents contains the depth/disparity information, which accounts for the perceptual process of binocular fusion. To comprehensively evaluate the quality of stereoscopic image, the depth/disparity information needs to be deeply investigated. In [6] the disparity information is adopted to enhance the SIQA metric. Since the ground truth disparity information is unavailable, the disparity map has to be estimated using stereo algorithm. The distortion in the stereo pairs will cause mismatches during the disparity extraction. Thus the inaccuracy of the disparity can be an indicator of the image quality.

Here we propose a Gaussian average SSIM [1] based disparity estimation metric in which the pixel neighborhood is taken into consideration. An example of the binocular disparity is shown in Fig. 3, where (a) is the left view of the stereo pair and (b) is the corresponding disparity map. For the pixel in one view to be searched, we will take a patch centered at the pixel as a template and then use the SSIM metric to find the corresponding patch in other view which has the largest similarity with the current patch. Finally, the center pixel of the matched patch is the pixel we need and the difference of horizontal coordinate of the two pixels is calculated as disparity.

(a) left view of the reference stereo pair   (b) disparity map

Fig. 3. Binocular disparity map of reference stereo pair.

2.4 Binocular Energy

Varies studies have been conducted towards understanding binocular rivalry/suppression. Briefly, when two individual images come into human eyes, HVS will unify the two views into a single generated stereoscopic view based on the relative stimulus energy of the two views. The region with stronger stimulus energy in one image will suppress the same region in another image and dominate the mergence process. If the two stimuli have the same energy but different contents, they will rival in the mergence process, which will cause viewing fatigue of observers. In order to model the energy of the image, we adopt the Gabor filter magnitude responses as image energy as [7]. The resulting energy is a map representing local energy in the image. Since the estimated disparity information between two views cannot achieve the satisfactory accuracy, we cannot compare the local energy between left and right views pointwise. So we collapse the energy map into a single value that can represent the energy of an image.

3 Proposed Algorithm

The flowchart of the proposed 3D image quality assessment method is shown in Fig. 4. Since the depth/disparity information which is a fundamental component of the cyclopean image cannot be accurately obtained, we evaluate the quality of stereo pairs based on left and right views rather than the cyclopean image. Given a stereoscopic image, we first extract image characteristics described in Sect. 2 respectively in both reference and distorted stereo pairs. Then the similarities or differences of these image characteristics between the reference and distorted images is calculated. Finally, machine learning is employed to map these similarities and differences into quality score.

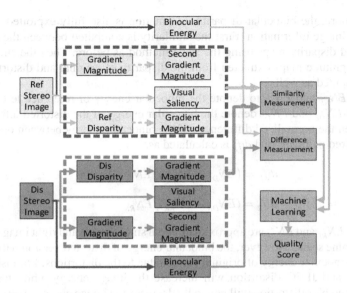

Fig. 4. Proposed framework for FR SIQA.

The similarity measurement for VS map $S_{VS}(x)$ of the reference and distorted stereo pairs is defined as,

$$S_{VS}(x) = \frac{2VS_1(x)VS_2(x) + C_1}{VS_1^2(x) + VS_2^2(x) + C_1} \qquad (4)$$

where $VS_1(x)$ and $VS_2(x)$ represent the reference and distorted images respectively. C_1 is a positive constant to increase the stability of $S_{VS}(x)$ when the denominator is close to zero. The VS similarity contains two values for left and right views, both of which is between 0 and 1.

The definition of the similarity of GM map and the second GM map is identical with the VS map,

$$S_{GM}(x) = \frac{2GM_1(x)GM_2(x) + C_2}{GM_1^2(x) + GM_2^2(x) + C_2} \qquad (5)$$

$$S_{GMM}(x) = \frac{2GMM_1(x)GMM_2(x) + C_2}{GMM_1^2(x) + GMM_2^2(x) + C_2} \qquad (6)$$

where $S_{GM}(x)$ is the similarity of GM map of left or right view between reference and distorted stereo pairs, and $GM_1(x)$ and $GM_2(x)$ represent GM maps of reference and distorted images respectively. $S_{GMM}(x)$ is the similarity of second GM map, and $GMM_1(x)$ and $GMM_2(x)$ represent the second GM map of reference and distorted image, respectively.

Furthermore, the binocular disparity information is also fully exploited since it is enriched of image information. First the similarity is computed between the reference and distorted disparity maps using the same method as before. Then the similarity of gradient magnitude maps extracted from the disparity of original and distorted stereo pairs is computed as well.

We use EN_{RL} and EN_{RR} to denote the binocular energy of reference left and right images, and EN_{DL} and EN_{DR} denote the binocular energy of the distorted left and right images. Then the normalized differences of the binocular energy between original and distorted stereo pairs dif_L and dif_R is calculated as,

$$dif_L = \left(EN_{DL} - EN_{RL}\right)/EN_{RL} \tag{7}$$

$$dif_R = (EN_{DR} - EN_{RR})/EN_{RR} \tag{8}$$

Usually, EN_{RL} and EN_{RR} are approximate equal since the left and right images capture the almost same scene. However, the binocular energy of distorted version will fluctuate around the binocular energy of original version due to the distortions. For instance, the white noise and JPEG distortion will increase the image energy while fast fading, JPEG2000 and blur distortion will generally decrease the image energy. Thus no matter the value of dif_L or dif_R is positive or negative, the relative value of the dif_L and dif_R can model the relative stimulus energy. The view with larger normalized difference tends to suppress the other one. On the other hand, the larger the absolute value of normalized differences imply the higher level distortion. Thus the normalized differences dif_L and dif_R can model both binocular rivalry/suppression and distortion level.

All those similarities and differences we acquired can independently predict the quality of the test stereo pairs in a certain extent. However, the performance is not satisfying when we combine all of them using an arithmetic way such as addition, multiplication or exponent. The performance degradation may be explained that these similarities and differences have information redundancies which may cause the reciprocal inhibition. Thus we employ the method of machine learning(ML) to derive the final quality score since ML can exploit all the advantages of these similarities and differences. In this paper we utilize LIBSVM package [15] to implement the SVR with a radial basis function (RBF) kernel.

4   Experimental Results and Analysis

4.1   Database and Evaluation Criteria

We test the proposed metric on two publicly available image quality databases: LIVE 3D IQA Database [16] containing two phases including Phase I and the Phase II. The LIVE 3D IQA Database I consists of 20 reference images and 365 distorted images which contain five types of distortions: JPEG and JPEG2000 (JP2K) compression, Gaussian blur (Blur), White noise (WN) and fast-fading (FF). The distortions are symmetrically applied to the left and right reference images at various levels. The Phase

II consists of 120 symmetrically and 240 asymmetrically polluted images generated from 8 reference images with the same distortions as Phase I.

We adopt three different criteria to evaluate the performance of the proposed algorithm including Spearman Rank Order Correlation Coefficient (SROCC), Pearson Linear Correlation Coefficient (PLCC) and Root Mean Squared Error (RMSE). PLCC and RMSE are used for evaluating the prediction accuracy of SIQA metrics, and SROCC is used for evaluation the prediction monotonicity. Before computing these performance criterions, a nonlinear regression analysis suggested by the video quality exports group [17] is utilized to provide a nonlinear mapping between the objective scores and subjective mean opinion scores (MOSs). For the nonlinear regression, a five-parameter logistic function [18] is used:

$$f(x) = \beta_1 \cdot \left(\frac{1}{2} - \frac{1}{1 + e^{\beta_2(x-\beta_3)}} \right) + \beta_4 x + \beta_5 \tag{9}$$

where β_i, i = 1, 2…5, are parameters determined by the best fit of subjective scores and the objective scores. Higher SROCC and PLCC and lower RMSE values suggest better objective SIQA metrics.

4.2 Performance Comparison

Since the proposed metric is based on machine learning, we randomly split the dataset into 80% and 20% subsets for training and testing sets with no overlap. To make the performance independent of the selection of the training and testing content, this procedure of train-test split is repeated 1000 times and we report the average result of the performance across these 1000 iterations.

We compare the proposed algorithm with several state-of-the-art FR-SIQA metrics, and the overall performance comparisons are shown in Tables 1 and 2. The top metric has been highlighted in boldface. It can be seen from Tables 1 and 2 that the proposed metric significantly outperforms all the compared metrics in both phase I and phase II. Gorley's method [4] assesses the quality by averaging the left and right view's quality computed based on 2D IQA metric. The stereoscopic properties are not taken into consideration, which leads to poor performance. You et al. take a step further to combine disparity into quality assessment and the algorithm [6] has gained improvement compared to Gorley's method. The schemes [7–9] are constructed based on cyclopean image. Chen's method [7] generate the cyclopean image by exploiting the properties of binocular fusion. However, this metric only evaluates the quality of cyclopean image and the performance is limited. Method [9] evaluates both the cyclopean image and the disparity map and the performance is better than [7]. The high performance of algorithm [8] may be attributed to the evaluation of both cyclopean image and two individual views. Although our method does not employ cyclopean image, by extracting image characteristics sophisticatedly, it turns to be more effective than the compared metrics. From the experimental results and analysis, we can draw a conclusion that the predicted objective quality scores from proposed algorithm achieve high consistency with the subjective ratings.

Table 1. PLCC, SROCC and RMSE on LIVE 3D IQA database phase I

	Algorithm	JP2K	JPEG	WN	Blur	FF	ALL
SROCC	Gorley [4]	0.4203	0.0152	0.7408	0.7498	0.3663	0.1419
	You [6]	0.8598	0.4388	0.9395	0.8822	0.5883	0.8789
	Chen [7]	0.8956	0.5582	0.9481	0.9261	0.6879	0.9157
	Zhang [8]	0.916	0.700	**0.950**	**0.942**	0.833	0.944
	Li [9]	0.9035	0.6623	0.9339	0.9299	0.7470	0.9302
	Proposed	**0.9248**	**0.7891**	0.9425	0.9382	**0.8372**	**0.9458**
PLCC	Gorley [4]	0.4853	0.3124	0.7961	0.8527	0.3648	0.4511
	You [6]	0.8778	0.4874	0.9412	0.9198	0.7300	0.8814
	Chen [7]	0.9289	0.6344	0.9568	0.9419	0.7608	0.9241
	Zhang [8]	–	–	–	–	–	0.951
	Li [9]	0.9463	0.7181	0.9308	0.9479	0.8129	0.9335
	Proposed	**0.9660**	**0.8315**	**0.9710**	**0.9772**	**0.8742**	**0.9540**
RMSE	Gorley [4]	11.323	6.2119	10.197	7.5622	11.569	14.635
	You [6]	6.2066	5.7097	5.6216	5.6798	8.4923	7.7463
	Chen [7]	4.7842	5.0681	4.8168	4.8063	8.0323	6.2404
	Zhang [8]	–	–	–	–	–	5.052
	Li [9]	4.1864	4.5511	6.0804	4.6876	7.2365	5.8789
	Proposed	**3.3931**	**3.4843**	**4.0599**	**2.9188**	**5.7040**	**4.9345**

Table 2. PLCC, SROCC and RMSE on LIVE 3D IQA database phase II

	Algorithm	JP0032K	JPEG	WN	Blur	FF	ALL
SROCC	Gorley [4]	0.110	0.027	0.875	0.770	0.601	0.146
	You [6]	0.894	0.795	0.909	0.813	0.891	0.786
	Chen [7]	0.814	0.843	0.940	0.908	0.884	0.889
	Zhang [8]	0.895	0.866	**0.952**	**0.942**	**0.922**	0.924
	Li [9]	–	–	–	–	–	0.912
	Proposed	**0.9226**	**0.8705**	0.9316	0.9321	0.8988	**0.9420**
PLCC	Gorley [4]	0.372	0.322	0.874	0.934	0.706	0.515
	You [6]	0.905	0.830	0.912	0.784	0.915	0.800
	Chen [7]	0.834	0.862	0.957	0.963	0.901	0.900
	Zhang [8]	–	–	–	–	–	0.927
	Li [9]	–	–	–	–	–	0.921
	Proposed	**0.9593**	**0.9221**	**0.9627**	**0.9895**	**0.9229**	**0.9485**
RMSE	Gorley [4]	9.113	6.940	5.202	4.988	8.155	9.675
	You [6]	4.186	4.086	4.396	8.649	4.649	6.772
	Chen [7]	5.562	3.865	3.368	3.747	4.966	4.987
	Zhang [8]	–	–	–	–	–	4.220
	Li [9]	–	–	–	–	–	5.01
	Proposed	**2.7473**	**2.7891**	**0.8747**	**2.1085**	**4.1581**	**3.5582**

5 Conclusion

In this paper, we propose a stereoscopic image quality assessment metric. The visual saliency, gradient magnitude and the second gradient magnitude are first extracted from both views of the stereo pairs. Then the binocular disparity between left and right views is computed, and the gradient magnitude information is extracted from the disparity map. Furthermore, the Gabor filter bank is utilized to derive the binocular energy of the image from which the normalized difference of binocular energy can be obtained. Finally, we compute the similarities of these characteristics between the original and distorted images. The support vector machine based regression module is utilized to derive final score based on these similarities and differences. We compare the proposed algorithm with 5 SIQA metrics on two publicly available databases. The experimental results demonstrate that the proposed algorithm outperforms the state-of-the-art quality assessment methods.

Acknowledgment. This work is sponsored by Shanghai Pujiang Program (15pjd015) and Innovation Program of Shanghai Municipal Education Commission (13ZZ069), and is supported by the National Natural Science Foundation of China under grant No. 61171084, 61172096, 61422111 and U1301257.

References

1. Wang, Z., Bovik, A.C., Sheikh, H.R., Simoncelli, E.P.: Image quality assessment: from error visibility to structural similarity. IEEE Trans. Image Process. **13**(4), 600–612 (2004)
2. Saad, M.A., Bovik, A.C., Charrier, C.: Blind image quality assessment: a natural scene statistics approach in the DCT domain. IEEE Trans. Image Process. **21**(8), 3339–3352 (2012)
3. Moorthy, A.K., Bovik, A.C.: Blind image quality assessment: from natural scene statistics to perceptual quality. IEEE Trans. Image Process. **20**(12), 3350–3364 (2011)
4. Gorley, P., Holliman, N.: Stereoscopic image quality metrics and compression. In: Electronic Imaging 2008, p. 680305. International Society for Optics and Photonics, February 2008
5. Campisi, P., Le Callet, P., Marini, E.: Stereoscopic images quality assessment. In: 15th European Signal Processing Conference, Poznan, pp. 2110–2114 (2007)
6. You, J., et al.: Perceptual quality assessment for stereoscopic images based on 2D image quality metrics and disparity analysis. In: Proceedings of International Workshop on Video Processing and Quality Metrics for Consumer Electronics, Scottsdale, AZ, USA (2010)
7. Chen, M.-J., et al.: Full-reference quality assessment of stereopairs accounting for rivalry. Sig. Process. Image Commun. **28**(9), 1143–1155 (2013)
8. Zhang, Y., Chandler, D.M.: 3D-MAD: a full reference stereoscopic image quality estimator based on binocular lightness and contrast perception. IEEE Trans. Image Process. **24**(11), 3810–3825 (2015)
9. Li, F., Shen, L., Wu, D., Fang, R.: Full-reference quality assessment of stereoscopic images using disparity-gradient-phase similarity. In: 2015 IEEE China Summit and International Conference on Signal and Information Processing (ChinaSIP), Chengdu, pp. 658–662 (2015)
10. Larson, E.C., Chandler, D.M.: Most apparent distortion: full-reference image quality assessment and the role of strategy. J. Electron. Imag. **19**(1), 011006 (2010)

11. Larson, E.C., Vu, C., Chandler, D.M.: Can visual fixation patterns improve image fidelity assessment? 2008 15th IEEE International Conference on Image Processing, San Diego, CA, pp. 2572–2575 (2008)
12. Moorthy, A.K., Bovik, A.C.: Visual importance pooling for image quality assessment. IEEE J. Sel. Top. Sig. Process. **3**(2), 193–201 (2009)
13. Zhang, L., Shen, Y., Li, H.: VSI: A Visual Saliency-Induced index for perceptual image quality assessment. IEEE Trans. Image Process. **23**(10), 4270–4281 (2014)
14. Zhang, L., Gu, Z., Li, H.: SDSP: a novel saliency detection method by combining simple priors. In: 2013 IEEE International Conference on Image Processing, Melbourne, VIC, pp. 171–175 (2013)
15. Chang, C.-C., Lin, C.-J.: LIBSVM: a library for support vector machines. ACM Trans. Intell. Syst. Technol. (TIST) **2**(3), 27 (2011)
16. Moorthy, A.K., et al.: Subjective evaluation of stereoscopic image quality. Sig. Process. Image Commun. **28**(8), 870–883 (2013)
17. Final Report From the Video Quality Experts Group on the Validation of Objective Models of Video Quality Assessment VQEG (2000). http://www.vqeg.org
18. Sheikh, H.R., Sabir, M.F., Bovik, A.C.: A statistical evaluation of recent full reference image quality assessment algorithms. IEEE Trans. Image Process. **15**(11), 3440–3451 (2006)

An Effective Crowd Property Analysis System for Video Surveillance Application

Shuying Yang[1]([✉]), Hua Yang[1,2], Jijia Li[1,2], and Ji Zhu[1,2]

[1] Institute of Image Communication and Network Engineering,
Shanghai Jiao Tong University, Shanghai, China
{labeouf,hyang}@sjtu.edu.cn
[2] Shanghai Key Laboratory of Digital Media Processing and Transmission,
Shanghai, People's Republic of China

Abstract. For public security, an intelligent video surveillance system that can analyze large-scale crowd scenes has become an urgent need. In this paper, we propose a system that integrates multiple crowd properties, including stationary and dynamic features, local and global characteristics, and historic statistics analysis in a unified framework. Specially our system consists of four modules. Crowd density module describes global density level and local density distribution with sparse spatial-temporal local binary pattern. Crowd segmentation module presents both global crowd grouping and local moving directions based on spatial-temporal dynamics. In crowd saliency module, salient regions are detected to alarm abnormal behaviors. At last, in order to analyze the historic features of video streaming, a historical statistics analysis module is introduced. Experiments on different crowd datasets show that our system is robust and feasible, and satisfies the requirements of video surveillance applications.

Keywords: Density distribution · Motion consistency · Crowd saliency · Historical statistics analysis

1 Introduction

With the rapid growth of population and human activities, video surveillance system for analysis of crowd scenes has attracted much attention in the field of computer vision. Public security or management in a high density crowd becomes a significant challenge, due to excessive number of individuals, extreme clutters and complexity of scenarios.

In the past decades, researchers have made great progress in the computer vision community for intelligent video surveillance. Automatic crowd analysis can be conducted at both microscopic level and macroscopic level. At the microscopic level, we concern about the movements of each individual. Mehran [1] detected abnormal behaviors in the crowd using the SFM and Zhou [2] proposed a dynamic pedestrian-agent model for semantic region analysis. Methods at microscopic level cannot adapt to high density crowds. To analyze crowd

© Springer Nature Singapore Pte Ltd. 2017
X. Yang and G. Zhai (Eds.): IFTC 2016, CCIS 685, pp. 115–127, 2017.
DOI: 10.1007/978-981-10-4211-9_12

scenes at the macroscopic level, Ali [3] designed a framework which is used to segment high density crowd scenes. In paper [4], a novel method was proposed to anomaly detection with crowd flow model. In order to analyze complex high density crowd scenes, many methods based on dynamics have been designed [5,6]. These methods are not applied in the real complex scenarios with heavy crowded scenes and can only achieve to analyze single kind of features. As for the intelligent surveillance system, it has gone through three stages, the analog video surveillance system, the analog-digital monitoring system, network video surveillance [7]. In [8], a dual-camera system was proposed to accomplish the vision-based recognition but it failed to detect the object when there are multiple moving objects. Carnegie Mellon University cooperated with DARPA and other institutes to develop an automatic video understanding technique for future city and war. University of Reading pursued research in tracking of pedestrian and vehicles and the interaction between them. Swedish Axis network communication company launched a product which includes an AXIS 242S IV video server and a people counting module application. Conventional surveillance systems fail to adopt to high density crowd scenes, regarding both accuracy and computation [9]. They only focus on specific scenes and are not applicable for large-scale crowd scenes. These crowd monitoring system cannot be applied in real scenarios because of the simplicity and the impractical assumptions of the modeling function.

Based on the need of public security, our goal is monitoring safety hazard in crowded scenes, and formulating specific technical routines with quantitative evaluation methods. Ideally we will help improve the public security departments capability of dealing with sudden mass disturbance, as well as surveillance on important events. The movements in crowded scenes are complicated, and thus it is difficult to characterize group behaviours. In order to gain effective and quick perception of abnormal group behaviours in large-scale crowd scenes, this paper proposes an intelligent surveillance system using multichannel videos, by leveraging the advanced technique of machine learning and computer vision. The system can not only estimate dynamic and stationary features, but also describe local and global characteristics in an unsupervised way.

The rest of this paper is organized as follows. In Sect. 2 we present the framework of our system and illustrate our system in detail. Section 3 describes software implementation of our system. In addition, the experiments and conclusions are presented in Sects. 4 and 5.

2   The Framework of Crowd Analysis System

In this paper, the novelty of our research is that we combine stationary and dynamic features, local and global characteristics, and historic statistics analysis in a unified framework, and design an intelligent video surveillance system as illustrated in Fig. 1. The proposed system consists of four main modules: crowd density module, crowd segmentation module, crowd saliency module, and historical statistics analysis module.

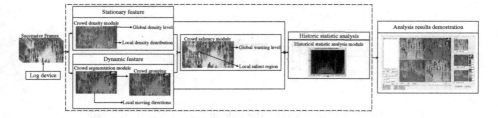

Fig. 1. Framework of the proposed system

These four modules cooperate with each other in the whole system. The crowd density module extracts stationary feature, sparse spatial-temporal local binary pattern (SST-LBP) [10], and provides local density distribution as well as global density level. The crowd segmentation module describes the whole crowd grouping with dynamic features including temporal motion grouping and distribution grouping. Meanwhile, this module also presents local moving direction of each grouping. The saliency module detects salient regions, where abnormal behaviors will happen. Abnormal activities can be detected with the density level results and the semantic segmentation, both locally and globally. The historical statistics analysis module can give out statistical distribution of crowd features, crowd density level and numbers of moving groups with different directions. In following sections, we provide the details on how to implement the four functional modules.

2.1 Crowd Density Module

As illustrated in Fig. 1, in our crowd density module stationary SST-LBP feature is extracted to deal with the crowd density, which contains two properties: local density distribution and global density level. We calculate the density level of crowd scenes and present crowd density spatial distribution. The density of crowd scene provides information for warning potential risk in the crowd due to the fact that panic-stricken stampede and overcrowding occur in large-scale crowd. In this module, we analyze distribution of different density levels for large-scale crowded scenes. The diagram of this module is shown in Fig. 2.

In real world crowd, there exist different crowd scenes with different density levels. An improved SST-LBP algorithm is applied to analyze crowd density in this module. Based on the original SST-LBP algorithm [10], which has good

Fig. 2. Pipeline of crowd density module.

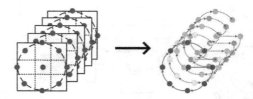

Fig. 3. Schematic diagram of the calculation of SST-LBP code.

performance on all density levels especially the large-scale crowd, we improve the calculation of spatial-temporal local binary as shown in Fig. 3. This method can present local density distribution. The volume to calculate SST-LBP code is set to $3 \times 3 \times 5$. The SST-LBP code is calculated along the helix. Also to improve the performance of density distribution, we sum up the Fourier coefficients of the center pixel and its neighboring pixels as the measure of the density of the center pixel and then apply Gaussian smoothing. The histogram of the spectrum analysis is the feature representation of the SVM model to specify the density of crowd.

Through above analysis, local density distribution can easily be found by labeling different colors and the places where there are more people are labeled with more attractive colors like red. We also obtain the global density level which is helpful for high-density crowd analysis and salient religions detection.

2.2   Crowd Segmentation Module

In this crowd segmentation module, crowd semantic segmentation based on spatial-temporal dynamics is used to perform both global and local grouping features. Global feature is addressed by segmenting, whereas local feature is performed using different directions of moving groups.

Individuals in a crowd interact with each other, whose trajectories are affected by both themselves and their neighbors. When two individuals are distant, there are few interactions between them. These two individuals cannot reflect each other. In this module, we propose crowd semantic segmentation based on spatial-temporal dynamics to achieve crowd segmentation as shown in Fig. 4. First, we use KLT algorithm [11] to detect trajectories of the crowd. In order to segment the crowd based on motion consistency, we cluster the trajectories with graph clustering algorithm proposed by [12]. After these steps, we obtain the temporal motion grouping. Then distribution grouping is processed to detect individuals with small distance and similar distribution, which are classified as one group. SST-LBP describes local particle distribution in neighbors. A set of Gaussian kernels with 5 different sizes are designed to organise the local distribution to generate the global distribution. After obtaining the density diffusion maps, k-means is used as a classifier to generate a 5-level grouping, which is called spatial distribution grouping. At last, we combine the spatial and temporal distribution group as semantic descriptions, which contain motion and

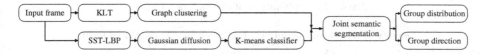

Fig. 4. Pipeline of crowd segmentation module.

distribution consistency. Group directions are defined as the mean velocity of individuals in one group. In this module, we utilize spatial-temporal distribution grouping to gather individuals with similar moving directions. The moving direction is divided into four groups, direction 3 o'clock, direction 6 o'clock, direction 9 o'clock and direction 12 o'clock. Also, individuals in the same group are labeled with the same color.

In summary, this module shows moving groups with different directions and the numbers of groups, which can reflect the degree of chaos of crowd motion. Masses of moving directions in a crowd scene lead to collision between individuals, which often cause abnormal behaviors. Moving groups with different directions are detected in this module to provide information for analysing interaction between individuals in crowd scenes, which makes contribution to detecting abnormal behaviors in crowd saliency and alarm module.

2.3   Crowd Saliency Module

Crowd saliency module detects salient regions and reports abnormal behaviors, such as an individual maneuvering through crowd, two groups meet and unstable regions. Different from traditional definition of saliency, our saliency based on abnormal behaviors detection describes possibility of unstable conditions. This module presents a warning level describing the salient degree. Based on the above two modules' results, we can analyze interactions between different groups and density of the crowd. Salient regions can be detected by combining density level and motion consistency.

A novel framework transforming low-level features into global similarity structure is applied to identify and localize salient regions proposed in [13]. The framework estimates crowd motion field to extract features to represent crowd dynamics, stability map and phase shift map. Stability map presents particle advection demonstrating spatial distribution and phase shift map describes the velocity phase similarity among individuals in a crowd scene. According to the novel framework, we can conclude that spatial distribution and velocity phrase difference can be applied to detect salient regions. Thus, density distribution which reflects spatial distribution can be denoted as stability map in this module. Motion consistency and directions of moving groupings presenting similarity of global motion field are related to phase shift map. Considering the density level and the motion consistency, we can detect salient regions, where there exist abnormal behaviors. When the salient regions are detected, the warning level are defined as in Table 1.

Table 1. Explanation of the saliency index.

Density level	Group numbers	Direction numbers	Warn level
<C	<5	<=2	1
<C	<5	<=2	2
>=C	<5	>=3	3
>=C	>=5	>=3	4

We propose this module for analysis of group behaviours in crowded scenes and application model, in order to analyze the characterization, categorization and evaluation of abnormal incidents, setting the foundation for alarming in public security video surveillance.

2.4   Historical Statistics Analysis Module

In order to observe both the trend of crowd density and the number of groups with different directions and report the level of crowd directly, a historical statistics analysis module is designed. This module presents the historic statistic analysis of our system. The interface of this module is shown in Fig. 5.

We choose NTGraph control to show the results from the query in the database of different periods as users set. There are three schemes showing different information of the selected channel. The first scheme describes the trends of density level. The second one depicts the changing proportion of different groups. The last one shows the changes in the number of groups with different moving directions. In this module, users can set the range of time they want to query. Then they can choose which kind of feature and which channel they inquire. This system shows different query results with regard to different users.

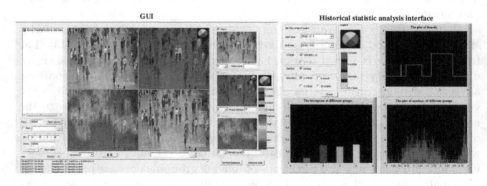

Fig. 5. The user interface of surveillance system.

3   Software Implementation of System

The user interface of our video surveillance is depicted by Fig. 5, including GUI and historical statistics analysis interface. After logging in device, video stream (as shown in Fig. 1) obtained from Hikvision IP camera located in East Nanjing Road and the Bund is transmitted to an analysis server, which provides analysis information. Its basic functions including playing videos, connecting to server, enrolling devices are implemented in Hikvision SDK. In following subsections, we will introduce software implementation of our system in detail.

3.1   Multichannel Monitoring

Multichannel monitoring plays a vital role in an effective iss. Our system can monitor 1, 4, 9, 16 channels simultaneously. In our system, the users need to firstly log in the system and then choose a channel to monitor. The GUI provides multiple windows to show multichannel video streaming with each window belonging to the same dialog class that can change the size of windows and play video. In addition, the analysis results of three video surveillance modules can all be shown in the windows.

3.2   Multithread and Buffer

Threads are designed to analyze different features of crowd scenes. Correspondingly, we utilize Hikvision SDK as the general framework and multithread is applied in historical statistics analysis module when users query data of different features. To avoid conflictions between writing and reading data, we create an array as a buffer, whose data queues depending on basic first-in-first-out structure. After the frame analysis we record the frame information into the buffer and then read data from it. It should be noted that in each thread, buffer should be locked when the process is reading or writing data.

3.3   Database Design and Statistics Display

Our system analyzes the density level, numbers of groups with different directions, and the crowd saliency level, all of which should be stored for historical statistics analysis module. We choose MySQL database and call MySQL statements in Visual Studio 2013. Moreover, in order to manage data effectively we design two tables.

To deal with the diversity of transmission channels and devices, a MySQL database is applied to record the information of channels, which can be mapped to 'deviceid' field in a table shown in Table 2. This table is used to store the information of channel and to avoid repeating storage the same channel. Another table as shown in Table 3 presents all properties of each frame, where the 'id' of each 'cameracode' has the same meaning as 'deviceid' in second table. When users select a channel to play video, the related information will be added to to the first table if the same channel is not stored.

Table 2. Device information.

Column	id	Cameracode	Name	Remarks
Meaning	Device id	Channel number	Camera name	Extra information

Table 3. Features information.

Column	Meaning	Column	Meaning
Timestamp	Time	imgpath	Image storage address
Deviceid	Device id	dirnum0	3 o'clock direction
Densitylevel	Density level	dirnum1	6 o'clock direction
Groupnum	Total groups	dirnum2	9 o'clock direction
Warnlevel	Salience	dirnum3	12 o'clock direction

3.4   Improvement of Speed Based on CUDA

The speed of segmentation and crowd density is mainly determined by k-Means and Gaussian blur process respectively. In this section, we propose parallel algorithms for k-Means Cluster and Gaussian blur and implement them on GPU, which can improve the processing speed of system.

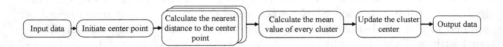

Fig. 6. Illustration of k-Means clustering algorithm.

In k-means algorithm the distance between each point to its corresponding cluster center is computed in step 3 as shown in Fig. 6, which is parallelized at patch-level. The kernel function computes the k-nearest points in different threads. In the Gaussian blur process, each point in original images is filtered in horizontal and vertical axis, the process of which includes lots of matrix calculations. CUDA has a good performance on matrix calculation so we can rewrite Gaussian blur as shown in Fig. 7 on CUDA to improve the speed of our system. Compared with traditional k-Means cluster and Gaussian blur, the CUDA implementation of the algorithms achieves a speedup over the CPU implementation.

4   Evaluations of System Performance

To evaluate our system performance, we conduct experiments on PETS, UFC, CUHK datasets and the real word datasets. In our system, the specifications of hardware are as follows, Core Intel i7-3770U 3.4 GHz and 8 GB RAM.

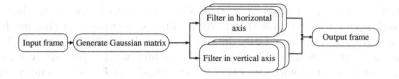

Fig. 7. Illustration of Gaussian blur algorithm.

Table 4. Experimental results of density level estimation.

Scene	Method	Density level accuracy			
		Free	Restricted	Dense	Jammed
PETS	Pixel statistic	0.923	0.87	0.82	0.79
	Texture feature	0.87	0.82	0.86	0.904
	Our system	0.92	0.89	0.87	0.89
Real Scenario	Our system	0.943	0.903	0.861	0.899

As for the crowd density module, we choose PETS dstaset and our own sets of video of East Nanjing Road and the Bund. In order to evaluate the density level accuracy of the proposed system, a quantitative comparison is conducted between different features based on effective region feature extration [14] and our system as shown in Table 4. The results indicate that our system achieves favorable performance on all density levels. The crowd density distribution is shown in Fig. 8, from which we can see that spatial distribution are presented accurately. The regions with more people are labeled with catchier colors.

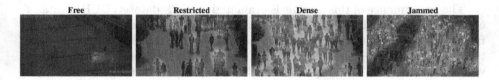

Fig. 8. The density distribution experimental results of the crowd density module.

As for the crowd segmentation module, we introduce Precision, Recall, F_1−score and segmentation accuracy to analyze the performance of our system. Definition of these metrics are given as below,

(1) Precision = Number of truly detected groups/Number of all detected groups;

(2) Recall = Number of truly detected groups/Number of all ground truth groups;

(3) F_1-score = $2 \times$ Precision $\times$ Recall/(Precision + Recall);

(4) Segmentation Accuracy = Number of truly labeled pixels/Number of all labeled ground truth pixels.

A truly detected group is defined as the group which has more than 50% area overlapping with ground truth group. The performance of this module is evaluated on UCF dataset, CUHK dataset compared with FTLE [3] and CF [15]. Evaluation results are shown in Table 5, from which we can see our system performs better compared with the other two methods on F_1−score and accuracy of segmentation areas. The qualitative segmentation results of datasets and real scenarios are shown in Fig. 9. We can see that our system segments crowd accurately with continuous and complete patches. Our system also provides moving directions of different groups.

Table 5. Results of different methods on the representative crowd datasets. The best results are marked in bold.

Method	Scene	Group detection			Group segmentation
		Precision	Recall	F_1-score	Accuracy
FTLE [3]	Mecca	0.33	0.48	0.39	0.86
	Crosswalk	0.45	0.66	0.54	0.76
	Pedestrians	0.24	0.24	0.24	0.53
CF [15]	Mecca	0.16	0.22	0.19	**0.93**
	Crosswalk	0.64	0.29	0.40	0.88
	Pedestrians	0.35	0.56	**0.43**	0.71
Our system	Mecca	0.42	0.50	**0.46**	0.90
	Crosswalk	0.62	0.54	**0.58**	**0.90**
	Pedestrians	0.33	0.63	**0.43**	**0.72**

The performance of this module is evaluated on UCF dataset, CUHK dataset compared with FTLE [3] and CF [15]. Evaluation results are shown in Table 5, from which we can see our system performs better compared with the other two methods on F_1−score and accuracy of segmentation areas. The qualitative segmentation results of datasets and real scenarios are shown in Fig. 9. We can see that our system segments crowd accurately with continuous and complete patches. Our system also provides moving directions of different groups.

Fig. 9. The grouping distribution experimental results of the crowd segmentation module.

Fig. 10. The salient regions detection experimental results of the crowd saliency module.

The crowd saliency module of this system can detect salient regions, where two different direction group meet, an individual maneuvering through crowd and some other unstable events happen as shown in Fig. 10. Our saliency is different from traditional definition of saliency and we focus on whether there exists abnormal behaviors. The historical statistics analysis module can show query results of numbers of moving groups with different directions as shown in Fig. 11. As Tables 6 and 7 show, implementing the k-means algorithms and Gaussian blur on CUDA can speed up our system. Comparing to the implementation on CPU, the parallelization of k-means algorithms cuts the runtime in half.

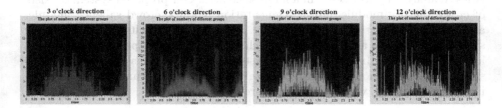

Fig. 11. The plot of different directions

Table 6. Comparison of the k-Means runtime of CPU and CUDA

Image no	CPU Runtime(ms)	CUDA runtime(ms)
1	3495	1503
2	3000	1430
3	3622	1595
4	3515	1444
5	3593	1437
6	4477	1892
7	4586	1782
8	4460	2019

Table 7. Comparison of the Gaussian runtime of CPU and CUDA

Image no	CPU runtime(ms)	CUDA runtime(ms)
5	1529	1278
6	928	882
7	922	883
8	921	883
9	927	882
10	924	882
11	922	882
12	927	881
13	933	884

5 Conclusion

In this paper, we develop a unified framework that combines multiple crowd properties including stationary and dynamic features, local and global characteristics to analyze crowd scenes in a large-scale area. Our proposed system consists of crowd density module, crowd segmentation module, crowd saliency module, and historical statistics analysis module. Experimental results demonstrate our system's robustness and feasibility, which achieve favorable performance in various crowd scenes. In this case, our system can only give a warning level for salient regions. Hence, how to recognize the type of abnormal behaviors is an important problem, which will be explored in further.

Acknowledgement. This work was supported in Science and Technology Commission of Shanghai Municipality (STCSM, Grant Nos.15DZ1207403).

References

1. Mehran, R., Oyama, A., Shah, M.: Abnormal crowd behavior detection using social force model. In: Conference on Computer Vision and Pattern Recognition, pp. 935–942 (2009)
2. Zhou, B., Wang, X., Tang, X.: Random field topic model for semantic region analysis in crowded scenes from tracklets. In: IEEE Conference on Computer Vision and Pattern Recognition, pp. 3441–3448 (2011)
3. Ali, S., Shah, M.: A lagrangian particle dynamics approach for crowd flow segmentation and stability analysis. In: IEEE Conference on Computer Vision and Pattern Recognition, pp. 1–6 (2007)
4. Wu, S., Moore, B.E., Shah, M.: Chaotic invariants of lagrangian particle trajectories for anomaly detection in crowded scenes. IEEE Conf. Comput. Vis. Pattern Recognit. **238**(6), 2054–2060 (2010)
5. Mehran, R., Moore, B.E., Shah, M.: A streakline representation of flow in crowded scenes. In: Daniilidis, K., Maragos, P., Paragios, N. (eds.) ECCV 2010. LNCS, vol. 6313, pp. 439–452. Springer, Heidelberg (2010). doi:10.1007/978-3-642-15558-1_32

6. Allain, P., Courty, N., Corpetti, T.: Crowd flow characterization with optimal control theory. Appl. Biochem. Microbiol. **51**(4), 432–441 (2010)
7. Raty, T.D.: Survey on contemporary remote surveillance systems for public safety. IEEE Trans. Syst. Man Cybern. C Appl. Rev. **40**(5), 493–515 (2010)
8. Bodor, R., Morlok, R., Papanikolopoulos, N.: Dual-camera system for multi-level activity recognition. In: IEEE/RSJ International Conference on Intelligent Robots and Systems, vol. 1, pp. 643–648 (2004)
9. Li, T., Chang, H., Wang, M., Ni, B., Hong, R., Yan, S.: Crowded scene analysis: a survey. IEEE Trans. Circ. Syst. Video Technol. **X**(1), 367–386 (2015)
10. Yang, H., Cao, Y., Su, H., Fan, Y., Zheng, S.: The large-scale crowd analysis based on sparse spatial-temporal local binary pattern. Multimedia Tools Appl. **73**(1), 41–60 (2014)
11. Tomasi, C.: Detection and tracking of point features. Technical report (1991). **9**(21), 9795–9802
12. Zhang, W., Wang, X., Zhao, D., Tang, X.: Graph degree linkage: agglomerative clustering on a directed graph. In: Fitzgibbon, A., Lazebnik, S., Perona, P., Sato, Y., Schmid, C. (eds.) ECCV 2012. LNCS, vol. 7572, pp. 428–441. Springer, Heidelberg (2012). doi:10.1007/978-3-642-33718-5_31
13. Mei, K.L., Kok, V.J., Chen, C.L., Chan, C.S.: Crowd saliency detection via global similarity structure. In: ICPR, pp. 3957–3962 (2014)
14. Su, H., Yang, H., Zheng, S.: The large-scale crowd density estimation based on effective region feature extraction method. In: Kimmel, R., Klette, R., Sugimoto, A. (eds.) ACCV 2010. LNCS, vol. 6494, pp. 302–313. Springer, Heidelberg (2011). doi:10.1007/978-3-642-19318-7_24
15. Zhou, B., Tang, X., Wang, X.: Coherent filtering: detecting coherent motions from crowd clutters. In: Fitzgibbon, A., Lazebnik, S., Perona, P., Sato, Y., Schmid, C. (eds.) ECCV 2012. LNCS, pp. 857–871. Springer, Heidelberg (2012). doi:10.1007/978-3-642-33709-3_61

Webpage Image Saliency Prediction via Adaptive SVM

Wei Shan[✉], Guangling Sun, and Zhi Liu

School of Communication and Information Engineering,
Shanghai University, Shanghai 200444, China
1449373534@qq.com

Abstract. In recent years, webpage is becoming an increasingly important visual information source, so it is meaningful to study human visual attention on webpage. However, the insufficiency of webpage image provided with eye tracking data has impeded performance improvement for its saliency prediction in the framework based on learning. Fortunately, we notice that the amount of natural image with eye tracking data is abundant. Although webpage image saliency could be predicted via direct learning from natural image, there is distribution discrepancy of visual features between webpage image and natural image. Thus, we propose to use adaptive SVM, which is learned from plenty of natural image and as well as adaptive learning from much less webpage images to boost the performance of webpage image saliency prediction. Experimental results demonstrate that the proposed adaptive SVM strategy has obtained better performance for webpage image saliency prediction.

Keywords: Webpage image · Natural image · Saliency prediction · Adaptive SVM

1 Introduction

Visual saliency prediction is a hot topic in computer vision and it includes two categories: human fixation prediction [1] and salient object detection [2]. In this paper, we focus on human fixation prediction.

With the wide spread of Internet in recent decades, webpage has become a more and more important source of information. In terms of survey, the number of Internet users has reached 3.2 billion in 2015. The fast growing trend of browsing webpage has greatly changed human living style and working pattern. Thus, studying of how human visual attention is guided and attracted by webpage has both academic and commercial values. Compared with natural image, webpage has different characteristics leading to direct using of existing saliency models for natural image ineffective. For example, webpage usually has rich visual elements such as text, computer graphics, logos and images [3]. From the point of view of fixation, webpage will be full of visual stimuli and competition among them happens everywhere. Undoubtedly, that fact will make webpage saliency prediction more challenge than and also different from that for natural image. In literature, there are two categories of models for webpage saliency prediction:

(1) Computational Models based on Non-Image Feature

© Springer Nature Singapore Pte Ltd. 2017
X. Yang and G. Zhai (Eds.): IFTC 2016, CCIS 685, pp. 128–136, 2017.
DOI: 10.1007/978-981-10-4211-9_13

Non-image feature refers to non-visual perception feature, such as HTML feature. Buscher *et al.* [4] utilized HTML-induced document object model (DOM) as features. They performed a linear regression on such features and decision trees to generated a model for predicting visual attention on webpage. Another example of this category model focus on a specific type of webpage [5].

(2) Computational Models based on Image Feature

Image feature refers to visual perception feature, such as color and luminance feature. One early effort utilizing Itti-Koch model [6] to predict saliency on webpage is from Still and Masciocchi [3]. The two recent works [7, 8] use image feature to learn and predict webpage saliency. The former use machine learning to predict webpage saliency and the latter use deep convolutional neural networks to extract features instead of handcrafted feature extraction by the former.

Inspired by [7], we also predict webpage saliency by machine learning scheme. However, the webpage image dataset labeled with eye tracking data is limited. It is seemingly that natural image with abundant labeled eye tracking data can be used to learn the saliency predictor, the low-level feature distribution differences between webpage image and natural image make the idea unsuccessful. Thus, we propose to predict webpage saliency via adaptive SVM. Specifically, we first use natural image to learn a SVM classifier; then we use much less webpage image to modify the decision hyperplane so as to let the original SVM classifier adapt to the feature distribution of webpage image. During testing, we use the adaptive SVM classifier to predict webpage saliency.

The remaining of the paper is organized as follows. Section 2 gives a brief introduction to adaptive SVM. Section 3 analyzes how to use adaptive SVM learning to predict webpage saliency. Section 4 demonstrates the promising experimental results. Section 5 is conclusion.

2 Adaptive SVM

Source domain has many labeled data while target domain has few labeled data, and the distribution of the two data set is different. The main idea of adaptive SVM is to learn a decision hyperplane using plenty of source domain data, then to search the changed part of the decision hyperplane with much less target domain data. The purpose of adaptive SVM is to improve the generalization of SVM for target domain. The following will elaborate the principle of adaptive SVM (Ref [9]).

The SVM classifier $f^s(\mathbf{x})$ is trained by source data. The adaptive SVM search the changed part on the basis of $f^s(\mathbf{x})$, so that improve the ability of generalization on the target data:

$$f(\mathbf{x}) = f^s(\mathbf{x}) + \Delta f(\mathbf{x}) = f^s(\mathbf{x}) + \mathbf{w}^T \varphi(\mathbf{x}) \tag{1}$$

where $\varphi(\mathbf{x})$ is the feature vector.

Thus, we define the objective function of adaptive SVM:

$$\min_{\mathbf{w}} \frac{1}{2}\|\mathbf{w}\|^2 + C\sum_{i=1}^{N} \xi_i$$

$$s.t.\ \xi_i \geq 0,$$

$$y_i f^s(\mathbf{x}_i) + y_i \mathbf{w}^T \varphi(\mathbf{x}_i) \geq 1 - \xi_i, \forall (\mathbf{x}_i, y_i) \in D_l^t$$

(2)

where $D_l^t = \{(\mathbf{x}_i, y_i)\}_{i=1}^{N}$ is the labeled target data, $\mathbf{x}_i$ and y_i represent ith feature vector and label data of target data. $\Sigma \xi_i$ measures the total classification error of target data, $\|\mathbf{w}\|^2$ is a regularization term. The purpose of minimal objective is seeking a new decision function $f(\mathbf{x})$ that is close to source classifier $f^s(\mathbf{x})$.

By introducing Lagrange multipliers, we can transfer Eq. (2) to dual space then get the model parameters:

$$\hat{\boldsymbol{\alpha}} = \arg\max_{\alpha} \left\{ \sum_{i=1}^{N} (1 - \lambda_i)\alpha_i - \frac{1}{2}\sum_{i=1}^{N}\sum_{j=1}^{N} \alpha_i \alpha_j y_i y_j K(\mathbf{x}_i, \mathbf{x}_j) \right\}$$

(3)

where $\lambda_i = y_i f^s(\mathbf{x}_i)$. Under the constraint $0 \leq \alpha_i \leq C$, estimating the $\hat{\boldsymbol{\alpha}}$ is a quadratic programming problem. Given the solutions $\hat{\boldsymbol{\alpha}}$, the adapted decision function is written as:

$$f(\mathbf{x}) = f^s(\mathbf{x}) + \sum_{i=1}^{N} \hat{\alpha}_i y_i K(\mathbf{x}, \mathbf{x}_i)$$

(4)

3   Proposed Method

The overview of the proposed method is illustrated in Fig. 1. Firstly we learn a SVM classifier $f^s(\mathbf{x})$ with natural image, then adapt it to a new classifier $f(\mathbf{x})$ using a spot of webpage image. The adapted classifier $f(\mathbf{x})$ is used to predict webpage image saliency.

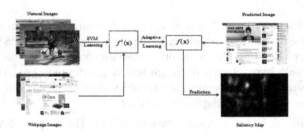

Fig. 1. Overview of proposed method

In this investigation, the natural image is source domain data and the webpage image is target domain data. For Eq. (1), the $f(\mathbf{x})$ is the final classification, the $\mathbf{x}$ denotes feature data of every pixel from webpage image. For Eq. (2), $\|\mathbf{w}\|^2$ is a regularization term and $\Sigma \xi_i$ measures the total error of webpage image saliency prediction. While

$D_l^t = \{(\mathbf{x}_i, y_i)\}_{i=1}^N$ is the labeled target data, $\mathbf{x}_i$ and y_i represent ith feature vector and label of webpage image, $y_i = \{0, 1\}$ indicates ith pixel is non-salient or salient. N is the number of pixels.

3.1 Features

A commonly referred line of early computational models that predict eye fixations on image was built upon low-level image statistics, such as luminance, color, edge and density [4, 6]. Those bottom-up saliency models can predict fixations in natural image in an effective way, indicating the importance of low-level features in driving attention. Recent studies, however, show that high-level features such as people and text also contribute a lot to predicting fixations [10–12]. Specifically, adding object detectors can dramatically improve performance of computational saliency models. So it is clear that both low-level feature and high-level feature play an important role in selective visual attention. So in this investigation, we use some low-level features and high-level features to predict webpage saliency.

Low-level features: Intensity, orientation and color contrast have long been seen as important features for bottom-up saliency. We include the three channels corresponding to these image features as calculated by Itti and Koch's saliency method [13]. We use the local energy of the steerable pyramid filters [14] as features. We also include features used in a simple saliency model described by Torralba [15] and Rosenholtz [16] based on subband pyramids.

High-level features: As we found that humans fixated so consistently on faces, we run the face detector and include this as feature to our model.

3.2 Learning and Prediction by Adaptive SVM

Our proposed method consists of two phases: one phase is adaptive SVM learning. We extract features from natural image and use it to train a classifier $f^s(\mathbf{x})$ firstly. Then extracting the same features from webpage image, and adapting $f^s(\mathbf{x})$ to a new classifier $f(\mathbf{x})$.

Another phase is webpage saliency prediction. First, we extract features from test webpage image, then feature vector of every pixel is input into the classifier $f(\mathbf{x})$. We can get salient value of all pixels from $f(\mathbf{x})$. This $\mathbf{x}$ denotes feature vector of every pixel in webpage image. In this way, we will get the final saliency map. The saliency map S can be obtained by

$$S = g * \max(f(\mathbf{x}), 0) \tag{5}$$

where g is a gaussian mask used to smooth the saliency map, '*' denotes convolution operator.

4 Experimental Results

4.1 Dataset

We involve two saliency datasets in this investigation: One is natural image (Object and Semantic Images and Eyetracking, OSIE) [17], that is source data D^s. Another is webpage image (Fixations on Webpage Image, FiWI) [7], that is target domain data D^t.

OSIE dataset with eye-tracking data from 15 participants for a full set of 700 natural images. Then the eye-track data is smoothed so that get ground truth of every image. Some images of the dataset is shown in following Fig. 2:

Fig. 2. Natural image samples in OSIE

FiWI is consist of 149 webpage images and corresponding eye-tracking data. Then the eye movement data of 11 participants are blurred by Gaussian filter so that we can get ground truth. These webpages were categorized as pictorial, text and mixed according to the different composition of text and pictures and each category contains around 50 images. Examples of webpage in each category are shown in Fig. 3.

Pictorial   Text   Mixed

Fig. 3. Webpage image samples

4.2 Saliency Evaluation Metrics

The saliency evaluation metrics we use include Linear Correlation Coefficient (CC), Normalized Scanpath Saliency (NSS) and shuffled Area Under Curve (sAUC).

CC measures the linear correlations between the estimated saliency map and the ground truth fixation map.

AUC is the most widely used score for saliency model evaluation. By varying the threshold on the saliency map, a Receiver Operating Characteristics (ROC) curve can then be plotted as the true positive rate vs. false negative rate. AUC is then calculated as the area under this curve. sAUC (shuffled AUC) is the same as AUC except using fixations of other images in the same dataset as negative.

NSS measures the average of the response values at fixation locations along the scanpath in the normalized saliency map.

All these three metrics have their advantages and limitations and a model that performs well should have relatively high score in all these three metrics.

4.3 Experiment Setup

We use $f^s(\mathbf{x})$, $f^T(\mathbf{x})$ and $f(\mathbf{x})$ to denote the classifier learned by source data, target data and the final classifier respectively.

First, we select 10 positive and negative samples respectively in all natural images to train a classifier $f^s(\mathbf{x})$, then predicting webpage saliency by this classifier. Second, webpage image sample set is randomly divided into 119 training images and 30 testing images and the final results were tested iteratively with different training and testing sets separation. The $f^T(\mathbf{x})$ is trained by 119 training images. Finally, we get $f(\mathbf{x})$ by adaptive SVM learning and sample selection is the same as first two experiments.

4.4 Results and Analysis

We use different classifier to predict webpage saliency. The results are shown in Table 1.

Table 1. The performance of different classifiers

Classifier	CC	sAUC	NSS
$f^s(\mathbf{x})$	0.3015	0.7112	0.7712
$f^T(\mathbf{x})$	0.3210	0.7283	0.8183
$f(\mathbf{x})$	**0.3447**	**0.7476**	**0.8792**

As been shown in Table 1, although labeled natural image is much more than labeled webpage image, the performance of $f^T(\mathbf{x})$ is better than $f^s(\mathbf{x})$. Therefore, there are big differences between data distribution of natural image and webpage image. We can't predict webpage saliency using the classifier trained by natural image. By comparing the results of $f(\mathbf{x})$ with $f^T(\mathbf{x})$ and $f^s(\mathbf{x})$, we find that adaptive SVM can solve the problems both labeled webpage image is short and the big difference between data distribution of two domains. Finally, our method improve the performance of predicting webpage saliency greatly. Besides, the $f^T(\mathbf{x})$ is a scheme proposed by Zhao *et al.* [7], which is the state-of-the-art method of webpage saliency prediction, the performance of our model is better than their model.

We still compare the performance of these classifiers by the T-test. We get two pairs of T-test by the results of three classifiers. In Table 2, $G_{f-f}{}^s$ and $G_{f-f}{}^T$ denotes the gain of $f(\mathbf{x})$ to $f^s(\mathbf{x})$ and $f^T(\mathbf{x})$ respectively. The evaluation shows that our model can improve the performance of predicting webpage saliency.

Table 2. Paired T-test

T-test pair	CC	sAUC	NSS
$G_{f-f}{}^T$	0.03	0.0229	0.0781
$G_{f-f}{}^s$	0.0567	0.0464	0.1434

As been shown in Table 3, low-level feature is important for saliency prediction. But the high-level feature still cannot be ignored.

Table 3. The performance of proposed method using different features

Feature	CC	sAUC	NSS
low-level	0.3159	0.7275	0.8047
low-level+high-level	0.3447	0.7476	0.8792

From Table 4, we could see that the performance on all the three categories are close, however, the performance on Text is a bit smaller than that on Pictorial and the performance on Mixed is between them. This results indicate that text might be a difficult part to predict saliency.

Table 4. The performance of proposed method on three different categories

Webpage categories	CC	sAUC	NSS
Text	0.3340	0.7420	0.8675
Mixed	0.3430	0.7490	0.8783
Pictorial	0.3578	0.7520	0.8924

Finally, we make subjective assessments for our model. From the Fig. 4, we could see that our model predict important texts like title or logo to be more salient than other objects and the background. It highlights all the regions where evident texts and objects locate.

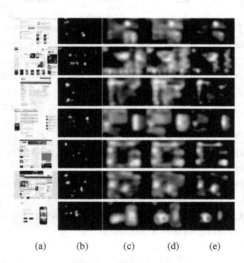

(a)   (b)   (c)   (d)   (e)

Fig. 4. Subjective assessments (a) webpage images; (b) ground truth; (c) saliency map predicted by $f^s(\mathbf{x})$; (d) saliency map predicted by $f^T(\mathbf{x})$; (e) saliency map predicted by $f(\mathbf{x})$.

5   Conclusion

Despite the abundant literature in saliency modeling that predicts where humans look at in a visual scene, there are few studies on saliency in webpage, and we make some exploration on this topic in this work. In this investigation, we proposed adaptive SVM to predict webpage saliency. Firstly, we train a SVM classifier by low-level features and high-level features of natural image, then we obtain a new SVM classifier by adapting the former SVM classifier using the corresponding features of webpage image. The results demonstrate our model improve the performance of webpage saliency prediction.

6   Acknowledgment

This work was supported by Shanghai Municipal Natural Science Foundation under Grant No. 16ZR1411100, National Natural Science Foundation of China under Grant No. 61471230, and the Program for Professor of Special Appointment (Eastern Scholar) at Shanghai Institutions of Higher Learning.

References

1. Borji, A., Itti, L.: State-of-the-art in visual attention modeling. IEEE Trans. Pattern Anal. Mach. Intell. **35**(1), 185–207 (2013)
2. Borji, A., Mingming, C., Huaizu, J., et al.: Salient object detection: a benchmark. IEEE Trans. Image Process. **24**(12), 5706–5722 (2015)
3. Still, J., Masciocchi, C.: A saliency model predicts fixations in web interfaces. In: 5th International Workshop on Model Driven Development of Advanced User Interfaces, Atlanta, Georgia, USA, pp. 25–28 (2010)
4. Buscher, G., Cutrell, E., Morris, M.: What do you see when you're surfing? Using eye tracking to predict salient regions of web pages. In: Proceedings of the SIGCHI Conference on Human Factors in Computing Systems, pp. 21–30. ACM, Boston (2009)
5. Cutrelle, E., Guan, Z.: What are you looking for? An eye-tracking study of information usage in web search. In: Proceedings of the SIGCHI Conference on Human Factors in Computing Systems, pp. 407–416. ACM, San Jose (2007)
6. Itti, L., Koch, C.A.: saliency-based search mechanism for overt and covert shifts of visual attention. Vis. Res. **40**(10), 1489–1506 (2000)
7. Shen, C., Zhao, Q.: Webpage saliency. In: European Conference on Computer Vision, Zurich, pp. 33–46 (2014)
8. Chengyao, S., Xun, H., Qi, Z.: Predicting eye fixations on webpage with an ensemble of early features and high-level representations from deep network. IEEE Trans. Multimed. **17**(11), 2084–2093 (2015)
9. Yang, J., Yan, R., Hauptmann, A.G.: Cross-domain video concept detection using adaptive SVMs. In: Proceedings of the 15th International Conference on Multimedia, pp. 188–197. ACM, Augsburg (2007)
10. Huang, X., Shen, C., Boix, X., et al.: SALICON: reducing the semantic gap in saliency prediction by adapting deep neural networks. In: Proceedings of the IEEE International Conference on Computer Vision, pp. 262–270 (2015)

11. Xu, M., Ren, Y., Wang, Z.: Learning to predict saliency on face images. In: Proceedings of the IEEE International Conference on Computer Vision, pp. 3907–3915 (2015)
12. Ming, L., Xiaolin, H.: Predicting eye fixations with higher-level visual features. IEEE Trans. Image Process. **24**(3), 1178–1189 (2015)
13. Itti, L., Koch, C.: Computational modelling of visual attention. Nat. Rev. Neurosci. **2**(3), 194–203 (2001)
14. Alioua, N., Amine, A., Bensrhair, A., et al.: Estimating driver head pose using steerable pyramid and probabilistic learning. Intl. J. Comput. Vis. Robot. **5**(4), 347–364 (2015)
15. Oliva, A., Torralba, A.: Modeling the shape of the scene: a holistic representation of the spatial envelope. Int. J. Comput. Vis. **42**(3), 145–175 (2001)
16. Rosenholtz, R.: A simple saliency model predicts a number of motion popout phenomena. Vis. Res. **39**(19), 3157–3163 (1999)
17. Xu, J., Jiang, M., Wang, S., et al.: Predicting human gaze beyond pixels. J. Vis. **14**(1), 1–20 (2014). Article 28

Face Recognition Based on Weighted Multi-order Feature Fusion of 2D-FrFT

Xu Wang$^{(\boxtimes)}$, Lin Qi, Yun Tie, and Enqing Chen

Information Engineering School, Zhengzhou University,
Zhengzhou 450001, China
iewxalex@163.com

Abstract. The fractional Fourier transform (FrFT) features have been known to be effective for face recognition. However, only a few approaches utilize phase feature and they usually perform worse than those using magnitude feature. To investigate the potential of FrFT phase and its fusion between different orders for face recognition, in this paper, we first propose weighted multi-order band fusion of generalized phase spectrum (WMFP) of 2D-FrFT. Compared with the conventional appearance-based face recognition method, the proposed method does not need to perform image-to-vector conversion and can well preserve the discriminative information of the original image. Different from the existing Fourier-based recognition approaches such as Fourier-LDA and local region histogram of 2D-FrFT magnitude and phase (LFMP), the proposed approach merges multiple orders' generalized phase spectrum of 2D-FrFT and gives different weights to different orders simultaneously. Experimental results on two benchmark face databases demonstrate the effectiveness of the proposed method and indicate that our method is better than Fourier-PCA and LFMP, as well as other popular face recognition methods such as Gabor-based linear discriminant analysis (GLDA) and local Gabor binary patterns (LGBP).

Keywords: Face recognition · Two dimensional fractional Fourier transform (2D-FrFT) · Generalized phase spectrum (GPS) · Fusion · Weighted multi-order band fusion of generalized phase spectrum (WMFP)

1 Introduction

Due to the advantages of non-intrusive natural and high uniqueness, as well as the increasing need for security-related applications, face recognition has been an active topic for researchers in the field of computer vision and pattern recognition [1]. A wide range of applications, from public security to personal consumer electronics, have made face recognition one of the most popular research topics. With the past decade, numerous face recognition approaches have been reported in the literature to handle variations in illumination, expression and occlusion etc. Despite a significant level of maturity and a few practical successes, finding efficient and robust algorithms for face recognition is still an active and challenging topic.

As a generalization of Fourier transform (FT), the fractional Fourier transform (FRFT) is a powerful signal analysis and processing tool. The Fourier analysis [2, 3] is

© Springer Nature Singapore Pte Ltd. 2017
X. Yang and G. Zhai (Eds.): IFTC 2016, CCIS 685, pp. 137–145, 2017.
DOI: 10.1007/978-981-10-4211-9_14

an effective analysis tool for facial images. However, it abnegates the time-domain information of images absolutely so that it will lose some significant information of faces inevitably. The conventional FT can be regard as a rotation in the frequency plane. However, FrFT performs a rotation of signal to any angle. Therefore, the two dimensional fractional Fourier transform (2D-FrFT) contains the time-frequency information of the signal simultaneously. Facial image can be regarded as a gradually changed signal. It has been shown that the 2D-FrFT is an effective analysis tool for facial images [6]. Gao et al. made use of the phase information of the 2D-FrFT for emotion recognition [4]. Wang et al. utilized the phase and Magnitude information of 2D-FrFT for face registration [15]. Kong et al. utilized 2D-FrFT with fuzzy fusion classification algorithm in human emotional state recognition [14].

Motivated by the above-mentioned reason, in this paper, we adopt 2D-FrFT phase information to improve the effect of face recognition. First, we extract the phase information of facial image in 2D-FrFT, which is called the generalized phase spectra (GPS). It has been shown that the lower frequency bands contain more smooth information, while high bands contain the edge information of a facial image [2]. Then, we present an improved two-dimensional separability judgment to select appropriate order parameters for 2D-FrFT. Through selecting the appropriate transform orders and choosing the optimal generalized phase spectrum band, a new spectrum feature can be extracted, which not only contains the smooth information but also includes the edge information of a facial image. In order to make full use of the discriminative information from different orders for face recognition, the proposed approach merges multiple orders' GPS band of 2D-FrFT and gives different weights to different orders simultaneously, as illustrated in Fig. 1. Finally, we perform the classification using the nearest neighbor classifier. In the experiments, two famous public face databases are employed as the test data.

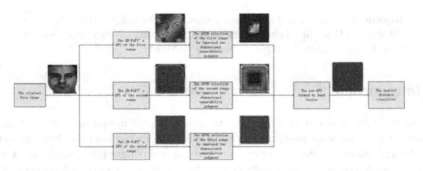

Fig. 1. Illustration of the WMFP.

In the following sections, we will first perform the analysis of FRFT and the definition of the GPS in Sect. 2. Then our face recognition approach is presented in Sect. 3. The experiment results based on the nearest neighbor classifier are summarized in Sect. 4. And finally, conclusions are drawn in Sect. 5.

2 Fractional Fourier Transform

The discrete FrFT [6] is a new time-frequency analysis tool which is developed and widely used in recent years. In essence, the signal representation in fractional Fourier domain integrates the information of time domain and frequency domain. The 2D-FrFT on each image is defined as follows:

$$X_{(\alpha,\beta)}(m, n) = \sum_{p=0}^{M-1} \sum_{q=0}^{N-1} x(p, q) K_{(\alpha,\beta)}(p, q, m, n) \tag{1}$$

$$K_{(\alpha,\beta)} = K_\alpha \otimes K_\beta \tag{2}$$

$$K_p = \frac{A_\alpha}{2\Delta x} \exp\left(\frac{j\pi(\cot\cot\alpha)m^2}{(2\Delta x)^2} - \frac{j2\pi(\csc\csc\alpha)mn}{(2\Delta x)^2} + \frac{j2\pi(\cot\cot\alpha)n^2}{(2\Delta x)^2} \right) \tag{3}$$

The transform kernel is $K_{(\alpha,\beta)}$, as defined as (2). 2D-FrFT is equivalent to apply discrete FrFT on the two parameters of a signal $x(p, q)$ successively. The separable kernel K_p with respect to different orders for x and y axes indicates additional degrees of freedom that can be used for specific applications in the feature extraction.

As we all know, two dimensional Fourier transform (2DFT) is not reality preserving. With the 2DFT, the original data is transformed into complex-value which contains both magnitude information and phase information. So does the 2D-FrFT, which is the generalized form of 2DFT. It is inflected in the phenomenon that the transform order can be selected according to different needs. In this paper, since the phase contains a large amount of edge information [4], it is more conducive to identify the face. It is extended from the phase spectrum by the FT. GPS means that a facial image with the 2D-FrFT phase information is distributed on the fractional domain.

3 Proposed Approach

It has been demonstrated that not all phase spectrum bands of FT are beneficial for face recognition [2]. This motivates us to exploit the discriminative nature of different GPS bands. Obviously, how to choose the appropriate GPS bands from different transform orders is the key question. According to the properties of FrFT [6], it is periodic with periodicity equal to 4. From the definition, we give detailed description about the transform order that changes from 0.1 to 1. Pei et al. has given some explanation about the phase information of different transform orders [6]. The transform order p changing from 0.1 to 1 is divided into three ranges according to the inter-class and intra-class difference of phase information. The orders can be divided into three ranges, small order range (0.1 to 0.4), middle order range (0.5 to 0.7) and large order range (0.8 to 1) respectively. The Fig. 2 indicates that the difference of inter-class figures from different ranges is obvious while the intra-class figures from the same range are similar.

As discussed in [3], the small transform orders will lose edge information of an image with the 2D-FrFT, and the large transform orders will contain much noise, such as illumination, expression and so on. As for the middle order, it is the low-abiding, but

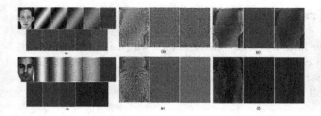

Fig. 2. (a) is the transformed face image from ORL database according to the orders changing from 0–1, (b) and (c) are the intra-class and inter-class average difference of three ranges based on ORL database, as well as (d), (e) and (f) are based on AR database.

Fig. 3. Illustration of the GPS bands.

we can also think that it cannot make full use of the low spectral phase band and the high spectral phase band yet. To make full use of the GPS bands of different ranges, we select the transform order from each range randomly and then choose the bands by the improved two-dimensional separability judgment. When the division of orders is completed, how to choose the GPS bands from the transform ranges is critical. The two-dimensional separability judgment [2] is adopted to select the frequency band, but it neglects the transformed data structure. In this paper, the improved two-dimensional separability judgment is proposed which takes the transformed data information into account instead of the face images. Suppose that the original image sample set is X, each gray image matrix is sized M ∗ N and expressed by $X(p, q)$, where $1 \leq p \leq M$, $1 \leq q \leq N$. We perform 2D-FrFT as depicted as the Eq. (4):

$$\mathbf{F}_{(\alpha,\beta)}(u, v) = \sum\nolimits_{p=0}^{M-1} \sum\nolimits_{q=0}^{N-1} \mathbf{X}(p, q)\mathbf{K}_{(\alpha,\beta)}(p, q, u, v) \tag{4}$$

For simplicity, we still use X to represent the transformed data. We will choose the GPS bands according to the properties of phase information from different ranges. Let $F_{(\alpha,\beta)}(\mu_0, v_0)$ indicates the zero PSB. Shift $F_{(\alpha,\beta)}(\mu_0, v_0)$ to the center of the image at $(M/2, N/2)$. Since the GPS domain is represented by the matrix form, we use a square ring Ring(k) to represent the kth GPS band, where $0 \leq k \leq M/2$. The four vertexes of Ring(k) are $(u - k, v - k)$, $(u + k, v - k)$, $(u - k, v + k)$ and $(u + k, v + k)$ respectively. So, the kth GPS band denotes:

$$F_{(\alpha,\beta)}(\mu, v) \in \text{Ring}(k) \tag{5}$$

Different GPS bands with the above expression way are illustrated in Fig. 3. If we select the GPS band, keep the original values of $F_{(\alpha,\beta)}(\mu, v)$, otherwise set the values of $F_{(\alpha,\beta)}(\mu, v)$ to be zero. The selection step can be expressed by the Eq. (6):

$$F_{(\alpha,\beta)}(\mu, v) = \begin{cases} \text{Original values} & \text{if } F_{(\alpha,\beta)}(\mu, v) \in \text{Ring}(k) \\ 0 & \text{if } F_{(\alpha,\beta)}(\mu, v) \notin \text{Ring}(k) \end{cases} \tag{6}$$

Then we can evaluate the separability J_k by the improved two-dimensional separability judgment. Let $A_i (i = 1, 2, \ldots, C)$ denote a mean value of w_i class and A denote the total mean value of X. A_i and A are in the form of the matrix. $F_{k(\alpha,\beta)}$ represents the kth GPS band. With regard to the kth GPS band, we can compute the within-class S_w matrix and between-class S_b matrix according to the Eqs. (7) and (8), and the trace ratio is calculated by the Eq. (9).

$$S_b = \sum\nolimits_{i=1}^{C} \left[(A_i - A)(A_i - A)^T \right] \tag{7}$$

$$S_w = \sum\nolimits_{i=1}^{C} \left[(A_i - F_{k(\alpha,\beta)})(A_i - F_{k(\alpha,\beta)})^T \right] \tag{8}$$

$$J_k = \frac{tr(S_b)}{tr(S_w)} \tag{9}$$

For all the GPS bands, we select the bands with high trace ratio by maximizing the between-class scatter while minimizing the within-class scatter.

4   Experimental Results

In this section, we present the experimental results on public available databases for face recognition, which serve to illustrate the efficacy of the proposed approach. The following describes the details of the experiments and results. The nearest neighbor classifier with the Euclidean distance is applied for recognition.

4.1   Experiments on the FERET Face Database

The FERET database consists of 13539 facial images corresponding to 1565 subjects, who are diverse across ethnicity, gender and age. From the FERET face database, we select a subset includes 1400 images of 200 individuals (each individual has seven images) in the experiment. There are 71 females and 129 males. This database involves the variations in facial expression, illumination and poses ($\pm 15°$ and $\pm 25°$). All the chosen images are resized to 64 * 64 with 256 gray levels per pixel. Figure 4 shows some sample images of one subject from the FERET database. In the experiment, the first three images of each person are used as training samples and the remainder as test samples. So, there are 600 (=200 * 3) training samples and 800(=200 * 4) test samples.

Fig. 4. The samples of cropped face images from the FERET database.

Tables 1 and 2 show the accuracy of different transform orders and the comparison between WMFP and Eigenface, Fisherface, SRC [10], LGBP [14], Fourier + PCA [2] and LFMP [15] separately on the FERET database. We implemented these methods ourselves and tuned the parameters for each method for fair comparison. The results verify the proposed method powerfully. Figure 5 indicates the identity of GPS bands from different transform orders, from which we select 0.4, 0.5 randomly and 0.9 as the band fusion orders. It is a positive correlation between color and the trace ratio of the GPSB. The closer to the white color, the higher trace ratio of GPSB.

Table 1. The recognition rate with the discrimination of different orders on the FERET database

Transform order	0.1	0.2	0.3	0.4	0.5	0.6	0.7	0.8	0.9	1.0	WMFP
Recognition rate	64%	64%	68%	67%	63%	58%	65%	65%	66%	63%	95%

Table 2. The comparison results on the FERET database

Different methods	Eigenface	Fisherface	SRC	LGBP	Fourier + PCA	LFMP	WMFP
Recognition rate	56.13%	61.2%	76.5%	80.4%	82.94%	90.5%	95%

Fig. 5. Illustration of the GPS bands according to different transform orders on the FERET database.

For the experiments on the FERET database, we test the effectiveness of our method to the overall problems. As can be seen from this table, the proposed WMFP outperforms the 6 compared methods with the lowest gains in accuracy of 5% on the FERET database. We have made three observations from the results listed in Tables 1 and 2: (1) Table 1 shows that different orders of 2D-FrFT may result in different recognition rates. However, the highest rate 68%, which is achieved in order 0.3, is still not satisfying, due to the fact that the single order 2D-FrFT feature is always not enough for recognition. Not only the amount of information, but also the redundancy is increasing when weighted multi-order bands are fused. (2) The Gabor method is very time consuming and more suitable for high-resolution image which imposes a heavy computational burden on the target device, in particular on mobile devices, which have low computational power. The proposed method is no need to construct the subspace through the feature extraction methods and has less computation cost. (3) WMFP obtains the best recognition performance on all the experiments, which implies that both edge and smooth information of facial image are important for recognition. Compared with other methods, the WMFP is more intuitive and effective with considerable results.

4.2 The Robustness to the Illumination Based on the Extended Yale-B Face Database

The Extended Yale-B database consists of 2414 frontal face images of 38 individuals under various laboratory-controlled lighting conditions. All the test images used in the experiments are manually aligned, cropped, and then resized to 64 * 64 images. The Extended Yale-B set only has little variability of expression, aging, etc. However, its extreme lighting conditions still make it a challenging task for most face recognition methods. The database is divided into five subsets, which can be seen from the Table 3. In this experiment, we select 0.2, 0.5 and 0.8 as the band fusion orders, which are selected randomly from the three transform ranges.

Table 3. Data partition on Extended Yale-B database for various experiments

Category	Training	Testing
Subset 1	Consisting of 266 images under normal lighting conditions	Consisting of 266 images under normal lighting conditions
Subset 2	Consisting of 266 images under normal lighting conditions	12 images per subject, characterize slight-to-moderate illumination variations
Subset 3	Consisting of 266 images under normal lighting conditions	12 images per subject, characterize moderate-to-drastic illumination variations
Subset 4	Consisting of 266 images under normal lighting conditions	14 images per person
Subset 5	Consisting of 266 images under normal lighting conditions	19 images per person

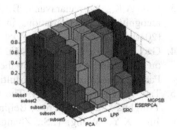

Fig. 6. The comparison on the Extended Yale-B database is revealed in this figure.

Figure 6 shows the performance for varying Subsets. We compare the proposed method with PCA, FLD, LPP, SRC and ESERPCA [11], in light of its capability of handling illumination changes. The three classical methods are sensitive to the illumination varying. Note that SRC, ESERPCA and the proposed method show excellent performance for moderate light variations, yielding 100%. In particular, WMFP obtains the best recognition rate of 62.36% on Subset 5. By contrast, recognition accuracy of the other approaches drops heavily in this Subset. It is not only more visualized to display the performance between different Subsets and methods, but also demonstrate the robustness of the proposed algorithm to the varying illumination.

5 Conclusion

This paper proposes a new method called WMFP which improve the phase information accuracy of 2D-FrFT significantly. The GPS bands are extracted from different orders of 2D-FrFT, which contains both the smooth information of small orders and the edge information of large orders. Following our method, the accuracy of the phase information achieves a preferred result. It also demonstrates the efficacy to the illumination varying which makes full use of the phase information of different transform orders. For future work, we are interested in designing effective classifiers to improve the recognition performance. Moreover, how to combine 2D-FrFT magnitude and phase of face images to further improve the face recognition accuracy appears to be another interesting direction of future work.

Acknowledgments. This work was supported in partly by the National Natural Science Foundation of China under Grant No. 61331201 and No. 61201251.

REFERENCES

1. Jain, A., Ross, A., Prabhakar, S.: An introduction to biometric recognition. IEEE Trans. Circ. Syst. Video Technol. **14**(1), 4–20 (2004)
2. Jing, X.Y., Tang, Y.Y., Zhang, D.: A Fourier-LDA approach for image recognition. Pattern Recogn. **38**(3), 453–457 (2005)
3. Sao, A.K., Yegnanarayana, B.: On the use of phase of the Fourier transform for face recognition under variations in illumination. Sig. Image Video Process. **4**(3), 353–358 (2010)
4. Gao, L., Qi, L., Chen, E.Q., Mu, X.M., Guan, L.: Recognizing human emotional state based on the phase information of the two dimensional fractional Fourier transform. In: 11th Pacific Rim Conference on Multimedia, pp. 694–794 (2010)
5. Tao, R., Qi, L., Wang, Y.: The theory and Applications of Fractional Fourier Transform. Tsinghua University Press, Beijing (2004)
6. Jing, X.Y., Wong, H.S., Zhang, D.: Face recognition based on discriminant fractional Fourier feature extraction. Pattern Recogn. Lett. **27**(13), 1465–1471 (2006)
7. Pei, S.C., Ding, J.J.: Relations between fractional operations and time-frequency distributions and their applications. IEEE Trans. Sig. Process. **49**(8), 1638–1655 (2001)
8. Choi, S.: Combined features for face recognition. Electron. Lett. **52**(1), 0013–5194 (2016)

9. Belhumeur, P.N., Hespanha, J.P., Kriegman, D.J.: Eigenfaces vs. Fisherfaces: recognition using class specific linear projection. IEEE Trans. Pattern Anal. Mach. Intell. **19**(7), 711–720 (1997)
10. Wright, J., Yang, A.Y., Ganesh, A., Sastry, S.S., Ma, Y.: Robust face recognition via sparse representation. IEEE Trans. Pattern Anal. Mach. Intell. **31**(2), 210–227 (2009)
11. Luan, X., Fang, B., Liu, L.H., Yang, W.B., Qian, J.: Extracting sparse error of robust PCA for face recognition in the presence of varying illumination and occlusion. Pattern Recogn. **47**(2), 495–508 (2014)
12. Liu, C., Wechsler, H.: Gabor feature based classification using the enhanced Fisher linear discriminant model for face recognition. IEEE Trans. Image Process. **11**, 467–476 (2002)
13. Zhang, W., Shan, S., Gao, W., et al.: Local Gabor Binary Pattern Histogram Sequence (LGBPHS): a novel non-statistical model for face representation and recognition. In: International Conference on Computer Vision, pp. 786–791 (2005)
14. Kong, M., Qi, L., Zheng, N., et al.: Application of the 2D-FrFT combined with fuzzy fusion classification algorithm in human emotional state recognition. In: TMEE, pp. 1094–1097 (2011)
15. Wang, Y.X., Qi, L., Guo, X., Gao, L.: Face recognition based on histogram of the 2DFrFT magnitude and phase. In: Information Science, Electronics and Electrical Engineering (ISEEE), vol. 3, pp. 1421–1425 (2014). doi:10.1109/6946154

Parallel-Friendly Frame Rate Up-Conversion Algorithm Based on Patch Match

Xu Jiang$^{(\boxtimes)}$, Li Chen, Zhiyong Gao, and Xiaoyun Zhang

Shanghai Jiao Tong University, Shanghai, 200240, China
{xu.jiang,hilichen,zhiyong.gao,xiaoyun.zhang}@sjtu.edu.cn

Abstract. In this paper, we propose a parallel-friendly frame rate up-conversion (FRUC) algorithm based on the patch match. The key points of the algorithm are the generation of self-similarity patch, parallel true motion estimation and motion vectors post-processing dealing with occlusion problem. Our algorithm is fully parallel at each step and can be implemented on GPU. The GPU implementation achieves up to 48 times speedup over its CPU implementation. Compared with the traditional FRUC algorithm based on 3-D Recursive Search, our algorithm has a good performance in handling the fine motion structure and occlusion problem.

Keywords: FRUC · Parallel true motion estimation · GPU · Patch Match

1 Introduction

Frame rate up-conversion (FRUC) is the technique that increases the frame rate by generating the intermediate frame between the original frame in the video. FRUC is commonly applied to increase the time resolution and reduce the effect of motion blur. The main approaches can be classified into three steps, motion estimation (ME), motion vectors post-processing (MVPP), and motion compensated interpolation (MCI). Among the three steps, ME is the most basic and important step. 3-D Recursive Search (3DRS) [1] is a good performing true-motion estimation algorithm with low computational complexity. And many improved methods [2, 3] based on 3DRS have been proposed. Because 3DRS is based on the assumption that most objects are much larger than a block, it recursively uses Motion Vectors (MVs) of spatial and temporal neighboring blocks to estimate the MV of a block [2]. The assumption indicates that it is not a good motion estimation method for a small object. And the spatial recursion, which depends on the precomputation of the spatial neighbor block, is obviously sequential execution. This prevents the algorithm to be applied in parallel computation. Besides 3DRS, optical flow estimation is a more accurate algorithm. But the high computational complexity limits the optical flow estimation in practical application.

Recently, numerous research proposed parallel-friendly algorithms which are suitable to be implemented on GPU to gain significant speedup [4]. In [7], this parallel true motion estimation algorithm adjust the 3DRS to use the temporal recursion only. But this result in more convergence time. In [8], the algorithm applies jump flooding scheme

© Springer Nature Singapore Pte Ltd. 2017
X. Yang and G. Zhai (Eds.): IFTC 2016, CCIS 685, pp. 146–154, 2017.
DOI: 10.1007/978-981-10-4211-9_15

proposed by Rong and Tan [5] for Patch Match. In [6], the Patch Match is applied in EPPM algorithm, and it proves that carefully crafted local methods can reach quality on par with global ones.

In this paper, we propose a parallel-friendly algorithm for FRUC, and implement it on GPU. We focus on improving the ME performance of the small object and handling the occlusion problem. Compared with 3DRS, proposed algorithm is based on dense Motion Vector Field (MVF), which can handle the fine motion structure. Compared with optical flow estimation, the adapted Patch Match in parallel reduces the high computational complexity. Our algorithm can also be divided into three steps. The detail of proposed algorithm is presented in Sect. 2. Section 3 describes the implementation of the proposed algorithm in CUDA. The result of the proposed algorithm is presented in Sect. 4. Section 5 concludes the paper.

2   Parallel-Friendly Frame Rate Up-Conversion Algorithm

Our algorithm can be classified into three steps: ME, MVPP and MCI. ME is based on Patch Match to realize parallelization, and through this step, we obtain the forward and backward MVF. Then MVPP is designed to eliminate and correct the outliers in forward and backward MVF. Finally, the MCI step generates the intermediate frame. The outline of proposed algorithm is depicted in Fig. 1.

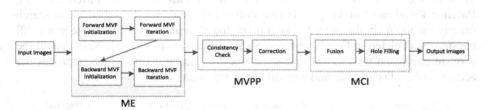

Fig. 1. Outline of the proposed algorithm.

2.1   Motion Estimation

The main idea of original Patch Match is to initialize a random correspondence field and then iteratively propagate good guesses among neighboring pixels [6]. The method has been adapted for the application of FRUC. Two significant changes are made to enhance the performance. Firstly, we change the block to self-similarity patch, which can improve the accuracy of ME. Secondly, we restrict the search range from the whole image to a certain window. Because it is impossible for the object in a video to move from one side to another side within two frames. The adapted Patch Match can be divided into 4 parts: Patch Generation, Initialization, Propagation and Random Search. The process of acquiring the forward MVF is presented as follow.

Patch Generation. To compute the matching cost the of a MV, we allocate a block $B(x,y)$ for each pixel (x,y) to compute the Sum of Absolute Differences (SAD). Notice that, with the increase of the radius, the computational load shows quadratic increase. This suggests a natural way to reduce the computational complexity which is that we only use the n most similar pixel to compute SAD. In other words, we ignore dissimilar pixel to the center pixel. For each pixel (x,y), we select the n most similar pixel from its neighborhood, store them in the array **Patch**(x,y), and only use the pixel belonging to the **Patch**(x,y) to compute the matching cost. Specifically, the matching cost is defined as follows,

$$D(\mathbf{a}, MV(\mathbf{a})) = \sum_{b \in Patch(a)} |F_t(\mathbf{b}) - F_{t+1}(\mathbf{b} + MV(\mathbf{a}))| \tag{1}$$

where $F_t(.)$ represents the frame at time t, $\mathbf{a}(x_a, y_a)$ is the pixel in F_t, $\mathbf{b}(x_b, y_b)$ represents the pixel belonging to **Patch(a)**, **MV(a)** is the motion vector at position **a**.

Then a problem raised is that the brute-force preselection of n similar pixels for each pixel actually can be too slow, especially when patch size is large, which may cancel out a large portion of the speed gain of the Patch Match [6]. Note that the straight implementation of the selection process takes $O(Mn)$ complexity for each pixel.

For the sake of speeding up, our algorithm utilize the similarity between the adjacent pixel to get the approximate n most similar pixel. The step of **Patch**(x,y) generation is as follows: For each pixel (x,y), we randomly select n pixels from its neighbor pixel and store them into a vector **Patch**(x,y) in order of their similarity to the center pixel (x,y); Then we merge the adjacent pixel similarity vector **Patch**$(x - 1,y)$, **Patch**$(x,y - 1)$, **Patch**$(x + 1,y)$ and **Patch**$(x,y + 1)$ into **Patch**(x,y). Since we do not intend to search exactly the top n similar pixel for each pixel, the algorithm does not iterate more. All the steps is depicted in Fig. 2, with $n = 50$ and patch size is 21×21. Note that all the pixel in one patch tend to own the same true MV intuitionally, which improves the accuracy of SAD criterion, and we will use this property in the MVPP step.

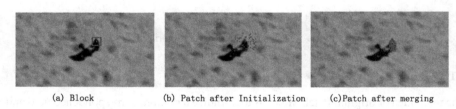

(a) Block   (b) Patch after Initialization   (c) Patch after merging

Fig. 2. Illustration of patch generation. (a) shows the 7×7 block around the center pixel. (b) shows the random initialization within 21×21 range around the center. (c) shows the final patch after merging. All the members belong to one patch can be seen as part of one object, so they usually own the same true motion vector.

Initialization. The MVF can be initialized by assigning random MV, or by using prior information. When initialize the forward MVF, we use the random values clamped to a certain value w (usually one eighth of the width of the image), because it is impossible for the object in a video to move from one side to another side within two frames. Then we use formula (1) to compute the matching cost for each MV. Note that after the acquirement of the forward MVF, we can use the prior information to initialize the backward MVF, which can reduce the number of iterations for backward MVF.

Iteration - Propagation. After initialization, we perform the iterative process of propagation to improve the accuracy of MVF. The propagation mode is based on jump flooding algorithm [5] to realize parallel computing, but we adapt the method for the FRUC. This process contains many rounds. For example, there are $\log l + 1$ rounds with halved step length of l, $l/2$, $l/4$, ..., 1. Figure 3 clarifies how the MVs is propagated. In each round with step l, we renew the **MV(a)** by **MV(a + b)**, as b satisfies the follow equation:

$$\mathbf{b} = arg\ min\ \mathrm{D}(\mathbf{a}, MV(\mathbf{a} + \mathbf{b})),\ \mathbf{b} \in \{(\pm l, 0), (0, \pm l), (0, 0)\} \tag{2}$$

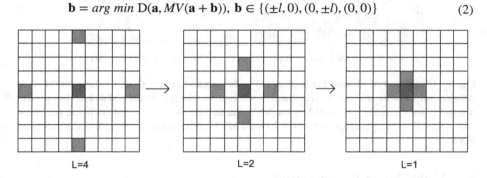

$$L=4 \qquad\qquad L=2 \qquad\qquad L=1$$

Fig. 3. Illustration of propagation. In each round, the red pixel inquiries the MVs of four blue neighbors as candidate MVs. (Color figure online)

Iteration - Random Search. Then we perform the iterative process of random search to improve the MVF. Let $\mathbf{mv}_0 = \mathbf{MV(a)}$. We attempt to improve $\mathbf{MV(a)}$ by testing a sequence of candidate MVs at an exponentially decreasing distance from $\mathbf{mv}_0$:

$$\mathbf{u}_i = \mathbf{mv}_0 + w\alpha^i \mathbf{R}_i \tag{3}$$

where $\mathbf{R}_i$ is a uniform random in $[-1,1] \times [-1,1]$, w is the clamped value mentioned above, and α is a fixed exponentially decreasing ratio. We examine $\mathbf{u}_i$ for $i = 0, 1, 2$. until $w\alpha^i$ is below 1 pixel. In our application, $\alpha = 1/2$.

After computing with 2–3 iterations, the forward MVF has almost always converged in practice. Then follow almost the same operations except the initialization step, computing 1–2 iterations, we can also get backward MVF. Figure 4 illustrates the intermediate result of all the steps in motion estimation.

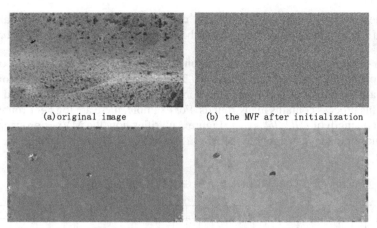

(a) original image   (b) the MVF after initialization

(c) the forward MVF after iteration   (d) the backward MVF after iteration

Fig. 4. Illustration of Motion Estimation. (a) is the original image. (b, c, d) show the MVF at different stages, with magnitude visualized as saturation and angle visualized as hue. For (c) and (d), there is some noise introduced by the SAD metric. But most noise gathers in the occlusion region (just like the up and left side of the forward MVF, and down and right side of the backward MVF).

2.2 Motion Vector Post-processing

After Motion Estimation, we can get the forward and backward MVF. As shown in Fig. 5, there are a lot of noise in both MVFs before MVPP. Because of the aperture problem, the SAD metric alone is not reliable enough to determine the true motion [3]. In addition to the noise introduced by SAD metric, there are many wrong MVs in occlusion region. So it is necessary to take MVPP step to eliminate outliers and to handle occlusion problem.

Consistency Check. After computing forward and backward MVFs between two frames, we explicitly perform forward-backward consistency check [9] to detect wrong MVs. All the inconsistent MVs is marked and wait to be corrected by the next step.

Correction. After the Consistency Check, we treat the consistent MVs as high-credibility MVs, and we will use these MVs to fix the wrong MVs. As we assumed in the Patch step, most pixels in the same Patch own the same true MV. So for each wrong $MV(x,y)$, we will select 5 alternative $MV(i,j)$, (i,j) belong to $Patch(x,y)$ and $MV(i,j)$ is high-credibility MVs. Vector Median Filter is applied to choose the fixing MV from 5 alternative MVs. The fixing result is depicted in Fig. 5.

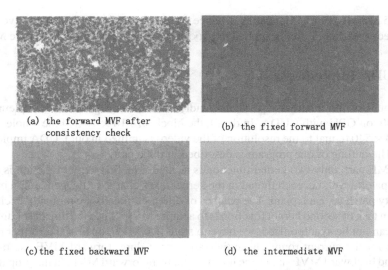

(a) the forward MVF after consistency check

(b) the fixed forward MVF

(c) the fixed backward MVF

(d) the intermediate MVF

Fig. 5. Illustration of MVPP and MCI. (a) shows the result of consistency check. All the blank region is the inconsistent region. (b) and (c) shows the MVF after correction. (d) shows the fusion result of the forward MVF and backward MVF.

2.3 Motion Compensated Interpolation

After the MVPP, we get two more reliable MVFs. Then we fuse the forward and backward MVFs into intermediate MVF for interpolation. But there may be still some holes remained after fusion. So we use the vector median filter again on the intermediate MVF to fill all the holes. The intermediate frame is constructed by the full intermediate MVF. Before outputting the intermediate frame, a 3×3 median filter is applied on the intermediate frame to filter the pepper noise along the motion edge of the object. The full intermediate MVF is shown in Fig. 5.

Fusion. For the pixel $\mathbf{a}(x_a, y_a)$ in F_t, and pixel $\mathbf{b}(x_b, y_b)$ in F_{t+1}, we define the intermediate MVF as follows:

$$
\begin{aligned}
MV_{inter}\left(\mathbf{a} + \frac{1}{2}MV_{forward}(\mathbf{a})\right) &= \frac{1}{2}MV_{forward}(\mathbf{a}) \ or \\
MV_{inter}\left(\mathbf{b} + \frac{1}{2}MV_{backward}(\mathbf{b})\right) &= -\frac{1}{2}MV_{backward}(\mathbf{b})
\end{aligned}
\tag{4}
$$

There may be conflicts in some positions. For example, pixel $\mathbf{a}$ and $\mathbf{b}$ may map to the same position. In order to avoid conflicts, we give first priority to the consistent MVs for selection and second priority to the fixed MVs. If two conflicted MVs are of the same priority, we will choose the one with smaller matching cost.

Hole Filling. There may be still some holes remained after fusion. So we use the Vector Median Filter again on the intermediate MVF to fill all the holes. For each hole, we will choose 5 nearest MVs in Manhattan distance on intermediate MVF as alternative MVs. Then Vector Median Filter is applied to choose the filling MV from alternative MVs.

3   CUDA Implementation

On account of the inherently parallel-friendly nature, our algorithm is implemented efficiently on GPU with CUDA. In detail, the block size 16×16 and the whole thread size 960×540 (equal to the resolution of the video) is unified in our CUDA implementation. The outline of our program is described in three part:

For ME part, only two kernel function is needed. The first kernel function is paralleled at patch-level, i.e. each thread in the kernel takes charge of the generation of self-similarity patch for each pixel. The patches of different threads are mutually exclusive. The main task of second kernel function is to acquire MVF. Since the threads of different blocks can not be synchronized, we have to store two MVF, one for the former round, and one for the current round. In initialization procedure, forward MVF use random MVs, and backward MVF shares the information from forward MVF. In the propagation procedure, each thread inquiries the MVs stored in the former round, compares it to the one in current round, and choose the best MVs for each pixel. After propagation, random search is applied to improve the MVF.

For MVPP part, two kernel function is designed for Consistency Check and Correction respectively. The Consistency Check function is paralleled at pixel-level, and each thread in the kernel check the consistency of the MV for the corresponding pixel. Then the Correction function is launched twice to correct the wrong MVs for forward MVF and backward MVF.

For MCI part, the Fusion and Hole Filling procedure correspond to two kernel function. The Fusion function is paralleled at MV-level, and each thread map the corresponding MV into the intermediate MVF. Then the Hole Filling function is launched to fill the holes remained in intermediate MVF.

4   Experiment Result

In our implementations, the hardware is Core^{TM} i7-3770 k 3.4 GHz and NVIDIA^{TM} GeForce GTX 780Ti with 1 GB dedicated graphic memory. Our algorithm is inherently parallel and can be implemented on GPU with CUDA as mentioned above. We choose the video with the resolution 960×540 for experiment. The GPU implementation takes 521 ms on average to generate an intermediate frame. Compared with 25 s for the CPU implementation, the GPU implementation achieves up to 48 times speedup over its CPU implementation. So far, the only parallel FRUC algorithm [7] has some defects, like long convergence time and less effective than the 3DRS. Therefore, the FRUC algorithm [10] based on 3DRS with 8×8 block is chosen as benchmark algorithm.

4.1 Subjective Evaluation

We choose three classic videos with different features to judge the performance of our FRUC algorithm. Figure 6 presents the results of our FRUC algorithm and benchmark algorithm mentioned above. For the first video, the most difficult part is to estimate the motion for the little black hawk on the top left corner, because it is very easy to be disturbed by the large background. Our algorithm shows a good performance for the fine motion structure. For the second video, the fast move of caterpillar and large occlusion region is a big challenge. The intermediate frame presents that our algorithm can tract the fast motion and handle occlusion well. For the third video, it is hard to keep the gird of window. As depicted in the result, we keep main grid, but still failed in some positions. It suggest that there is still a potential for improvement.

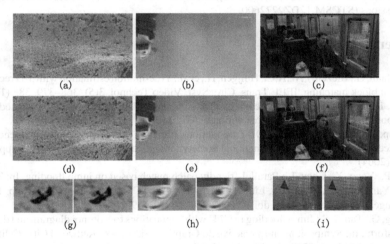

Fig. 6. Visual comparison of interpolated frames by different FRUC algorithms. (a, b, c) benchmark algorithm. (d, e, f) proposed algorithm. (g, h, i) are the partial enlarged details of the result. Left side is from benchmark algorithm, and right side is from proposed algorithm.

4.2 Objective Evaluation

PSNR is applied to evaluate the objective quality of the proposed algorithm and the benchmark algorithm. Table 1 presents the PSNR of the first 30 interpolated frames (to avoid the influence of the scene change) of the attackOfTheHawks, HMoveFast, and COMTrain sequences. As shown in the table, the proposed algorithm provides better PSNR performance than the benchmark algorithm.

Table 1. Average PSNR (dB) obtained by proposed algorithm and bench mark algorithm.

Sequences	attackOfTheHawks	HMoveFast	COMTrain
Proposed	28.23	36.57	24.28
Benchmark	26.34	34.23	23.36
Gain	1.89	2.34	0.92

5   Conclusion

In this paper, we propose a parallel-friendly FRUC algorithm based on patch match. This algorithm is inherently parallel and can be implemented on GPU with CUDA. The speedup and the quality of intermediate frame are analyzed. The GPU implementation achieves up to 48 times speedup over its CPU implementation. Compared with the FRUC based on 3DRS, proposed algorithm has advantage in the fine motion structure and occlusion problem.

Acknowledgment. This work was supported in part by Chinese National Key S&T Special Program (2013ZX01033001-002-002), National Natural Science Foundation of China (61133009, 61221001, 61301116), the Shanghai Key Laboratory of Digital Media Processing and Transmissions (STCSM 12DZ2272600).

References

1. De Haan, G., Biezen, P.W.A.C., Huijgen, H., et al.: True-motion estimation with 3-D recursive search block matching. IEEE Trans. Circ. Syst. Video Technol. **3**(5), 368–379, 388 (1993)
2. Kim, D.Y., Park, H.W.: An efficient motion-compensated frame interpolation method using temporal, information for high-resolution videos. J. Disp. Technol. **11**(7), 1 (2015)
3. Braspenning, R.A.C., Haan, G.D.: True-motion estimation using feature correspondences. In: Proceedings of SPIE - The International Society for Optical Engineering, vol. 5308, pp. 396–407 (2004)
4. Yu, P., Yang, X., Chen, L.: Parallel-friendly patch match based on jump flooding. In: Zhang, W., Yang, X., Xu, Z., An, P., Liu, Q., Lu, Y. (eds.) IFTC 2012. CCIS, vol. 331, pp. 15–21. Springer, Heidelberg (2012). doi:10.1007/978-3-642-34595-1_3
5. Rong, G., Tan, T.S.: Jump flooding in GPU with applications to Voronoi diagram and distance transform. In: Symposium on Interactive 3d Graphics, Si3d 2006, Redwood City, California, USA, 14–17 March 2006, pp. 109–116 (2006)
6. Bao, L., Yang, Q., Jin, H.: Fast edge-preserving patchmatch for large displacement optical flow. IEEE Trans. Image Process. **23**(12), 4996–5006 (2014). A Publication of the IEEE Signal Processing Society
7. Michielin, F., Calvagno, G., Sartor, P., et al.: A parallel true motion estimation method based on binarized cross correlation. In: IEEE Third International Conference on Consumer Electronics, Berlin, pp. 1198–1202 (2013)
8. Barnes, C., Shechtman, E., Finkelstein, A., et al.: PatchMatch: a randomized correspondence algorithm for structural image editing. Acm Trans. Graph. **28**(3), 341–352 (2009). Article 24
9. Hosni, A., Rhemann, C., Bleyer, M., et al.: Fast cost-volume filtering for visual correspondence and beyond. IEEE Trans. Pattern Anal. Mach. Intell. **35**(2), 504–511 (2013)
10. Guo, Y., Chen, L., Gao, Z., et al.: Frame rate up-conversion method for video processing applications. IEEE Trans. Broadcast. **60**(4), 659–669 (2014)

Automatic Exudate Detection in Color Fundus Images

Fucong Qi, Guo Li, and Shibao Zheng[✉]

Institute of Image Communication and Network Engineering,
Shanghai Key Labs of Digital Media Processing and Transmission,
Shanghai Jiao Tong University, Shanghai 200240, China
{fucongq,li_guo,sbzh}@sjtu.edu.cn

Abstract. Diabetic retinopathy is a major cause of blindness in working age population and exudates are considered the most significant characteristics of diabetic retinopathy. Therefore, automatic exudate detection is beneficial to large-scale diabetic retinopathy screening. In this paper, an automatic approach for detection of exudates on color fundus images is presented and discussed, which is based on the thresholding technique and Kirsch's edge detection. Besides, a color space conversion step (from RGB to YIQ) is utilized to improve the detection performance. The method is evaluated on a public dataset of fundus images from various ethnic groups. We obtain an average sensitivity of 75.17% and an average specificity of 97.98%, which outperforms the baseline method and validates the effectiveness of the proposed method.

Keywords: Exudate detection · Thresholding · Background estimation · Kirsch edge detection

1 Introduction

Diabetes is a worldwide-spreading disease and it has multiple effects on the eyes, heart and other organs. Diabetic retinopathy is a common complication of diabetes that is caused by changes in the blood vessels of the retina and one third of the diabetics suffer from this disease. Diabetic retinopathy can cause visual impairment and is considered as the most common cause of blindness among adults aged between 30 and 69 years old [12]. The early stage of diabetic retinopathy is asymptomatic. But once the vision loss occurs, it is irreversible. The laser treatment can help to prevent visual loss when diabetic retinopathy is not very serious. Therefore the early diagnosis of diabetic retinopathy is of great importance for diabetics. The traditional manual diagnosis method is supported by ophthalmologist, but the number of ophthalmologists needed is far from enough compared to the large number of diabetes patients, especially in the rural areas. Therefore, it is necessary to develop an automatic DR diagnosis system to save time, cost and labour.

Diabetic retinopathy can lead to several retinal abnormalities, including microaneurysms, hemorrhages, cotton wool spots and exudates. This paper

© Springer Nature Singapore Pte Ltd. 2017
X. Yang and G. Zhai (Eds.): IFTC 2016, CCIS 685, pp. 155–165, 2017.
DOI: 10.1007/978-981-10-4211-9_16

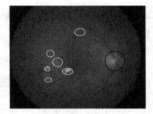

Fig. 1. Fundus image with DR, including optic disk marked with a black circle and exudates marked with white circles.

focuses on the detection of exudates, since exudates are one of the most prevalent lesions in the early stages of diabetic retinopathy. Exudates are also the specific marker for the existence of macular oedema, which has great effect on vision. Figure 1 shows a typical color fundus image labeled with exudates and optic disk and as we can see from it, exudates are yellowish lipid leaks from blood vessel with varying sizes, shapes and locations. Optic disk is the bright circular region from where blood vessels emanate. Since the color of optic disk is similar with exudates, optic disk will interfere with the detection of exudates. Therefore, optic disk must be removed from the fundus image before detecting exudates. Furthermore, the diversities of fundus images from different ethnic groups bring extra difficulty to exudate detection.

The method for exudate detection proposed in this paper is based on the thresholding technique and Kirsch's edge detection. Exudate candidates are first extracted by estimating the background with a large median filter and then exudates are extracted from exudate candidates by using edge detectors after the optic disk is removed from the fundus image.

The remainder of this paper is organized as follows: Sect. 2 briefly introduces related methods. Section 3 presents the proposed method for exudates detection. In Sect. 4, we conduct experiments on public databases and make performance comparisons with the existing method. Finally, Section 5 concludes the paper.

2   Related Work

Research on automatic detection of exudates can be roughly divided into two categories, unsupervised classification methods and supervised ones. Compared with supervised classification, unsupervised classification methods avoid tedious data labelling, which is of great importance in practical applications and can be further divided into three subcategories, including thresholding methods, region growing methods and morphology methods [2].

Thresholding methods are straightforward, but a universal optimal threshold for each image does not exist. Sánchez et al. [8] apply Gaussian mixture models to extract exudate candidates and an edge detector to localize exudates. Region growing methods are more time-consuming when they are employed in the whole fundus image. Li et al. [4] first locate the optic disk by principal component analysis (PCA) and then a combined method of region growing and edge detection is employed to detect exudates. Morphology methods are convenient to identify structures from fundus images using various morphological operators. Walter et al. [11] extract candidate regions by using the high grey level variation of exudate regions and the contours of exudates are determined by morphological reconstruction. Ravishankar et al. [7] use the operators of mathematical morphology to extract different structures of the retina. In supervised classification methods, ground-truth images must be provided in order to train a classifier, but selecting features that can present the properties of exudates is not an easy task. Selvathi et al. [9] detect anatomical structures in fundus images via morphological techniques and then features are extracted from these structures to train a classifier.

In fact, the above-mentioned methods are not isolated and they can be combined into one new method to achieve better performance. Hussain et al. [3] combine the thresholding and morphology methods to detect exudates. An adaptive thresholding method are first used to get candidates and then a morphological operation is used to refine the adaptive thresholding results. Sopharak et al. [10] propose an method for the exudate detection using morphology and thresholding methods. A morphological close operator and a local variation operator are first applied to get a standard deviation image and then the Otsu algorithm [6] is used to threshold the resulting image to get rid of all regions with low local variation.

3   Proposed Method

The method for exudate detection proposed in this paper is based on the thresholding technique and Kirsch's edge detection and this method can be divided into four stages. At the first stage, a preprocessing of the fundus images is performed, which refers to a color space transformation. At the second stage, background estimation is performed and exudate candidates are obtained by subtracting the background from the original image. At the third stage, optic disk is removed from the fundus image. Finally, exudates are extracted from exudate candidates by using edge detectors. The overall procedure of exudate detection is demonstrated in Fig. 2.

3.1   Preprocessing

Before starting processing the fundus images for contrast enhancement, we first need to crop the images to remove the dark background that we do not need. Since the dark background in corners of images, which is a large cluster of pixels, can influence the accuracy of our results. We choose the minimum bounding box that contains the circular region with the eye fundus information. The original image and the corresponding cropped image are shown in Fig. 3.

Step 1 Preprocessing   Step 2 Candidate Extraction

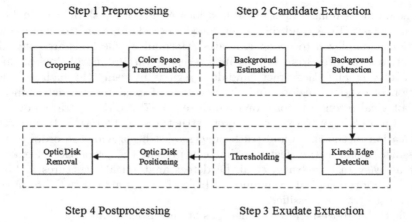

Step 4 Postprocessing   Step 3 Exudate Extraction

Fig. 2. Procedure of the proposed exudate detection method

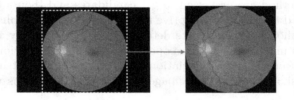

Fig. 3. Illustration of cropping.

Considering the poor quality of the fundus images, we need to enhance the contrast of the images before starting the detection of exudates to improve the difference between exudates and non-exudates. In this paper, we adopt a color space transformation method, which is first proposed by Sánchez et al. [8], to make exudates more prominent from the background. First, we convert the fundus images from RGB color space to YIQ color space, in which Y means luminance, I and Q mean hue. Then we update the Y as follows:

$$Y_{new} = 1.5Y - I - Q. \tag{1}$$

Finally, we convert the image back into the RGB color space to get the resulting image. As we can see in Fig. 4(b), the resulting image shows an improvement in the contrast between exudates and blood vessels. The exudate areas become much brighter and the blood vessel areas become darker at the same time, which is beneficial to detection of exudates.

3.2 Candidate Extraction

Background estimation and background subtraction are performed to extract exudate candidates. We will first introduce how the background of the fundus

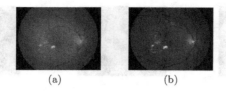

(a)   (b)

Fig. 4. Preprocessing. (a) Original image. (b) Resulting image after contrast enhancement.

image is estimated. First, we extract the I channel of the HSI color space as shown in Fig. 5(b) and a large median filter on the image of I channel is employed to get the initial background as shown in Fig. 5(c). In order to improve the accuracy of the background estimation, a morphological reconstruction [2] step is added. Comparing I with initial background, bigger pixel values are taken to get a new image to act as the mask for the morphological reconstruction, which is shown in Fig. 5(d). After the morphological reconstruction of the initial background using the mask, the final background is obtained for next stage of the background subtraction, which is shown in Fig. 5(e).

In the background subtraction stage, the final background is subtracted from the original image. The histogram of the image obtained shown in Fig. 5(f) shows a constant distribution: its highest peak is always centered on zero. Dark structures of fundus image, including blood vessels and red lesions, are located on the left side of the histogram and bright structures, including exudates and optic disk, are located on the right. We can distinguish between dark structures and bright structures of the fundus images with this characteristic. We get the dark structures with the threshold of -3, which is shown in Fig. 5(g) and we employ a hard threshold of 3 to select all exudate candidates, which is shown in Fig. 5(h).

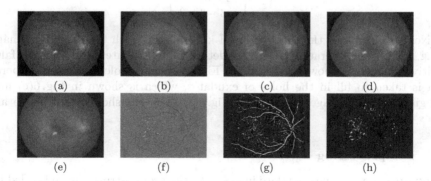

(a)   (b)   (c)   (d)

(e)   (f)   (g)   (h)

Fig. 5. Illustration of candidates extraction procedure. (a) Original image. (b) I channel. (c) Initial background. (d) Mask image. (e) Final background. (f) Subtraction image. (g) Blood vessels. (h) Exudate candidates.

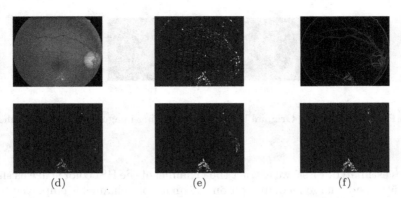

Fig. 6. Exudate extraction. (a) Original image. (b) Exudate candidates. (c) Kirsch image. (d) Exudate borders. (e) Detected exudates. (f) Ground-truth image.

3.3   Exudate Extraction

Considering exudates have clear borders compared with vascular reflections, which always appear in exudate candidates, we extract exudates from exudate candidates by means of edge detection. In our case, We employ the Kirschs mask as shown in Eq. (2) and 7 different rotations of it on the green channel of the fundus image, and the maximum value of the masked images is selected to act as the edge strength for each pixel. The result is stored in the final I-kirsch image and then we employ consecutive integer thresholds to threshold the I-kirsch image to obtain objects with sharpest edges, which is shown in Fig. 6(c) with the threshold of 10.

$$k = \begin{pmatrix} 5 & 5 & -3 \\ 5 & 0 & -3 \\ -3 & -3 & -3 \end{pmatrix} \tag{2}$$

Next, we combine the thresholding I-kirsch image with the candidate image using a boolean operation AND to detect only exudates and remove false positives, which is shown in Fig. 6(d). Finally, a morphological closing operation is taken to fill in the holes of exudates, which is shown in Fig. 6(e) and the ground-truth image is shown in Fig. 6(f). The thresholds used above are $thres = \{40 : -1 : 0\}$.

3.4   Postprocessing

Comparing the obtained exudate image with the ground-truth image labeled by experts, we can find that there are false positives in the optic disk area. Therefore further process steps need to be conducted to remove the optic disk from the fundus image. As we know, the optic disk belongs to the brightest parts of the fundus image and the vessel structures are dark, therefore we follow the method proposed by Watler et al. [11] to detect optic disk, in which local grey level

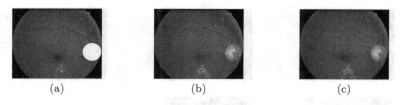

(a)   (b)   (c)

Fig. 7. Exudate detection. (a) Optic disk detection. (b) Detected image with optic disk. (c) Detected image without optic disk.

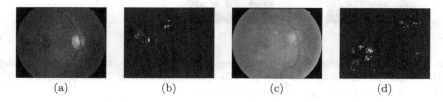

(a)   (b)   (c)   (d)

Fig. 8. Dataset for exudate detection. (a) Original image from the e-ophtha EX dataset. (b) Ground-truth for (a). (c) Original image from the e-ophtha EX dataset. (d) Ground-truth for (c).

variation is used to find the location of the optic disk. We remove the optic disk from the obtained exudate image and the result image is shown in Fig. 7(c). We can clearly see that false positives in the optic disk disappear.

4   Experimental Results

4.1   Datasets

The accuracy of the exudate detection method presented in this paper is tested on the public dataset e-ophtha EX, which is first introduced by Zhang et al. [13]. The e-ophtha EX dataset is composed of 47 fundus images containing exudates and 35 normal fundus images. The 47 images containing exudates are randomly chosen by an ophthalmologist from the e-ophtha dataset [1], which is constituted by all the fundus images acquired by OPHDIAT telemedical network for DR screening [5] between January 2008 and December 2009. These 35 normal fundus image, without exudates, are first chosen from the e-ophtha dataset by image processing experts and then are checked by ophthalmologists to make sure that there are no exudates in these images. These images in the e-ophtha EX dataset have four different sizes, ranging from 1440 × 960 pixels to 2544 × 1696 pixels and precise exudate segmentations are provided for these images as shown in Fig. 8.

4.2   Evaluated Methods

In this paper, we evaluate the performance of the exudate detection method on pixel level for each fundus image from the e-ophtha dataset and the sensitivity

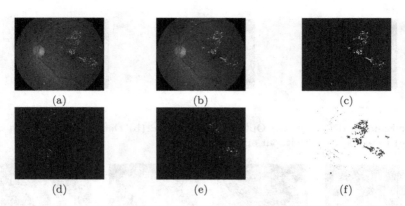

Fig. 9. Illustration of false positives/negatives and true positives/negatives. (a) Ground truth image. (b) Exudates detected. (c) True positive pixels. (d) False positive pixels. (e) False negative pixels. (g) True negative pixels.

Table 1. Values of TP, FN, FP and TN.

Threshold	TP pixels	TN pixels	FN pixels	FP pixels	Sensitivity (%)	Specificity (%)
0	5591	672969	226	22078	96.11	96.82
5	5472	691554	345	3493	94.07	99.5
10	4994	694127	823	920	85.85	99.87
20	2559	694775	3258	272	43.99	99.96

and specificity measures are used to evaluate the performance of the proposed method. The sensitivity and specificity are both calculated by four elements, which are true positive(TP), false negative(FN), true negative(TN) and false positive(FP). A pixel of lesion which is segmented as exudates in the ground-truth image is considered a true positive (TP) if it is also detected as exudates in the automatic detection method; a false negative (FN) if no corresponding lesion is found in the automatic detection method. A pixel of background is considered a true negative (TN) if it is detected as background in the automatic detection method; a false positive (FP) if an lesion is found in the automatic detection method but no corresponding lesion has been manually segmented.

The sensitivity is defined as the ability of a screening to correctly detect people with a disease and it is calculated according to Eq. (3). The specificity is defined as the ability of a screening to properly exclude people without a disease and it is calculated according to Eq. (4).

$$sensitivity = \frac{TP}{TP + FN} \tag{3}$$

$$specificity = \frac{TN}{TN + FP} \tag{4}$$

4.3   Evaluation Results

The amount of pixels belonging to TP, FN, FP and TN are calculated for each resulting image of the method to get the final sensitivity and specificity. Table 1 shows the values of TP, FN, FP and TN for one fundus image with different thresholds and the corresponding images with the threshold of 5 are shown in Fig. 9.

We can see from Table 1 that the sensitivity decreases and the specificity increases as the increase of the threshold. The average sensitivities and specificities of 47 fundus images from e-ophtha database are calculated and presented in Fig. 10. We can see from Fig. 10 that there is a great increasing on sensitivity with the preprocessing of the YIQ color space transformation. This proves that the preprocessing method we added is beneficial and can improve the performance of the exudate detection.

Also we can see from Fig. 10 that as the threshold varies, the sensitivity and specificity change simultaneously. Therefore an appropriate threshold should be chosen to keep balance between sensitivity and specificity. Here we choose the threshold of 8 to get our final result. Sensitivity increases from 74.65% to 75.17% and specificity increases from 97.91% to 97.98% by employing the ntsc transform. Table 2 gives quantized results.

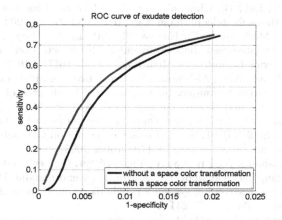

Fig. 10. Exudate detection performances.

Table 2. Final results of SE and SP.

Measures	Original method	With a preprocessing step
SE	74.65%	75.17%
SP	97.91%	97.98%

5   Conclusion

In this paper, a method for exudate detection on color fundus images has been introduced. The exudates are identified by its high intensity and its sharpness of its edges with a Kirsch operator. Candidate extraction and exudate extraction are two main steps for our method. A preprocessing method is added before background estimation to improve the performance of the method and pixel-level evaluation is introduced. After applying our method to 47 fundus images from the e-ophtha dataset, the average sensitivity increases from 74.65% to 75.17% and the averaged specificity increases from 97.91% to 97.98% respectively. Our results suggest that the method is effective in detecting exudates and can help ophthalmologists to localize exudates since it is robust on different fundus images from various ethnic groups. In future work, we will improve the specificity by removing reflection light of blood vessels and try to locate all exudates to improve the sensitivity.

References

1. Decencière, E., Cazuguel, G., Zhang, X., Thibault, G., Klein, J.C., Meyer, F., Marcotegui, B., Quellec, G., Lamard, M., Danno, R., Elie, D., Massin, P., Viktor, Z., Erginay, A., Laÿ, B., Chabouis, A.: Teleophta: machine learning and image processing methods for teleophthalmology. IRBM **34**(2), 196–203 (2013)
2. Giancardo, L., Mériaudeau, F., Karnowski, T.P., Li, Y., Garg, S., Tobin, K.W., Chaum, E.: Exudate-based diabetic macular edema detection in fundus images using publicly available datasets. Med. Image Anal. **16**(1), 216–226 (2012)
3. Jaafar, H.F., Nandi, A.K., Al-Nuaimy, W.: Detection of exudates in retinal images using a pure splitting technique. In: International Conference of the IEEE Engineering in Medicine and Biology Society, pp. 6745–6748 (2010)
4. Li, H., Chutatape, O.: A model-based approach for automated feature extraction in fundus images. In: 9th IEEE International Conference on Computer Vision (ICCV 2003), Nice, France, pp. 394–399, 14–17 October 2003
5. Massin, P., Chabouis, A., Erginay, A., Viens-Bitker, C., Lecleire-Collet, A., Meas, T., Guillausseau, P.J., Choupot, G., André, B., Denormandie, P.: OPHDIAT: a telemedical network screening system for diabetic retinopathy in the ile-de-France. Diabetes Metabol. **34**(3), 227–234 (2008)
6. Otsu, N.: An automatic threshold selection method based on discriminate and least squares criteria. Denshi Tsushin Gakkai Ronbunshi **63**, 349–356 (1979)
7. Ravishankar, S., Jain, A., Mittal, A.: Automated feature extraction for early detection of diabetic retinopathy in fundus images. In: 2009 IEEE Computer Society Conference on Computer Vision and Pattern Recognition (CVPR 2009), 20–25 June 2009, Miami, Florida, USA, pp. 210–217 (2009)
8. Sánchez, C.I., Hornero, R., Lopez, M.I., Poza, J.: Retinal image analysis to detect and quantify lesions associated with diabetic retinopathy. In: International Conference of the IEEE Engineering in Medicine and Biology Society, pp. 1624–1627 (2004)
9. Selvathi, D., Prakash, N.B., Balagopal, N.: Automated detection of diabetic retinopathy for early diagnosis using feature extraction and support vector machine (2012)

10. Sopharak, A., Uyyanonvara, B., Barman, S., Williamson, T.H.: Automatic detection of diabetic retinopathy exudates from non-dilated retinal images using mathematical morphology methods. Comp. Med. Imag. Graph. **32**(8), 720–727 (2008)
11. Walter, T., Klein, J.C., Massin, P., Erginay, A.: A contribution of image processing to the diagnosis of diabetic retinopathy-detection of exudates in color fundus images of the human retina. IEEE Trans. Med. Imag. **21**(10), 1236–1243 (2002)
12. Watkins, P.J.: ABC of diabetes: retinopathy. BMJ Br. Med. J. **326**(7395), 924–926 (2003)
13. Zhang, X., Thibault, G., Decencière, E., Marcotegui, B., Lay, B., Danno, R., Cazuguel, G., Quellec, G., Lamard, M., Massin, P., Chabouis, A., Victor, Z., Erginay, A.: Exudate detection in color retinal images for mass screening of diabetic retinopathy. Med. Image Anal. **18**(7), 1026–1043 (2014)

View-Specific Based Error Concealment Scheme for Multi-view Plus Depth Video

Ran Ma[1,2(✉)], Xiangyu Hu[1,2], Deyang Liu[1,2], Yu Hou[1,2], and Ping An[1,2]

[1] School of Communication and Information Engineering,
Shanghai University, Shanghai 200072, China
maran@shu.edu.cn
[2] Key Laboratory of Advanced Display and System Application,
Ministry of Education, Shanghai 200072, China

Abstract. Multi-view video plus depth (MVD) is an efficient format of 3D video. MVD video can be encoded by either H.264/AVC or HEVC standard to gain higher compression ratio, which benefits their broadcasting over the Internet. However, the encoded and transferred MVD video tends to develop worse visual quality degradation caused by lossy network channel. Therefore, error concealment is here to help refrain this problem. In this paper, we propose a classification-related error concealment method for MVD video. Within our method, motion-based classification is used to judge whether the corrupted blocks are static or not. If so, the blocks from reference frames are adopted to conceal the corrupted blocks. Otherwise, view-specific based concealment procedures, which are designed in accordance with view features, are used to conceal the corrupted blocks in different views. Experimental results on AVC-based Test Model (ATM) show the superiority of this concealment scheme to several other error concealment methods in PSNR along with acceptable execution time increase.

Keywords: Multi-view video plus depth · AVC-based Test Model · Error concealment · View-Specific

1 Introduction

Customers' passion for 3D video has constantly driven the advancement of 3D video coding technology. Two major 3D video formats have emerged for this demand, which are multi-view coding (MVC) and multi-view plus depth (MVD) [1]. The MVD format wins the other one at reconstructed visual quality of complex scene due to its extra depth maps that help synthesize virtual views, thus gaining increasing focus of the academic research and commercial solutions. However, compared to the traditional 2D video, the transferred MVD video is prone to develop heavier quality degradation caused by lossy networks for its extra views in single frame. Therefore, error concealment (EC) on received MVD videos is rather necessary to help mitigate this problem.

Related works about error concealment on MVD date back to early 2007. Depth-based boundary matching algorithm (DBMA) [2] was proposed, in which boundary matching algorithm (BMA) [3] was used to find candidate motion vector (MV) in depth

© Springer Nature Singapore Pte Ltd. 2017
X. Yang and G. Zhai (Eds.): IFTC 2016, CCIS 685, pp. 166–175, 2017.
DOI: 10.1007/978-981-10-4211-9_17

view for recovering the corrupted texture view block. Similar works appeared lately, where MVs of the corrupted blocks in texture/depth view were fixed by using their correspondence in depth/texture view [4, 5]. However, the inconsistency between MVs in texture view and their correspondence in depth view was ignored in the above three methods. To overcome this, certain kinds of block classification were applied for better performance. Method in [6] classified the corrupted blocks into homogeneous blocks and boundary blocks, then used BMA and decoder motion vector estimation (DMVE) [7] to fix the homogeneous or boundary blocks respectively. It achieved better conceal- ment quality compared to previous ones, but still lacked further exploiting relations between texture and depth views in MVD video. Methods in [8, 9] predicted the corrupted blocks' prediction models by exploring relations between the 2 views, then proposed different concealment method for different prediction models. Furtherly, they gained increased concealment quality, but with the unacceptable computation time addition.

Our proposed method, which was enlightened by [9], makes further improvements on concealment efficiency. Instead of dividing corrupted blocks into simple or complex ones as described in [9], a second motion-based block type classification is carried out in our purposed view-specific methods. This classification varies in each of the views, catering each view' own characteristics. In our method, firstly, corrupted blocks are classified into two major kinds, static blocks and motional blocks. Static blocks are concealed by simply reusing collocated contents (MVs or pixel patches) from their reference frames, which largely reduce the complexity of our method. The concealment of motional blocks is related to the unique characteristics of the views they belong to. Specifically, motional blocks in different views should be concealed in view-specific ways for better overall quality enhancement and lower computation time. As texture views include complex color pattern and splines, for blocks in texture views, further size classification is executed instead to exploit the spatial relations of each block for better concealment quality. Contrary, depth views only contain simple objects and splines, so blocks in depth views should receive a secondary MV-related classification to further exploit temporal relations inside the video, attempting to reduce the overall time cost of our proposed method.

This paper is organized as follows. Section 2 describes the proposed hybrid error concealment method for MVD video. Experimental results are presented and analyzed in Sect. 3. Section 4 is the final conclusion part.

2   The Proposed Error Concealment Method

2.1   Frame Structure of MVD

Figure 1 describes the overall frame structure of typical multi-view plus depth (MVD) video, in which 6 views are included in a single video frame. The texture center (TC) view can be regarded as single frame in 2D videos. The depth center (DC) view that accompa- nies the TC view can increase the synthesized view quality during the display process. The texture/depth left (TL/DL) views and the texture/depth right (TR/DR) views provide more perspective angles of the MVD video, giving us more vivid 3D experience. These views are processed with various order by different codecs. For example, in H.264/AVC codecs, TC view is encoded first, then DC view, followed by DL and DR views and finally TL and TR views. On the HEVC codecs, TL and TR views are just ahead of DL and DR views.

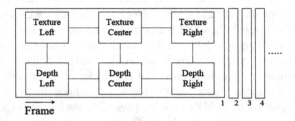

Fig. 1. MVD frame structure

Generally, like traditional 2D video frames, the texture views are color pictures that consist of complicated color patterns, multiple object edges and complex texture splines, while depth views are grey-level pictures only contain large object contours and plain areas. Figure 2 is an example of these 2 views.

Fig. 2. Example texture and depth views of a MVD frame

2.2 The Initial Block Classification

For error concealment, the computational complexity is a crucial requirement for real-life application. Therefore, initial block classification is to help reduce complexity by judging what kind of blocks can be concealed with lower computational method, and this classification of the corrupted blocks is firstly implied in every view.

As is shown in Fig. 3, corrupted blocks are classified into static and motional blocks. Static blocks are detected in large uniform regions with less details. Concealing these blocks with simpler method won't cause apparent video quality loss. Meanwhile, the time cost for the whole method can be largely decreased due to this. Contrarily, the motional blocks are discovered in regions with complex splines and figures, and should be concealed with the more effective, but complicated methods to ensure the overall concealment quality. In our case, the motional blocks are processed by the proposed view-specific methods for better quality assurance.

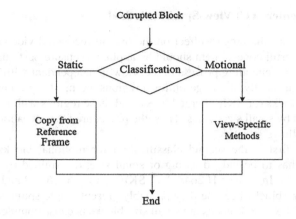

Fig. 3. General structure of proposed method

The initial classification process is as follows. Let the corrupted block be MB_0 and its eight-neighboring blocks be MB_1 to MB_8. The average of all the correctly received motion vectors (mv_i) from MB_1 to MB_8 is calculated according to Eq. 1. Where, the parameter p_i is used to mark whether the MB_i is correctly received or not (equals 1 if the MB_i is received correctly, otherwise it equals 0).

$$mv_{avg} = \frac{\sum_{i=0}^{8} mv_i \times p_i}{\sum_{i=0}^{8} p_i} \tag{1}$$

If this average vector (mv_{arg}) is 0, this corrupted block is a static block and is directly recovered by using its collocated block in the reference frame or view. Otherwise, it should be the motional bock.

Motional block usually indicates the movements of foreground objects and has its unique features inherited from the view who owns it. These features, in fact, represent the differences as well as similarities in each view according to the previous work by Liu [8, 9]. One of features for similarities is that motion vectors in TC or DC view should be identical to those in TL/TR or DL/DR views. On the other hand, the features for splines and textures can be greatly differed in different views, as we can find those to be much complex in texture views but very simple, even not exist in depth views.

Due to these features, view-specific concealment methods for motional blocks are proposed for better complying with view integrity, so as to acquire better concealment quality. Moreover, for the purpose of better trade-off between complexity and quality, at the beginning of the methods, a second block classification is carried out. TC, DC, DL/DR and TL/TR views are assigned to their respective view-specific methods described as follows.

2.3 Texture Center (TC) View-Specific Method

TC view usually has the biggest effect on the overall recovered video quality, so the efficient and powerful concealment should be applied to ensure best quality. For most codec standards, the encoding process of TC view is independent with other views in MVD video. Additionally, the large uniform regions are mostly presented by comparably big sized blocks (or SKIP/merge block), and those regions with many details are likely segmented by small sized ones. Thus, the procedure for concealment motional in TC view is as follows.

What comes first is the second classification for motional blocks in TC view. Motional block has to be judged as big or small size, determined by the size of its neighboring blocks. In case of H.264/AVC, SKIP, 16×16, 16×8 and 8×16 blocks belong to big size blocks because they probably present single spline and color. And 8×8, 4×8, 8×4 & 4×4 blocks are small size blocks because complex textures may be presented in these blocks.

Big size blocks usually have perfect resemblance in the reference views according to [9], so for its concealment, OBMA method is applied on previous and next reference views to get two candidate MVs. Then the best one is chosen by lowest minimum square sum of difference (SSD), to finally conceal the block. SSD determines the best vector that has the minimum difference between the outer bound of corrupted block and the outer bound of the regions it refers to.

Small size blocks usually contain more splines and colors, so it's necessary to segment these blocks into 4×4 sub-blocks and recover them separately. The vector mv_{arg} by Eq. 1 and the candidate vector by DMVE [7], which is applied on present view, are prepared, and the optimal one is chosen using SSD to finish concealing each sub-blocks.

2.4 Depth Center (DC) View-Specific Method

Since both DC and TC views present the same scene, many regions in DC view have strong motion homogeneousness with their collocated ones in TC View. This makes the reduction of method's complexity possible while maintaining its overall recovering quality. During the DC view-specific method, motional block's vector mv_{arg} by Eq. 1 and the one from its collocated block in TC view are subtracted for the second block classification in DC view method.

If the subtraction is 0, it is classified as consistent block, which means the motion similarity between the block and its collocated one in TC view is very likely to valid. Using contents referred by mv_{arg} to conceal this block is effective enough. Otherwise, it should be classified as inconsistent one, and both the spatial and temporal correlation of this block should be exploited. In most codec systems, two temporal reference views and one spatial reference view are referenced when processing DC view, which is described in Fig. 4.

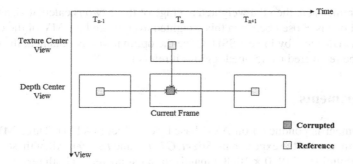

Fig. 4. Reference map of DC view

For dealing with blocks whose subtraction are not 0, three candidate vectors $(mv_{argTC}, mv_{argDC+}, mv_{argDC-})$ are calculated by using Eq. 1 on its collocated blocks in TC view at current frame, as well as in DC views at post and next frame, respectively. Then the optimal of these three vectors is chosen by SSD denoted in Sect. 2.3. Finally, the block is recovered using OBMA method on the view where the optimal vector is from.

2.5 Depth Left/Right (DL/DR) View-Specific Method

In most codec standard, DL/DR view has three reference views: DL/DR view at post and next frame, and DC view at current frame. Moreover, similar to DC view, DL/DR view has only contours of scene objects and large plain areas. This indicates strong relations between the motional block and its neighbors. Thus, simple concealment may achieve the satisfying recovering quality, as well as largely-reduced complexity.

DL/DR view-specific method is described as follows. For all motional blocks in DL/DR view, first, three average vectors, calculated by Eq. 1 on its collocated blocks in DC view at current frame, and in DL/DR views at post and next frame each, are prepared. Then, the optimal vector is chosen by lowest SSD from these three average vectors. Finally, the block is concealed using regions where the optimal vector refers to.

2.6 Texture Left/Right (TL/TR) View-Specific Method

Like DL/DR view, TL/TR view also has three reference views: DL/DR view at current frame and TL/TR view at post and next frame, which is similar to DC view. Furthermore, TL/TR view contains texture patterns while DL/DR view doesn't. Therefore, compared to DL/DR view, the concealment of TL/TR view need some additional steps to receive plausible quality.

Firstly, the block classification for TL/TR view method relies on motion subtraction. The subtraction of the average vectors, one acquired by Eq. 1 from the block itself and the other from its collocated block in DL/DR view, is calculated. If this subtraction is 0, the corrupted block is concealed with regions this vector refers to. Otherwise, OBMA is used to find the two best candidate vectors from TL/TR views at post and next reference frame each, then the weighted average of these two is calculated, and finally, the optimal one is chosen between this weighted average and the MV of the collocated block in DL/DR view by lowest SSD. Once the optimal MV is obtained, the corrupted block can be recovered using pixel regions it refers to.

3   Experiments

Our experiment is conducted on AVC-based Test Model (ATM). Three MVD video sequences are used in the experiment: *Street*, *GT_Fly* and *Dancer*. All of these sequences have the resolution of 1920 × 1088. Quantization parameters in both texture and depth view are configured as 28. The Hierarchy-B prediction structure and P-I-P view prediction structure are separately applied at intra-view prediction and inter-view prediction. I frame is assumed to be correctly received and the Flexible Macroblock Ordering (FMO) [12] is enable at NAL level.

To validate the improvements of the proposed error concealment scheme, its performance is compared with the traditional OBMA [11] method's and Liu's [9] method's, which is also implemented on ATM.

Table 1 shows PSNR results which represent the overall concealment quality for the above 3 methods. Each of the test videos had suffered from 3%, 5% and 10% packet loss rate (PLR) and was recovered by OBMA, Liu's and the proposed method respectively. Also, the averages for each methods' performance at each view is also listed. Our results prove that the proposed scheme outperforms the other two schemes for better concealment quality in all views. Compared to OBMA, the proposed scheme has PSNR increase in average 0.24 dB, 0.31 dB and 0.38 dB for 3%, 5% and 10% PLR, respectively. For Liu's method, the increase is in average 0.12 dB, 0.22 dB and 0.23 dB for 3%, 5% and 10% PLR. In case of 3% PLR, the TL/TR view-specific method achieves the biggest PSNR average increases, which are 0.3 dB to OBMA, and 0.2 dB to Liu's method. Meanwhile, for 5% and 10% PLR, DC view-specific method instead, gains biggest increases, which are 0.21 dB and 0.35 dB to Liu's method at 5% and 10% PLR respectively. These results indicate better designed view-specific methods for TL/TR view and DC view, compared to ones for the other views. Since both methods carry out the second block classification using motion subtraction, one can infer that the classification by motion subtraction is more capable of eliminating scene inconsistency that exists in one view.

Another interesting fact from the results is that, the PSNR for proposed method has the lowest decrease with the PLR increases. From 3% to 10% PLR, the average PSNR decrease for OBMA and Liu's method are 2.08 dB and 2.04 dB respectively, while 1.94 dB is decreased for the proposed method. So, the proposed method has better error resilient performance compared to OBMA and Liu's.

Table 1. PSNR comparison under different packet loss rate

Sequence & view		PLR								
		3%			5%			10%		
		OBMA (dB)	Liu (dB)	Proposed (dB)	OBMA (dB)	Liu (dB)	Proposed (dB)	OBMA (dB)	Liu (dB)	Proposed (dB)
Street	TC	36.56	36.83	36.93	35.73	36.08	36.12	34.14	34.62	34.83
	TL	34.13	34.21	34.46	33.03	33.15	33.41	30.75	30.83	30.92
	TR	34.11	34.20	34.33	33.28	33.38	33.50	30.65	30.70	30.85
	DC	40.12	40.42	40.54	39.74	39.76	40.42	38.67	38.70	39.15
	DL	39.44	39.47	39.57	39.11	39.19	39.29	37.54	37.60	37.71
	DR	39.89	40.04	40.13	39.20	39.32	39.40	37.53	37.90	38.15
GT_Fly	TC	37.99	38.06	38.17	37.29	37.44	37.59	35.87	36.07	36.22
	TL	36.91	36.95	37.19	36.26	36.32	36.62	34.64	34.68	35.14
	TR	37.16	37.18	37.45	36.30	36.36	36.77	34.67	34.71	35.29
	DC	41.45	41.49	41.64	41.33	41.42	41.60	40.88	40.97	41.23
	DL	41.79	41.82	41.86	41.48	41.56	41.70	40.90	40.96	41.17
	DR	41.91	41.90	41.98	41.55	41.57	41.65	40.89	40.91	41.08
Dancer	TC	34.10	34.21	34.35	33.19	33.24	33.54	31.00	31.22	31.52
	TL	32.04	32.14	32.32	31.12	31.23	31.31	29.63	29.76	29.91
	TR	31.93	32.18	32.30	31.21	31.26	31.33	29.71	29.91	30.01
	DC	38.92	39.06	39.17	38.83	38.68	39.03	37.83	37.92	38.04
	DL	37.29	37.35	37.49	36.06	36.24	36.47	34.90	35.09	35.32
	DR	37.22	37.33	37.37	35.79	35.88	36.16	35.24	35.58	35.76
Average	TC	36.22	36.37	36.48	35.40	35.59	35.75	33.67	33.97	34.19
	TL	34.36	34.43	34.66	33.47	33.57	33.78	31.67	31.76	31.99
	TR	34.40	34.52	34.69	33.60	33.67	33.87	31.68	31.77	32.05
	DC	40.16	40.32	40.45	39.97	39.95	40.35	39.13	39.20	39.47
	DL	39.51	39.55	39.64	38.88	39.00	39.15	37.78	37.88	38.07
	DR	39.67	39.76	39.83	38.85	38.92	39.07	37.89	38.13	38.33

Table 2 shows us the OBMA, Liu's & proposed methods' execution time, along with the Liu's & proposed methods' time increments compared to classic OBMA method. Apparently, the time consumption for our proposed method is just slightly higher than Liu's & OBMA method with acceptable, even negligible time increments, despite the classification and view-specific method applied on each view, making the proposed method be more complicated than the other two.

Table 2. Comparison for time consumption under different packet loss rate (PLR)

Sequence	PLR (%)	OBMA	Liu		Proposed	
		Time (s)	Time (s)	Increment (s)	Time (s)	Increment (s)
Street	3	4.63	4.80	0.17	4.78	0.15
	5	4.75	5.04	0.29	4.83	0.08
	10	4.83	5.13	0.30	5.01	0.18
GT_Fly	3	4.63	4.78	0.15	4.81	0.18
	5	4.75	4.83	0.08	4.89	0.12
	10	4.83	5.02	0.19	5.10	0.27
Dancer	3	4.99	5.21	0.23	5.22	0.24
	5	5.23	5.41	0.18	5.48	0.25
	10	5.40	5.99	0.59	5.93	0.53

This is mainly due to the classification of the motional or static blocks applied before view-specific methods. The classification gives a chance to most of these corrupted blocks of much easier copying concealment, if they are classified as static. The experiment results give the proof of the certain extent of computation reduction that the classification brings to proposed method.

4 Conclusion

We proposed a new view-specific based error concealment scheme for MVD. During the overall method, two unique classifications are conducted in turn, for judging the most suitable concealment for each corrupted block. Also, different view-specific methods are executed in different views according to different view features. The first classification helps us reducing time that is wasted on concealing corrupted blocks. The second classification helps improving the video quality for better catering each view's own characteristics. Compared to previous methods, we achieved a better trade-off between concealment quality and time consumption, which can be proved by our experiment results.

Acknowledgements. This work was supported in part by the National Natural Science Foundation of China, under Grants 161301112 and the 2016 peak discipline of filmology of Shanghai University.

References

1. Merkle, P., Smolic, A., Muller, K., Wiegand, T.: Multi-view video plus depth representation and coding. In: 2007 IEEE International Conference on Image Processing, vol. 1, pp. 201–204 (2007)
2. Yan, B.: A novel H.264 based motion vector recovery method for 3D video transmission. IEEE Trans. Consum. Electron. **53**(4), 1546–1552 (2007)
3. Lam, W.M., Reibman, A.R., Liu, B.: Recovery of lost or erroneously received motion vectors. In: 1993 IEEE International Conference on Acoustics, Speech, and Signal Processing, vol. 5, pp. 417–420 (1993)
4. Hewage, C.T.E.R., Worrall, S.T., Dogan, S., Kondoz, A.M.: A novel frame concealment method for depth maps using corresponding color motion vectors. In: 3DTV Conference: The True Vision - Capture, Transmission and Display of 3D Video, pp. 149–152 (2008)
5. Hewage, C.T.E.R., Martini, M.G.: Joint error concealment method for backward compatible 3D video transmission. In: 2011 IEEE 73rd Vehicular Technology Conference (VTC Spring), pp. 1–5 (2011)
6. Liu, Y., Wang, J., Zhang, H.: Depth image-based temporal error concealment for 3-D video transmission. IEEE Trans. Circ. Syst. Video Technol. **20**(4), 600–604 (2010)
7. Zhang, J., Arnold, J.F., Frater, M.R.: A cell-loss concealment technique for MPEG-2 coded video. IEEE Trans. Circ. Syst. Video Technol. **10**(4), 659–665 (2000)
8. Liu, D., Ma, R., Shi, N.D., et al.: An error concealment method for multi-view video plus depth. J. Optoelectron. Laser **24**(8), 1548–1591 (2013)
9. Liu, D., Ma, R., Shi, N.D., et al.: An error concealment method for multi-view video plus depth coding. J. Optoelectron. Laser **25**(8), 756–763 (2014)

10. Su, W., Rusanovskyy, D., Hannuksela, M.M., Li, H.: Depth-based motion vector prediction in 3D video coding. In: Picture Coding Symposium (PCS), pp. 37–40 (2012)
11. Thaipanich, T., Wu, P.-H.,. Kuo, C.-C.J: Video error concealment with outer and inner boundary matching algorithms. In: Proceedings of SPIE, vol. 6696, p. 669607. The International Society for Optical Engineering (2007)
12. Dhondt, Y., Mys, S., De Zutter, S., Van de Walle, R.: An alternative scattered pattern for flexible macroblock ordering in H.264/AVC. In: Eighth International Workshop on Image Analysis for Multimedia Interactive Services, pp. 57–57 (2007)

Mesh Denoising with Local Guided Normal Filtering and Non-local Similarity

Wenbo Zhao[1], Xianming Liu[1(✉)], Jiantao Zhou[2], Debin Zhao[1], and Wen Gao[3]

[1] School of Computer Science and Technology,
Harbin Institute of Technology, Harbin, China
{wbzhao,dbzhao}@hit.edu.cn, xmliu.hit@gmail.com
[2] Department of CIS, University of Macau, Macau, China
jtzhou@umac.mo
[3] School of Electrical Engineering and Computer Science,
Peking University, Beijing, China
wgao@pku.edu.cn

Abstract. Most of existing mesh denoising schemes are inspired by the techniques of conventional 2D image denoising. However, due to the significant difference between 3D mesh and 2D image, the employment of some well-known natural image priors, such as non-local similarity, are not straightforward in mesh denoising. In this paper, we revisit natural priors in the context of mesh denoising, and propose an effective mesh denoising scheme by combining local normal smoothness and non-local self-similarity. Specifically, the normals of neighboring faces and the current face are weighted combined to suppress noise, according to the distances to the current face and their guidance normals. Furthermore, the normals of non-local faces with similar structures are exploited. To find similar structures and calculate the similarity, the concept of k-ring patch is introduced for each face, in which the consistency and average normals of patches are used for finding similar patches. At last, the distance and normal difference between faces are used in calculating similarity between patches and non-local normals will be weighted by similarity. Experimental results show that the proposed scheme outperforms the state-of-the-art techniques, in terms of both objective and perceptual metrics, especially for the meshes with regular structures.

Keywords: Mesh denoising · Normal filtering · Similarity · Guidance normal

1 Introduction

3D surface mesh models have been widely used in many practical industry and entertainment applications, such as CAD, architectural design, virtual reality, and computer games. However, due to the limitation of the accuracy of scanning devices and digitization processes, noises are inevitably introduced into the acquired raw mesh data. Hence, mesh denoising is needed to improve the quality of imperfect meshes for further geometry processing.

© Springer Nature Singapore Pte Ltd. 2017
X. Yang and G. Zhai (Eds.): IFTC 2016, CCIS 685, pp. 176–184, 2017.
DOI: 10.1007/978-981-10-4211-9_18

Though a variety of mesh denoising algorithms have yielded promising results, how to distinguish high-frequency features such as sharp edges and corners from noises remains a challenging task. Some schemes borrowed the idea of filtering from the counterpart 2D image denoising, which worked in a two-step approach: filtering normals firstly and then updating vertex positions. Different filters have been applied on face normals. Zheng et al. [15] employed the bilateral filter on the normals; In [12], the mean and median filters were used; Zhang et al. [14] exploited a joint bilateral normal filter, in which the guidance normals are used in evaluating weights instead of the original normals. Similar approaches are also used in [7,8]. However, these filtering-based schemes do not take good advantage of similarity in mesh, which can be helpful to recover noisy features.

Non-local similarity has been extensively studied in image denoising, and many previous works [4,5] have achieved satisfying results. Some schemes try to make use of similarity in mesh denoising. Yoshizawa et al. [13] defined a similarity kernel and performed mesh denoising by non-local means. Digne et al. [2] built a local descriptor for each point in mesh and computed the weights by this descriptor. Rosman et al. [6] proposed a patch-based self-similarity point cloud denoising scheme, which extended the well-known BM3D [1] algorithm in 2D image denoising to mesh denoising. Most of existing similarity-based schemes are point-based, and it is hard to use these schemes in face normal filtering.

With the ever increasing popularity of signal sparse representation, the sparsity prior has also been introduced into mesh denoising. Due to the sparse property of sharp features, He et al. [3] applied the L0 minimization to mesh denoising. Similar idea also appeared in [9]. Wang et al. [11] presented an approach for decoupling noises and features with L1-analysis compressed sensing optimization. However, these schemes are based on the assumption that the noises are independent and identically distributed. When this assumption is not satisfied, the performance of these schemes drops significantly.

In this paper, we revisit the local smoothness and non-local self-similarity priors, which are popular in 2D image denoising, in the context of mesh denoising, and propose a novel mesh denoising scheme by combining local guided normal filtering and non-local face-based similarity. Specifically, the normals of neighboring faces and the current face are weighted combined to suppress noises, according to the distances to the current face and their guidance normals. Furthermore, the normals of non-local faces with similar structures are exploited. To find similar structures and calculate the similarity, the concept of k-ring patch is introduced for each face. The consistency and average normals of patches are used for finding similar patches. At last, the distance and normal difference between faces are used in calculating similarity between patches, and non-local normals will be weighted by similarity. Experimental results show the superiority of our scheme.

The rest of this paper is organized as follows. In Sect. 2, we introduce the proposed mesh denoising scheme in details. In Sect. 3, we present the experimental results and comparative studies, and Sect. 4 concludes.

2   The Proposed Mesh Denoising Scheme

In this section, we will introduce the proposed mesh denoising scheme in details. Firstly, the k-ring patch is proposed, then a review of the guided normal filtering [14] will be presented, after that we will show the features of patch and how to calculate the similarity between patches. At last, we will give the framework of our mesh denoising scheme.

2.1   The K-Ring Patch

When dealing with a noisy mesh, most similarity-based schemes choose to build local descriptors to describe the surface around point. However, our scheme is face-based and those schemes are unsatisfactory, hence the k-ring patch is introduced for each face to describe local structure around face. A patch that contains only one face f_i is defined as 0-ring patch, and f_i is the central face of the patch. Two faces are adjacent if they share at least one vertex, and k-ring patch is built by repeating adding all the adjacent faces into patch for k times. A face is defined as n-ring face if it is added to the patch at the n time process, and the set of n-ring faces are named by n-ring. A 2-ring patch is illustrated in Fig. 1, 0-ring; 1-ring and 2-ring are colored by red; blue and green separately.

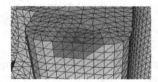

Fig. 1. A case of a 2-ring patch (Color figure online)

2.2   Guided Normal Filtering

The joint bilateral filter is a local smooth filter that can preserve sharp features, the main idea of it is using guidance signal in weighting instead of original signal. The authors in [14] extend it to mesh denoising. Given a noisy mesh, the normal and the centroid of each face are denoted as n_i and c_i. Then the filtered normal n_i' is computed from guided normal filtering:

$$n_i' = e_i \sum_{f_j \in N_i} a_j W_s\left(c_i, c_j\right) W_r\left(g_i, g_j\right) n_j, \tag{1}$$

where N_i is the neighborhood faces of f_i, a_j stands for the area of f_j, g_i is the guidance normal of f_i, e_i is the normalization factor to ensure n_i' is a unit vector. W_s and W_r are the Gaussian kernels [10]:

$$W_s\left(c_i, c_j\right) = \exp\left(-\frac{\|c_i, c_j\|^2}{2\sigma_s^2}\right), \tag{2}$$

$$W_r\left(g_i, g_j\right) = \exp\left(-\frac{\|g_i, g_j\|^2}{2\sigma_r^2}\right), \tag{3}$$

where σ_s and σ_r are Gaussian weight parameters.

The author defines that g_i is the normalized area-weighted average normal of a 1-ring patch p which contains f_i. and p should contain faces with similar normals. Such a guidance normal can provide more accurate weight in filtering than the original normal. The following function is introduced to measure the consistency of the normals to select p:

$$C\left(p\right) = \phi\left(p\right) R\left(p\right), \tag{4}$$

where $\phi\left(p\right)$ is the maximum difference of normals in the patch:

$$\phi\left(p\right) = \max_{f_i, f_j \in p} \|n_i, n_j\|. \tag{5}$$

$R\left(p\right)$ represents the saliency of a patch, it is computed by the saliency of the edges in it. For a edge e_i, the edge's saliency is defined as:

$$\varphi\left(e_i\right) = \|n_{i1}, n_{i2}\|, \tag{6}$$

where n_{i1}, n_{i2} are the normals of the incident faces of e_i. Then we can calculate $R\left(p\right)$ by:

$$R\left(p\right) = \frac{\max_{e_i \in p} \varphi\left(e_i\right)}{\varepsilon + \sum\limits_{e_i \in p} \varphi\left(e_i\right)}, \tag{7}$$

where ε is a small positive value to avoid $\sum\limits_{e_i \in p} \varphi\left(e_i\right)$ is zero.

To get the guidance normal g_i of face f_i, we traversal all the patches that contain f_i, find the patch which has the minimum $C\left(p\right)$, and calculate the normalized area-weighted average normal of the patch as g_i.

2.3   Definition of Feature and Similarity

As mentioned before, local filter lacks the usage of non-local similarity, which is helpful to preserve features. To use similarity in face normal filter, we define the features of patch and give the method to calculate the similarity between patches.

Given a k-ring patch p, robust local features are needed to describe the patch for finding similar patches. The consistency defined in Sect. 2.2 can describe the shape of 1-ring patch, so we extend it to k-ring patch to give a brief description of local structure. The consistency of each ring in k-ring patch p is defined as:

$$C_n\left(p\right) = \phi_n\left(p\right) R_n\left(p\right), 1 \leq n \leq k, \tag{8}$$

$\phi_n\left(p\right)$ means the maximum normals difference of n-ring faces:

$$\phi_n\left(p\right) = \max_{f_i, f_j \in n-ring} \|n_i, n_j\|. \tag{9}$$

$R_n(p)$ means the saliency of n-ring:

$$R_n(p) = \frac{\max_{e_i \in E_n} \varphi(e_i)}{\varepsilon + \sum\limits_{e_i \in E_n} \varphi(e_i)}, \tag{10}$$

where E_n is an edge set in which the incident faces of each edge are n-ring faces or one of the faces is $(n-1)$-ring face.

Notice that most point-based local descriptors use normal direction. Though $C_n(p)$ can describe the shape of n-ring patch, the directions of face normals have not been taken into considered, so the normalized area-weighted average normal w_i of the patch is also regarded as a feature. Then we can compute the distance of features between two k-ring patches by:

$$D(p_1, p_2) = \sum_{i=1}^{k} |C_i(p_1) - C_i(p_2)| \, \|w_{p1}, w_{p2}\|, \tag{11}$$

With (11) we can quickly find similar patches in a search window. But it cannot give an accurate estimation of similarity and is unsuitable in weighting normals. Hence we consider both the distance and the normal difference between faces, and use the following steps to calculate similarity of two k-ring patches p_1, p_2:

(1) Move the centroid of the central face of p_1 coinciding with the centroid of the central face of p_2.

(2) For each centroid c_i in p_1, find a face f_j in p_2 that the distance between c_i and f_j is minimum. Then the similarity is calculated by:

$$S(p_1, p_2) = \frac{\sum\limits_{f_i \in p_1, f_j \in p_2} dist(c_i, f_j) \, \|n_i, n_j\| \, a_j}{\sum\limits_{f_j \in p_2} a_j}. \tag{12}$$

With these features and similarity, for each patch we can find several most similar patches in mesh, and the normals in those patches will be used in filtering.

2.4   The Proposed Denoising Scheme

Combining above methods, our mesh denoising scheme is achieved by the following process, and the process will iterate N_{iter} times: First 1-ring and k-ring patch are built for each face. Second, we use the scheme introduced in Sect. 2.2 to compute the guidance normals. Third, the most n similar patches are found for each patch and the similarity between them are calculated. Since the faces that come from two patches are not corresponding except the central faces, only the central faces' normals of similar patches will be weighted in filtering, then noisy normals are filtered by the following formula:

$$n'_i = e_i \left(\sum_{f_j \in N_i} a_j W_s(c_i, c_j) W_r(g_i, g_j) n_j + \sum_{f_k \in G_i} a_k W_m(S(p_i, p_k)) n_k \right), \tag{13}$$

where p_k is one of the most n similar patches, G_i is the set of the central faces of those similar patches, W_m is the Gaussian kernel:

$$W_m\left(S\left(p_i, p_k\right)\right) = \exp\left(-\frac{S(p_i, p_k)^2}{2\sigma_m^2}\right), \tag{14}$$

where σ_m is weight parameter.

At last, The scheme in [7] is employed to update the vertexes' positions according to the denoised normals. It will iterate V_{iter} times to get a good result.

3 Experimental Results

In this section, experimental results are provided to demonstrate the superiority of the proposed scheme.

3.1 Parameters Setting

First, we discuss the parameters setting in our scheme. The proposed scheme involves the following parameters: the ring number of each patch k_{rnum}, the number of similar patches used in filtering n_{snum}, the weight parameters of Gaussian kernels σ_s, σ_r, σ_m and the number of iterations N_{iter}, V_{iter}. We use the same parameters σ_s, σ_r, V_{iter} in [14] because we use similar local guided normal filtering in denoising. The ring number of patch k_{rnum} controls the number of features of patch, we observe in experiments that $k_{rnum} = 2$ are enough for well performing, and larger k_{rnum} only increases the computation cost. The number of similar patches n_{snum} means the number of non-local faces used in normal filtering, we always set $n_{snum} = 5$ to avoid over-smoothed. The choice of σ_m and N_{iter} is shown in Table 1.

Table 1. Parameters' setting in our scheme

Parameter	Fand(0.3)	Fand(0.7)	Julius	Sphere	Bunny	Twelve
σ_m	0.08	0.06	0.02	0.02	0.02	0.12
N_{iter}	20	40	3	15	2	50

For a fair comparison, the parameters used in other schemes are as same as [14] to ensure the results of other schemes are the best results.

3.2 Objective and Subjective Comparison

We compare our scheme with the state-of-the-art denoising schemes in [3, 7, 14, 15], and evaluate the results with two error metrics E_a and E_v in [7]: E_a is the mean square angular error (MASE), and E_v is the L2 vertex-based error. In

Table 2. Comparison of error metrics

Mesh	Error	[7]	[15]	[3]	[14]	Ours
Fand(0.3)	E_a	10.763	8.094	10.141	7.615	**7.375**
	E_v	2.21×10^{-3}	2.07×10^{-3}	2.55×10^{-3}	2.01×10^{-3}	$\mathbf{1.93 \times 10^{-3}}$
Fand(0.7)	E_a	23.283	24.835	20.929	17.697	**16.568**
	E_v	3.26×10^{-3}	3.30×10^{-3}	2.83×10^{-3}	2.54×10^{-3}	$\mathbf{2.48 \times 10^{-3}}$
Julius	E_a	10.393	9.167	10.664	8.203	**8.012**
	E_v	$\mathbf{2.14 \times 10^{-5}}$	2.17×10^{-5}	2.26×10^{-5}	2.19×10^{-5}	2.19×10^{-5}
Sphere	E_a	21.797	**14.144**	20.868	20.842	16.334
	E_v	1.02×10^{-3}	9.54×10^{-4}	1.07×10^{-3}	9.52×10^{-4}	$\mathbf{9.06 \times 10^{-4}}$
Bunny	E_a	7.413	7.808	9.359	7.379	**7.203**
	E_v	$\mathbf{1.08 \times 10^{-5}}$	1.10×10^{-5}	1.11×10^{-5}	1.10×10^{-5}	1.10×10^{-5}
Twelve	E_a	11.557	13.465	12.147	11.099	**6.297**
	E_v	1.69×10^{-2}	1.75×10^{-2}	2.79×10^{-2}	8.38×10^{-3}	$\mathbf{6.82 \times 10^{-3}}$

Table 2, we show the error metrics results, where the best error metric values are bold. It can be observed that our scheme achieves better results in most cases.

Figures 2, 3 and 4 show the visually comparison between different schemes. In Figs. 2 and 3, the input meshes are generated by adding Gaussian noise, and in Fig. 4 the noise is impulsive noise. We could observe that our scheme preserve both sharp and smooth features well. In Fig. 2, our scheme succeeds in recovering structure, while other results are either over smoothed or fail on recovering the long edge. In Fig. 3, [7, 15] also perform good smooth results but fail on recovering edges. In Fig. 4, both [14] and our scheme recover the corner, but the edges recovered by [14] is curved.

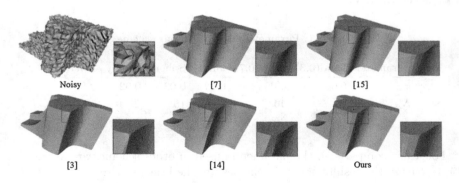

Fig. 2. Denoising results of Fand, the intensity of noise is 0.3.

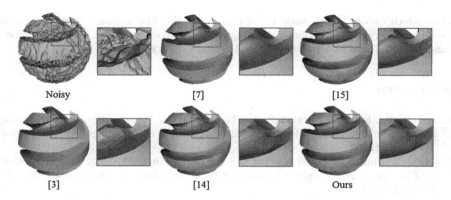

Fig. 3. Denoising results of Sphere, the intensity of noise is 0.3.

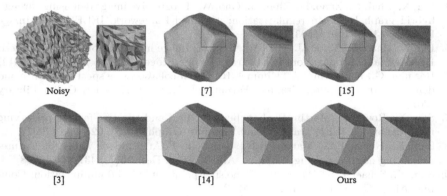

Fig. 4. Denoising results of Twelve, the intensity of noise is 0.5.

4   Conclusion

In this paper, we propose a novel mesh denoising scheme that using both local guided normal filtering and non-local face-based similarity. Specifically, Local normals are weighted by guidance normals and distance, while non-local normals are weighted by similarity. To find and weight the face-based similar structure, the k-ring patch is introduced to describe the local structure around face, then the consistency and average normals of patches are employed to find similar patches. At last distance and normal difference between faces are used in calculating the similarity between patches. The experiment results show that combining similarity and guidance normals in face normal filtering can achieve both visually and numerically better denoising results, especially for those meshes with regular structures such as long edge or smooth surface.

Acknowledgments. This work is supported by the Major State Basic Research Development Program of China (973 Program 2015CB351804), the National Science Foundation of China under Grants 61300110 and 61672193.

References

1. Dabov, K., Foi, A., Katkovnik, V., Egiazarian, K.: Image denoising by sparse 3-D transform-domain collaborative filtering. IEEE Trans. Image Process. **16**(8), 2080–2095 (2007)
2. Digne, J.: Similarity based filtering of point clouds. In: 2012 IEEE Computer Society Conference on Computer Vision and Pattern Recognition Workshops, pp. 73–79. IEEE (2012)
3. He, L., Schaefer, S.: Mesh denoising via l0 minimization. ACM Trans. Graph. (TOG) **32**(4), 64 (2013)
4. Liu, X., Zhai, D., Zhao, D., Zhai, G., Gao, W.: Progressive image denoising through hybrid graph laplacian regularization: a unified framework. IEEE Trans. Image Process. **23**(4), 1491–1503 (2014)
5. Liu, X., Zhao, D., Zhou, J., Gao, W., Sun, H.: Image interpolation via graph-based Bayesian label propagation. IEEE Trans. Image Process. **23**(3), 1084–1096 (2014)
6. Rosman, G., Dubrovina, A., Kimmel, R.: Patch-collaborative spectral point-cloud denoising. In: Computer Graphics Forum, vol. 32, pp. 1–12. Wiley Online Library (2013)
7. Sun, X., Rosin, P., Martin, R., Langbein, F.: Fast and effective feature-preserving mesh denoising. IEEE Trans. Visual. Comput. Graph. **13**(5), 925–938 (2007)
8. Sun, X., Rosin, P.L., Martin, R.R., Langbein, F.C.: Random walks for feature-preserving mesh denoising. Comput. Aided Geom. Des. **25**(7), 437–456 (2008)
9. Sun, Y., Schaefer, S., Wang, W.: Denoising point sets via L0 minimization. Comput. Aided Geom. Des. **35**, 2–15 (2015)
10. Tomasi, C., Manduchi, R.: Bilateral filtering for gray and color images. In: Sixth International Conference on Computer Vision, pp. 839–846. IEEE (1998)
11. Wang, R., Yang, Z., Liu, L., Deng, J., Chen, F.: Decoupling noise and features via weighted L1-analysis compressed sensing. ACM Trans. Graph. (TOG) **33**(2), 18 (2014)
12. Yagou, H., Ohtake, Y., Belyaev, A.: Mesh smoothing via mean and median filtering applied to face normals. In: Proceedings of the Geometric Modeling and Processing, pp. 124–131. IEEE (2002)
13. Yoshizawa, S., Belyaev, A., Seidel, H.P.: Smoothing by example: Mesh denoising by averaging with similarity-based weights. In: IEEE International Conference on Shape Modeling and Applications (SMI 2006), p. 9. IEEE (2006)
14. Zhang, W., Deng, B., Zhang, J., Bouaziz, S., Liu, L.: Guided mesh normal filtering. In: Computer Graphics Forum, vol. 34, pp. 23–34. Wiley Online Library (2015)
15. Zheng, Y., Fu, H., Au, O.K.C., Tai, C.L.: Bilateral normal filtering for mesh denoising. IEEE Trans. Visual Comput. Graph. **17**(10), 1521–1530 (2011)

BD_CNN Based Pedestrians and Vehicle Recognition in Video Surveillance

Xueqin Zhang[1(✉)], Ting Fang[1], and Qiuchen Gu[2]

[1] Institute of Information Science and Technology,
East China University of Science and Technology, Shanghai, China
zxq@ecust.edu.cn
[2] Institute of Business, East China University of Science and Technology,
Shanghai, China

Abstract. Intelligent video analysis technology has been widely used to detect moving vehicles and pedestrians in huge volume video record. In order to find a unified solution to moving vehicles and pedestrians detection in videos, BD_CNN (Background Difference_Convolutional Neural Network) algorithm is proposed in this paper, which applies background difference technology to recognize moving objects, adopts convolutional neural network algorithm to extract features of vehicle and pedestrian automatically, and builds unified vehicle and pedestrian classifier. The multi-scale detection method and reasonable decision mechanics are designed to improve the detection accuracy. Experimental results validate the algorithm's availability and efficiency in the moving objects detection.

Keywords: Pedestrian and vehicle detection · Convolutional neural network · Background difference algorithm

1 Introduction

Video surveillance system has become an important auxiliary means of criminal investigation. At present, the police usually find the detection object by reviewing the recordings manually, which has low efficiency and high cost. Intelligent video analysis technology [1], which can detect moving objects and find pedestrians and vehicle automatically, has become a research hotspot. kNN (k-NearestNeighbor) classifier has proposed by Komaropoulos and Tsakalides [2] which is based on a variation of k-nearest neighbor algorithm. Cheng et al. [3] has presented accelerating a sliding-window based vehicle detection algorithm on a heterogeneous multicore systems using OpenCL designs which reduce search space. A novel pedestrian detection algorithm has proposed by Lin et al. [4] which uses novel outline features and a three-layer back-propagation feed-forward neural network as the classifier for the real-time pedestrian detection system at night. Wang [5] has proposed a general ternary classification framework which is based on cascade classification framework and each stage is a ternary detection pattern for pedestrian detection in changing scenes.

© Springer Nature Singapore Pte Ltd. 2017
X. Yang and G. Zhai (Eds.): IFTC 2016, CCIS 685, pp. 185–196, 2017.
DOI: 10.1007/978-981-10-4211-9_19

The methods mentioned above focus on realizing detection for the single moving object well. But for multi-object detection, extracting the suitable characteristics for a unified classifier is the bottleneck. Deep learning is put forward by Hinton et al. [6] in 2006. One of the important characteristics of this kind of deep learning method is that it can realize the automatic extraction of the features without manual intervention. In order to find a unified solution to the moving vehicle and pedestrian detection in videos, this paper proposed using background difference technology to recognize moving object and adopting convolutional neural network (CNN) algorithm to extract features of vehicles and pedestrians and build classifier.

2   Basic Knowledge of Algorithms Used

2.1   Introduction of Convolutional Neural Network

Convolutional Neural Network (CNN) is proposed by LeCun [7] in 1998. It has been widely applied in image recognition, audio intelligent, document analysis, behavior recognition, etc. Similar to a traditional neural network, a classic convolutional neural network structure [8,9] has input layer, hidden layer and output layer. But the hidden layer of it contains the convolution layer and sampling layer, which can extract and optimize classification features respectively. Convolutional neural network has three most important characteristics: local sensing, shared weights, sub-sampling. These characteristics make it combine with the local information to get global information, reduce the required parameters, the model complexity and have better anti-noise ability.

Convolution and sub-sampling process of CNN are described as below. As shown in Fig. 1, input an image or a feature map p, M_j is the local awareness of input layer. The process of convolution layer is

$$C_x = \text{sigmoid}(\sum_{i \in M_j} p_i f_x + b_x) \tag{1}$$

where C_x represents the feature map, f_x denotes convolution kernel, b_x is bias; sigmoid() is the activation function of neurons. In CNN, a feature map is formed by one kind of kernels. Therefore, if more features are needed, various convolution kernels can be selected.

Formula of sub-sampling is

$$S_{x+1} = f(W_{x+1} \sum_{i \in N \times N} C_i + b_{x+1}) \tag{2}$$

where W_{x+1} is trainable weights.

Generally, the gradient descent method with fast convergence speed is used in the training of convolutional neural network. The weight w of convolution kernel is updated according to:

$$W_{x+1} = W_x - alpha \times \frac{de}{dW_x} \tag{3}$$

where $alpha$ represents learning rate, $\frac{de}{dW_x}$ denotes error function, e is the derivative about the weight parameters.

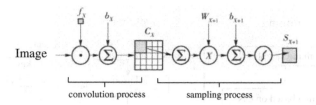

Fig. 1. Convolution and sampling process

2.2   Introduction of Background Difference

Background difference [10], namely, background subtraction. The difference image is generated from subtracting the current frame and background frame. The algorithm can extract the moving object accurately and excluding background interference.

The steps of extracting the background image are described as below:

$\{I_k(x,y)\}_{k=1}^{M}$ is the input video sequence, M is total frame number of video, k is the sequence of frame, T represents threshold of background updating, $D(x,y)$ denotes background frame.

Step1: Make gray processing for video frame and background frame respectively to get image $I_{k-ray}(x,y)$ and $D_{ray}(x,y)$.

Step2: Subtract the background gray frame from the current gray frame to get difference image $MD_{k-ray}(x,y)$.

$$MD_{k-ray}(x,y) = |I_{k-ray}(x,y) - D_{ray}(x,y)| \tag{4}$$

Step3: Get binaryzation image through adaptive threshold adjustment.

$$MD_k(x,y) = \begin{cases} 255, \ MD_{k-ray}(x,y) \geq TS \\ 0, \ MD_{k-ray}(x,y) < TS \end{cases} \tag{5}$$

where TS is the threshold, the value of $MD_k(x,y)$ is 255 representing the region of moving object.

3   Pedestrian and Vehicle Detection Algorithm Based on CNN and Background Difference (BD_CNN Algorithm)

3.1   BD_CNN Arithmetic Statement

The frame of BD_CNN algorithm is shown in Fig. 2.

BD_CNN arithmetic statement is described as below:

Step1: Make gray processing for video frame and background frame respectively to get image $I_{k-ray}(x,y)$ and $D_{ray}(x,y)$. Two grayscale images are subtracted to get difference image $MD_{k-ray}(x,y)$.

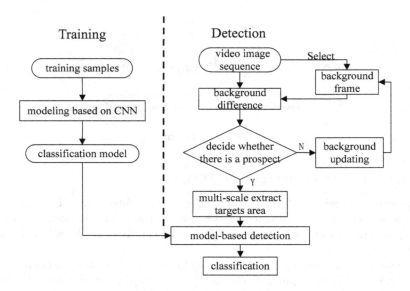

Fig. 2. BD_CNN algorithm framework

Step2: Get image MD from $MD_{k-ray}(x, y)$ by binaryzation operation.

Step3: Traverse the binary image $MD_k(x, y)$, and sum up the number of white pixels pix (x, y).

Step4: When $P > T$, the current frame is argued as motion frame. Otherwise, this frame is regarded as non-sports frame, update the background frame with this frame and then read the next video frame and return to step1.

Step5: Record centroid position $m_i(x_i, y_i)$ of enclosed area of each motion frame (i is the number of enclosed area). The number of pixels of these areas is recorded as num_i.

Step6: When $num\ i < 100$, ignore the small plots. Otherwise, dig out several different grid regions according to the position of centroid $m_i(x_i, y_i)$ to do multi-scale detecting furthermore.

Step7: Apply voting mechanism on the multi-scale detection result to get finally classify decision.

3.2   The Network Structure of CNN Classifier

The architecture of CNN is shown in Fig. 3. The first input layer is used to obtain the training sample. The last output layer plays the role of traditional back propagation neural network. The rest layers are convolution layers and sub-sampling layers. A classic six layer network structure is: input layer, convolution layer, sub-sampling layer, convolution layer, sub-sampling layer and the fully connection layer. Usually, the sub-sampling layer adopts an average sampling method.

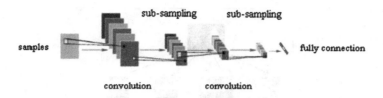

Fig. 3. CNN network structrue

Once the network structure is determined, the following parameters still need to be considered to get the optima model: the size of convolution kernel, the number of network layer, the times of training, the learning rate and the transfer function. Especially, the size of the convolution kernel is an important factor. Undersize will cause difficulty in extracting the data structure from the image, while oversize will cause greater computational and time cost.

3.3 Multi-scale Detection

In order to improve detection accuracy, image multi-scale detection is usually adopted. This method is also named as "pyramid" multi-scale transformation, which detects object by traversing the scaling images to get more detail of image. However, the method needs to scale the image and traverse the graph, which results long time consume.

Therefore, a multi-scale detection based on identifying window is proposed here. Firstly, the region of moving objects are found by background difference method, and the foreground image are dug out with initial identifying window size according to the centroid of moving objects. Then the size of identifying window are changed, the sub-images are dug out from the foreground image, which size are the same as the identifying windows. Finally, these sub-images are adjusted to a unified scale, and sent to CNN classifier.

The advantage of this method is that it just operates on foreground image and doesn't need to traverse the image for several times. So, the detection time can be reduced. Also, this method can get more image details, thus the detection accuracy can be improved.

3.4 Voting Mechanisms

Vehicle detection or pedestrian detection is two-classification problem. Vehicle and Pedestrian mixed detection is three-classification problem. The voting mechanisms based on multi-scale detection are designed as follow (Fig. 4):

For two-classification problem, the unequal voting mechanism is adopted. That is, if the multi-scale detection model returns N results, one of them decides the moving object is vehicle or pedestrian, the final decision is vehicle or pedestrian accordingly.

For three-classification problem, the average voting mechanism is adopted. That is, if the multi-scale detection model returns N results, more than half of

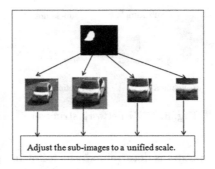

Adjust the sub-images to a unified scale.

Fig. 4. The method of multi-scale recognition

them are vehicles or pedestrians, the final decision is a vehicle or pedestrian accordingly.

4   Experiment and Results

4.1   Experimental Data and Environment Description

Experimental Data. Three datasets containing vehicles, pedestrians, roads, buildings, windows and etc. are collected from the Internet to train three different BD_CNN models respectively, including vehicle classifier, pedestrian classifier and vehicle-pedestrian mixed classifier. There are 6000 positive samples which contains vehicle under different scenarios, and 6000 negative samples for vehicle detection. Training samples of pedestrian detection are similar to it. The training samples of vehicle and pedestrian mixed classifier contain 6000 vehicle samples, 6000 pedestrian samples and 6000 samples without pedestrians and vehicles.

Five short videos are selected as test videos. The scenarios of these videos are respectively a crossroads, front of a shopping mall, straight road, road on campus and a bend. The description of these videos is illustrated in Table 1:

In the table, #frame is the total number of frame, #fr_pe, #fr_no_pe represent the number of frame with or without pedestrians respectively. #fr_ve, #fr_no_ve represent the number of frame with or without vehicle respectively.

Table 1. Information of test videos

	#frame	#fr_pe	#fr_no_pe	#fr_ve	#fr_no_ve	Moving state
V_crossroad	910	422	488	376	534	Straight, turning
V_mall	1077	893	184	154	923	Straight, turning
V_straight	415	149	266	98	317	Straight
V_campus	799	757	42	0	799	Straight, turning
V_bend	563	48	515	532	31	Turning

Experimental Observation Indication. In order to verify the validity of the BD-CNN algorithm for vehicle or pedestrian detection, detection rate (h_r), false alarm rate (f_r) and false negative rate (m_r) are considered:

$$h_r = \frac{x_1 + x_2}{m_1 + m_2}, \; f_r = \frac{y_2}{m_2}, \; m_r = \frac{y_1}{m_1} \tag{6}$$

where m_1, m_2 are the total number of frames with or without vehicle in test video respectively. x_1 is the number of correct detection frames with vehicle, x_2 is the number of correct detection frames without vehicle. y_1 is the number of missed frame with vehicle, y_2 is the number of frame which is identified mistakenly.

For vehicle and pedestrian mixed detection, the correct rate (h_r) is considered:

$$h_r = \frac{N\_Accurate_1 + N\_Accurate_2}{N\_veh\_ped_1 + N\_veh\_ped_2} \tag{7}$$

where $N\_veh\_ped_1$, $N\_veh\_ped_2$ represents the total number of frame with or without pedestrian or vehicle respectively; $N\_Accurate_1$, $N\_Accurate_2$ is the number of correct detection frame which with or without pedestrian or vehicle respectively.

Experimental Environment. The experiment CPU is Intel(R) Core(TM) i5-3230M the OS is Windows 7 the development tool is Matlab 2012(b).

4.2   Experiments and Results

Experiment 1: The Selection of Convolution Kernel Size. Set the times of training as 10, the number of network layers as 6, the value of learning rate as 0.06. Select sigmoid function, three kinds of convolution kernel size are tested: 13×13, 9×9 and 5×5.

For vehicle classification, model VehModel_1, VehModel_2 and VehModel_3 were built. For pedestrian classification, model PeoModel_1, PeoModel_2, Peo-Model_3 were trained. For vehicle and pedestrian mixed classification model VePe_1, VePe_2, VePe_3 were made.

The experiment results on test videos with single-scale detection are shown in Tables 2, 3 and 4.

Table 2. Detection results on different models (vehicle detection)

	VehModel_1			VehModel_2			VehModel_3		
	m_r (%)	f_r (%)	h_r (%)	m_r (%)	f_r (%)	H_r (%)	m_r (%)	f_r (%)	h_r (%)
V_crossroad	9.04	43.07	70.99	15.43	0	93.63	*9.31*	*0.37*	*95.93*
V_mall	0	0	100	0	0	100	*0*	*0*	*100*
V_straight	16.33	11.36	87.47	28.57	11.36	84.58	*31.6*	*11.36*	*83.86*

Table 3. Detection results on different models (pedestrian detection)

	PeoModel_1			PeoModel_2			PeoModel_3		
	m_r (%)	f_r (%)	h_r (%)	m_r (%)	f_r (%)	h_r (%)	m_r (%)	f_r (%)	h_r (%)
V_crossroad	1.18	0.61	99.12	0.95	0.61	99.23	*0.59*	*1.22*	*99.07*
V_mall	30.57	0	74.65	31.13	0	74.19	*20.16*	*0*	*83.29*
V_straight	63.09	0	77.35	49.66	0	82.17	*20.13*	*0*	*92.77*

Table 4. Detection results on different models (mixed detection)

	h_r (%)		
	VePe_1	VePe_2	VePe_3
V_crossroad	90.11	*95.05*	93.98
V_mall	71.03	*88.07*	88.07
V_straight	90.6	*93.98*	92.53

It can be seen that the detection rate of VehModel_3, PeoModel_3 and VePe_2 are the highest. The convolution kernel size should be 5×5, 5×5 and 9×9 respectively.

Experiment 2: The Selection of Learning Rate (*alpha*). Learning rate influences the weights updating. In order to determine the appropriate value of *alpha*, set the times of training as 10, the number of network layers as 6, the transfer function as sigmoid function, the size of convolution kernel as the value got in 4.2.1.

The experiment results on test videos with single-scale detection are shown in Tables 5, 6 and 7.

This indicates that, for vehicle detection, when *alpha* is 0.01, the detection rate is the highest. And for pedestrian and mixed detection, when *alpha* is 0.06, the detection rate is the highest.

Multi-scale Experiment: Selecting the optima parameter determined in the above experiment and adopting single-scale detection and multi-scale detection

Table 5. Detection results on different learning rate (vehicle detection)

	$alpha = 0.01$			$alpha = 0.06$			$alpha = 0.1$		
	m_r (%)	f_r (%)	h_r (%)	m_r (%)	f_r (%)	h_r (%)	m_r (%)	f_r (%)	h_r (%)
V_crossroad	*10.1*	*0*	*95.82*	9.31	0.37	95.93	17.42	0	92.8
V_mall	*0*	*0*	*100*	0	0	100	0	0	100
V_straight	*38.76*	*5.68*	*86.51*	31.6	11.36	83.86	28.57	11.67	84.34

Table 6. Detection results on different learning rate (pedestrian detection)

| | alpha = 0.01 | | | alpha = 0.06 | | | alpha = 0.1 | | |
	m_r (%)	f_r (%)	h_r (%)	m_r (%)	f_r (%)	h_r (%)	m_r (%)	f_r (%)	h_r (%)
V_crossroad	0.95	2.25	98.35	*0.59*	*1.22*	*99.07*	0.95	1.43	98.79
V_mall	38.75	6.52	66.76	*20.16*	*0*	*83.29*	25.64	1.09	78.55
V_straight	0	10.53	94.46	*20.13*	*0*	*92.77*	43.62	0	84.34

Table 7. Detection results on different learning rate (mixed detection)

| | h_r (%) | | |
	alpha=0.01	alpha=0.06	alpha=0.1
V_crossroad	89.51	*95.05*	88.35
V_mall	65.66	*88.07*	78.46
V_straight	84.58	*93.98*	91.08

separately on test videos. The experimental results are shown in Tables 8, 9 and 10:

Thus it can be seen, the time of multi-scale detection is increased slightly, but the false-negative-rate is reduced greatly for vehicle and pedestrian detection. And the detection rate is increased in three kinds of detection.

Comparison Experiments: Typically, the Haar feature and the HOG feature are selected for vehicle and pedestrian classification respectively. So, in

Table 8. Comparisons of detection results and time (vehicle detection)

| | Multi-scale | | | | Single-scale | | | |
	m_r (%)	f_r (%)	h_r (%)	t_f (ms)	m_r (%)	f_r (%)	h_r (%)	t_f (ms)
V_crossroad	*6.65*	*0*	*97.25*	95.04	10.1	0	95.82	81.34
V_mall	*0*	*0*	*100*	80.08	0	0	100	63.87
V_straight	*11.22*	*4.85*	*93.01*	103.7	38.76	5.68	86.51	90.22

Table 9. Comparisons of detection results and time (pedestrian detection)

| | Multi-scale | | | | Single-scale | | | |
	m_r (%)	f_r (%)	h_r (%)	t_f (ms)	m_r (%)	f_r (%)	h_r (%)	t_f (ms)
V_crossroad	*0.71*	*0*	*99.67*	87.62	0.59	1.22	99.07	68.67
V_mall	*1.01*	*1.63*	*98.89*	77.91	20.16	0	83.29	63.78
V_straight	*7.38*	*0*	*97.35*	96.89	20.13	0	92.77	77.15

Table 10. Comparisons of detection results and time (mixed detection)

	Multi-scale		Single-scale	
	h_r (%)	t_f (ms)	h_r (%)	t_f (ms)
V_crossroad	**95.71**	108.23	95.05	95.55
V_mall	**91.2**	84.1	88.07	75.64
V_straight	**99.76**	118.89	93.98	103.36

Table 11. Comparisons of pedestrain detection results

	BD_CNN				HOG_SVM			
	m_r (%)	f_r (%)	h_r (%)	t_f (ms)	m_r (%)	f_r (%)	h_r (%)	t_f (ms)
V_crossroad	**0.71**	**0**	**99.67**	**87.62**	5.5	8.2	93.08	296.32
V_mall	**1.01**	**1.63**	**98.89**	**77.91**	7.84	21.74	89.79	284.82
V_straight	**7.38**	**0**	**97.35**	**96.89**	6.71	7.14	93.01	294.69
V_campus	**4.62**	**0**	**95.62**	**77.35**	10.57	4.7	89.74	295.17

Table 12. Comparisons of vehicle detection results

	BD_CNN				Haar_Adaboost			
	m_r (%)	f_r (%)	h_r (%)	t_f (ms)	m_r (%)	f_r (%)	h_r (%)	t_f (ms)
V_crossroad	**6.65**	**0**	**97.25**	95.04	0.27	10.3	93.85	**66.5**
V_mall	**0**	**0**	**100**	80.08	1.3	4	94.06	**88.72**
V_straight	**11.22**	**4.85**	**93.01**	103.7	0	17.35	86.75	**88.52**
V_bend	**6.58**	**0**	**93.78**	85.59	33.21	93.55	63.4	**78.88**

this experiment, BD_CNN algorithm is compared with HOG_SVM algorithm in pedestrian detection, and Haar_AdaBoost algorithm in vehicle detection. The HOG_SVM algorithm is based on HOG feature and SVM classifier and the Haar_AdaBoost algorithm is based on Haar_like feature and AdaBoost classifier. Due to the little number of pedestrians in V_bend, it is not adopted in the experiment of pedestrian detection. Similarly, v_campus is not adopted in the experiment of vehicle detection because there are no vehicles. The experiment results on vehicle and pedestrian are listed in Tables 11 and 12.

Experimental results show that BD_CNN algorithm has better detection rate and shorter detection time than HOG_SVM. The detection time of BD_CNN is a little longer than Haar_Adaboost, however, it has better and more steady detection performance.

Some experimental results are depicted in Fig. 5. Figure (a), (b), (c) represent mixed detection, pedestrian detection and vehicle detection respectively. Here, Green box is draw for vehicle and red for pedestrian.

Fig. 5. Some experimental results (Color figure online)

5   Conclusion

It is difficult to find the unified feature of vehicle and pedestrian for traditional pattern classification problem. With the aid of advantage that convolutional neural network can extract feature automatically, combining CNN with background difference method is proposed in this paper to accomplish the pedestrian and vehicle mixed detection by building an unify model. At the same time, with the help of multi-scale window technology, the detection accuracy is improved. Experiments show that the BD_CNN algorithm is an effective method to detection the vehicle and pedestrian in surveillance video.

References

1. Lizhong L, Zhiguo L, Yubin Z.: Research on detection and tracking of moving target in intelligent video surveillance. In: 2012 International Conference on Computer Science and Electronics Engineering (ICCSEE), vol. 3, pp. 477–481. IEEE (2012)
2. Komaropulos, E.M., Tsakalides, P.: A novel KNN classifier for acoustic vehicle classification based on alpha-stable statistical modeling. In: Proceeding of the 15th Workshop on Statistical Signal Processing, pp. 1–4. IEEE, Cardiff (2009)
3. Cheng, K.M., Lin, C.Y., Chen, Y.C., et al.: Design of vehicle detection methods with OpenCL programming on multi-core systems. In: IEEE Symposium on Embedded Systems for Real-Time Multimedia, pp. 88–95. IEEE (2013)
4. Lin, C.F., Lin, S.F., Hwang, C.H.: Real-time pedestrian detection system with novel thermal features at night. In: Proceedings of the 2014 IEEE International Instrumentation and Measurement Technology Conference (I2MTC), pp. 1329–1333. IEEE (2014)
5. Wang, Z., Cao, X.B.: Rapid classification based pedestrian detection in changing scenes. In: 2010 IEEE International Conference on Systems Man and Cybernetics (SMC), pp. 1591–1596. IEEE (2010)
6. Hinton, G.E., Salakhutdinov, R.R.: Reducing the dimensionality of data with neural networks. Science **313**(5786), 504–507 (2006)

7. LeCun, Y., Bottou, L., Bengio, Y., et al.: Gradient-based learning applied to document recognition. Proc. IEEE **86**(11), 2278–2324 (1998)
8. Nebauer, C.: Evaluation of convolutional neural networks for visual recognition. IEEE Trans. Neural Netw. **9**(4), 685–696 (1998)
9. Chen, Y.N., Han, C.C., Wang, C.T., et al.: The application of a convolution neural network on face and license plate detection. In: 18th International Conference on Pattern Recognition, ICPR 2006, vol. 3, pp. 552–555. IEEE (2006)
10. Xu, Y., Zhou, C., Xu, S., et al.: Moving region detection based on background difference. In: IEEE Workshop on Electronics, Computer and Applications, pp. 518–521 (2014)

The Subway Pantograph Detection Using Modified Faster R-CNN

Ruimin Ge[1], Yu Zhu[1(✉)], Yuling Xiao[2], and Zhihua Chen[1]

[1] School of Information Science and Engineering,
East China University of Science and Technology, Shanghai, China
Y45140087@mail.ecust.edu.cn, {zhuyu,czh}@ecust.edu.cn
[2] Henan Chemical Industry Vocational College, Henan University of Technology,
Zhengzhou, China
xiaoyuling2000@163.com

Abstract. To ensure the safe operation of the train in metro system, catenary anomaly detection and alerting security have become a major issue to be resolved. Moreover, effective pantograph detection is an important foundation of catenary anomaly detection. In this paper, we present a novel computer vision pantograph detection system involving Faster R-CNN object detection method. Based on the architecture of deep Convolution Neural Network (CNN), we modify the Faster R-CNN to real-time detect the subway pantograph. It combines region proposal generation with object detection. The results reveal that the approach achieves inspiring detection accuracy with over 94.9%. The system can work in different environment of the subway's train, at different times throughout the day. It provides important reference for subsequent anomaly detection of catenary.

Keywords: Computer vision · Pantograph detection · Object detection · Faster R-CNN

1 Introduction

The electric transmission system for modern electric rail systems consists of an upper, weight-carrying wire (known as a catenary) from which is suspended a contact wire. The pantograph is spring-loaded and pushes a contact shoe up against the underside of the catenary wire to draw the current needed to run the train. It is a common type of current collector. The most common type of pantograph today is the so-called 'Z'-shaped pantograph, shown as Fig. 1 left. A considerable proportion of running accidents are caused by the abnormal power supply of catenary among high-speed railways and urban subways. In order to prevent train safety hazards, the anomaly detection of the catenary has become quite important and necessary. The anomaly detection [1] includes the foreign object debris and the electric spark for catenary. Now, the anomaly detection mostly rely on labor job. This way is time-consuming and miss detection easily happens due to eye fatigue. Thus, intelligent anomaly detection for catenary has

© Springer Nature Singapore Pte Ltd. 2017
X. Yang and G. Zhai (Eds.): IFTC 2016, CCIS 685, pp. 197–204, 2017.
DOI: 10.1007/978-981-10-4211-9_20

become quite important. In order to more accurately detect the electric spark and foreign object debris, we concentrated on computer vision method to solve the problem of the subway pantograph associated with the catenary wire in this paper.

Computer vision-based object detection is a very challenge task but with important applications. The traditional object detection is based on image color, shape and texture with the common methods of extracting the feature points, such as speeded up robust features (SURF) [2], deformable part model (DPM) [3] based on histogram of oriented gradients (HOG) [4]. Because of complex work environment of the train, various backgrounds, diverse interference (Fig. 1, right), conventional methods can't achieve good performance. The rapid development of deep learning [5] and convolutional neural networks [6] has dramatically improved object detection performance. Recently, Faster R-CNN [7] was proposed for real-time object detection in pictures. It achieved a mean average precision (mAP) of 73.2% on the PASCAL VOC 2007 and 2012 dataset.

Fig. 1. Left: the asymmetrical 'Z'-shaped pantograph of the electric transmission system. Right: the selected example of video images during driving

In this paper, we applied the modified Faster R-CNN model to detect the pantograph. With merging region proposal network (RPN) [7] and Fast R-CNN [8] into a single network by sharing their convolutional (Conv) layers, it is able to automatically learn good feature representations for the task. Experiments show that the modified Faster R-CNN performs very well in the detection of pantograph during different illumination and background. The results suggest that the method is a cost-efficient and effective reference for practical application.

2   Method

2.1   Fast R-CNN

Fast R-CNN is an improvement on the original R-CNN [9] designed to speed up the detection network. The architecture of Fast R-CNN is shown in Fig. 2.

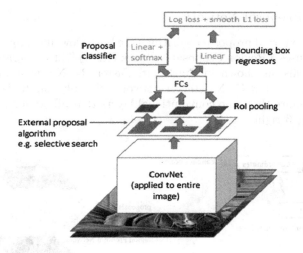

Fig. 2. Fast R-CNN architecture

It reuses the same Conv features for each bounding box. First, bounding boxes are generated for the image using bounding box proposal methods like Selective Search [10] or Edge Boxes [11]. Next, the entire image is passed into the CNN, up through the last Conv layer. Then for each bounding box, the region of interest (RoI) pooling is applied to the final layer Conv features to create a fixed size vector. This RoI vector is then passed to a classification network and regression network. The classification layer is fully connected layers followed by a softmax layer over all object classes. The regression network is fully connected layer network that fine-tunes the bounding box coordinates. The fine-tuning produces notably improved bounding boxes.

The network is trained with a multi-task loss function for an image (Fig. 2). The loss consists of the proposal classification loss and the box-regression loss. The classification loss L_{cls} is the log loss over two classes (object vs. not object). The regression loss $L_{reg}(t, t^*)$ is defined by smooth L_1:

$$L_{cls}(p, p^*) = -\log[p * p + (1 - p^*)(1 - p)] \tag{1}$$

$$L_{reg}(t, t^*) = \text{smooth}_{L_1}(t - t^*) \tag{2}$$

$$L(p, p^*, t, t^*) = L_{cls}(p, p^*) + \lambda p^* L_{reg}(t, t^*) \tag{3}$$

Here, p is the probability vector being objects and background predicted by classifier. t is the coordinates vector of the bounding box predicted by the regression network. p^* is the ground-truth label and t^* is the ground-truth bounding box. The value of p^* is 0 when the proposed bounding box is a background bounding box. L_{reg} is not used for training on background bounding boxes.

2.2   Region Proposal Network

Unfortunately, external proposal algorithms are both slow and suboptimal. Thus, Faster R-CNN uses a Region Proposal Network (RPN) [7] to generate the bounding box proposals, as shown in Fig. 3 left. Faster R-CNN is simply the RPN combined with a Fast R-CNN detector network. Notably, the RPN and Fast R-CNN network share the same convolutional layers that allows for joint training, as shown in Fig. 3 right.

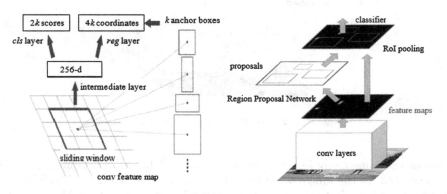

Fig. 3. Left: Region Proposal Network (RPN). Right: Faster R-CNN is a single unified network for object detection. The RPN module serves for region proposal (credit [7]).

The RPN utilizes a sliding window approach to generate k bounding boxes for each position in the last layer Conv feature map. First, an n by n filter is convolved with last layer Conv feature map. Then the result is projected to a lower dimensional space resulting in a fixed-size vector for each position. The vector is separately passed into a box-regression layer and a box-classification layer.

To reduce the number of bounding box proposals, non-maxima suppression (NMS) [12] is used on proposals that have high intersection-over-union (IoU). The boxes are ranked based on the object probability score. Finally, the top N proposals are taken from the remaining proposals, again ranked by object probability score. These proposals are then passed into the Fast R-CNN detector network and classified as described in the previous section.

2.3   Modified Faster R-CNN Model

In this paper, our task is defined as real-time detecting of the subway pantograph on the dynamic videos. In every frame, the pantograph area is the detected object and the other parts is defined as background. Since the requirement is video real-time detecting, the processing speed must be concerned. Therefore, to conform to the problem, we modified the Faster R-CNN to simplify the model from the original one. In the specific methods we remove some convolution layer and local response normalization (LRN) layer. We use simple notations to represent parameters in the network: (1) $Conv(N, K, S)$ for convolutional layers with N outputs, kernel size K, stride S and, (2) ReLU for the activation functions with rectified linear unit, (3) $Pool(T, K, S)$ for pooling layers with the T type, pool size K, stride S, (4) $ROIPool(P, S)$ for the ROIPooling layer with pool size P and spatial scale S, (5) $Dropout(R)$ for the dropout ratio, (6) $FC(N)$ for fully - connected layers with N outputs. The network has parameters:

$Conv(96, 7, 2) - ReLU - Pool(\max, 3, 2) - conv(256, 5, 2) - ReLU - Pool$ $(\max, 3, 2) - Conv(384, 3, 1) - ReLU - Conv(256, 3, 1) - ReLU - conv(256, 3, 1) -$ $conv(6, 1, 1) - (Softmax, Conv(12, 1, 1)) - ROIPool(6, 0.0625) - FC(4096) -$ $ReLU - Dropout(0.5) - FC(4096) - ReLU - Dropout(0.5) - (FC(2)FC(8))$.

In the subway pantograph detection work, the subway pantograph's size stays all the same without any scaling because the surveillance system is located on the subway train and the relative position of the camera with the subway pantograph is fixed. It is unnecessary to predict region proposals with different aspect ratio at each sliding-window location. Hence, the aspect ratio in settings of anchors only takes a value (1:1) and the anchor scale takes the values ($128^2, 256^2, 512^2$). We train Fast R-CNN using 2000 RPN proposals.

In the training, we adopt the 4-Step Alternating Training [2] method to fine-tune the model. The pre-trained ImageNet network is used to initialize the network parameters. First, the RPN is trained on the dataset (RPN Stage 1). Then, the fast R-CNN is trained using the RPN's proposals (fast R-CNN Stage 1); Afterwards, we refine the RPN by fixed the convolutional layers to be those of the trained fast R-CNN (RPN Stage 2); Finally, the fast R-CNN's fully connected layers are fine-tuned, using the new RPN's proposals (fast R-CNN Stage 2).

3   Experimental Results

We comprehensively evaluate the utility on our own datasets. This dataset consists of about 5380 images. We split all the images randomly into training, validation, and test sets with a ratio of 5 : 2 : 3. We only detect the subway pantograph in every image. All visible objects in every frame are annotated with a pantograph class label and bounding box coordinates.

The result of the loss vs. iteration number during training is shown in Fig. 4. The loss vs. iterations indicates that the entire network is convergent.

Figure 5 shows the convolutional kernels learned by stochastic gradient descent (SGD) with back propagation. The network has learned a variety of frequency and orientation-selective kernels, as well as various colored blob.

Next, we investigated the mAP of the entire object detecting system. Since the work environment of the subway train is quite distinct under different scenes. We take five 10-min videos for every scene. The frame rate is 25 fps. It can be divided into following scenes: (1) Underground environment; (2) Above-ground environment (night); (3) Above-ground environment (day); (4) Access tunnel; (5) Passing viaduct; (6) Above-ground passageway. The detailed detection result

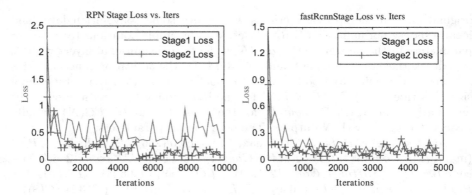

Fig. 4. The loss vs. iterations during training

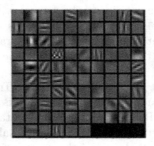

Fig. 5. 96 convolutional kernels of size $7 \times 7 \times 3$ learned by the first convolutional layer on the $224 \times 224 \times 3$ input images.

Table 1. Detection mAP (%) of the system

Scene	mAP
Underground environment	95.1
Above-ground environment (night)	96.4
Above-ground environment (day)	93.5
Access tunnel	92.7
Passing viaduct	94.6
Above-ground passageway	97.4
All scenes average	94.9

is shown in Table 1 and Fig. 6 illustrates some selected frame examples in different scenes.

The result in Table 1 indicates that the pantograph detection method performs excellent even if the subway work environment is complicated. The NVIDIA GTX 1070 is used for the experiment. The entire pantograph detection system takes 45 ms to detect one image and has a frame-rate of 22 fps.

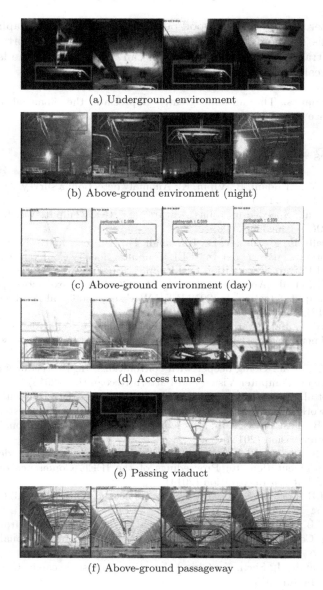

(a) Underground environment

(b) Above-ground environment (night)

(c) Above-ground environment (day)

(d) Access tunnel

(e) Passing viaduct

(f) Above-ground passageway

Fig. 6. Selected examples of pantograph detection using the modified Faster R-CNN.

4   Conclusion

We have developed a subway pantograph detection system based on computer vision. The state-of-the-art object detection architecture of Faster R-CNN is the strong baseline of the system. To fit in with the real-time video processing requirement, we modified the architecture of convolutional feature extracting layers in Faster R-CNN and get good performance in the pantograph detection. It is the basis of anomaly detection of the catenary and important for safe operation of trains. The detection solution can greatly reduce the labor input, and achieve real-time detection of subway train operation status.

Acknowledgments. The authors greatly appreciate the financial supports of National Science Foundation of China (No. 61370174).

References

1. Chandola, V., Arindam, B., Vipin, K.: Anomaly detection: a survey. ACM Comput. Surveys (CSUR) **41**(3), 15 (2009)
2. Bay, H., et al.: Speeded-up robust features (SURF). Comput. Vis. Image Understand. **110**(3), 346–359 (2008)
3. Felzenszwalb, P., Mcallester, D., Ramanan, D.: A discriminatively trained, multi-scale, deformable part model. In: IEEE Computer Society Conference on Computer Vision and Pattern Recognition DBLP, pp. 1–8 (2008)
4. Mizuno, K., et al.: Architectural study of HOG feature extraction processor for real-time object detection. In: 2012 IEEE Workshop on Signal Processing Systems. IEEE (2012)
5. Krizhevsky, A., Sutskever, I., Hinton, G.E.: Imagenet classification with deep convolutional neural networks. In: Advances in Neural Information Processing Systems (2012)
6. Szegedy, C., et al.: Going deeper with convolutions. In: Proceedings of the IEEE Conference on Computer Vision and Pattern Recognition (2015)
7. Ren, S., et al.: Faster R-CNN: towards real-time object detection with region proposal networks. In: Advances in Neural Information Processing Systems (2015)
8. Girshick, R.: Fast R-CNN. In: Proceedings of the IEEE International Conference on Computer Vision (2015)
9. Girshick, R., et al.: Rich feature hierarchies for accurate object detection and semantic segmentation. In: Proceedings of the IEEE Conference on Computer Vision and Pattern Recognition (2014)
10. Uijlings, J.R.R., et al.: Selective search for object recognition. Intl. J. Comput. Vis. **104**(2), 154–171 (2013)
11. Zitnick, C.L., Dollár, P.: Edge boxes: locating object proposals from edges. In: European Conference on Computer Vision. Springer International Publishing (2014)
12. Lin, Z., Brandt, J., Shen, X.: Object detection via visual search. U.S. Patent No. 9,081,800, 14 Jul 2015

Multi-scale Deep Residual Networks
for Fine-Grained Image Classification

Xiangyang Wang[1(✉)], Yusu Jin[1], Zhi Liu[1], Yadong Zhao[1],
Xiaoqiang Zhu[1], and Juan Zhang[2]

[1] School of Communication and Information Engineering,
Shanghai University, Shanghai 200444, China
{wangxiangyang,xqzhu}@shu.edu.cn, liuzhi@staff.shu.edu.cn,
iejinyusu@gmail.com, zhaoyadong2009@gmail.com
[2] School of Electronic and Electrical Engineering,
Shanghai University of Engineering Science, Shanghai 201620, China
zhang-j@foxmail.com

Abstract. Fine-grained image classification aims at distinguishing very similar images, i.e., the subcategories in one class. Compared with generic object recognition, fine-grained image classification is much more challenging due to the small inter-class variance. Deep Residual Networks (ResNet) is a recently proposed deep Convolution Neural Networks (CNN) model, and has achieved the excellent performance on image classification. Though powerful, like other contemporary CNN models, ResNet only exploits the features extracted from the last output layer for classification, which may be insufficient for fine-grained classification. In this paper, we propose a Multi-scale Residual Networks (Multi-scale ResNet) to further improve the fine-grained image classification performance. Based on the ResNet model, we extract features from multiple CNN layers, add these high-level and mid-level features together with different weights for final classification. We compare our proposed model with some state-of-the-art models on two fine-grained image dataset, Stanford Cars and Dogs, and experimental results validate the efficacy of our method.

Keywords: Convolution Neural Networks (CNN) · Residual learning · Multi-scale residual networks · Fine-grained image classification

1 Introduction

Fine-grained visual recognition is a challenging problem in computer vision community, which aims at recognizing the subcategories in one object class. For instance, it may be practically useful to recognize the dog or bird species, or car models [1, 2, 6]. Such objects are both semantically and visually similar to each other.

Fine-grained image classification has attracted much attention in the past few years [3–5]. Usually, fine-grained recognition is more difficult than common image classification. For example, fine-grained categorization of car models (or bird species) would be a more difficult task than distinguishing people from dogs. Fine-grained recognition

© Springer Nature Singapore Pte Ltd. 2017
X. Yang and G. Zhai (Eds.): IFTC 2016, CCIS 685, pp. 205–217, 2017.
DOI: 10.1007/978-981-10-4211-9_21

is quite challenging because visual differences between the categories are small, and the recognition accuracy may be affected by factors such as pose, viewpoint, or location of the object in the image.

Convolutional Neural Networks (CNNs). In recent years, deep Convolutional Neural Networks (CNNs) [7, 32] have gained great success in the area of machine learning and computer vision, especially because of their surprising achievements in image classification tasks [8, 9]. From the AlexNet [8] with 8 layers to the VGG net [10] with 16 or 19 layers, the CNN classification accuracy increases with the network going deeper [11]. CNNs can learn robust features and do end-to-end classification. They greatly surpass traditional classification methods, as long as large image datasets are available. CNNs trained on large-scale image classification datasets, such as ImageNet [9], have been transferred well to other vision tasks such as object detection [12], semantic segmentation [13], and edge detection [14], etc.

Many works have also adopted CNNs for fine-grained visual recognition [1, 6, 15, 16] with results better than previous traditional methods [2, 3]. Current fine-grained image classification methods are mostly based on the VGG net [10] pre-trained on the large image dataset, ImageNet, and then fine-tuned on specific fine-grained data.

Residual Networks. Recently, He et al. [17] proposed a novel deep network structure, named as Deep Residual Networks (ResNet), which is based on the observation of the "degradation" problem: with the network depth increasing, the accuracy gets saturated. They address the degradation problem by introducing a deep residual learning framework. ResNet makes it possible to train very deep network structures and gain rather better image recognition accuracy. ResNet exhibits the excellent characteristics and won the 1st places on the ILSVRC2015 ImageNet classification tasks.

Multi-scale CNN features have been used for visual recognition [18], edge detection [14], saliency detection [19], and even visual tracking [20]. It is based on the observation that, the last convolutional layers encode the high-level semantic information of the objects and such representations are robust to significant appearance variations, while earlier layers can capture fine-grained low-level visual information details [20] such as the object shapes or parts which may be important for fine-grained image classification. Using the CNN features from multi-scale layers together with the last layer for image classification will greatly improve the image classification accuracy.

Our proposed: Multi-scale Deep Residual Networks (Multi-scale ResNet). We expect to get attractive fine-grained image classification performance in virtue of the novel ResNet model. In our experiments, we find that although ResNet can achieve better classification accuracy than previous deep network models, however, for fine-grained recognition task, by integrating multi-scale deep features we can further improve the classification performance. In this paper, we propose a multi-scale Deep Residual Networks (multi-scale ResNet) model for fine-grained image classification.

The rest of this paper is organized as follows. In Sect. 2, we review the Deep Residual networks. In Sect. 3 we describe our proposed Multi-scale Deep Residual Networks. Experimental results on the fine-grained classification dataset are given in Sect. 4. Section 5 concludes this paper.

2   ResNet: Deep Residual Networks

When deep neural networks go deeper, it will be more difficult to train. Because they will suffer the degradation problem, that is, with the network depth increasing, the accuracy gets saturated; the deeper network has the higher training error and test error.

Deep Residual Networks (ResNet) [17] adopts a deep residual learning framework to ease the training of very deep networks. They can tackle the degradation problem, and gain the higher accuracy on very deep network structures. The residual nets trained on the ImageNet dataset are with 152 layers, which is 8 times deeper than VGG nets [10] but still has the lower complexity and the higher accuracy.

Formally, a building block of Residual networks is defined as (shown in Fig. 1)

$$y = \mathcal{F}\big(\{W_i\}, x\big) + x \tag{1}$$

where x and y are the input and output vectors of the considered layers. $\mathcal{F}\big(\{W_i\}, x\big)$ is the residual mapping function to be learned. In Fig. 1, we have two layers, $\mathcal{F} = W_2 \text{ReLU}\big(W_1 x\big)$, in which ReLU is defined as $\text{ReLU}(x) = \max\{0, x\}$ [21]. The operation $\mathcal{F} + x$ is performed by a shortcut connection and element-wise addition.

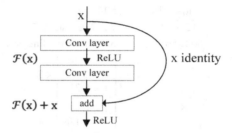

Fig. 1.   The building block of residual networks [17]

The building block of Residual learning reformulates the layers as learning residual functions with reference to the layer inputs, instead of learning unreferenced functions. It lets the stacked layers fit a residual mapping. It would be easier to optimize the residual mapping than to optimize the original unreferenced mapping.

We will illustrate the idea of the residual learning as follows. Formally, let $\mathcal{H}(x)$ be an underlying mapping to be fit by a few stacked layers (not necessarily the entire net), with x denoting the inputs to the first of these layers. Since multiple nonlinear layers can asymptotically approximate complicated functions, they can also asymptotically approximate the residual functions, i.e., $\mathcal{H}(x) - x$ (assuming that the input and output are of the same dimensions). So rather than expect stacked layers to approximate $\mathcal{H}(x)$, the residual learning lets the stacked nonlinear layers fit another residual mapping function $\mathcal{F}(x): = \mathcal{H}(x) - x$. Then the original mapping function becomes $\mathcal{F}(x) + x$.

This reformulation is motivated by the counterintuitive phenomena about the degradation problem. If the added layers can be constructed as identity mappings, a deeper model should have the training error not greater than its shallower counterpart. The degradation problem suggests that the solvers might have difficulties in approximating identity mappings by multiple nonlinear layers. With the residual learning reformulation, if identity mappings are optimal, the solvers may simply drive the weights of the multiple nonlinear layers toward zero to approach identity mappings.

The formulation $\mathcal{F}(x) + x$ can be realized by feedforward neural networks with "shortcut connections". Shortcut connections are those skipping one or more layers. In Residual Networks, the shortcut connections simply perform identity mapping, and their outputs are added to the outputs of the stacked layers (Fig. 1). Identity shortcut connections add neither extra parameter nor computational complexity. The entire network can still be trained end-to-end by stochastic gradient descent (SGD) [7, 23] with backpropagation, and can be easily implemented using deep leaning libraries such as Caffe [22].

In our work, we use the 50-layer ResNet (Fig. 2(a)) as the baseline network. The detailed information of the 50-layer ResNet (ResNet-50) architectures for ImageNet is summarized in Table 1. Building blocks are shown in brackets, with the numbers of blocks stacked. Down-sampling is performed by conv3_1, conv4_1 and conv5_1 with a stride of 2.

Table 1. ResNet-50 architectures for ImageNet.

Layer name	Output size	50-layer
Conv1	112×112	7×7, 64, stride 2
Conv2_x	56×56	3×3 max pooling, stride 2
		$\begin{bmatrix} 1 \times 1, 64 \\ 3 \times 3, 64 \\ 1 \times 1, 256 \end{bmatrix} \times 3$
Conv3_x	28×28	$\begin{bmatrix} 1 \times 1, 128 \\ 3 \times 3, 128 \\ 1 \times 1, 512 \end{bmatrix} \times 4$
Conv4_x	14×14	$\begin{bmatrix} 1 \times 1, 256 \\ 3 \times 3, 256 \\ 1 \times 1, 1024 \end{bmatrix} \times 6$
Conv5_x	7×7	$\begin{bmatrix} 1 \times 1, 512 \\ 3 \times 3, 512 \\ 1 \times 1, 2048 \end{bmatrix} \times 3$
	1×1	Average pooling, 1000-d fc, softmax

In Residual networks, we use the 3-layer building block scheme, that is, each residual unit consists of 3 layers, 1×1, 3×3 and 1×1 convolutions. In fact, each such layer still contains three sub-layers as illustrated in Fig. 2(b), i.e., convolutions (Conv), batch normalization (BN) [24] and ReLU.

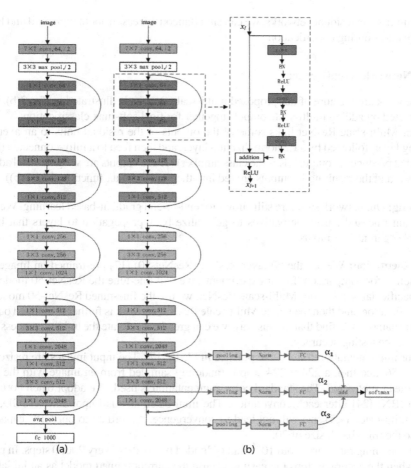

Fig. 2. Example network architectures of (a) residual network and (b) multi-scale residual network

3   Multi-scale Deep Residual Networks (Multi-scale ResNet)

As has been stated before, features from the last CNN layer can capture the high-level global semantic information of the image, which will be useful for coarse classification tasks such as distinguishing between different object classes (i.e., people and dogs). On the other hand, features from earlier CNN layers may also be useful, as they can capture the mid or low-level information of the image, such as the object shape and local parts, which are important for fine-grained classification tasks such as recognizing the subcategories in one object class (i.e., species of dogs or birds, car models). Usually, previous works just use the features from the last CNN layer for classification.

In this paper, we explore a multi-scale residual networks (Multi-scale ResNet) for fine-grained image classification, which use features from multiple layers for output prediction.

With multi-scale residual networks, we can simultaneously reason about high, mid and low-level features during classification.

3.1 Network Architecture

The network architecture of our proposed multi-scale ResNet is illustrated in Fig. 2(b). It is constructed by adding multi-scale outputs together for final soft-max classification.

Our Multi-scale ResNet links some of the outputs of the residual units to an average pooling layer, followed by a L2 normalization layer, and then feed to a fully-connected (FC) layer that produces K outputs (K is the class number). These outputs are weighted and added together, and the resulting K outputs are fed into the final softmax function (Fig. 2(b)).

Training: Our network structure still allows for end-to-end gradient-based learning. We use the chain rule and partial derivatives to generalize back-propagation to layers that have multiple "parents" or inputs.

Implementation: We use the 50-layer ResNet (ResNet-50) [17] pre-trained on ImageNet as baseline for comparison. In our experiments, we will fine-tune the ResNet-50 model on our specific dataset. For our Multi-scale ResNet, we use the fine-tuned ResNet-50 model as an initialization, and then the whole Multi-scale ResNet network is further fine-tuned on the specific dataset. We find that, in this way, we can greatly accelerate the training process and improve the testing accuracy.

Our implementation follows the practice in [8, 10, 17]. The input images are resized to 256×256, and then a 224×224 crop is randomly sampled from an image with the per-pixel mean subtracted. The standard color augmentation is used. We adopt batch normalization (BN) [24] after each convolution. The mini-batch size is important for SGD, too small mini-batch (<5) size will not lead to convergence. According to our GPU capacity, we use the mini-batch size of 20.

The learning rate starts from 10^{-5}, and is divided by 10 after every 20000 steps. In practice, when the accuracy stops increasing, we use the current trained model as an initialization and increase the learning rate (i.e. 10^{-3}) for the next training stage.

The models are trained for up to 50×10^4 iterations. We use a weight decay of 0.0005 and a momentum of 0.9. As the practice in [24], we do not use dropout [25].

4   Experimental Results

Our experiments are carried out on a workstation with 2 Intel Xeon E5-2620v3, 2.4 GHz CPUs, 32 GB RAM, a single NVIDIA GeForce Titan X 12 GB GPU, on Windows 7 operation systems. We implement our CNN models using the publicly available Caffe Library [22].

We compare our proposed Multi-scale ResNet with the baseline ResNet model, and previous CNN models, AlexNet [8] and VGG [10], and other traditional fine-grained image classification methods, such as SPM-3D-L&BB-3D-G [2], LLC [26] and ELLF [27]. We evaluate these models on two benchmark fine-grained visual recognition dataset: Stanford Cars dataset [2], Stanford Dogs dataset [9, 28]. The example data for the two datasets are shown in Fig. 3.

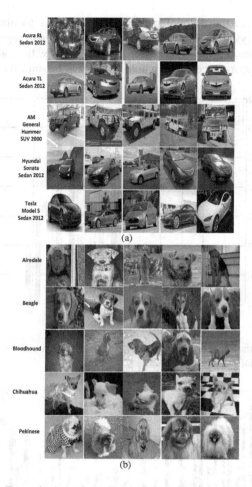

Fig. 3. Example data of: (a) Stanford Cars and (b) Stanford Dogs.

4.1 Analysis of Multi-scale Feature Classification and Selection

We do some experiments to explore the classification performance of our Multi-scale CNN model by using the pooled features extracted from multiple layers. Because the last layer usually has a strong classification performance (indeed, most previous methods only use the features from the last layer), we use it as the starting feature layer, and then iteratively add more layers to evaluate the performance. Our experimental results verify that if we add some intermediate layers, the performance will increase. But when more earlier layers are added, on the contrary the classification accuracy will decrease. So features at high-level and mid-level layers (i.e., parts and shape) are more useful than features at low-level layers for fine-grained classification.

We prefer to select the optimal combination of layers to maximize our model performance. By analysis, we select some layers and add them together with different weights to form the multi-scale CNN features. We will show that, with the multi-scale CNN features, the performance of the whole model will be improved.

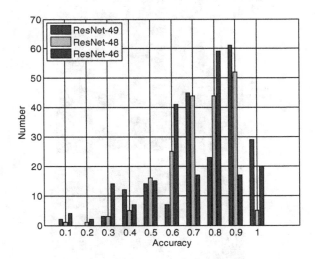

Fig. 4. Histogram of the classification accuracy of the 49th, 48th and 46th layer of ResNet on total 196 classes of Stanford cars dataset [2]

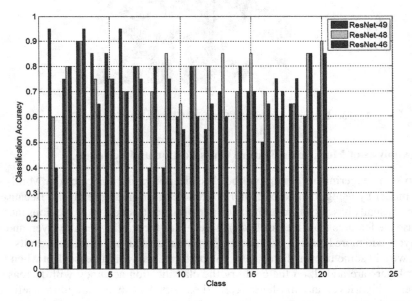

Fig. 5. Classification accuracy of the 49th, 48th and 46th layer of ResNet on 20 classes of Stanford cars dataset [2]

Figures 4 and 5 are the histograms of our experimental results on Stanford cars dataset [2]. Stanford Cars dataset consists of 196 classes of 16,185 images. We apply the 49, 48 and 46 layer of ResNet, respectively, for classification of total 196 classes. In Fig. 4, the X-axis represents the classification accuracy, and the Y-axis counts the number of classes. Figure 5 compares the classification accuracy of the 49, 48 and 46 layers of ResNet individually on some 20 classes in detail.

We can see that while high-level features (i.e., 49-layer at accuracy of 0.9) gain high accuracy on most of the classes, their performances are less satisfied than intermediate-level features (i.e., 48 and 46-layer at accuracy 0.8 and 0.6) on some other classes. Such an observation suggests that multi-scale CNN features should be fused to further improve the performance.

In the following, we further investigate the performance of multi-scale ResNet model. Figure 6 illustrates the effect of different layers on the whole model. We start with the 49-layer, and iteratively add the previous layers. The "+" sign on the X-axis means the recent-most added layer.

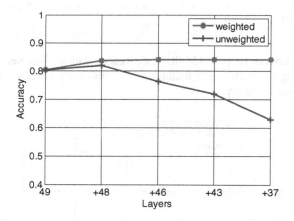

Fig. 6. The performance of the multi-scale CNN model varies as adding more layer-specific features.

We first use simple unweighted adding, that is we firstly add 48-layer to 49-layer, and then add 46, 43 and 37-layers in sequence. We find that the accuracy increases when adding 48-layer, but continuously decreases while adding other layers. This implies that some earlier layers are less helpful, and even degrades the performance of model.

Next, we apply the weighted adding, which gives each layer an appropriate weight while adding to previous layers. Figure 6 shows that, when 48-layer is weighted added to 49-layer, the accuracy improves obviously. Then we add the 46-layer with a small weight and the accuracy increases a little. The performance will not be improved by adding other earlier layers. Keep on adding other earlier-layer features will not improve, and even slightly decrease the performance.

From our experimental analysis, we adopt the weighted adding scheme for multi-scale ResNet model. We assign the higher weights for high-level layers with good capacities (i.e., 49 and 48-layers), and lower weights for lower-level layers (i.e., 46-layer). We do not use other layers, because they may have less contribution to the whole performance. In the following experiments, the weights for the three layers, 49, 48 and 46-layer, are empirically set as 1, 0.5 and 0.01, respectively.

4.2   Results on Stanford Cars Dataset

Stanford Cars dataset consists of 16,185 images of 196 classes, with about 80 images per category. We use the official training/testing splitting. Following the approach used by others (e.g., [2, 10]), we crop the images to their bounding boxes, train on 40 images per category using the official training partition, and test on the remaining images. We have not augmented the training dataset. Our results are given in Table 2. Using our full model, we achieve 84.2% accuracy, outperforming the previous best result, 75.6% in [2].

Table 2. Classification accuracy (%) on Stanford Cars dataset [2]

Methods	SPM-3D-L & BB-3D-G [9]	LLC [18]	ELLF [19]	AlexNet [8]	VGG [10]	ResNet [17]	Multi-scale ResNet(ous)
Accuracy	75.5	69.5	73.9	68.6	75.6	80.5	84.2

We also compare our proposed Multi-scale ResNet with the ResNet model in Fig. 7. It can be seen that, the multi-scale features can significantly improve the fine-grained image classification accuracy.

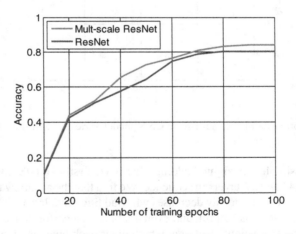

Fig. 7. Comparison of multi-scale ResNet with ResNet on Stanford Cars dataset.

4.3   Results on Stanford Dogs Dataset

The Stanford Dogs dataset contains 20,580 images from 120 fine-grained classes. These images were taken from ImageNet [9] for fine-grained image categorization. We use the official training/testing splitting. The comparison methods include some traditional fine-grained image classification approaches on this Stanford Dogs dataset, including

SIFT + Gaussian Kernel [28], Selective Pooling Vectors [30], Unsupervised Grid Alignment [29], and Gnostic Fields [31].

The experimental results are shown in Table 3. Note that the recent method based on unsupervised grid alignment [29] reports an accuracy of 57.0%. It extracts multi-channel local descriptors and utilizes unsupervised part detection and segmentation. However, our proposed method can benefit both from the end-to-end deep learning ResNet framework and the multi-scale features, and achieves the accuracy of 76.1%, much better than other models. Compare to ResNet, with the accuracy of 72.1%, we still have the relative 4% improvement, which validates that our model with multi-scale features can further improve the performance of CNN models.

Table 3. Classification accuracy (%) on Stanford Dogs dataset [9, 28]

Methods	SIFT+Gaussian Kernel [28]	Selective Pooling Vectors [30]	Unsupervised Grid Alignment [29]	Gnostic Fields [31]
Accuracy	22.0	52.0	57.0	47.7
Methods	AlexNet [8]	VGG [10]	ResNet [17]	Multi-scale ResNet(ous)
Accuracy	42.3	70.9	72.1	76.1

5   Conclusion

In this paper, we propose a Multi-scale Residual networks (Multi-scale ResNet) for fine-grained image classification. We explore multi-scale features extracted from multi-layers of the ResNet, and add them together with different weights for final fine-grained classification tasks.

It has been verified from the experiments that the high-level CNN features (i.e., the last layer) appear to focus on global statistics and high-level semantic information of the whole image, while the mid-level features emphasize parts or shape of objects. As fine-grained image classification tasks usually aim at distinguishing very similar images, i.e., the subcategories in one class, it will be insufficient to only use the high-level CNN features. Multi-scale CNN features, which include both the high-level and mid-level features, may be helpful to improve the classification accuracy.

Very deep CNN models always suffer from the degradation problem, that is, the training and testing errors increase with the networks depth going deeper. Deep Residual Networks adopt the residual learning strategy to tackle the degeneration problem. Currently, with the most deep network structures, deep residual networks have exhibited very excellent characteristics in image classification.

Our Multi-scale ResNet benefits the virtues from both the deep Residual Networks and Multi-scale CNN features. We present extensive analysis and experiments on two fine-grained image dataset, Stanford Cars and Dogs. We compare our proposed model with some state-of-the art fine-grained classification methods including traditional ones and CNN models. Our experimental results show that our model achieves the better accuracy than others, and can significantly improve the fine-grained image classification performance.

Acknowledgements. This work was supported by the National Natural Science Foundation of China under Grants 61471230, 61402277, the Program for Professor of Special Appointment (Eastern Scholar) at Shanghai Institutions of Higher Learning, the Innovation Program of Shanghai Municipal Education Commission (15ZZ044), and the Open Project Program of the State Key Lab of CAD&CG (Grant No. 1507), Zhejiang University, the Project of Local Colleges' and Universities' Capacity Construction of Science and Technology Commission in Shanghai (Grant No. 15590501300). We also thank NVIDIA Corporation for their GPU donation.

References

1. Krause, J., Jin, H., Yang, J., Fei-Fei, L.: Fine-grained recognition without part annotations. In: CVPR (2015)
2. Krause, J., Stark, M., Deng, J., Fei-Fei, L.: 3D object representations for fine-grained categorization. In: 3D Representation and Recognition Workshop at ICCV (2013)
3. Yao, B., Khosla, A., Fei-Fei, L.: Combining randomization and discrimination for fine-grained image categorization. In: IEEE Conference on Computer Vision and Pattern Recognition (CVPR), pp. 1577–1584 (2011)
4. Zhang, N., Farrell, R., Iandola, F., Darrell, T.: Deformable part descriptors for fine-grained recognition and attribute prediction. In: IEEE International Conference on Computer Vision (ICCV), pp. 729–736 (2013)
5. Yang, S., Bo, L., Wang, J., Shapiro, L.G.: Unsupervised template learning for fine-grained object recognition. In: Advances in Neural Information Processing Systems (NIPS), pp. 3122–3130 (2012)
6. Yang, L., Luo, P., Loy, C.C., Tang, X.: A large-scale car dataset for fine-grained categorization and verification. In: CVPR (2015)
7. LeCun, Y., Bottou, L., Bengio, Y., Haffner, P.: Gradient based learning applied to document recognition. Proc. IEEE **86**(11), 2278–2324 (1998)
8. Krizhevsky, A., Sutskever, I., Hinton, G.E.: Imagenet classification with deep convolutional neural networks. In: NIPS (2012)
9. Deng, J., Dong, W., Socher, R., Li, L.-J., Li, K., Fei-Fei, L.: ImageNet: a large-scale hierarchical image database. In: CVPR (2009)
10. Simonyan, K., Zisserman, A.: Very deep convolutional networks for large-scale image recognition. In: ICLR (2015)
11. Szegedy, C., Liu, W., Jia, Y., Sermanet, P., Reed, S., Anguelov, D., Erhan, D., Vanhoucke, V., Rabinovich, A.: Going deeper with convolutions. In: CVPR (2015)
12. Girshick, R.B., Donahue, J., Darrell, T., Malik, J.: Rich feature hierarchies for accurate object detection and semantic segmentation. In: CVPR (2014)
13. Long, J., Shelhamer, E., Darrell, T.: Fully convolutional networks for semantic segmentation. In: CVPR (2015)
14. Xie, S., Tu, Z.: Holistically-nested edge detection. In: ICCV (2015)
15. Lin, T.-Y., RoyChowdhury, A., Maji, S.: Bilinear CNN models for fine-grained visual recognition. In: ICCV (2015)
16. Xie, S., Yang, T., Wang, X., Lin, Y.: Hyper-class augmented and regularized deep learning for fine-grained image classification. In: CVPR (2015)
17. He, K., Zhang, X., Ren, S., Sun, J.: Deep residual learning for image recognition. In: CVPR 2016. arXiv:1512.03385. 10 December 2015
18. Yang, S., Ramanan, D.: Multi-scale recognition with DAG-CNNs. In: ICCV (2015)
19. Li, G., Yu, Y.: Visual saliency based on multiscale deep features. In: CVPR (2015)

20. Ma, C., Huang, J.-B., Yang, X., Yang, M.-H.: Hierarchical convolutional features for visual tracking. In: ICCV (2015)
21. Nair, V., Hinton, G.E.: Rectified linear units improve restricted boltzmann machines. In: ICML (2010)
22. Jia, Y., Shelhamer, E., Donahue, J., Karayev, S., Long, J., Girshick, R., Guadarrama, S., Darrell, T.: Caffe: convolutional architecture for fast feature embedding. In: ACM Multimedia, pp. 675–678 (2014)
23. LeCun, Y., Boser, B., Denker, J.S., Henderson, D., Howard, R.E., Hubbard, W., Jackel, L.D.: Backpropagation applied to handwritten zip code recognition. Neural Comput. $1(4)$, 541–551 (1989)
24. Ioffe, S., Szegedy, C.: Batch normalization: accelerating deep network training by reducing internal covariate shift. In: ICML (2015)
25. Hinton, G.E., Srivastava, N., Krizhevsky, A., Sutskever, I., Salakhutdinov, R.R.: Improving neural networks by preventing coadaptation of feature detectors. arXiv:1207.0580 (2012)
26. Krause, M.S.J., Deng, J., Fei-Fei, L.: Collecting a large-scale dataset of fine-grained cars. In: The Second Workshop on Fine-Grained Visual Categorization (2013)
27. Krause, J., Gebru, T., Deng, J., Li, L.-J., Fei-Fei, L.: Learning features and parts for fine-grained recognition. In: IEEE 22nd International Conference on Pattern Recognition (ICPR), pp. 26–33 (2014)
28. Khosla, A., Jayadevaprakash, N., Yao, B., Fei-Fei, L.: Novel dataset for fine-grained image categorization. In: First Workshop on Fine-Grained Visual Categorization (FGVC), IEEE Conference on Computer Vision and Pattern Recognition (CVPR) (2011)
29. Gavves, E., Fernando, B., Snoek, C.G., Smeulders, A.W., Tuytelaars, T.: Local alignments for fine-grained categorization. Int. J. Comput. Vision $111(2)$, 1–22 (2014)
30. Chen, G., Yang, J., Jin, H., Shechtman, E., Brandt, J., Han, T.: Selective pooling vector for fine-grained recognition. In: 2015 IEEE Winter Conference on Applications of Computer Vision (WACV2015)
31. Kanan, C.: Fine-grained object recognition with Gnostic fields. In: 2014 IEEE Winter Conference on Applications of Computer Vision (WACV2014)
32. LeCun, Y., Bengio, Y., Hinton, G.: Deep learning. Nature 521, 436–444 (2015)

Cross-Media Retrieval by Multimodal Representation Fusion with Deep Networks

Jinwei Qi, Xin Huang, and Yuxin Peng[✉]

Institute of Computer Science and Technology, Peking University,
Beijing 100871, China
{qijinwei,huangxin_14,pengyuxin}@pku.edu.cn

Abstract. With the development of computer network, multimedia and digital transmission technology in recent years, the traditional form of information dissemination which mainly depends on text has changed to the multimedia form including texts, images, videos, audios and so on. Under this situation, to meet the growing demand of users for access to multimedia information, cross-media retrieval has become a key problem of research and application. Given queries of any media type, cross-media retrieval can return all relevant media types as results with similar semantics. For measuring the similarity between different media types, it is important to learn better shared representation for multimedia data. Existing methods mainly extract single modal representation for each media type and then learn the cross-media correlations with pairwise similar constraint, which cannot make full use of the rich information within each media type and ignore the dissimilar constraints between different media types. For addressing the above problems, this paper proposes a deep multimodal learning method (DML) for cross-media shared representation learning. First, we adopt two different deep networks for each media type with multimodal learning, which can obtain the high-level semantic representation of single media. Then, a two-pathway network is constructed by jointly modeling the pairwise similar and dissimilar constraints with a contrastive loss to get the shared representation. The experiments are conducted on two widely-used cross-media datasets, which shows the effectiveness of our proposed method. *abstract environment.*

Keywords: Cross-media retrieval · Representation learning · Deep networks

1 Introduction

Nowadays, the Internet has stored various multimedia data, including texts, images, videos, audios, 3D models and so on, influencing everyone's daily life deeply. How to manage and utilize the multimedia more efficiently has become a hot research topic in multimedia field. Traditional multimedia retrieval methods mainly focus on the text retrieval, which require the manual annotations

© Springer Nature Singapore Pte Ltd. 2017
X. Yang and G. Zhai (Eds.): IFTC 2016, CCIS 685, pp. 218–227, 2017.
DOI: 10.1007/978-981-10-4211-9_22

of data and then perform multimedia retrieval by text matching when given keywords. But the low scalability of manual annotation restricts the flexibility of those methods. In order to overcome this disadvantage and realize automatic retrieval, content-based multimedia retrieval has been proposed. Compared with the traditional methods which cannot support to retrieve the relevant data by an image query, content-based methods can search the results directly by feature extraction, similarity computation and similarity ranking.

However, the above methods can only be used for single-media retrieval [9,14,18]. In other words, the retrieval results and user query must have the same media type, which restricts the comprehensiveness and flexibility of information retrieval. To overcome this shortage and make the retrieval results more comprehensive, cross-media retrieval has been proposed. This retrieval method can return the relevant samples with all media types. For example, if you want to search the relevant items to an image, the retrieval results may include texts, images, videos etc. Some of the existing cross-media retrieval methods mainly map data of different media types into one common feature space to get the shared representations, thus the similarity between different media types can be measured. As we known, the cross-media correlations are very complex, and different media types have different feature representations, so it is important to project those features to a common space more effectively and accurately.

In view of the above problems, this paper proposes a deep multimodal learning method (DML) for cross-media shared representation learning. First, we adopt two different deep networks for each media type with multimodal learning, which can obtain the high-level semantic representation of single media. Then, a two-pathway network is constructed by jointly modeling the pairwise similar and dissimilar constraints with a contrastive loss to get the shared representation. The experiment is conducted on two widely-used cross-media datasets, which proves the effectiveness of our proposed method.

2   Related Works

In this section, we briefly review some representative methods of cross-media retrieval based on shared representation learning, which can be divided into two categories. One strategy is to project the data of different media types into one common space with traditional linear projection. The other is based on deep learning, which adopts deep networks to model the correlations between different media types to learn the shared representation. We will describe these two strategies of methods as follows.

2.1   Traditional Cross-Media Shared Representation Learning Methods

Traditional statistical correlation analysis methods learn linear project function for given training pairs, which maximize the pairwise correlations between the projected training pairs. Canonical Correlation Analysis (CCA) [6] is one of the most representative methods, which is a natural solution to learn the shared representation. Specifically, after extracting features for each media type, CCA is adopted to learn the mapping matrices for different media types, which can build a low-dimensional common space where the projected media data has the maximum correlations. Later works, such as Semantic Correlation Matching (SCM) [10] proposed by Rasiwasia et al., attempt to introduce the semantic information on the common space learned by CCA to further improve the performance of cross-media retrieval.

Besides, Cross-modal Factor Analysis (CFA) [7] is an alternative method which minimizes the Frobenius norm between the pairwise data to learn a common space for different media types. The joint graph regularized heterogeneous metric learning (JGRHML) [19] proposed by Zhai et al. uses the data in learned metric space to construct the joint graph regularization, and this work is further improved as joint representation learning (JRL) [20] which proposes a unified framework to jointly model the semantic and correlation information.

2.2 Cross-Media Shared Representation Learning with Deep Networks

Recent years, single-media retrieval and classification have made great progress because of the strong ability of deep neural network (DNN) in feature representation learning. Some representative deep networks such as Stacked Autoencoders (SAE) [15], Deep Belief Network (DBN) [5] and Deep Boltzmann Machines (DBM) [12] are proposed.

Inspired by these, researchers attempt to apply DNN to model the correlations between different media types to perform cross-media retrieval. Bimodal Autoencoders (Bimodal AE) [8] extends the Restricted Boltzmann Machine (RBM), taking features of two media types as input to generate the shared representation at the code layer, which can also reconstruct both two media types at the reconstruction layer. Srivastava et al. [13] propose Multimodal DBN to model the joint distribution over multiple media types to get the shared representation. Besides, Deep Canonical Correlation Analysis (DCCA) [1,17] and Correspondence Autoencoder (Corr-AE) [3] have similar deep architectures composed of two linked networks. DCCA extends CCA to learn two correlated deep encodings, while Corr-AE minimizes the correlation learning error and reconstruction error at the same time to boost the accuracy of cross-media retrieval.

3　Our DML Model

Our DML model consists of two stages. First, we adopt two deep models, DBN and SAE, to obtain two kinds of high-level semantic representation and combine them by a joint RBM to get the separate representation for each media type, which can fully explore the rich semantic information within each media type. Second, a two-pathway network is constructed with the contrastive loss

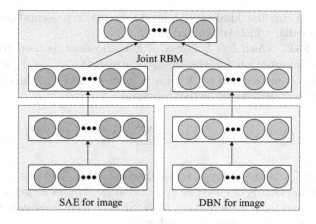

Fig. 1. Network of separate representation learning for image data.

by modeling the pairwise similar and dissimilar constraints to get the shared representation.

Formally, the cross-media dataset is denoted as $D = \{D^i, D^t\}$ which contains two media types, image and text. For image data, $D^i = \{x_p^i, y_p^i\}_{p=1}^n$, $x_p^i \in R^{d^{(i)}}$ denotes the p-th image instance which has $d^{(i)}$ dimension with the corresponding label y_p^i. Similarly, the text data is denoted as $D^t = \{x_p^t, y_p^t\}_{p=1}^n$.

3.1   Multimodal Separate Representation Learning

Two deep models, DBN and SAE, are adopted for multimodal separate representation learning. Specifically, DBN is used to model the distribution over the feature of each media type, and we use SAE to get the high-level semantic representation by minimizing the reconstruction error.

For image data, as shown in Fig. 1, we first use Gaussian RBM [16] to form the two-layer DBN, which models the distribution over the image feature $X^i = \{x_p^i\}$. Here, the RBM model is an undirected graphical model which has visible units v connected to the hidden units h. The following equations define the energy function and joint distribution respectively:

$$E(v, h; \theta) = -a^{\mathrm{T}}v - b^{\mathrm{T}}h - v^{\mathrm{T}}Wh \tag{1}$$

$$P(v, h; \theta) = \frac{1}{Z(\theta)} exp(-E(v, h; \theta)) \tag{2}$$

where the three parameters a, b, W are contained in θ, and $Z(\theta)$ is the normalizing constant. Then DBN model assigns the probability to the input image feature as follows:

$$P(v_i) = \sum_{h^{(1)}, h^{(2)}} P(h^{(2)}, h^{(1)})P(v_i|h^{(1)}) \tag{3}$$

So we can obtain the first kind of high-level semantic representation from DBN for the image media, which is denoted as Y_1^i.

Then, the SAE, which has h layers of autoencoders, is used to model the reconstruction information for the image features $X^i = \{x_p^i\}$, while X_{2h}^i is denoted as the reconstruction of X^i. Each layer of SAE is trained separately by minimizing the following objective function:

$$L(X^i) = L_r(X^i, X_{2h}^i) + \alpha \sum_{p=1}^{h} (\|W_{ie}^p\|_2^2 + \|W_{id}^p\|_2^2) \tag{4}$$

where $L_r(X^i, X_{2h}^i)$ is the average reconstruction error, and the parameters of the activation function is denoted as W_{ie} and W_{id}. So we can get another kind of high-level semantic representation from SAE, which preserves the original characteristic of image features, denoted as Y_2^i.

Finally, we combine the two kinds of high-level representation Y_1^i and Y_2^i for image data by adopting a joint RBM, which can model the joint distribution between them and be defined as follows:

$$P(v_1, v_2) = \sum_{h_1^{(1)}, h_2^{(1)}, h^{(2)}} P(h_1^{(1)}, h_2^{(1)}, h^{(2)}) \times \sum_{h_1^{(1)}} P(v_1 \mid h_1^{(1)}) \times \sum_{h_2^{(1)}} P(v_2 \mid h_2^{(1)}).$$

$$\tag{5}$$

where v_1 and v_2 denote the two kind of representation Y_1^i and Y_2^i. The output of the joint RBM can be collected as the separate representation for image data, which is denoted as S^i.

As for the text data, we also use DBN which contains two layers of Replicated Softmax model [11], and SAE with h layers of autoencoders. Similarly, the separated representation for text can be also collected from the joint RBM, which is denoted as S^t.

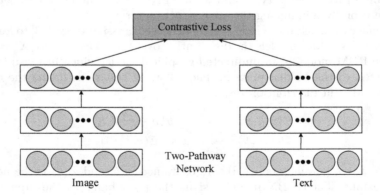

Fig. 2. Two-pathway network for shared representation learning with contrastive loss.

3.2 Two-Pathway Network with Contrastive Loss

As shown in Fig. 2, to learn the shared representation for different media types, we adopt a two-pathway network, which consists of three fully-connected layers on each pathway and a contrastive loss connected on the top of them to train the whole network.

For the training stage, we construct a neighborhood graph $G = (V, E)$, where V denotes the image and text data, and E denotes the similarity matrix, which is constructed according to the labels as follows:

$$E(p,q) = \begin{cases} 1 & y_p^i = y_q^t \\ 0 & y_p^i \neq y_q^t \end{cases} \tag{6}$$

To model the pairwise similar and dissimilar correlations, we consider the following two constraints. First, the distance between image and text which have the same label should be minimized. Second, the distance between image and text which have different labels should be maximized. So the contrastive loss is defined as follows:

$$L_e(p,q) = \begin{cases} \left\| f(s_p^i) - g(s_q^t) \right\|^2 & E(p,q) = 1 \\ max(0, \alpha - \left\| f(s_p^i) - g(s_q^t) \right\|)^2 & E(p,q) = 0 \end{cases} \tag{7}$$

where s_p^i and s_p^t denote the image and text data, and α is set to be the margin parameter. $f(.)$ and $g(.)$ denote the non-linear mapping of the two-pathway network. By applying back propagation, we can get the optimized shared representations $f(S^i)$ and $g(S^t)$, denoted as M^i and M^t, which can preserve the pairwise similar and dissimilar correlations for further boosting the cross-media retrieval.

4 Experiment

In this section, we will introduce the experiment to show the effectiveness of our method. In the experiment, the cross-media retrieval has two tasks: retrieve text by image query (Image→Text) and retrieval image by text query (Text→Image).

4.1 Dataset

Two datasets Wikipedia and NUS-WIDE-10k are chosen for the experiment, which are widely used in cross-media retrieval. We will briefly introduce these two datasets as follows:

Wikipedia dataset [10] is widely used in the cross-media retrieval problem. The dataset contains a total of 2866 image–text pairs and some examples are shown in Fig. 3. It is randomly split into a training set of 2173 documents, a testing set of 462 documents and a validation set of 231 documents. In terms of feature extraction, we extract the feature of images and texts respectively

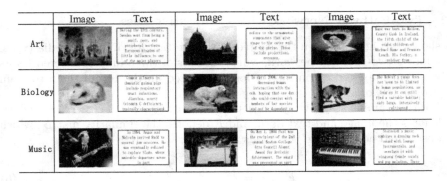

Fig. 3. Examples from Wikipedia dataset.

with the method illustrated in [3]. For images, the feature is the concatenation of three parts: 1000 dimensional Pyramid Histogram of Words (PHOW), 512 dimensional GIST, and 784 dimensional MPEG-7. For texts, the representation is 3000 dimensional bag of words vector.

NUS-WIDE-10k dataset [2] contains totally 10,000 image–text pairs divided into 10 classes, which is selected from NUS-WIDE dataset. 1000 image–text pairs are contained in each class. The image is organized as follows: 64 dimensional color histogram, 144 dimensional color correlogram, 73 dimensional edge direction histogram, 128 dimensional wavelet texture, 225 dimensional block-wise color moments and 500 dimensional SIFT-based bag of words features, which has totally 1134 dimension. And 1000 dimensional bag of words feature is used to represent the text data. The dataset is also randomly split into three parts: 8000 documents as training set, 1000 documents as test set, and 1000 documents as validation set.

4.2   Compared Methods and Evaluation Metric

In the experiment, we compare our proposed method with 5 existing cross-media retrieval methods, which will be briefly introduced as follows.

- **Canonical Correlation Analysis** [6]: CCA learns mapping matrix for each media type to maximize the pairwise correlation in the common space.
- **Cross-modal Factor Analysis** [7]: CFA learns a common space for different media types by minimizing the Frobenius norm between the pairwise cross-media data.
- **Kernel Canonical Correlation Analysis** [4]: KCCA adopts kernel functions to project the data into the common space, which is a non-linear extension of CCA. In the experiment, we choose polynomial kernel (Poly) and radial basis function (RBF) as the kernel functions.
- **Bimodal Autoencoders** [8]: Bimodal AE generates the shared representation at the code layer and also has reconstruction layers with the ability to reconstruct both two media types.

- **Multimodal Deep Belief Network** [13]: Multimodal DBN first adopts two separate DBN to model the distribution over each media type and then uses a joint RBM to learn the shared representation.

The retrieval results will be evaluated using the mean average precision (MAP) score, which is widely used in information retrieval. The MAP score for a set of queries is the mean of the average precision (AP) for each query.

4.3   Experiment Results

Now we will show the experiment results of our proposed method compared with 5 existing cross-media retrieval methods and give brief analysis for them. Tables 1 and 2 show the MAP scores of two cross-media retrieval tasks and their average results on Wikipedia and NUS-WIDE-10k dataset. We can see that our DML method outperforms all the compared methods and achieves significant improvement on the average result.

As for the traditional cross-media retrieval methods, CFA outperforms CCA by minimizing the Frobenius norm to project the pairwise data into one common space. And KCCA achieves the best results among the three traditional methods because kernel functions are used to effectively model the high nonlinear characteristics of multimedia data. Then, for the two methods based on DNN, the

Table 1. The MAP scores on Wikipedia dataset.

Method	Image→Text	Text→Image	Average
CCA	0.124	0.120	0.122
CFA	0.236	0.211	0.224
KCCA(Poly)	0.200	0.185	0.193
KCCA(RBF)	0.245	0.219	0.232
Bimodal AE	0.236	0.208	0.222
Multimodal DBN	0.149	0.150	0.150
DML	**0.255**	**0.285**	**0.270**

Table 2. The MAP scores on NUS-WDIE-10k Dataset.

Method	Image→Text	Text→Image	Average
CCA	0.120	0.120	0.120
CFA	0.211	0.188	0.200
KCCA(Poly)	0.150	0.149	0.150
KCCA(RBF)	0.232	0.213	0.223
Bimodal AE	0.159	0.172	0.166
Multimodal DBN	0.158	0.130	0.144
DML	**0.261**	**0.278**	**0.270**

performance of both Bimodal AE and Multimodal DBN are not so good because they directly use single modal representation for each media type as input and only model the cross-media correlations with pairwise similar constraint. Additionally, Bimodal AE minimizes the reconstruction error, which makes it perform better than Multimodal DBN. Compared with the above methods, Our DML method first uses two different deep networks for each media type with multimodal learning, which can obtain the high-level semantic representation of single media. Then, a two-pathway network is constructed by jointly modeling the pairwise similar and dissimilar constraints with a contrastive loss to get the shared representation. Our proposed method learns the cross-media shared representation with deep multimodal learning method, which can further improve the accuracy of cross-media retrieval.

5   Conclusion

This paper has proposed a deep multimodal learning method (DML) for cross-media shared representation learning. First, two different deep networks are adopted for each media type with multimodal learning, which can obtain the high-level semantic representation of single media. Then, we design a two-pathway network by jointly modeling the pairwise similar and dissimilar constraints with a contrastive loss to get the shared representation. The experiment is conducted on two widely-used cross-media datasets, which proves the effectiveness of our proposed method. For the future work, we attempt to apply semi-supervised learning into our framework to further exploit the unlabeled data for improving the effectiveness of cross-media retrieval.

Acknowledgments. This work was supported by National Hi-Tech Research and Development Program of China (863 Program) under Grant 2014AA015102, and National Natural Science Foundation of China under Grants 61371128 and 61532005.

References

1. Andrew, G., Arora, R., Bilmes, J.A., Livescu, K.: Deep canonical correlation analysis. In: International Conference on Machine Learning (ICML), pp. 1247–1255 (2013)
2. Chua, T.-S., Tang, J., Hong, R., Li, H., Luo, Z., Zheng, Y.: Nus-wide: a real-world web image database from national university of singapore. In: ACM International Conference on Image and Video Retrieval (ACM-CIVR), pp. 1–9 (2009)
3. Feng, F., Wang, X., Li, R.: Cross-modal retrieval with correspondence autoencoder. In: ACM International Conference on Multimedia (ACM-MM), pp. 7–16 (2014)
4. Hardoon, D.R., Szedmák, S., Shawe-Taylor, J.: Canonical correlation analysis: an overview with application to learning methods. Neural Comput. **16**(12), 2639–2664 (2004)
5. Hinton, G.E., Osindero, S., Teh, Y.W.: A fast learning algorithm for deep belief nets. Neural Comput. **18**(7), 1527–1554 (2006)

6. Hotelling, H.: Relations between two sets of variates. Biometrika **28**, 321–377 (1936)
7. Li, D., Dimitrova, N., Li, M., Sethi, I.K.: Multimedia content processing through cross-modal association. In: ACM International Conference on Multimedia (ACM-MM), pp. 604–611 (2003)
8. Ngiam, J., Khosla, A., Kim, M., Nam, J., Lee, H., Ng, A.Y.: Multimodal deep learning. In: International Conference on Machine Learning (ICML), pp. 689–696 (2011)
9. Peng, Y., Ngo, C.-W.: Clip-based similarity measure for query-dependent clip retrieval and video summarization. IEEE Trans. Circ. Syst. Video Technol. (TCSVT) **16**(5), 612–627 (2006)
10. Rasiwasia, N., Costa Pereira, J., Coviello, E., Doyle, G., Lanckriet, G.R.G., Levy, R., Vasconcelos, N.: A new approach to cross-modal multimedia retrieval. In: ACM International Conference on Multimedia (ACM-MM), pp. 251–260 (2010)
11. Salakhutdinov, R., Hinton, G.E.: Replicated softmax: an undirected topic model. In: Advances in Neural Information Processing Systems (NIPS), pp. 1607–1614 (2009)
12. Salakhutdinov, R., Hinton, G.E.: An efficient learning procedure for deep Boltzmann machines. Neural Comput. **24**(8), 1967–2006 (2012)
13. Srivastava, N., Salakhutdinov, R.: Learning representations for multimodal data with deep belief nets. In: International Conference on Machine Learning (ICML) Workshop (2012)
14. Typke, R., Wiering, F., Veltkamp, R.C.: A survey of music information retrieval systems. In: The International Society for Music Information Retrieval (ISMIR), pp. 153–160 (2005)
15. Vincent, P., Larochelle, H., Bengio, Y., Manzagol, P.-A.: Extracting and composing robust features with denoising autoencoders. In: International Conference on Machine Learning (ICML), pp. 1096–1103 (2008)
16. Welling, M., Rosen-Zvi, M., Hinton, G.E.: Exponential family harmoniums with an application to information retrieval. In: Advances in Neural Information Processing Systems (NIPS), pp. 1481–1488 (2004)
17. Yan, F., Mikolajczyk, K.: Deep correlation for matching images and text. In: IEEE Conference on Computer Vision and Pattern Recognition (CVPR), pp. 3441–3450 (2015)
18. Jie, Y., Tian, Q.: Semantic subspace projection and its applications in image retrieval. IEEE Trans. Circ. Syst. Video Technol. (TCSVT) **18**(4), 544–548 (2008)
19. Zhai, X., Peng, Y., Xiao, J.: Heterogeneous metric learning with joint graph regularization for cross-media retrieval. In: AAAI Conference on Artificial Intelligence (AAAI), pp. 1198–1204 (2013)
20. Zhai, X., Peng, Y.X., Xiao, J.: Learning cross-media joint representation with sparse and semi-supervised regularization. IEEE Trans. Circ. Syst. Video Technol. (TCSVT) **24**(6), 965–978 (2014)

Audio Processing

Blind Estimation of Spectral Standard Deviation from Room Impulse Response for Reverberation Level Recognition Based on Linear Prediction

Sai Ma[✉] and Xi Xie[✉]

Communication University of China, Beijing, China
{saima,cici.xie}@cuc.edu.cn

Abstract. Reverberation is an important factor affecting speech quality and intelligibility, Reverberation Time (RT) and Direct-to-Reverberant Ratio (DRR) are the primary parameters for reverberation strength judgement, spectral standard deviation (SSD) from room impulse response (RIR) and DRR exist as monotonic relationships to some extent which means that SSD can also be an indicator of reverberation characteristics. We propose a blind estimation of spectral standard deviation (BESSD) that is obtained directly from reverberant speech signals. Experiments prove BESSD can be used as an index for male reverberation level recognition.

Keywords: Reverberation · Linear prediction · Room impulse response · Direct-to-reverberant ratio

1 Introduction

When speech signals propagate in an enclosed environment, they are distorted by the features of room acoustics, including room dimension, reflection path and sound absorption of the enclosure which make them reverberate. Reverberation has an important influence on perceived speech quality and intelligibility. The image-source model (ISM) [1] represents an essential practical application for reverberant speech signal processing technologies. Numerous reverberation parameters can be predicted from room impulse response (RIR) generated with the ISM, e.g. Direct-to-Reverberant Ratio (DRR) [2] and Reverberation Time (RT) [3]. ISM approach has been foundational to a broad domain of related research on acoustic problems, including blind source separation [4], channel identification and equalization [5], acoustic source localization and tracking [6], speech enhancement [7], and speech recognition [8]. Furthermore, RT and DRR are significant indicators of room reverberation characteristics. Sabine formula [9] is widely used for RT prediction and is based on room geometrical features. In [10], an estimate of DRR is made from a multi-channel system with an arbitrary number of microphones with the selection of an appropriate beamformer. Falk proposed an estimator by using temporal dynamics information for blind

© Springer Nature Singapore Pte Ltd. 2017
X. Yang and G. Zhai (Eds.): IFTC 2016, CCIS 685, pp. 231–241, 2017.
DOI: 10.1007/978-981-10-4211-9_23

measurement of room RT and DRR [11]. In addition, blind estimation of RT by the kurtosis of linear prediction (LP) residuals was introduced in [12], while LP based methods have also been successfully used for reverberation suppression [13,14].

In this paper we propose a blind measurement for the ground truth of spectral standard deviation from room impulse response, which indicates reverberation intensity of the environment. The paper is organized as follows: In Sect. 2, we simulate human vocal tract model by LP coefficients. A reverberant speech signal database is synthesized in Sect. 3. In Sect. 4, we illustrate the algorithm of blind estimation of spectral standard deviation (BESSD), and experiments are done in Sect. 5 which show how BESSD can be as a cue for reverberation level recognition. Conclusions are drawn in Sect. 6.

2   Vocal Tract Model

LP analysis constitute the source-filter production model of speech. The filter is considered to be an all-pole filter, and the source is assumed to be a periodic pulse train for voiced speech or white noise for unvoiced speech. According to the human speech generation mechanism, these all-pole filters can be used to model the vocal tract. LP analysis is used to obtain all-pole filter parameters to characterize the shape of vocal tract spectrum.

We perform LP analysis on a segment (with 25 ms Hamming window) of a clean speech signal. Adapting commonly used LP analysis methods: autocorrelation, covariance and lattice [15], we compared variation in prediction error with LP analysis ordered by Normalized Mean Square Error (NMSE). Empirical results shown in Fig. 1. Identify autocorrelation as the LP analysis method which has a lower NMSE.

In order to get sufficient frequency domain sampling of the vocal tract frequency response, we detect pitch frequency of every frame, and choose the one

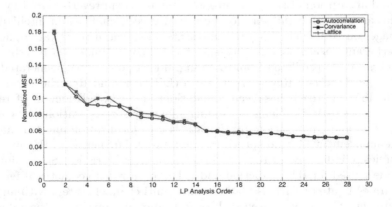

Fig. 1. Prediction error comparison

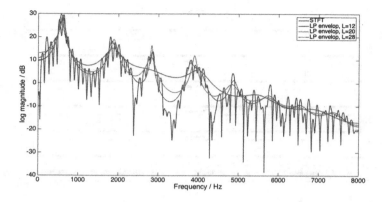

Fig. 2. STFT and LP envelop for selected frame

around 100 Hz. For 16 kHz sampled speech, we used the LP analysis order $L = 12$, 20, 28. Fig. 2 depicts short-time Fourier transform (STFT) for selected frames, and associated LP envelops which are also indicative of the vocal tract spectrum.

3 Database Description

Taking the three sets of LP coefficients from the above analysis, and implementing an all-pole filter for each, respectively. Three unique vocal tract models are obtained.

3.1 Synthesized Speech Signals

Synthesize voiced and unvoiced speech signals were then processed using these filters. For voiced speech, the all-pole filter was excited with a periodic pulse train wherein consecutive pulses are separated by the pitch period. Synthesis over a range of pitch frequencies, e.g. 50, 80, 120, 180, 250, 350 Hz, was conducted in order to cover most of the range of human pitch [16]. For unvoiced speech, we excite the filter using white noise. The first 50 ms of excitation pulses are described in Fig. 3.

To make each synthesized speech long enough (e.g. around 5 s), the entire file would have only the active speech, and no pauses. There would be a total of $3 * 7 = 21$ files. The all-pole filter has zero-state at time zero. We omit the onset and decay of the all-pole filter from the synthesized signals, for e.g., by starting to collect samples from the all-pole filter only after running it for 50 ms and stop collecting samples from it at time $= 4.55$ s.

3.2 Room Reverberation Property

We use the image method to generate different room impulse response (RIR). Reverberation Time (RT) is roughly a function of the room size (for reflection

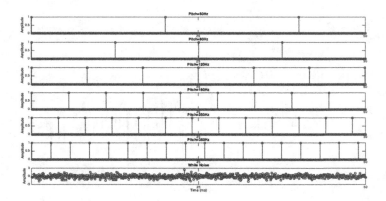

Fig. 3. Excitation signals for synthesized voiced and unvoiced speech signals

constant) but not the source-microphone distances (SMDs), taking three different RTs, (e.g. 300 ms, 600 ms and 1000 ms). Table 1 illustrates a number of SMDs which make the direct-to-reverberant energy ratio (DRR) span from 15 to -15 dB, where the room dimensions (length * width * height) $= 9 * 4 * 6$ m^3. Therefore, 33 room impulse response are generated. DRR comparison of these room impulse response are shown in Fig. 4.

Table 1. SMD and corresponding DRR

RT $= 300$ ms		RT $= 600$ ms		RT $= 1000$ ms	
SMD (m)	DRR (dB)	SMD (m)	DRR (dB)	SMD (m)	DRR (dB)
0.174	15.0403	0.101	15.0083	0.072	15.0710
0.262	12.0170	0.151	12.0281	0.105	12.0789
0.387	9.0259	0.217	9.0200	0.155	9.0290
0.578	6.0290	0.315	6.0321	0.219	6.0517
0.857	3.0026	0.456	3.0044	0.314	3.0279
1.275	0.0030	0.647	0.0183	0.466	0.0196
1.877	-3.0042	0.954	-3.0067	0.645	-3.0011
2.848	-6.0006	1.376	-6.0011	0.945	-6.0007
4.580	-9.0420	1.980	-9.0121	1.360	-9.0273
6.962	-12.0011	2.831	-12.0080	1.867	-12.0033
7.999	-15.0290	3.985	-15.0254	2.806	-15.1267

We perform convolution to produce reverberated speech signals [17]. With the above procedure, $21 * 33 = 693$ reverberant speech files are synthesized, and only use the first 3 s of the reverberant speech for analysis. This is the database for the following experiments.

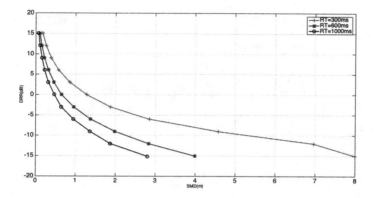

Fig. 4. DRR comparison of simulated room

4   Algorithm

4.1   Spectral Standard Deviation (SSD) from Room Impulse Response

The reverberant speech signals are obtained by

$$x(n) = s(n) * h(n) \tag{1}$$

where $s(n)$ is synthesized speech signal, $h(n)$ is RIR for the specific room, and $*$ indicates convolution.

First, spectral standard deviation (SSD) is calculated from the magnitude frequency response of the RIRs generated in Sect. 3. N points discrete fourier transform of $h(n)$ is,

$$H(k) = DFT[h(n)] = \sum_{n=0}^{N-1} h(n) W_N^{kn}, \quad 0 \leq k \leq N - 1 \tag{2}$$

note power spectrum of $H(k)$,

$$P(k) = |H(k)|^2, \quad 0 \leq k \leq N - 1 \tag{3}$$

corresponding SSD in logarithm is,

$$SSD = \sqrt{\frac{1}{N} \sum_{k=0}^{N-1} (10 \log_{10} P(k) - \mu)^2} \tag{4}$$

$$\mu = \frac{\sum_{k=0}^{N-1} 10 \log_{10} P(k)}{N} \tag{5}$$

The relationship of RIRs frequency response to direct-to-reverberant ratio is illustrated in Fig. 5, in which we randomly choose two cases at the same Reverberation Time (RT = 300 ms). The degree of RIRs frequency response fluctuate

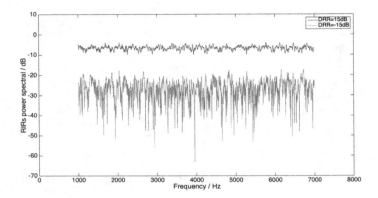

Fig. 5. RIRs frequency response

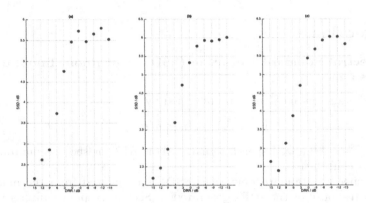

Fig. 6. SSD vs. DRR. (a) RT = 300 ms. (b) RT = 600 ms. (c) RT = 1000 ms

with different DRR values which is in accordance with the results in [18]. SSD measures how much the frequency response fluctuates around a constant value, apparently, the top plot has a smaller SSD than the bottom plot.

Computing the SSDs from these RIRs, the relevance between SSD versus DRR at RT = 300 ms, RT = 600 ms and RT = 1000 ms are shown in Fig. 6. SSD is calculated directly from room impulse response, according to the above analysis, we can see SSD increases monotonically with the decrease of DDR, which appears to saturate at roughly 6 dB as DRR drops below 0.

Focusing on the region DRR > 0 dB, SSD is thus considered to be a property of room reverberation, the goal then, is to blindly estimate SSD from speech signals that have been reverberated by the room.

4.2   Blind Estimation of Spectral Standard Deviation (BESSD)

The original speech signal $x(n)$ discrete fourier transform is,

$$X(k) = DFT[x(n)] = \sum_{n=0}^{N-1} x(n)W_N^{kn}, \quad 0 \le k \le N-1 \qquad (6)$$

while the power spectrum of $X(k)$ is,

$$Q(k) = |X(k)|^2, \quad 0 \le k \le N-1 \qquad (7)$$

By LP analysis model, $x(n)$ and excitation signal $u(n)$ are in the equation,

$$x(n) = \sum_{i=1}^{p} a_i x(n-i) + Gu(n) \qquad (8)$$

the z transform is,

$$X(z) = \frac{G}{1 - \sum_{i=1}^{p} a_i z^{-i}} U(z) \qquad (9)$$

substitue z by $e^{j\omega}$,

$$X(e^{j\omega}) = \frac{G}{1 - \sum_{i=1}^{p} a_i e^{-ji\omega}} \cdot U(e^{j\omega}) \qquad (10)$$

$u(n)$ is the excitation signal, it would be periodic pulses or white noise, therefore, its spectrum, $U(e^{j\omega})$, is to some extent a flat spectrum, so that the signal spectrum $X(e^{j\omega})$ could be represented by the model transfer function (where G is constant),

$$X(e^{j\omega}) = \frac{G}{1 - \sum_{i=1}^{p} a_i e^{-ji\omega}} \qquad (11)$$

Let $\widehat{Q(e^{j\omega})}$ express the power spectrum of LP modeled speech signal,

$$\widehat{Q(e^{j\omega})} = |X(e^{j\omega})|^2 = \frac{G^2}{|1 - \sum_{i=1}^{p} a_i e^{-ji\omega}|^2} \qquad (12)$$

and sampling the power spectrum in frequency domain by $\omega = \frac{2\pi}{N}k$,

$$\widehat{Q(k)} = Q(\widehat{\frac{2\pi}{N}k}) = \left| X\left(\frac{2\pi}{N}k\right) \right|^2 = \frac{G^2}{|1 - \sum_{i=1}^{p} a_i e^{-ji\frac{2\pi}{N}k}|^2}, \quad k = 0, 1, ..., N-1 \qquad (13)$$

we transform to logarithm and take the difference with power spectrum of original speech signal discrete fourier transform,

$$\varepsilon^2 = \frac{1}{|R|} \sum_{k \in R} (10\log_{10}(\widehat{Q(k)}) - 10\log_{10}(Q(k)))^2 \qquad (14)$$

Table 2. BESSD analysis groups

1	RT = 300 ms, BESSD LP analysis order M = 12
2	RT = 300 ms, BESSD LP analysis order M = 20
3	RT = 300 ms, BESSD LP analysis order M = 28
4	RT = 600 ms, BESSD LP analysis order M = 12
5	RT = 600 ms, BESSD LP analysis order M = 20
6	RT = 600 ms, BESSD LP analysis order M = 28
7	RT = 1000 ms, BESSD LP analysis order M = 12
8	RT = 1000 ms, BESSD LP analysis order M = 20
9	RT = 1000 ms, BESSD LP analysis order M = 28

R refers to the frequency range of the spectrum. This can be calculated for e.g., with a starting frequency of $f_1 = 150$ Hz (which contains no more than 5% of the total energy), and ending at $f_2 = 7000$ Hz (which covers more than 95% of the total energy) when sampling frequency is 16 kHz, and using the first half for computation because of the symmetrical characteristic of the spectrum.

Let,

$$\varepsilon^{*2} = \min(\varepsilon^2) \tag{15}$$

and then we define blind estimation of spectral standard deviation,

$$BESSD = \sqrt{\varepsilon^{*2}} \tag{16}$$

We perform LP analysis on the reverberant database, using the same analysis window and BESSD LP analysis order $M = L$ as applied in Sect. 2, in order to reduce the number of combinations. Table 2 divides the database to 9 groups according to their Reverberation Time (RT) and BESSD LP analysis order M.

5   Experiments

5.1   Pearson Correlation Coefficients

Using Pearson correlation coefficients to measure the strength of a linear association between SSD and BESSD, and calculated by pitch frequency for every group as illustrated in Fig. 7. Obviously, there is a linear relation between SSD and BESSD for pitch frequency = 50, 80 and 120 Hz which cover most of male pitch frequencies and for white noise.

Figure 8 shows SSD and BESSD scatter at reverberant speech signal pitch frequency = 50, 80, 120 Hz and white noise, respectively.

5.2   Relation Between BESSD and DRR at Linear Condition

For RT = 300 ms, 600 ms and 1000 ms, BESSD LP analysis order M = 12, 20 and 28, Fig. 9 describe the relation between BESSD and DRR at pitch frequency = 50, 80, 120 Hz and white noise which is similar to the relation between SSD and DRR in Fig. 6.

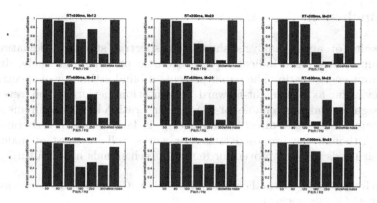

Fig. 7. Pearson correlation coefficients between SSD and BESSD. (a) RT = 300 ms, BESSD LP analysis order M = 12, 20, 28. (b) RT = 600 ms, BESSD LP analysis order M = 12, 20, 28. (c) RT = 1000 ms, BESSD LP analysis order M = 12, 20, 28.

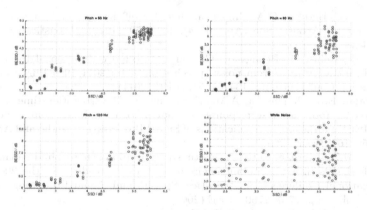

Fig. 8. SSD and BESSD scatter at linear condition

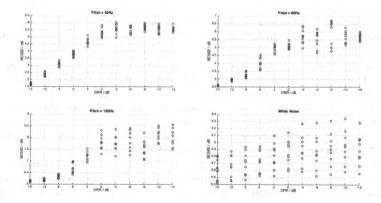

Fig. 9. BESSD vs. DRR at linear condition

6   Conclusion

The results of above analysis show that spectral standard deviation from room impulse response indicates room acoustic parameter, namely, direct-to-reverberant energy ratio. The paper presents a blind estimator of spectral standard deviation as a straight-forward computation performed on reverberant speech signals, and it is reliable for room reverberation level measurement under the circumstances that direct sound energy is larger than reverberant sound energy. Although the proposed estimator works well for most of male speech signals, it needs to be improved for female speech signals in the future.

Acknowledgments. The authors thank Prof. W.-Y. Chan for his guidance, assistance and support for this research.

References

1. Allen, J.B., Berkley, D.A.: Image method for efficiently simulating small-room acoustics. J. Acoust. Soc. Am. **65**(4), 943–950 (1979). Acoustical Society of America
2. Jeub, M., Nelke, C., Beaugeant, C., Vary, P.: Blind estimation of the coherent-to-diffuse energy ratio from noisy speech signals. In: 2011 19th European Signal Processing Conference, pp. 1347–1351. IEEE (2011)
3. Lehmann, E.A., Johansson, A.M., Nordholm, S.: Reverberation-time prediction method for room impulse responses simulated with the image-source model. In: 2007 IEEE Workshop on Applications of Signal Processing to Audio and Acoustics, pp. 159–162. IEEE (2007)
4. Ikram, M.Z., Morgan, D.R.: A Multiresolution approach to blind separation of speech signals in a reverberant environment. In: Proceedings of the 2001 IEEE International Conference on Acoustics, Speech, and Signal Processing (ICASSP 2001), vol. 5, pp. 2757–2760. IEEE (2001)
5. Radlovic, B.D., Williamson, R.C., Kennedy, R.A.: Equalization in an acoustic reverberant environment: robustness results. IEEE Trans. Speech Audio Process. **8**(3), 311–319 (2000). IEEE
6. Lehmann, E.A., Johansson, A.M.: Particle filter with integrated voice activity detection for acoustic source tracking. EURASIP J. Adv. Sig. Process. **2007**(1), 1–11 (2006). Springer
7. Aarabi, P., Shi, G.: Phase-based dual-microphone robust speech enhancement. IEEE Trans. Syst. Man Cybern. Part B (Cybern.) **34**(4), 1763–1773 (2004). IEEE
8. Palomäki, K.J., Brown, G.J., Wang, D.: A binaural processor for missing data speech recognition in the presence of noise and small-room reverberation. Speech Commun. **43**(4), 361–378 (2004). Elsevier
9. Joyce, W.B.: Sabine's reverberation time and ergodic auditoriums. J. Acoust. Soc. Am. **58**(3), 643–655 (1975). Acoustical Society of America
10. Eaton, J., Moore, A.H., Naylor, P.A., Skoglund, J.: Direct-to-reverberant ratio estimation using a null-steered beamformer. In: 2015 IEEE International Conference on Acoustics, Speech and Signal Processing (ICASSP), pp. 46–50. IEEE (2015)
11. Falk, T.H., Chan, W.-Y.: Temporal dynamics for blind measurement of room acoustical parameters. IEEE Trans. Instrum. Meas. **59**(4), 978–989 (2010). IEEE

12. Gillespie, B.W., Malvar, H.S., Florêncio, D.A.F.: Speech dereverberation via maximum-kurtosis subband adaptive filtering. In: Proceedings of the 2001 IEEE International Conference on Acoustics, Speech, and Signal Processing (ICASSP 2001), vol. 6, pp. 3701–3704. IEEE (2001)

13. Gaubitch, N.D., Ward, D.B., Naylor, P.A.: Statistical analysis of the autoregressive modeling of reverberant speech. J. Acoust. Soc. Am. **120**(6), 4031–4039 (2006). Acoustical Society of America

14. Yegnanarayana, B., Murthy, P.S.: Enhancement of reverberant speech using LP residual signal. IEEE Trans. Speech Audio Process. **8**(3), 267–281 (2000). IEEE

15. Vaidyanathan, P.P.: The theory of linear prediction. Synth. Lect. Sig. Process. **2**(1), 1–184 (2007). Morgan & Claypool Publishers

16. Peterson, G.E., Barney, H.L.: Control methods used in a study of the vowels. J. Acoust. Soc. Am. **24**(2), 175–184 (1952). Acoustical Society of America

17. Habets, E.A.P., Gannot, S., Cohen, I.: Late reverberant spectral variance estimation based on a statistical model. IEEE Sig. Process. Lett. **16**(9), 770–773 (2009). IEEE

18. Jetzt, J.J.: Critical distance measurement of rooms from the sound energy spectral response. J. Acoust. Soc. Am. **65**(5), 1204–1211 (1979). Acoustical Society of America

Deep Learning Based Language Modeling for Domain-Specific Speech Recognition

Jing Zhu, Xinwei Gong, and Guilin Chen$^{(\boxtimes)}$

Shanghai YoungTone Technologies Co. Ltd., Shanghai, China
zhujing@sjtu.edu.cn,
{xinwei.gong,guilin.chen}@youngtone.cn

Abstract. Recurrent neural network (RNN) applied as language model of automatic speech recognition (ASR) can capture all previous history of word sequences and is theoretically superior to the N-gram language model. RNN has successfully applied in acoustic model of ASR and greatly improved the performance. In this paper, we combine RNN and N-gram language models and apply to a domain-specific speech recognition task. A rectification mechanism was introduced during RNN language model training procedure to prevent early stop and tried to deal with gradient vanishing issue. For Chinese word segmentation, a universal algorithm was designed for identifying proper name automatically, which improves word segmentation accuracy by 2.0–3.0%. Our experimental results show the new ASR system combing N-gram language model and domain-specific neural network language model can achieve lower word error rate than that with standard N-gram language model significantly.

Keywords: Recurrent neural network · Language model · Automatic speech recognition · Deep learning

1 Introduction

The goal of automatic speech recognition (ASR) research is to address the problem of automatic transcription of speech by building systems that map from an acoustic signal to a string of words. ASR has been investigated for several decades and its performance has been improved steadily. Both acoustic model and language model are important components of a modern ASR system. Deep-learning-based acoustic modeling method has improved the performance of ASR system significantly [1]. As for language model, N-gram language modeling is a mainstream modeling technology in ASR system development and has dominated this area over the past two decades. Recently, several researchers have reported promising results for reducing speech recognition error further by combining N-gram language model and deep neural network language model, for instance recurrent neural network language model (RNNLM).

In this paper, we investigated the performance of ASR system with combined N-gram language model and RNNLM, especially for domain-specific speech recognition and transcription task. The current target domain is banking industry. During RNNLM training procedure, we introduced rectification mechanism to prevent early stop and tried to deal with gradient vanishing issue. We conducted a series of experiments on

© Springer Nature Singapore Pte Ltd. 2017
X. Yang and G. Zhai (Eds.): IFTC 2016, CCIS 685, pp. 242–251, 2017.
DOI: 10.1007/978-981-10-4211-9_24

general-purpose N-gram language model, domain-specific N-gram language model interpolation and RNNLM rescoring to evaluate their performance, respectively. Especially for Chinese word segmentation, we designed a universal algorithm for identifying proper name automatically, which improves word segmentation accuracy by 2.0–3.0%. We will present our work in great detail in the following sections.

2 Chinese Word Segmentation

For Chinese Mandarin ASR system, word-based language model always demonstrates higher performance than character-based one to some degree when language model size is comparable. The difference can range from 1.0–3.0% in terms of word error rate (WER). Hence, it has become a common way for industrial community to build up word-based language model nowadays. One potential reason is that most of the frequently used Chinese characters are polyphonic while polyphonic Chinese words are rarely seen. For example, "中" is polyphonic while "中国" is not polyphonic. Considering that there is no explicit boundary between Chinese words at text level, we regard word segmentation as one of fundamental tasks in a Chinese Mandarin ASR system and other Chinese natural language processing (NLP) systems.

Strictly speaking, Chinese word segmentation is still an open issue due to its inherent hardness. Overall, the main challenges come from two aspects. One is to resolve ambiguity (about 1%); the other is to identify non-standard word (NSW, about 3–4%) such as proper name and abbreviation etc. For the former, resolution accuracy of about 90% can be achieved on average. For the latter, people classified NSW into different types and investigated several methods for each type, respectively. Generally speaking, NSW includes person name, place name, organization name, brand name and abbreviation etc.

We studied a general-purpose method for identifying NSW automatically, which combines bi-gram and hidden Markov model (HMM).

2.1 Bi-gram Model for Single-Character Word

Firstly, we employ bi-gram to model the probability that two consecutive single–character words form a word pair. Intuitively speaking, if the probability of two words' co-occurrence is very large, the possibility of forming an OOV word by their combination is relatively low, which helps to avoid plausible combinations, like Chinese word "family (家)" and "have (有)". The following calculation is used to approximate this probability of co-occurrence.

$$P(W_j|W_{j-1}) \approx \frac{C(W_{j-1}, W_j)}{C(W_{j-1})} \tag{1}$$

Where $C(W_{j-1}, W_j)$ is the number of co-occurrences of single-character words W_{j-1} and W_j in text; $C(W_{j-1})$ is the number of occurrences of single-character word W_{j-1} in text.

2.2   HMM for Character

HMM is a kind of statistical model, which can be employed to choose the optimum state consequence for given observation consequence according to an optimization criteria and has been used successfully in speech recognition. Recently, many researchers have applied it to the area of natural language processing, such as part-of-speech tagging and semantic tagging. For discrete observation consequence $O = o_1 o_2 \cdots o_T$, the elements of HMM are defined as follows [2]:

N: the number of states in the model
$Q = \{i\}$: state set, where $1 \leq i \leq N$
M: different number of observations for each state, namely the size of discrete symbol table $V = \{v_k\}$, $1 \leq k \leq M$.
$A = \{a_{ij}\}$: state transition matrix, where $a_{ij} = P[q_{t+1} = j | q_t = i]$, $1 \leq i,j \leq N$, q_t represents the state at time instant t
$B = \{b_j(k)\}$: observational probability distribution matrix, where $b_j(k) = P[o_t = V_k | q_t = j]$.
$\pi = \{\pi_i\}$: initial probability distribution matrix

In the process of automatic identification, we put the focus on the capability of word forming in NSW for each character, and on its capability of word-forming singly. The practice shows that if the proportion of a character serves as a single-character word is very high, then its probability of occurrence in NSW is relatively low, such as "of (的)"、"yes (是)". This distribution information can be quantitatively reflected via probability. By contrast, rule set mainly provides qualitative knowledge, which lacks detailed description. Specifically speaking, we regard Chinese character set as V, and define the following four states according to situations where a character forms word separately or occurs in NSW: state 1 for single-character word(singleton); state 2 for word initial; state 3 for word medial and state 4 for word final.

Therefore, the state set $Q = \{1, 2, 3, 4\}$

The state transition matrix $A = \{a_{ij}\}$, $1 \leq i \leq N, 1 \leq j \leq N$. If $a_{ij} = 0$, then it means that valid transition exists; if $a_{ij} = -\infty$, it means that the corresponding state transition is invalid.

2.3   The Training Procedure

We follow the standard procedure to estimate bi-gram probability and HMM parameters [3, 4].

2.4   The Automatic Identification of NSW

After the baseline segmentation (lexicon-based bi-directional maximum matching), for $T(T \geq 2)$ consecutive single-character word sequence, $H_1 H_2 \cdots \cdots H_T$, we can treat them as an observation of HMM, and build up a trellis accordingly, as shown in Fig. 1.

Now, we convert the problem of automatic identification of NSW into a search problem. Since each arc in the trellis has a weight, we can choose an optimum state

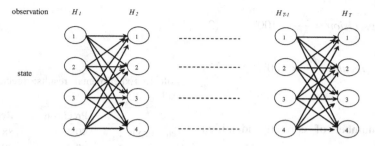

Fig. 1. Observation and state transition of HMM

sequence according to certain optimization standard. The common search methods include Viterbi and Forward-Backward, etc. Considering that there is no circle in this trellis, we can also treat it as a directed acyclic graph (DAG). Thus, the search for optimal state sequence has been converted into an optimal path problem. In this paper, we propose a Viterbi-like search algorithm based on dynamic programming as Algorithm one, which is a deterministic algorithm.

In the trellis of Fig. 1, a virtual starting node q_s is added, which corresponds to time instant 0. The weight for all nodes from q_s to time instant 1 are constants. The optimal path from q_s to node q_i at time instant t is denoted as *path(t,i)*, which is a state sequence. Accordingly, the sum of its weight is denoted as *s(t,i)*. The induction process is shown as algorithm one:

Algorithm one

```
Initialization:
    s(0,i) = c, 1 ≤ i ≤ N
    path(0,i) = {qₛ}.
Induction:
    given j, s(t,j) = max[s(t-1,i)+Sₜⱼ+aᵢⱼ], 1 ≤ t ≤ T ,
                      1≤i≤N
    denote u = arg max [s(t-1,i)+Sₜⱼ+aᵢⱼ], then
                    1≤i≤N
        path(t,j) = path(t-1,u) ∪ {u}.
end:
    at time T, u = arg max s(T,i).
                    1≤i≤N
    Then path(T,u) - {qₛ} is the optimal path.
```

2.5   Word Segmentation Test and Analysis

The definitions of precision and recall are defined as follows:

$$precision = \frac{N_c}{N_T} \times 100\% \qquad (2)$$

$$recall = \frac{N_c}{N_a} \times 100\% \qquad (3)$$

Where,

N_c: number of correctly identified NSWs

N_T: total number of identified NSWs

N_a: number of NSWs in test material

Table 1. Experimental results: precision and recall

	Precision	Recall
Test corpus 1	90.43%	88.80%
Test corpus 2	90.46%	90.66%
Test corpus 3	88.09%	90.76%

From the Table 1, it can be seen that the best precision is 90.46%, while the highest recall is 90.76%. Some Japanese person names, like "松永光" and "神崎武法" etc. have been identified correctly.

3   Language Model

A statistical language model is a probability distribution over sequences of words. Language model can be applied in wide range of tasks such as speech recognition, machine translation and input method etc.

3.1   *N*-gram Language Model

N-gram language model is the most frequently used statistical language model in modern automatic speech recognition. In *N*-gram language model the next word is predicted from its previous $n - 1$ words. The probability of a sequence of words is computed using a chain rule as

$$P(w_1^n) = \prod_{k=1}^{n} P(w_k|w_1^{k-1}) \qquad (4)$$

where $w_1^n = w_1 w_2 \cdots w_n$ is a sequence of words.

The simplest and most intuitive way to estimate *N*-gram probabilities is Maximum Likelihood Estimation (MLE). The problem of sparse data with the MLE may occur for training the parameters of an *N*-gram model, techniques like smoothing, interpolation or Katz backoff can be adopt to estimate unseen word sequences in the training data [2].

3.2   Domain-Specific *N*-gram Language Model

Generally speaking, different industries/sectors have their own terminologies. A general-purpose language model does not demonstrate high performance when recognizing speech data from a specific domain. One reason is that ASR is essentially a search procedure among a huge network (say a static weighted finite state transducer, WFST) based on an optimization criteria. Such kind of search network depends on lexicon, language model, acoustic model and decision tree etc. For a specific domain such as banking and finance industry, the general-purpose lexicon only contains a small part of banking and finance terminologies in most cases, which degrades speech recognition accuracy substantially. To relieve such kind of problem, we need to build up a domain-specific *N*-gram language model.

We use the open-source SRI language modeling toolkit (SRILM) [3] to train general-purpose *N*-gram model and domain-specific language model.

3.3   Domain-Specific RNNLM

Most of the state-of-the-art large-vocabulary continuous speech recognition (LVCSR) systems leverage WFST as a static search framework, which can be very huge, say 60 GB or above in memory. *N*-gram language model, lexicon, decision tree and HMM can be composed into a WFST. Considering that RNNLM demonstrates promising performance in modeling word probability distribution, we are interested in using this method to build domain-specific language model. RNNLMs work well in a state-of-the-art speech recognition systems, and are complementary to standard *N*-gram models [5]. Why can it serve as complement only? It is still very challenging to choose an RNNLM model as a replacement of *N*-gram language model and compose the RNNLM into the final WFST. Considering that RNNLM outperforms *N*-gram language model in terms of perplexity, researchers apply it to improve rescoring result rather than utilize neural network information in decoding phase directly.

The architecture of RNNLM is shown in Fig. 2. The network is represented by input, hidden and output layers and corresponding weight matrices - matrices $\mathbf{U}$ and $\mathbf{W}$ between the input and the hidden layer, and matrix $\mathbf{V}$ between the hidden and the output layer. The input layer consists of a vector $\mathbf{w}(t)$ that represents the current word w_t encoded as 1 of V_L (the size of the vocabulary), and of vector $\mathbf{s}(t-1)$ that represents output values in the hidden layer from the previous time step. The output layer $\mathbf{y}$ represents a probability distribution of the next word w_{t+1} given the history. After the network is trained, the output layer $\mathbf{y}(t)$ represents $P(w_{t+1}|w_t, \mathbf{s}(t-1))$. (Fig. 3)

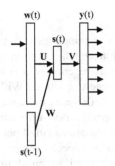

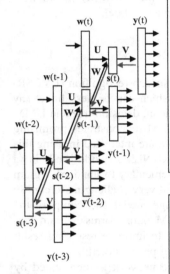

Fig. 2. Architecture of RNN

Fig. 3. Example of batch mode training with BPTT. Blue arrows indicate how the gradients are propagated through the unfolded recurrent neural network. (Color figure online)

RNN Training phase
Forward:

$$s(t) = f(\mathbf{U}\mathbf{w}(t) + \mathbf{W}\mathbf{s}(t-1)) \qquad (5)$$

$$\mathbf{y}(t) = g(\mathbf{V}\mathbf{s}(t)) \qquad (6)$$

Where $f(z) = \frac{1}{1+e^{-z}}$ is a sigmoid function, $g(z_m) = \frac{e^{z_m}}{\sum_k e^{z_k}}$ is a softmax function. $\mathbf{w}(t)$ and $\mathbf{y}(t)$ is encoded as $1 - of - V_L$ vector, where V_L is vocabulary size.

BP (Backpropagation):

$$\mathbf{e}_0(t) = \mathbf{d}(t) - \mathbf{y}(t) \qquad (7)$$

$$\mathbf{V}(t+1) = \mathbf{V}(t) + \mathbf{s}(t)\mathbf{e}_0(t)^T\alpha \qquad (8)$$

$$\mathbf{U}(t+1) = \mathbf{U}(t) + \mathbf{w}(t)\left[\mathbf{e}_0(t)^T\mathbf{V}\mathbf{s}(t)(1-\mathbf{s}(t))\right]\alpha \qquad (9)$$

$$\mathbf{W}(t+1) = \mathbf{W}(t) + \mathbf{s}(t-1)[\mathbf{e}_0(t)^T\mathbf{V}\mathbf{s}(t)(1-\mathbf{s}(t))]\alpha \qquad (10)$$

BPTT (Backpropagation through time):

$$\mathbf{W}(t+1) = \mathbf{W}(t) + \sum_{z=0}^{T} \beta_{tz}\mathbf{e}_h(t-z)^T\alpha \qquad (11)$$

$$\mathbf{e}_h(t-z-1) = \mathbf{e}_h(t-z)\mathbf{W}\beta_{tz}(1-\beta_{tz}) \qquad (12)$$

$$\mathbf{e}_h(t) = \mathbf{e}_0(t)^T\mathbf{V}\mathbf{s}(t)(1-\mathbf{s}(t)) \qquad (13)$$

where $\beta_{tz} = \mathbf{s}(t-z-1)$

The training of RNNLM is performed by the standard stochastic gradient descent (SGD) algorithm, and the matrix $\mathbf{W}$ that represents recurrent weights is trained by the backpropagation through time (BPTT) algorithm [6]. In the practical usage a truncated BPTT is applied - the network is unfolded in time for a specified amount of time steps.

Alternatively, training RNNLM is a very time-consuming procedure. For data sets with 100–1000 million of words, it is still possible to train RNN models with a small hidden layer in a reasonable time. However, this choice severely degrades the final performance, as networks trained on large amounts of data with small hidden layers have insufficient capacity to store information. Also it can result in gradient vanishing or divergence in some cases. We deal with these issues by modifying network architecture and weight update.

To speed up the training procedure, we introduce word class to factorize the output $y(t)$ illustrated as Fig. 4:

$$\mathbf{y}(t) \rightarrow \mathbf{y}(t) \cup \mathbf{c}(t) \tag{14}$$

Thus we can improve training speed by 100 times roughly at the cost of 5–10% perplexity increase.

For gradient vanishing or divergence issue, we propose a rectification mechanism like rectified linear unit (ReLU), which means that units in a neural net use the activation function $y = \max(0, x)$ to replace the standard sigmoid function in RNNLM training. This nonlinearity is quite simple. However, it can avoid gradient vanishing effectively. Figure 5 illustrates ReLU behavior.

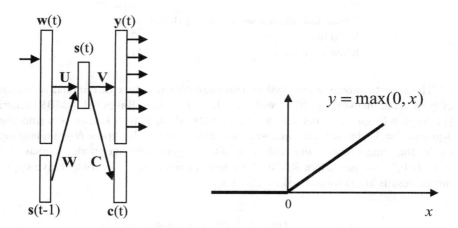

Fig. 4. Factorization of the output layer.   **Fig. 5.** ReLU illustration.

ReLU activation can decrease perplexity by 7–10% further on the basis of standard RNNLM.

A typical usage of RNNLM in an ASR system consists of these steps:

- train RNN language model(s)
- decode utterances, produce lattices.
- extract n-best lists from lattices
- compute sentence-level scores given by the baseline N-gram model and RNNLM
- perform weighted linear interpolation of log-scores given by various LMs (the weights should be tuned on the development data)
- re-rank the n-best lists using the new LM scores.

So RNNLM is usually introduced to reduce WER further in the post-processing stage of ASR system.

4   Experimental Results

The text corpus used for language model training contains 2 datasets as follows.

- general-purpose text corpus, roughly 300 GB
- domain-specific text corpus (collected from Chinese finance and banking related websites), roughly 1.38 GB

The test speech database comes from SpeechOcean (www.speechocean.com), which includes about 100-hour data and 230 speakers.

The RNNLM can lower the perplexity significantly, especially the one with ReLU activation function. Table 2 presents the detailed perplexity information.

Table 2. Perplexity comparison

Model	Perplexity
3-gram LM, Kneser-Ney smoothing (KN3)	147.6
RNNLM (sigmoid)	123.9
RNNLM (ReLU)	112.8

The acoustic model in our ASR system employs a sequence-discriminative training of deep neural networks (DNNs) with state-level minimum Bayes risk (sMBR) criteria [7]. N-gram language model was built using SRILM [3, 8] with Kneser-Ney smoothed 3-gram ($N = 3$, trigram). The interpolation factor for general-purpose N-gram language model (baseline version) and domain-specific N-gram language model (domain version) is 0.5. We just adopt RNNLM to perform rescoring. The comparative experimental results are demonstrated as Table 3.

Table 3. WER comparison

Language model combination	WER
Baseline	22.8%
Baseline + domain interpolation	7.6%
Baseline + domain interpolation + RNNLM rescoring	4.9%

5   Conclusion

In the work, speech recognition is performed with deep learning based language model to evaluate its performance on domain-specific application. The combined deep-learning-based language model RNNLM and N-gram on the domain-specific finance dataset got a WER of 4.9%, which is 34.2% relative decrease compared to the result without RNNLM rescoring. It can even achieve 78.5% relative decrease compared to the baseline result. The improvement introduced by RNNLM is significant and is worth further investigating to improve its performance.

References

1. Hinton, G., Deng, L., Yu, D., Dahl, G.E., Mohamed, A., Jaitly, N., Senior, A., Vanhoucke, V., Nguyen, P., Sainath, T.N., Kingsbury, B.: Deep neural networks for acoustic modeling in speech recognition: the shared views of four research groups. IEEE Sig. Process. Mag. **29**(6), 82–97 (2012)
2. Daniel, J., James, H.M.: Speech and language processing: an introduction to natural language processing. In: Computational Linguistics and Speech Recognition, 2nd edn. Prentice Hall (2009)
3. Stolcke, A.: SRILM-an extensible language modeling toolkit. In: Interspeech (2002)
4. Young, S., Evermann, G., Gales, M., Hain, T., Kershaw, D., Liu, X., Moore, G., Odell, J., Ollason, D., Povey, D.: The HTK Book, vol. 3, p. 175. Cambridge University Engineering Department, Cambridge (2002)
5. Schwenk, H., Gauvain, J.-L.: Training neural network language models on very large corpora. In: Proceedings of the Conference on Human Language Technology and Empirical Methods in Natural Language Processing. Association for Computational Linguistics (2005)
6. Rumelhart, D.E., Hinton, G.E., Williams, R.J.: Learning internal representations by error propagation. DTIC Document (1985)
7. Veselý, K., Ghoshal, A. Burget, L., Povey, D.: Sequence-discriminative training of deep neural networks. In: Interspeech (2013)
8. Stolcke, A., Zheng, J., Wang, W., Abrash, V.: SRILM at sixteen: update and outlook. In: Proceedings of IEEE Automatic Speech Recognition and Understanding Workshop (2011)

Image and Video Compression

Fast Intra Encoding Decisions Based on Horizontal-Vertical Progressive Gradient Accumulation for HEVC

Zhenglong Yang[✉], Guozhong Wang, Tao Fan, and Guowei Teng

School of Communication and Information Engineering,
Shanghai University, Shanghai, China
yangzlxy1@sina.com

Abstract. High Efficiency Video Coding (HEVC) employs a flexible quad-tree structure for intra prediction. It enables up to 35 prediction modes with using all the possible depth levels and prediction modes to obtain the optimal CU (coding unit) and PU (prediction unit) mode. However, these characteristics bring great computational complexity. To address this issue, we propose a progressive gradient accumulation strategy for intra encoding decisions. The horizontal and vertical progressive gradient values will be obtained by adding up all the differences of every adjacent column and row. Then, the maximum optimal depth of the neighboring CU with similar vector is used for current CU early termination, and the vector direction is used for current PU mode decision. In the process of arithmetic, the accumulative values will be simplified into only calculating the difference of edge pixels. Experimental results verify that the proposed algorithm can reduce 21.82% coding time with 3.89% BDBR increasing.

Keywords: HEVC · Horizontal-vertical · Progressive gradient · The difference · Edge pixels

1 Introduction

High efficiency video coding (HEVC) is the latest video coding standing developed by ISO/IEC Moving Picture Experts Group (MPEG) and ITU-T Video Coding Experts Group (VCEG) standardization organizations, working together in a partnership known as the Joint Collaborative Team on Video Coding (JCT-VC) [1]. Compared with its predecessor H.264/AVC, it has obtained great performance gains. Though the video coding layer of HEVC employs the same hybrid approach (inter/intra picture prediction and 2-D transform coding) used in all video compression standards since H.261, several improvements and new techniques are adopted in HEVC, such as multi-sized coding units (CUs), more prediction modes, sample adaptive offset and others. These changes increase quality and coding efficiency but with drastically increased complexity.

© Springer Nature Singapore Pte Ltd. 2017
X. Yang and G. Zhai (Eds.): IFTC 2016, CCIS 685, pp. 255–264, 2017.
DOI: 10.1007/978-981-10-4211-9_25

The core of the coding layer structure in HEVC is the coding tree unit (CTU). A CTU consists of a luma CTB, the corresponding chroma CTBs and syntax elements. The size L × L of a luma CTB can be chosen as L = 16, 32, or 64. HEVC supports a partitioning of a CTB into smaller blocks as coding units (CUs) using a flexible quad-tree structure. A CU may be split to form multiple smaller CUs, and it consists of one luma coding block (CB), ordinarily two chroma CBs and the associated syntax elements. The size of a CU can be from 64 × 64 to 8 × 8 with depth from 0 to 3. Each CU has an associated partitioning into prediction units (PUs) and a tree of transform units (TUs). HEVC supports variable PU sizes from 64 × 64 down to 4 × 4 samples, and the square TU sizes from 32 × 32 down to 4 × 4 samples [2,3]. The recursive coding structure is shown in Fig. 1.

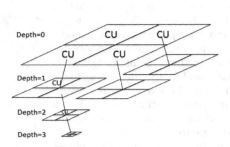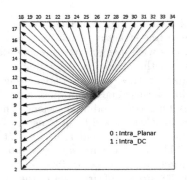

Fig. 1. Illustration of recursive coding structure

Fig. 2. Intra prediction modes in HEVC

In HEVC, intra prediction is applicable to CU, but the prediction is done in PU. Intra prediction supports 33 angular modes, a planar mode and a DC mode. Each number from 2 to 34 represents a distinct direction. 0 and 1 represent planar and DC mode respectively. All intra prediction modes are shown in Fig. 2.

The rest of this paper is organized as follows. Section 2 reviews related works. In Sect. 3, we introduce and analyze the algorithm model. The proposed algorithm is described in Sect. 4. Section 5 presents the experimental results. The conclusions are given in Sect. 6.

2   Related Works

Many excellent fast intra prediction algorithms are proposed before. [4] gives a intra gradient-based fast decision for HEVC. It gives a PU size and PU mode decision with the intensity gradient to decide the texture complexity and texture prediction for PU. Shen et al. [5] finds that the optimal size of current CU can be predicted by using the optimal size of spatially neighboring CUs. Based on the optimal size of left, up, left-up and right-up CUs, the RD cost check of some CU sizes can be skipped. [6] gives a fast intra mode decision using matching edge detector and kernel density estimation alike histogram generation algorithm. This paper introduces a conception of the fix-point arithmetic based on edge detector and using the kernel density estimation into the histogram calculation. [7] proposes a fast intra encoding decisions for HEVC, For fast CU skip decision, it gives several standard deviations for CU skip and CU early termination. For fast PU mode decision, this paper always selects the minimum RMD cost mode from different sets until the final set G is built as the candidate set. [8] gives a fast intra mode decision algorithm based on dominant edge assent (DEA) distribution. It computes four DEAs in the directions of $0°$, $45°$, $90°$ and $135°$. Then, the dominant edge is decided by the minimum DEA and a subset of prediction modes is chosen for the RMD process. However, these algorithms always can improve coding efficiency, but they can't perform sufficient complexity reduction due to the required pre-calculations. In this paper, we propose a fast intra encoding decisions only using the edge pixels of every CU. It will reduce the computational complexity sufficiently without losing coding efficiency.

3 Proposed Algorithm Model and Analysis

3.1 Proposed Algorithm Model

In an orthonormal coordinate system (O, X, Y), the origin locates at the left-up corner of current CU, X represents the horizontal direction to the right, Y represents the vertical direction to the bottom. a_{ks} ($k = 1, 2, 3, ...,$ m and $s = 1, 2, 3, ...,$ n) represents the pixel value of the current CU. The model is shown in Fig. 3.

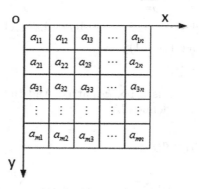

Fig. 3. Proposed algorithm model

Now, we map the model (shown in Fig. 3) to a $m \times n$ matrix A, which can be written as:

$$\mathbf{A} = \begin{pmatrix} a_{11} & a_{12} & a_{13} & \cdots & a_{1n} \\ a_{21} & a_{22} & a_{23} & \cdots & a_{2n} \\ a_{31} & a_{32} & a_{33} & \cdots & a_{3n} \\ \vdots & \vdots & \vdots & \vdots & \vdots \\ a_{m1} & a_{m2} & a_{m3} & \cdots & a_{mn} \end{pmatrix} \qquad (1)$$

Then, let A_k denote a $1 \times n$ matrix and B_s is a $m \times 1$ matrix, which can be written as:

$$A_k = \begin{pmatrix} a_{k1} & a_{k2} & a_{k3} & \cdots & a_{kn} \end{pmatrix} \qquad (2)$$

where A_k represents the k-th row of A, and

$$B_s = \begin{pmatrix} a_{1s} & a_{2s} & a_{3s} & \cdots & a_{ms} \end{pmatrix}^T \qquad (3)$$

represents the s-th column of A. Thus

$$\mathbf{A} = \begin{pmatrix} a_{11} & a_{12} & a_{13} & \cdots & a_{1n} \\ a_{21} & a_{22} & a_{23} & \cdots & a_{2n} \\ a_{31} & a_{32} & a_{33} & \cdots & a_{3n} \\ \vdots & \vdots & \vdots & \vdots & \vdots \\ a_{m1} & a_{m2} & a_{m3} & \cdots & a_{mn} \end{pmatrix} = \begin{pmatrix} A_1 \\ A_2 \\ A_3 \\ \vdots \\ A_m \end{pmatrix} = \begin{pmatrix} B_1 & B_2 & B_3 & \cdots & B_n \end{pmatrix} \qquad (4)$$

The vertical progressive gradient accumulation Y is defined by:

$$\begin{aligned} Y &= \sum_{j=1}^{n} \sum_{i=2}^{m} (a_{ij} - a_{i-1j}) \\ &= \sum_{j=1}^{n} (a_{2j} - a_{1j}) + \sum_{j=1}^{n} (a_{3j} - a_{2j}) + \cdots + \sum_{j=1}^{n} (a_{mj} - a_{m-1j}) \\ &= (A_2 - A_1 + A_3 - A_2 + \cdots + A_m - A_{m-1})(1\ 1\ \cdots\ 1)_n^T \qquad (5) \\ &= (A_m - A_1)(1\ 1\ \cdots\ 1)_n^T \\ &= (A_m - A_1)I_n^T \end{aligned}$$

where $I_k = (1\ 1\ \ldots\ 1)_k$ is a $1 \times k$ matrix. And the horizontal progressive gradient accumulation X is defined by:

$$\begin{aligned} X &= \sum_{i=1}^{m} \sum_{j=2}^{n} (a_{ij} - a_{ij-1}) \\ &= \sum_{i=1}^{m} (a_{i2} - a_{i1}) + \sum_{i=1}^{m} (a_{i3} - a_{i2}) + \cdots + \sum_{i=1}^{m} (a_{in} - a_{in-1}) \\ &= (1\ 1\ \cdots\ 1)_m (B_2 - B_1 + B_3 - B_2 + \cdots + B_n - B_{n-1}) \qquad (6) \\ &= (1\ 1\ \cdots\ 1)_m (B_n - B_1) \\ &= I_m(B_n - B_1) \end{aligned}$$

Thus, the vector of current CU is:

$$\overrightarrow{OP} = X \cdot \overrightarrow{i} + Y \cdot \overrightarrow{j}$$
$$= I_m(B_n - B_1) \cdot \overrightarrow{i} + (A_m - A_1)I_n^T \cdot \overrightarrow{j} \tag{7}$$

where $\overrightarrow{i}$ and $\overrightarrow{j}$ are the two unit vectors in the X and Y direction respectively. From (7), we can see that only the edge pixels of current CU are used for calculating.

The direction of this CU is:

$$Ang(\overrightarrow{OP}) = -\frac{180}{\pi} \arctan(\frac{X}{Y}) \tag{8}$$

3.2   Model Analysis

A sample frame of Johnny_1280 × 720 with its typical texture maps is shown in Fig. 4. Now we analyze the reasonableness of (7) and (8).

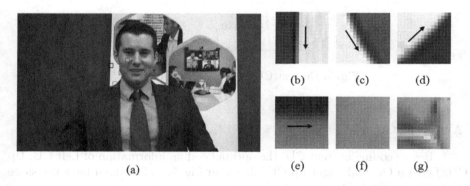

Fig. 4. (a) Sample frame of Johnny_1280 × 720 sequence, (b)(c)(d)(e)(f)(g) Typical texture maps (Color figure online)

Six 16×16 typical texture maps are took from (a) and marked with the black, red, green, pink, blue and yellow box respectively.

For (b), we can obtain $|X| > 0$, $|Y| \to 0$, so the direction of this CU is nearby $90°$ (as the arrow pointing).

For (c), we can obtain $0 < |Y| < |X|$, so the direction of this CU is $45° < Ang() < 90°$.

For (d), we can obtain $0 < |X| \approx |Y|$, so the direction of this CU is nearby $-45°$.

For (e), we can obtain $|X| \to 0$, $|Y| > 0$, so the direction of this CU is nearby $0°$.

For (f), we can obtain $X \to 0$ and $Y \to 0$, the results getting from (7) and (8) can't indicate the CU's direction. The optimal mode of this texture should be the DC or Planar mode. The same to (g), this CU has a complex texture. So the DC and Planar mode should be always added to the candidate mode set.

With (7) and (8), we can obtain the vector of current CU. This result will be used for CU similarity measurement and PU direction decision.

4   Proposed Algorithm

4.1   Fast CU Early Termination

In natural pictures, the optimal size of current CU may have a strong correlation with its neighboring CUs [5].

Based on this concept, the information of current CU can be predicted using spatially nearby CUs as follows,

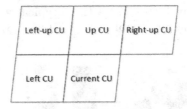

Fig. 5. Current CU and its neighboring CUs

(A) 64 × 64 CU

1. Before coding current CU, the optimal coding information of Left CU, Up CU, Left-up CU and Right-up CU, shown in Fig. 5, (all of them have the same size with current CU) can be obtained.

2. The vectors of the five CUs can be obtained by (7). If the neighboring CUs' vector values are equal to current CU's, these CUs are similar with current CU, then go to step 3. If there are no vector values equal to current CU's, it will be split recursively and go to (B).

3. Obtain current CU's depth D_c and the maximum optimal depth D_i of neighboring CUs which are similar with current CU. (i∈ {Right-up CU, Left CU, Left-up CU, Up CU})

4. If $D_c < D_i$, current CU will be split recursively, then go to (B). If $D_c \geq D_i$, stop splitting current CU, then calculate the next 64 × 64 CU.

(B) 32 × 32 CU

1. Make sure the four 32 × 32 neighboring CUs' optimal information can be obtained.

2. Obtain the similar neighboring CUs by (7). If there are no similar CUs, split current CU recursively and go to (C). Otherwise, go to step 3.

3. The same as (A): step 3.

4. If $D_c < D_i$, split current CU recursively, then go to (C). If $D_c \geq D_i$, stop splitting current CU and calculate the next 32×32 CU.

(C) 16×16 CU and 8×8 CU

It has the same process as (A) and (B) until the size of current CU is 8×8. Since 8×8 CU is the minimum size, encode current CU as traditional.

4.2   Fast PU Mode Decision

Since X and Y can be obtained by (5) and (6) to calculate the direction $Ang()$ by (8) of current PU. Several prediction modes will be checked. The $Ang()$ is chosen as the temporary optimal direction of current PU, and the corresponding temporary optimal angular mode is mode n $(2 < n < 34)$. The details are described as follows:

(A) 64×64 PU

1. Check DC, Planar, MPMs, mode n, mode(n − 4), mode(n + 4) for RDO process.

2. If the minimum RDcost mode is one of DC, Planar, MPMs or mode n, this mode is the optimal mode.

3. If the minimum RDcost mode is mode(n − 4) or mode(n + 4), check the two second adjacent modes, which are mode(n − 2) and mode(n − 6) or mode(n + 2) and mode(n + 6).

4. If the minimum RDcost mode is also mode(n − 4) or mode(n + 4), this mode is the optimal mode. Otherwise, check the two adjacent modes, which are mode(n − 1) and mode(n − 3) or mode(n − 5) and mode(n − 7) or mode(n + 1) and mode(n + 3) or mode(n + 5) and mode(n + 7).

5. Select the optimal mode from the three adjacent modes.

(B) 32×32 PU

1. Check DC, Planar, MPMs, mode n, mode(n − 2) and mode(n + 2) for RDO process.

2. If the minimum RDcost mode is one of DC, Planar, MPMs or mode n, this mode is the optimal mode.

3. If the minimum RDcost mode is mode(n − 2) or mode(n + 2), check the two adjacent modes, which are mode(n − 1) and mode(n − 3) or mode(n + 1) and mode(n + 3).

4. Select the optimal mode from the three adjacent modes.

(C) 16×16 PU

1. Check DC, Planar, MPMs, mode n, mode(n − 1) and mode(n + 1).
2. Select the optimal mode from them.

(D) 8×8 PU and 4×4 PU

1. Check DC, Planar, MPMs and mode n.
2. Select the optimal mode from them.

4.3 Overall Algorithm

As the aforementioned analysis, including the fast CU early termination and PU mode decision, the fast intra encoding decisions algorithm is as follow:

Step 1: Start intra prediction for a CU.

Step 2: Calculate the spatially nearby CUs based on (7) to find the similar CUs. If the similar CUs can be obtained, go to Step 3. If there are no similar CUs, go to Step 4.

Step 3: Obtain the maximum optimal depth of the similar neighboring CUs. If current depth is smaller than the maximum optimal depth, split current CU, and then go to Step 1. Otherwise, stop splitting current CU, then go to Step 7.

Step 4: Start PU mode decision process.

Step 5: Obtain the direction of current PU based on (8). Then select some special modes (proposed in Sect. 4.2) for RDO process.

Step 6: Loop all the PUs as Step 5.

Step 7: Go to step 1 and proceed with the next CU.

5 Experimental Results

The proposed algorithm is implemented in the test model HM15, and the experiments are carried out for all I-frames sequences. We use the intra Main Profile configurations [9] with QP = 22, 27, 32 and 37 in five resolutions (2560×1600, 1920×1080, 1280×720, 832×480, 416×240 formats). Maximum CU size is 64×64 and maximum depth level is 4. Coding efficiency is measured with BDBR(%) [10] and $TS(\%)$ is used to indicate time savings. $T_{proposed}$ and T_{HM15} are the coding time of the proposed algorithm and HM15 respectively. The BDBR(%) metric is calculated using the bit rates and the PSNR.

The TS metric is defined by:

$$TS = \frac{T_{proposed} - T_{HM15}}{T_{HM15}} \times 100\% \tag{9}$$

The RD performance of CU early termination, PU mode decision and fast intra encoding decisions algorithm compared with original HM15 software is shown in Tables 1 and 2 respectively.

The results shown in Table 1 indicate that the CU early termination algorithm can save 15.48% coding time on average with 2.49% BDBR increasing. The PU mode decision algorithm can save 5.28% coding time without losing coding efficiency, where BDBR increases 0.67% on average.

Table 2 shows the performances of the proposed fast intra encoding decisions algorithm. The results indicate that it can save 21.82% coding time with 3.89% BDBR increasing and 0.26 dB BDPSNR decreasing. We can conclude that no matter the texture of the picture is complex or smooth, our proposed algorithm has a stable performance on BDBR, BDPSNR or TS index. However, the reasons of BDBR increasing are mainly about:

Table 1. RD performance of CU early termination and PU mode decision algorithm

Sequences	CU early termination		PU mode decision	
	BDBR(%)	TS(%)	BDBR(%)	TS(%)
Class A	0.89	−12.1	0.04	−4.63
Class B	4.05	−15.22	0.69	−5.2
Class C	3.18	−16.2	0.85	−6.2
Class D	2.16	−15.3	0.96	−6.22
Class E	2.19	−16.6	0.78	−4.13
Average	2.49	−15.48	0.67	−5.28

1. Some large CUs, such as 32 × 32 and 16 × 16, need to be further split but their similar neighboring CUs are already the optimal mode under current size. So current CU stops splitting when its mode isn't optimal.

2. Based on the fast PU mode decision algorithm, the temporary optimal angular mode and its two n-th adjacent modes are selected as the most probable modes. However, the result may be a locally optimal mode.

Above all, these are the main reasons of BDBR increasing, but they are also the reasons for coding time saving.

Table 2. RD performance of fast intra encoding decisions algorithm

Sequences	Size	BDBR(%)	BDPSNR(dB)	TS(%)
NebutaFestival	2560 × 1600	4.38	−0.83	−19.99
PeopleOnStreet	2560 × 1600	3.5	−0.2	−21.82
BasketballDrive	1920 × 1080	4.86	−0.12	−19.45
BQTerrace	1920 × 1080	5.58	−0.39	−23.7
BasketballDrill	832 × 480	3.97	−0.19	−22.07
BQMall	832 × 480	4.19	−0.26	−20.48
PartyScene	832 × 480	3.19	−0.27	−23.67
BasketballPass	416 × 240	3.63	−0.21	−24.91
BlowingBubbles	416 × 240	3.73	−0.22	−25.5
RaceHorses	416 × 240	2.91	−0.21	−20.2
FourPeople	1280 × 720	2.86	−0.16	−17.93
Johnny	1280 × 720	3.92	−0.16	−22.17
Average		3.89	−0.26	−21.82

6   Conclusion

This paper proposes a fast intra encoding decisions algorithm which calculates the difference of edge pixels to obtain the vector of every CU. The measurement of the similarity between the current CU and its neighboring CUs is based on the vector. Then, the maximum optimal depth obtained from similar neighboring CUs is used for current CU early termination and the vector direction is used for fast PU mode decision.

As the future work, the prediction precision and the reduction of coding time should be further improved.

Acknowledgment. This work is supported by National Science Foundation of China under Grant No. 61271212. National High-tech R&D Program (863 Program) under Grant No. 2015AA015903. National Science Foundation of Shanghai under Grant No. 14ZR1415200.

References

1. Bross, B., Han, W.-J., Sullivan, G.J., Ohm, J.-R., Wiegand, T.: High Efficiency Video Coding (HEVC) Text Specification Draft 9, document JCTVC-K1003, ITU-T/ISO/IEC Joint Collaborative Team on Video Coding (JCT-VC), October 2012
2. Sullivan, G.J., Boyce, J.M., Chen, Y., et al.: Standardized extensions of high efficiency video coding (HEVC). IEEE J. Sel. Top. Sig. Process. **7**(6), 1001–1016 (2013)
3. Sullivan, G.J., Ohm, J.-R., Han, W.-J., Wiegand, T.: Overview of the high efficiency video coding (HEVC) standard. IEEE Trans. Circ. Syst. Video Technol. **22**(12), 1648–1667 (2012)
4. Zhang, Y., Li, Z., Li, B.: Gradient-based fast decision for intra prediction in HEVC. In: IEEE Visual Communications and Image Processing (VCIP), pp. 1–6, November 2012
5. Shen, L., Zhang, Z., An, P.: Fast CU size decision and mode decision algorithm for HEVC intra coding. IEEE Trans. Consum. Electron. **59**(1), 207–213 (2013)
6. Chen, G., et al.: Fast HEVC intra mode decision using matching edge detector and kernel density estimation alike histogram generation. In: 2013 IEEE International Symposium on Circuits and Systems (ISCAS2013). IEEE (2013)
7. Yang, M., Grecos, C.: Fast intra encoding decisions for high efficiency video coding standard. J. Real-Time Image Process. 1–10 (2014)
8. Yao, Y., Li, X., Lu, Y.: Fast intra mode decision algorithm for HEVC based on dominant edge assent distribution. Multimedia Tools Appl. **75**(4), 1–19 (2014)
9. Bossen, F.: Common HM test conditions and software reference configurations. JCT-VC Doc. L1100 (2013)
10. Bjontegaard, G.: Calculation of average PSNR difference between RD-curves. In: 13th VCEG-M33 Meeting, Austin, TX, 2–4 April 2001

An Efficient Optimization of Real-Time AVS+ Encoder in Low Bitrate Condition

Li Cao$^{(\boxtimes)}$, Xiaoyun Zhang, and Zhiyong Gao

Institute of Image Communication and Information Processing,
Shanghai Jiao Tong University, Shanghai, China
{iceload,xiaoyun.zhang,zhiyong.gao}@sjtu.edu.cn

Abstract. AVS+ is a national standard for audio and video compression in China, which has been widely used for broadcasting and survillance. Compution complexity and coding effiency are always the main concern in real-time practical applications. And image quality becomes critical and sensitice when coding at low bitrates. In this paper, we analysis the influence of skip mode in low bitrate condition and propose a novel fast skip decision scheme to achieve good trade-off between encoding speed and quality. We employ visual coding based on just noticeable distortion (JND) model to suppress residues for non-skip macroblocks. Simulated results show the proposed method can achieve 0.5 dB average gain in BDPSNR while maintaining real-time speed.

Keywords: AVS+ · Low bitrate · Real-time · Skip mode decision · Just noticeable distortion

1 Introduction

AVS+, as an industrial standard of source encoding, is developed by Audio and Video Coding Standard Working Group of China [1]. It targets at high compression capability for audio and video sources, which has been widely used for various scenarios such as broadcasting, video-surveillance and high-definition DVD [2]. Comparing to H.264/AVC, AVS+ charges low for its patent, which would benefit related industry in China. Much work has been done to enhance the performance of AVS+ encoder. Comparing to AVS, Advanced Entropy Coding, Adaptive Weighting Quantization and Enhanced PB Field Coding techniques are added to improve compression efficiency. Some optimizations of motion estimation have been proposed to reduce computation complexity for AVS+ encoder [3]. Some work also aims at integrating efficient visual perceptual cues into AVS+ encoder to improve the visual quality [4].

In many application scenarios of AVS+, real-time encoding speed is needed. Hardware real-time encoder is one major solution, which possesses typical forms as FPGA platform or the encoder hardcore in System on Chip (SoC). Many hardware devices supporting AVS+ standard have been produced for specific commercial use in the past years. However, it can hardly be changed once a

© Springer Nature Singapore Pte Ltd. 2017
X. Yang and G. Zhai (Eds.): IFTC 2016, CCIS 685, pp. 265–275, 2017.
DOI: 10.1007/978-981-10-4211-9_26

hardware encoder is designed. Instead, software encoder has notable superiority in flexibility. Software encoder is usually based on certain processor platform, such as Personal Computer (PC), Acorn RISC Machine (ARM) and Digital Signal Processor (DSP). The speed of software encoder not only depends on the coding algorithms but also the processing speed of platform. With the development of processors, software based AVS+ encoder now can achieve stable real-time speed with good encoding performance.

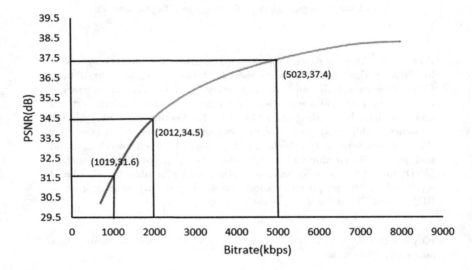

Fig. 1. The R-D curve of BasketBallDrive.yuv using GDM (Color figure online)

Another key factor in practical applications is the encoding bitrate. Considering limited network bandwidth and cost issues, low bitrate is preferred and popularly used. For example, the video bitrate of the popular video service websites in China for standard definition videos is usually no more than 1 Mbps, which is quite low and critical for the encoder. It is also found the encoding quality is more sensitive in low bitrate interval. As shown in Fig. 1, the R-D curve located in low bitrate interval (red color) for BasketballDrive has a steep section which means the PSNR improves fast as the bitrate increases. But as the bitrate increases at the higher bitrate interval, the improvement of PSNR turns slow. Therefore, the encoding optimization at low bitrate condition is quite necessary and meaningful.

In this paper, we concentrate on the optimization of real-time AVS+ software encoder in low bitrate condition. In this occasion, skip prediction mode has great influence on the performance of the encoder. On the one hand, skip mode takes up a large proportion in low bitrate condition and inappropriate skip mode seriously affects the encoding quality. On the other hand, fast-skip decision is frequently used in real-time encoder to reduce computational complexity, which raises up a trade-off problem between speed and accuracy. More detailed analyses are present in Sect. 2. An optimization method is then proposed in Sect. 3. Experiment results are shown in Sect. 4 while conclusions are drawn in Sect. 5.

2 Low Bitrate Skip Mode Analysis in Real-Time AVS+ Encoder

Lagrangian based RDO is widely used for real video encoder, in which the final prediction mode chosen for one coding block should minimize the following cost function

$$J = \lambda R + D \qquad (1)$$

where λ is Lagrange multiplier depending on quantization step size; D is distortion metric between an original block and its reconstructed block; R is the cost of bits for encoding the block with corresponding prediction mode. Since in low bitrate condition the quantization step is usually large, the Lagrange multiplier λ increases, which means the encoder prefers saving bits R rather than limiting distortion D. Among all the prediction modes in AVS+, skip prediction mode saves bits most because the encoder does not need to encode the residues and the motion vector of a skip block. In fact, skip mode takes up a large proportion in low bitrate condition. Figure 2 show the percentage of P/B skip modes used in AVS+ encoder for sequences CREW and HARBOUR using low bitrates. The percentage of the skip blocks increases significantly as the bitrate decreases.

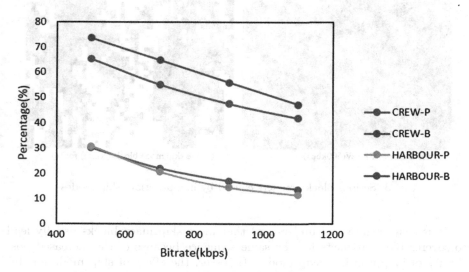

Fig. 2. The skip mode percentage for sequence CREW and HARBOUR

In practical real-time video encoders, several fast-skip methods are used before or within motion estimation process to reduce computational complexity.

A fast skip-mode selection algorithm based on all-zero block check is proposed in [5]. The information of neighboring blocks is also used to guide the mode decision of the current block [6]. These proposed methods claim negligible decrease in image quality and good accuracy of skip-mode detection. However, fast skip mode decision has the risk of causing block artifact which is unacceptable to human visual system, especially in low bitrate condition. Figure 3 shows the images encoded at the low bitrate 500kps, and it can be seen that block artifacts generally occur at the area encoded by skip prediction mode.

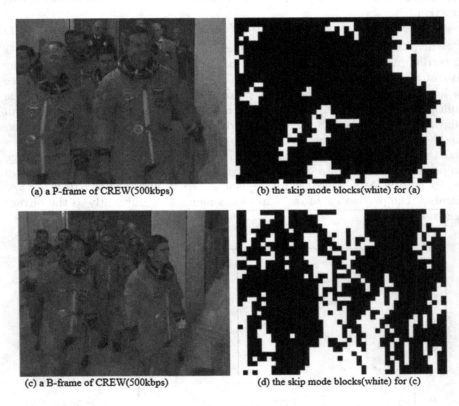

(a) a P-frame of CREW(500kbps)   (b) the skip mode blocks(white) for (a)

(c) a B-frame of CREW(500kbps)   (d) the skip mode blocks(white) for (c)

Fig. 3. Serious block artifacts caused by inappropriate skip modes

It is easy to find and understand that more skip macroblocks usually lead to severer block artifacts for the same sequence because of the increased possibility of inappropriate skip modes. However, the effect of skip mode for different sequences is different and related with the video content. For example, the encoder uses more skip modes for HARBOUR than CREW as Fig. 2 shows, but the decoded frames of HARBOUR show no siginificant block artifacts and the subjective quality is even better than CREW. More sequences are tested in low bitrate condition to further study the property of skip mode. It is found sequences with large variation between adjacent frames are sensitive to increased skip macroblocks such as CREW, BasketballDrive, SOCCER, Pedestrain, etc. These sequences contain obvious moving targets and complex behavioral activities which are difficult for encoders to handle. On the contrary, sequences with little variation between adjacent frames are not sensitive to increased skip macroblocks and might be even better with more skip macroblocks such as HARBOUR, FourPeople, Johnny, etc. These sequences contain large areas of static background without significant movement and therefore the use of skip mode seldom causes serious block artifacts.

It is also found that the P-skip mode has more influence on the encoding performance than B-skip mode. The image quality of reconstructed frames decreases quickly as P-skip modes increase, while the influence of increased B-skip modes is relatively small. This is because P-frames is used as reference frames and if an inappropriate P-skip mode is used, it will further influence the encoding process of the following B-frames and the next P-frame.

Based on these analyses, the fast skip-mode decision should be improved and optimized at low bitrate by considering the effect of sequences' content and the differences between P-frames and B-frames. On the other hand, we also need to maintain the balance between encoding quality and computational complexity at the same time. This leads to our proposed algorithm in Sect. 3.

3   Proposed method

In this section, we propose a hybrid optimization method for AVS+ real-time encoder from two aspects. Firstly, the skip mode decision should be well designed considering the effect of video contents to ensure both the encoding speed and quality. Secondly, since the bits are very tense in low bitrate condition, Just-Noticeable-Distortion (JND) model based perceptual coding technique is used to further improve the visual coding quality. The details are described as follows.

3.1   Speed and Quality Trade-Off Using Content-Based Skip Mode Decision

For a hypothetical and ideal AVS+ encoder, whether a block should be encoded as skip prediction mode can only be judged after all prediction modes have been analyzed. A block will be considered as skip mode only if the skip mode has the minimum RDCost among all prediction modes. In practical application, fast skip decision tries to predict if a block can be coded as skip mode before the whole mode decision process is done. As a result, the encoder does not need to do motion estimation for the skip blocks, which is the most time-consuming part for the encoder.

A regular method for fast skip mode decision is as follows: Using the predicted MV as the final MV to do the motion compensation, if residues become all-zero after DCT transform and quantizer, the block is considered as skip mode. A much looser skip mode decision method even does not require all-zero coefficients but very few non-zero coefficients. This brings higher speed but also more wrong decisions. In fact, there are many different skip mode decision methods, most of which face the trade-off between the encoding speed and image quality.

In this paper, we implement our method based on open source AVS encoder XAVS [7]. Similar to x264, XAVS provides several presets for users which can be seen as different trade-offs between encoding speed and image quality. In fact, different presets use different strategies for skip mode decision process. For P frames, the placebo preset does not use any fast algorithms, which we define as the strict skip mode decision. The veryfast preset recognizes a block as P-skip mode if the residues after DCT transform and quantizer using predicted MV contains relative few no-zero coefficients (judged by a score function). It can be defined as the loose skip mode decision. The medium preset is similar to veryfast preset but with additional limits which require that the best MV for 16×16 blocks should be very close to predicted MV and the corresponding distortion should be under certain threshold. It can be defined as the eclectic skip mode decision.

For B frames, the method used in veryfast preset is still seen as the loose skip mode decision. The medium preset recognizes a block as B-skip mode if the sum of squared differences (SSD) using predicted MV is under the theoretical minimum cost for other prediction mode. It can be seen as the strict skip mode decision for B frames. The eclectic skip mode decision for B frames can be extended from medium preset with a higher threshold value for SSD in the final step.

According to the analysis in Sect. 2, the variation between frames should be considered when designing skip mode decision scheme. For sequences with large variation between frames, since wrong skip mode would bring serious block arti-facts, relative strict skip mode decision should be applied. For sequences with little variation between frames, since skip mode does not have great influence on the image quality, relative loose skip mode decision can be applied to save more encoding time. For sequences with medium variation between frames, eclectic skip mode decision can be used to achieve the balance between speed and quality. To give a quantitative representation of the variation between frames, V is defined as:

$$V_n = \frac{\sum_W \sum_H |F_n(i,j) - F_{n-1}(i,j)|}{W \times H} \tag{2}$$

where W and H are the width and height of the frame, Fn represents the nth frame. Then the proposed Content-based skip-mode decision can be described as:

If Vn>Thα, then use strict skip-mode decision;

If Vn<=Tlα, then use loose skip-mode decision.

If Tlα<Vn<=Thα, then use eclectic skip-mode decision.

Where α can be either P or B depend on the slice type of the frame. Considering that we should treat P-frames more carefully than B-frames, TlP should be much smaller than TlB while Thp should be much smaller than ThB. In this paper, TlP and ThP are set to 1 and 3 while TlB and ThB are set to 6 and 10.

3.2   Visual Coding Based on JND Model and Its Real-Time Implement

For sequences with large variation between frames, we reduce the number of skip macro-blocks by using stricter fast-skip decision method. However, when in low bitrate condition, the increased non-skip macroblocks bring more pressure on bit allocation. To solve this problem and further improve the performance of the encoder, Just-Noticeable-Distortion (JND) model is introduced to our encoding scheme. JND measures the smallest detectable difference between two signals therefore can be utilized to quantify the perceivable distortion in the noise contaminated image [8]. Chou [9] proposed a spatial domain perceptual model based on luminance masking and contrast masking. Yang et al. [10] developed a new spatial JND estimator with the nonlinear additivity model for masking (NAMM) and proposed a spatial-temporal JND profile. An image-domain JND based perceptual video coding scheme was also proposed, which contains JND-adaptive motion estimation and residue filter.

In this paper, we use the spatial-temporal JND model refer to [9,10]. Then we use JND-adaptive residue filter mentioned in [10] to suppress the residues that needed to be DCT-transformed. Since we consider P-frames more important than B-frames and do not want to introduce extra deviation to P-frames, this manipulation is only done when a frame is B-frame.

However, the complexity of calculating JND model is relative high for real-time AVS+ encoder. If using C Language, pixel-wise computation is quite time-consuming. Instead of pixel-wise computation, Streaming SIMD Extensions 2 (SSE2) instructions are used to speed up the computation process. SSE2 instructions set to execute a large number of small-size native data type operations in parallel to improve the real-time multimedia data processing capability [11]. When dealing with 8-bit-depth data, 16 pixels can be handled at the same time since SSE2 instructions support 128-bit registers. To use SSE2 instructions for JND model computation, integer arithmetic and bits shift are used instead of float arithmetic. This could bring some deviation to the final JND value but the possibility is small and the deviation is proved no more than 1, which is acceptable considering the improvement in computation speed. Since integer arithmetic is used, Look-Up-Table (LUT) technique can be included to further speed up the calculation. Some intermediate products can be precomputed and restored in Look-Up-Table to omit the calculation process later. Moreover, we simplify the computation of background luminance and texture detection (see details in [9,10]) by reducing the size of convolution mask from 5×5 to 3×3. This manipulation not only reduces the computation complexity, but also improves the computation efficiency by a good design of data reuse in SSE2 implement. All these efforts contribute to the significant acceleration in JND computation.

The overall flow of the proposed algorithm is shown in Fig. 4. Firstly, the variation between frames is calculated for each frame. Secondly, different skip mode decision methods are chosen based on the variation. Then normal mode decision process is applied to find the best prediction mode for each block. Finally, JND-adaptive residue filter is used when encoding non-skip blocks for B-frames.

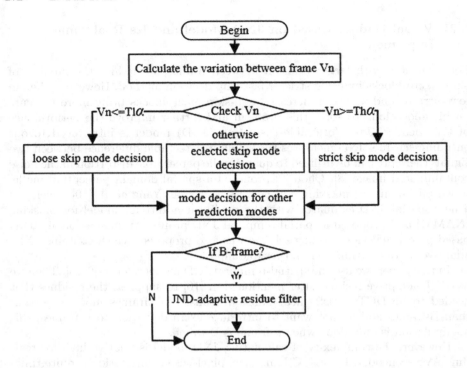

Fig. 4. The overall flow of the proposed algorithm

4   Experiment Result

The proposed method is incorporated into AVS open source reference software XAVS. Advanced Entropy Coding and Adaptive Weighting Quantization are developed according to AVS+ standard. The performance of proposed method is tested against the XAVS veryfast preset considering similar complexity. The GOP structure is set as IPBB.

Table 1 presents the simulation results for four 704×576 video sequences and six 1920×1080 video sequences. The bitrates of 704×576 sequences are chosen as 500, 600, 700, 800 kbps and the bitrates of 1920×1080 sequences are chosen as 2, 2.5, 3, 3.5 Mbps. The table gives average PSNR gain in dB (at the same bitrates) and percentage decrease in bitrate (at the same PSNR) with respect to XAVS veryfast preset. According to the table, the objective quality of the decoded video increased prominently. The proposed method contributed to 0.51 dB improvement in PSNR and 13.8% reduction in bitrate. The method is very successful for videos with obvious changes between frames, such as Crew, Soccer and BasketballDrive. Experiments also show the PSNR gain increases as bitrate decreases, which validates the improved performance of the proposed method in low bitrate condition.

Table 1. Performance evaluation of proposed method

Videos	Resolution	BDPSNR	BDBR	SPEED
Crew	704 × 576	0.65	−15.41	29.76
Harbour	704 × 576	0.30	−9.74	32.35
Soccer	704 × 576	0.78	−17.23	29.32
Ice	704 × 576	0.62	−15.72	34.09
BasketballDrive	1920 × 1080	0.76	−19.03	24.89
BQTerrace	1920 × 1080	0.29	−14.52	25.37
Cactus	1920 × 1080	0.28	−9.34	27.11
Kimomo1	1920 × 1080	0.50	−13.17	25.91
ParkScene	1920 × 1080	0.42	−13.06	27.24
Pedestrian	1920 × 1080	0.45	−10.86	24.36
Average	-	0.51	−13.81	28.04

(a) XAVS-veryfast(500kps)   (b) proposed method(500kps)

(c) XAVS-veryfast(2Mbps)   (d) proposed method(2Mbps)

Fig. 5. Visual comparisons for sequence Crew and Pedestrian

Visual comparisons also confirm the superiority of the proposed method. Figure 5 shows the frames of Crew and Pedestrian. In Fig. 5(a), obvious block artifacts occurs at the middle right area of the image while in Fig. 5(b), most of these artifacts have been corrected. In Fig. 5(d), the white T-shirt/black bag of the woman and the face of the biking man show significant visual improvement comparing to Fig. 5(c).

With both objective and subjective quality improvements, the proposed method still maintains a high encoding speed to satisfy real-time applications. The encoding speed tests are carried out on the computer equipped with I7-4770 Central Processing Unit. For sequences with 704×576 resolution, we build 8-channel encoder system which runs 8 AVS+ encoders at the same time. For sequences with 1920×1080 resolution, we build 2-channel encoder system which runs 2 AVS+ encoders at the same time. The last column of Table 1 presents the average encoding speed of each channel for different sequences. It is found the proposed method can achieve the speed of over 25 frames per second, which meets the requirements for most real-time applications.

5   Conclusion

In this paper, we proposed an efficient optimization of real time AVS+ encoder in low bitrate condition. In the proposed algorithm, the feature of video content is considered and then guides the skip-mode decision to achieve a good trade-off between encoding speed and quality. JND-adaptive residue filter is also used to further save bits for non-skip macroblocks as well as to enhance visual quality. Some efforts are done to speed up JND computation to make it meet real-time requirement. Simulation results show our method has significant improvement in both objective quality and visual quality, especially in the low bitrate region. In addition, the optimized encoder can still maintain real-time speed, which is important in practical applications.

Acknowledgement. This work was supported in part by National Natural Science Foundation of China (61133009,61301116,61221001), the Shanghai Key Laboratory of Digital Media Processing and Transmissions(STCSM 12DZ2272600).

References

1. Zhang, Q., Fang, Y., Wang, C.: A novel rate control algorithm for AVS video coding. In: International Conference on Wireless Communications, NETWORKING and Mobile Computing, pp. 2900–2902 (2007)
2. Gao, W., Ngan, K.N., Yu, L.: Special issue on AVS and its applications: guest editorial. Sig. Process. Image Commun. **24**(4), 245–246 (2009)
3. Wang, S., Xue, Y.: Optimization of Umhexagons Algorithm for AVS+. In: IEEE International Symposium on Broadband Multimedia Systems and Broadcasting (2015)
4. Cai, Q., Song, L.: AVS encoding optimization with perceptual just noticeable distortion model. In: International Conference on Information, Communications and Signal Processing, pp. 1–4 (2013)

5. Ma, L., Song, J., Xiao, L., Li, P.: A fast skip-mode selection algorithm based on all-zero block check in H. 264. In: International Conference on E-Business and E-Government, pp. 3498–3501 (2010)
6. Jo, Y., You, J., Kim, W., Jeong, J.: Fast mode decision algorithm using efficient block skip techniques for H. 264 P slices. In: International Conference on Advances in Multimedia, pp. 92–97 (2009)
7. http://xavs.sourceforge.net. AVS open source software
8. Chen, Z.: JND modeling: Approaches and applications (2014)
9. Chou, C.H., Li, Y.C.: A perceptually tuned subband image coder based on the measure of just-noticeable-distortion profile. IEEE Trans. Circ. Syst. Video Technol. **5**(6), 467–476 (1996)
10. Yang, X.K., Ling, W.S., Lu, Z.K., Ong, E.P., Yao, S.S.: Just noticeable distortion model and its applications in video coding. Sig. Process. Image Commun. **20**(7), 662–680 (2005)
11. Xiang, Y., Zhang, H., Chen, D., Xiang, X., Xiong, L.: Optimization of H. 264 encoder based on SSE2. In: IEEE International Conference on Progress in Informatics and Computing, pp. 752–755 (2010)

An Improved 3D Holoscopic Image Coding Scheme Using HEVC Based on Gaussian Mixture Models

Deyang Liu[1,2], Ping An[1,2(✉)], Tengyue Du[1,2], Ran Ma[1,2], and Liquan Shen[1,2]

[1] School of Communication and Information Engineering,
Shanghai University, Shanghai 200072, China
anping@shu.edu.cn
[2] Key Laboratory of Advanced Displays and System Application,
Ministry of Education, Shanghai 200072, China

Abstract. 3D holoscopic system can provide continuous motion parallax throughout the viewing zone with precise convergence and depth perception, for which it is regarded as a promising technique for future 3D TV. In this paper, a 3D holoscopic image coding scheme based on Gaussian mixture models (GMM) is introduced firstly, taking full advantage of the intrinsic characteristic of such particular type of content. Due to the shortcomings of GMM based method, an improved method is thereafter put forward, in which many parameters that are insignificant in the final estimator of GMM based method are avoided, and more surrounding pixels are used to obtain the model parameters with the help of the least square method. Experimental results indicate that the improved method can obtain considerable gains over HEVC intra prediction and several other prediction methods.

Keywords: 3D holoscopic image · Image prediction · Image coding · GMM · HEVC

1 Introduction

Holoscopic imaging, also referred to as integral imaging, light field imaging or plenoptic imaging, is an autostereoscopic light field technology, which is capable of recreating and transmitting the intensity and light direction information coming from 3D scene to user's eyes providing a more immersive experience. In the process of content acquisition and display, an array of micro convex lens, known as a "flys-eye" lens array, is utilized to record and reproduce the light rays of 3D objects in different direction. Therefore, 3D holoscopic systems can provide continuous motion parallax throughout the viewing zone with precise convergence and depth perception, for which it can minimize some uncomfortable feelings such as eye strain or headache when people focus on the screen for a long time and is regarded as a promising technique for future 3D TV.

© Springer Nature Singapore Pte Ltd. 2017
X. Yang and G. Zhai (Eds.): IFTC 2016, CCIS 685, pp. 276–285, 2017.
DOI: 10.1007/978-981-10-4211-9_27

For the purpose of supplying immersive experience and fitting high definition (HD) demand, much higher image resolution is needed and, consequently, effective coding tools are desirable for such particular type of content.

Several 3D holoscopic image coding frameworks have been proposed based on the new standard, High Efficient Video Coding (HEVC) [1], which is developed by Joint Collaborative Team on Video Coding (JCT-VC). In [2,3], a prediction coding work is proposed, in which new prediction modes are incorporated into HEVC to explore the self-similarity of the particular structure of 3D holoscopic content. In [4], a locally linear embedding (LLE)-based prediction algorithm is introduced into the HEVC encoder to handle 3D holoscopic image, which is an improved algorithm based on template matching prediction (TMP) [5]. A disparity compensation based 3D holoscopic image coding algorithm using HEVC is put forward in [6], in which the shifting vector is extracted and then the obtained disparity information is utilized to predict the coding block. In [7], the compression of holoscopic image is handled by introducing the full inter-prediction scheme in HEVC into intra-prediction.

The main idea of the most above mentioned schemes is to use a linear model to estimate a prediction of the coding block given a best matched block or k-nearest neighbor (k-NN) patches set. However, the linear model is ineffective for some texture and edge regions. The Gaussian mixture model (GMM) plays significant role in non-Gaussian image modeling, and may approximate distributions arbitrarily well through amending the number of mixture components. As a result, the GMM is widely used in image processing, including object detection in images [8], video compressive sensing [9] and video error concealment [10]. In this paper, a 3D holoscopic image prediction algorithm based on GMM is introduced firstly and, thereafter, an improved scheme based on GMM is put forward to get a better prediction motivated by discussion of the shortcoming of the GMM based method. The advantages of the improved method are twofold. Firstly, we do not need to set an initial value of the current coding block in prediction analytic expression. Due to this reason, we can achieve a better prediction to some extent. Secondly, many parameters that are insignificant in the final prediction in GMM based method are avoided. Therefore, the complexity of the total prediction scheme can be considerably reduced.

The remainder of the paper is organized as follows. Section 2 briefly introduces the 3D holoscopic image prediction algorithm based on GMM. An improved scheme is put forward based on the shortcoming of the GMM based method in Sect. 3. Section 4 presents the experimental results and analysis, and Sect. 5 concludes the paper.

2   Prediction Based on GMM

In this section, we will introduce the prediction of the coding block based on the GMM. The GMM based coding scheme for 3D holoscopic image includes two parts: First, derive the patch dictionary stacked with the k-NN patches of the current coding block, where the patch dictionary is determined in the specified causal coded and reconstructed region of the image. Second, construct a block-based GMM based on the patch dictionary and deduce the analytic expression of the optimal prediction to predict the current coding block.

2.1   Construction of k-NN patches dictionary

As we all known, the holoscopic image is composed of numerous elemental images (EIs) and each EI shows a slightly different view of 3D scene. Therefore, the holoscopic image has a high self-similarity. In this paper, the k-NN patches dictionary of the current coding block is obtained in vertical and horizontal directions with the help of neighboring blocks of coding block, shown in Fig. 1, under Euclidean distance.

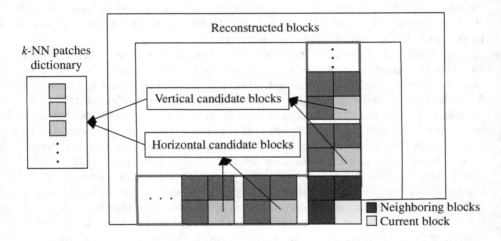

Fig. 1. Deriving of the k-NN patches dictionary

Let current coding block is stacked in a column vector $\mathbf{X}_0$, and neighboring blocks of current coding block are represented by a vector $\mathbf{X}_p$. Let $\mathbf{C}_{Hor} = [\mathbf{C}_{Hor}^0, \mathbf{C}_{Hor}^p]^{\mathrm{T}}$ and $\mathbf{C}_{Var} = [\mathbf{C}_{Var}^0, \mathbf{C}_{Var}^p]^{\mathrm{T}}$, where $\mathbf{C}_{Hor}^0$ and $\mathbf{C}_{Var}^0$ denote dictionaries stacked by all the possible patches that having the same geometric shape as current coding block in horizontal and vertical searching windows, shown in Fig. 1, respectively. While $\mathbf{C}_{Hor}^p$ and $\mathbf{C}_{Var}^p$ are constructed by all the patches that having the same geometric shape as the neighboring blocks of current coding block in horizontal and vertical searching windows, respectively. Therefore, the problem of finding the k-NN patches can be formulated as searching for k atoms $\mathbf{c}_{0m}$ in $\mathbf{C}_{Hor}^0$ and $\mathbf{C}_{Var}^0$ with the corresponding atoms $\mathbf{c}_{pm}$ in $\mathbf{C}_{Hor}^p$ and $\mathbf{C}_{Var}^p$ under the matching criterion given by

$$D = \|\mathbf{X}_p - \mathbf{c}_{pm}\|_2^2 \tag{1}$$

Suppose vector $\mathbf{Y}_0$ is stacked by k atoms $\mathbf{c}_{0m}$ and $\mathbf{Y}_p$ represents the k corresponding atoms $\mathbf{c}_{pm}$. Therefore, the k-NN patches dictionary $\mathbf{S} = [\mathbf{X}_0, \mathbf{Y}_0]^{\mathrm{T}}$ is derived. Thereafter, the vector $\mathbf{S}$ can be used to formulate a Gaussian mixture models to predict the current coding block. In next section, we will deduce the prediction analytic expression and give the process of GMM parameter estimation.

2.2 Prediction Analytic Expression

The main idea of the GMM based prediction is to take full advantage of the k-NN patches to derive a better estimate $\widehat{\mathbf{X}}_0 = \mathcal{K}(\mathbf{Y}_0)$, where $\mathcal{K}()$ is an estimating equation. Therefore, the optimal prediction for the current coding block is found by solving an MMSE problem, given by

$$\mathcal{K}^*(\mathbf{Y}_0) = \underset{\mathcal{K}(\mathbf{Y}_0)}{\mathrm{argmin}} \, E[\|\mathbf{X}_0 - \mathcal{K}(\mathbf{Y}_0)\|_2^2] \tag{2}$$

The solution of (2) can be written as

$$\mathcal{K}^*(\mathbf{Y}_0) = E[\mathbf{X}_0|\mathbf{Y}_0] = \int x_0 f_{\mathbf{X}_0|\mathbf{Y}_0}(x_0|y_0)dx_0 \tag{3}$$

Here the probability density function $f_{\mathbf{X}_0,\mathbf{Y}_0}(x_0, y_0)$ is formulated as a GMM, which is given by

$$f_\mathbf{S}(s) = \sum_{n=1}^{N} \pi^n p^n(s), \mathbf{S}^{\mathrm{T}} = [\mathbf{X}_0^{\mathrm{T}}, \mathbf{Y}_0^{\mathrm{T}}] \tag{4}$$

where $p^n(s)$ is Gaussian density with mean $\mu_\mathbf{S}^n$ and covariance $\mathbf{C}_\mathbf{S}^n$, s is the atom of vector $\mathbf{S}$ and the weights π^n are all positive and sum to one.

$$\mu_\mathbf{S}^n = \begin{bmatrix} \mu_{\mathbf{X}_0}^n \\ \mu_{\mathbf{Y}_0}^n \end{bmatrix}, \mathbf{C}_\mathbf{SS}^n = \begin{bmatrix} \mathbf{C}_{\mathbf{X}_0\mathbf{X}_0}^n & \mathbf{C}_{\mathbf{X}_0\mathbf{Y}_0}^n \\ \mathbf{C}_{\mathbf{Y}_0\mathbf{X}_0}^n & \mathbf{C}_{\mathbf{Y}_0\mathbf{Y}_0}^n \end{bmatrix} \tag{5}$$

Based on (3), (4) and (5), we can deduce that the optimal prediction for the current coding block can be expressed as

$$\widehat{\mathbf{X}}_0 = \sum_{n=1}^{N} \pi^n(\mathbf{Y}_0)(\mu_{\mathbf{X}_0}^n + \mathbf{C}_{\mathbf{X}_0\mathbf{Y}_0}^n(\mathbf{C}_{\mathbf{Y}_0\mathbf{Y}_0}^n)^{-1}(\mathbf{Y}_0 - \mu_{\mathbf{Y}_0}^n)) \tag{6}$$

where

$$\pi^n(\mathbf{Y}_0) = \frac{\pi^n p_{\mathbf{Y}_0}^n}{\sum_{m=1}^{N} \pi^m p_{\mathbf{Y}_0}^m} \tag{7}$$

The expectation-maximization (EM) algorithm [11] is a classical method to estimate the GMM parameters and performs well. Therefore, the standard EM algorithm can be utilized to obtain the GMM parameters here.

It is worth mentioning that the EM method can be started by either initializing the weights of each Gaussian component and conducting M-step, or doing E-step with a set of initial means and covariance. In this paper, we choose the former and the weights are given random.

3   Improved Prediction Scheme Based on GMM

GMM based prediction is an effective way to handle 3D holoscopic image coding and outperforms the HEVC standard and many other schemes with considerable gains. However, a few remarks about its shortcomings should be made. First, in the final prediction function, the GMM based method has to set an initial value of the current coding block in order to calculate the $\mu_{\mathbf{X}_0}^n$ and $\mathbf{C}_{\mathbf{X}_0\mathbf{Y}_0}^n$, and the estimate depends on the initial value of the current coding block to some extent. Second, in this paper, EM algorithm is used to obtain the GMM parameters. Therefore, the computational complexity is high, even though we can send some priori information to the decoder to reduce complexity.

According to the analysis above, we improve the GMM based scheme in order to shun the shortcomings of GMM based method. In the improved method, the prediction expression (6) is rewritten as follows.

$$\widehat{\mathbf{X}}_0 = \sum_{n=1}^{N} \pi^n(\mathbf{Y}_0)(\mathbf{C}_{\mathbf{X}_0\mathbf{Y}_0}^n(\mathbf{C}_{\mathbf{Y}_0\mathbf{Y}_0}^n)^{-1}\mathbf{Y}_0) \tag{8}$$

In the improved prediction scheme, the means $\mu_{\mathbf{X}_0}^n$ and $\mu_{\mathbf{Y}_0}^n$ are removed. We rewrite the Eq. (8) into a matrix form.

$$\widehat{\mathbf{X}}_0 = \pi\mathbf{C}_{\mathbf{X}_0\mathbf{Y}_0}(\mathbf{C}_{\mathbf{Y}_0\mathbf{Y}_0})^{-1}\mathbf{Y}_0 \tag{9}$$

where $\pi = [\pi^0(\mathbf{Y}_0), \pi^1(\mathbf{Y}_0), ..., \pi^N(\mathbf{Y}_0)]$ is a matrix of dimension $1 \times N$ and $\mathbf{C}_{\mathbf{X}_0\mathbf{Y}_0} = [\mathbf{C}_{\mathbf{X}_0\mathbf{Y}_0}^0, \mathbf{C}_{\mathbf{X}_0\mathbf{Y}_0}^1, ..., \mathbf{C}_{\mathbf{X}_0\mathbf{Y}_0}^N]^{\mathrm{T}}$ is a matrix of dimension of $N \times K$. As can be seen in (9), if we can obtain parameter matrices π and $\mathbf{C}_{\mathbf{X}_0\mathbf{Y}_0}^0$, then the estimator of the current coding block can be got. In order to derive a better prediction, vector $\mathbf{X}_p$ and $\mathbf{Y}_p$ are used as a training set to calculate the parameters with the help of the least square method. It is worth mentioning here that it is hardly to directly acquire π and $\mathbf{C}_{\mathbf{X}_0\mathbf{Y}_0}^0$. Therefore, $\pi\mathbf{C}_{\mathbf{X}_0\mathbf{Y}_0}^0$ is as a whole and the calculated $\pi\mathbf{C}_{\mathbf{X}_0\mathbf{Y}_0}^0$ is then used to predict the current coding block.

4   Experimental Results

The performance of the proposed coding framework is compared with the original HEVC standard (referred to as HEVC), as well as the method in [6]. HEVC Test Model (HM) reference software version 13.0 is modified for the proposed scheme. The configuration parameter used in the paper is the "Intra, main", which is defined in [12]. Four tested Quantization Parameters (22, 27, 32, and 37) are adopted. Four holoscopic test images [13] are used in the test, as shown in Fig. 2: Fredo, Laura, Plenoptic2 and Seagull. For simplicity, we cut all the test images into size of 3840 × 2160, and all images are transformed into YUV 4:2:0 formats. The proposed improved prediction method (referred to as "GMM-Improved") is evaluated against three prediction schemes: the original HEVC intra standard (referred to as "HEVC"), the disparity compensation based

3D holoscopic image coding method proposed in [6] (referred to as "DCCM") and the GMM based prediction method with 3 components (referred to as "GMM-3").

The dimensions defined for the search window is the same as in [6]. In our experiments, HEVC intra mode 4 is replaced by the proposed approach. We choose 6 nearest neighbour patches, 3 in each direction, to constitute the k-NN patches dictionary. In GMM based scheme, the number of the components of GMM based method is set to 3, and the weight of the nth Gaussian component π^n is random, and sums to one. In order to obtain the mean and covariance matrix of p_s^n, an initial value for $\mathbf{X}_0$ is needed. In our experience, $\mathbf{X}_0$ is initialized by the optimal one in k-NN patches dictionary, which approximates the coding block best. The EM algorithm guarantees an increasing log-likelihood from iteration to iteration. As a result, the termination criterion for iteration in the experience is that the number of iteration is equal to 10 or the log-likelihood is convergent according to EM method. All experiments were performed on a computer with an Intel i5-2310 CPU 2.9 GHz and 8-GB RAM. The program developing environment is Visual Studio C++ 2008 with the Microsoft Windows 7 operating system.

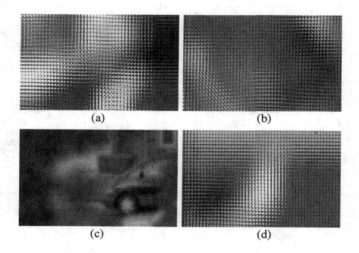

Fig. 2. 3D holoscopic images used in the test set: (a) Fredo, (b) Laura, (c) Plenoptic2, (d) Seagull

Table 1 shows the rate distortion gains of three prediction methods over HEVC. From Table 1, we can see that the GMM based coding scheme with 3 components is clearly advantageous, outperforming the original HEVC intra-prediction and the DCCM proposed in [6]. The BD-PSNR (BD-rate) of the proposed GMM with 3 components over method in [6] are 0.22 dB (−2.47%) for Fredo, 0.36 dB (−4.56%) for Laura, 0.26 dB (−2.84%) for Plenoptic2, and 0.25 dB (−3.47%) for Seagull. The reason for the improvement is that the GMM

Table 1. BD-PSNR/Rate: compared to HEVC intra prediction

Images	Coding methods	BD-PSNR (dB)	BD-Rate (%)
Fredo	DCCM	1.90	−28.98
	GMM-3	2.11	−31.45
	GMM-Improved	2.69	−37.49
Laura	DCCM	1.46	−20.17
	GMM-3	1.82	−24.73
	GMM-Improved	2.73	−35.41
Plenoptic2	DCCM	0.85	−10.09
	GMM-3	1.11	−12.93
	GMM-Improved	1.55	−18.51
Seagull	DCCM	1.39	−23.10
	GMM-3	1.64	−26.57
	GMM-Improved	2.72	−39.53

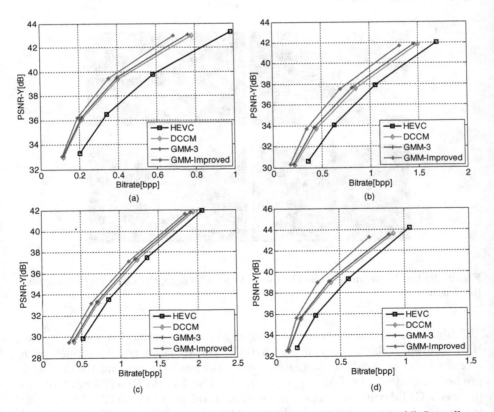

Fig. 3. Rate-distortion results: (a) Fredo, (b) Laura, (c) Plenoptic2, (d) Seagull

based method takes full advantage the intrinsic characteristic of such particular type of content to derive k-NN patches of the current coding block, which are used to construct GMM to predict the coding block. However, an initial value of the current coding block is needed, and the iteration in EM method increases the computational complexity.

The proposed improved scheme shuns the shortcomings of GMM based method. From Table 1, it is clearly to see that the BD-PSNR (BD-rate) of the improved method over GMM with 3 components are 0.57 dB (-6.04%) for Fredo, 0.91 dB (-10.68%) for Laura, 0.44 dB (-5.58%) for Plenoptic2, and 1.08 dB (-12.96%) for Seagull. The achievements over GMM based scheme are twofold. On the one hand, the improved method does not need to initialize the coding block which can reduce the estimation errors. On the other hand, more surrounding pixels are used to obtain the model parameters which can increase the estimation accuracy.

Figure 3 shows the rate-distortion curve of the test image set using different coding schemes, which further confirms that the proposed coding scheme performs better than other prediction methods.

Table 2 gives the detail execution times of proposed prediction method and HEVC both on encoder and decoder sides for all the test images. From Table 2, we can see that more execution times are needed by using the proposed method both on encoder and decoder sides compared to HEVC. For all the test images, over three times execution time are needed by the GMM-Improved method

Table 2. Run-time comparison at the encoder side and decoder side

Images	Coding methods	Encoding time (s)	Decoding time (s)
Fredo	HEVC	72.2	0.82
	DCCM	228.2	4.00
	GMM-3	15548.5	793.3
	GMM-Improved	262.6	11.42
Laura	HEVC	82.6	1.03
	DCCM	243.1	11.09
	GMM-3	16636.1	824.2
	GMM-Improved	297.8	14.27
Plenoptic2	HEVC	89.5	1.18
	DCCM	230.6	8.37
	GMM-3	13993.2	574.5
	GMM-Improved	299.9	12.99
Seagull	HEVC	72.4	0.80
	DCCM	233.4	10.59
	GMM-3	15623.1	853.5
	GMM-Improved	281.9	13.67

compared to HEVC. Since the decoder side has to perform the same prediction process as the encoder side in the proposed method, the time ratio in the decoder side is higher then that in the encoder side. From Table 2, we find that over ten times execution time are required by the GMM-Improved scheme compared to HEVC in the decoder side. When compared to DCCM, similar execution times are needed by the GMM-Improved method both on encoder and decoder sides. However, the computation complexity can be reduced more than 90% by the improved method compared to GMM-3 method.

5   Conclusion

In this paper, a 3D holoscopic image prediction algorithm based on GMM is firstly introduced. Thereafter, an improved scheme is put forward to achieve a better prediction motivated by the discussion of the shortcoming of the GMM based method. In the improved method, many parameters that are insignificant in the final estimator of GMM based method are avoided, and more surrounding pixels are used to obtain the model parameters with the help of the least square method. Future work will include the prediction modes analysis of such particular type of content in HEVC to further decrease the computational complexity.

Acknowledgment. This work was supported in part by the National Natural Science Foundation of China, under Grants 61571285, U1301257, 61422111, and 61301112.

References

1. Sullivan, G.J., Ohm, J., Han, W.J., Wiegand, T.: Overview of the high efficiency video coding (HEVC) standard. IEEE Trans. Circuits Syst. Video Technol. **22**(12), 1649–1668 (2012)
2. Conti, C., Nunes, P., Soares, L.D.: New HEVC prediction modes for 3D holoscopic video coding. In: IEEE International Conference on Image Processing (ICIP), pp. 1325–1328 (2012)
3. Agooun, A., Fatah, O.A., Fernandez, J.C., Conti, C., Nunes, P., Soares, L.D.: Acquisition, processing and coding of 3D holoscopic content for immersive video systems. In: 3DTV-Conference: The True Vision Capture, Transmission and Display of 3D Video (3DTV-CON), pp. 1–4 (2013)
4. Lucas, L.F.R., Conti, C., Nunes, P., Soares, L.D., Rodrigues, N.M.M., Pagliari, C.L., da Silva, E.A.B., de Faria, S.M.M.: Locally linear embedding-based prediction for 3D holoscopic image coding using HEVC. In: 2014 Proceedings of the 22nd European Signal Processing Conference (EUSIPCO), pp. 11–15, 1–5 (2014)
5. Tan, T.K., Boon, C.S., Suzuki, Y.: Intra prediction by template matching. In: IEEE International Conference on Image Processing (ICIP), pp. 1693–1696 (2006)
6. Liu, D., An, P., Ma, R., Shen, L.: Disparity compensation based 3D holoscopic image coding using HEVC. In: 2015 IEEE China Summit and International Conference on Signal and Information Processing (ChinaSIP), pp. 201–205 (2015)
7. Li, Y., Sjostrom, M., Olsson, R., Jennehag, U.: Efficient intra prediction scheme for light field image compression. In: IEEE International Conference on Acoustics, Speech and Signal Processing (ICASSP), pp. 539–543, 4–9 (2014)

8. Zhang, J., Ma, D.: Nonlinear prediction for Gaussian mixture image models. IEEE Trans. Image Process. **13**(6), 836–847 (2004)

9. Yang, J., et al.: Video compressive sensing using Gaussian mixture models. IEEE Trans. Image Process. **23**(11), 4863–4878 (2014)

10. Persson, D., Eriksson, T., Hedelin, P.: Packet video error concealment with Gaussian mixture models. IEEE Trans. Image Process. **17**(2), 145–154 (2008)

11. Redner, A., Walker, H.F.: Mixture densities, maximum likelihood and the EM algorithm. SIAM Rev. **26**, 195–239 (1984)

12. Bossen, F.: Common HM test conditions and soft-ware reference configurations, Document JCTVC-L1100 (2013)

13. Georgiev, T.: Jan 2013. http://www.tgeorgiev.net/

A Novel Image Coding Framework
Based on Content Similarity Analysis

Qianhan Liu, Long Ye[✉], Jingling Wang, and Qin Zhang

Key Laboratory Media Audio and Video, Communication University of China,
Ministry of Education, Beijing 100024, China
liuqianhancuc@qq.com, {yelong,wjl,zhangqin}@cuc.edu.cn

Abstract. Because of not considering the correlations among images, current image coding technologies result in an unnecessary waste of storage space. This paper proposed a novel image coding framework based on content analysis, which can help to elevate the storing efficiency by utilizing the removal of spatial correlations within the image set composed by similar images. In our method, SVM algorithm is used to classify similar images after extracting image features of BOF (Bag of Feature). All images of each category are considered as a GOP (Group of Pictures) within MPEG-2 standard, and then each of them will be further compressed with predictive coding. Experimental results demonstrate that the proposed method can improve coding efficiency by reducing redundancy of correlated images, and further greatly saving the storage space.

Keywords: Image compression · Content similarity analysis · Image coding · Image classification · Support Vector Machine (SVM)

1 Introduction

Huge numbers of photos and videos have posted a great challenge on storage space, meantime bring about higher requirement for the image compression efficiency. The compression process is based on reducing the redundancy of the image to be stored or transmitted in an efficient form [1]. Earlier image coding technologies, such as Huffman and vector quantization coding methods have almost touched their limitations of coding efficiency. In the mid-1980s, ISO and CCITT jointly formulate a general image compression standard named the JPEG standard [2], the core algorithm of this standard is based on Discrete Cosine Transform (DCT), uniform quantization and Huffman coding. It has been widely used and continuously upgraded. In 1993, embedded zero-tree wavelet coding proposed by Shapiro [3] greatly improved the efficiency of image coding, hence become the mainstream. In 1997, the Joint photographic expert group developed a new

This work is supported by the National Natural Science Foundation of China under Grant Nos. 61201236 and 61371191, and the Project of State Administration of Press, Publication, Radio, Film and Television under Grant No. 2015-53.

© Springer Nature Singapore Pte Ltd. 2017
X. Yang and G. Zhai (Eds.): IFTC 2016, CCIS 685, pp. 286–295, 2017.
DOI: 10.1007/978-981-10-4211-9_28

static image compression standard named JPEG2000 [4]. This new JPEG standard can achieve higher compression ratio and robustness.

The image compression standards mentioned above have enjoyed tremendous success during the past decades. Though these conventional image coding are mature ways to use the correlations of pixels in the same image for compression, they also have limitations to exploit the correlations of external images and significantly reduce compressed data size.

Many databases, even with personal devices that contain a significant number of similar images, due to the large quantities of taken photos, the storage of such data can be expensive. Therefore, compression task to store images efficiently is needed more than ever to reduce the cost of saving images [5]. But if the picture is stored alone using existed image compression standards, the correlations between images may be ignored, thus much precious storage space is occupied by useless redundant information. Recent researches on image processing using a large-scale image database have emerged in exploiting the correlations of external images and significantly reduce compressed data size. In particular, Wu *et al.* have introduced a cloud-based image coding scheme [6], when the large-scale database of images is available in the cloud, the proposed coding scheme can retrieve near and similar images, thus exploiting the correlations of external images and reconstructing the original image. Song *et al.* [7] proposed a cloud-based distributed image coding (Cloud-DIC) schemes to exploit external correlations for mobile photo uploading. For each input image, a thumbnail is transmitted to retrieve correlated images and reconstruct it in the cloud by geometrical and illumination registrations.

These image coding schemes conducted cloud-based searching for the original images to obtain the similar ones for reference and reconstruction. We propose to classify these similar images within specific image datasets. Furthermore, the classified images are compressed as categories. There are three main problems needed to be solved in our method. At first, we know that in video coding the correlation between images exist in consecutive frames, but in image coding, it's difficult for us to identify the similar images in local storage when we attempt to code a new image. Secondly, the choice of image features is also an important factor which influences the classified effect. Finally, we need to design a compression coding method to get more coding efficiently than the traditional coding algorithm such as JPEG.

To solve the above problems, we propose a novel image coding framework based on content similarity analysis, the basic idea mimics inter-frame coding in video. When it comes to video which is composed of time-sequence images, the similarity between successive frames can be applied to exploit the temporal redundancy. Motion estimation is a critical component of video compression for its simplicity and coding efficiency of motion vectors [8]. Support Vector Machine (SVM) [9] is used to construct the image library of classified scenes by utilizing the BOF [10] image descriptors, and an effective coding method is achieved based on the similarity content analysis of each class. The rest of this paper is organized as follows. Section 2 gives a detailed description of our coding framework. Section 3 explains how to classify images into clusters so as to exploit optimized correlation between pictures. The experimental results are presented in Sect. 4 and Sect. 5 concludes the paper.

2   Image Coding Framework Based on Content Similarity

The coding framework based on content similarity is shown in Fig. 1. In the part of Image classification, we acquire the visual features of images and classify all the pictures by using a supervised learning algorithm. And in the part of Image coding, we select a reference picture in every cluster and reconstruct the other pictures using the motion vector and residual information compared with the reference image.

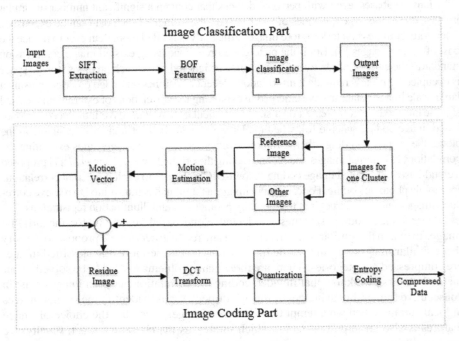

Fig. 1.   Coding framework based on content similarity analysis

2.1   Image Coding Based on Content Similarity

Unlike video frames, images do not have temporal property. It is necessary for us to cluster images with similar contents in storage space before we imitate the way to remove video's temporal redundancy.

Besides clustering, another important work in our image coding framework is to find a reference image in every cluster shown in Fig. 2. The function of reference image just like I-frame in inter-prediction coding adopted by MPEG-2.

Let $g(i,j)$ represents the Mean-Square-Error (MSE) value between image i and image j. i, j denote the image index in a given image cluster, especially when $i = j, g(i,j) = 0$. By denoting the reference image as I_{re}, we can calculate every MSE value of the images in the library, and find out which image owns the minimum MSE value as the reference picture, as Eq. (1). MSE as the arithmetic factor of PSNR, is the mean square error

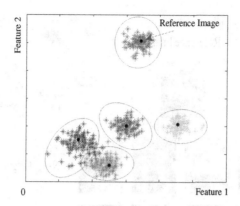

Fig. 2. Reference image from the classification results

between original image and the processed image, which can measure the image quality. Assume that each image in image library is a separate point, those points can be divided into different clusters according to their visual features.

$$I_{re} = arg \min_{j} \left[\sum_{i=1}^{N} g(i,j) \right] \tag{1}$$

2.2 Block Matching Based Motion Estimation

In inter-frame prediction algorithm, a frame image is divided into many non-overlapping blocks after the block-matching based on motion estimation. Each pixel in the same block has the same displacement in the preference frame, so the block can find a most similar block in it according to a given principle. The displacement between the matching block and original block is called motion vector. One of the widely used principles to blocks matching is Least-Mean-Square-Error (LMSE), as Eq. (2).

$$MSE(i,j) = \frac{1}{MN} \sum_{m=1}^{M} \sum_{n=1}^{N} \left[f_k(m,n) - f_{k-1}(m+i,n+j) \right]^2 \tag{2}$$

After motion estimation, we can get a set of motion vectors D for every image in each cluster. Through the help of I_{re} and D, we can reconstruct every image in the cluster and acquire the residual information between reconstruction and original picture.

Through DCT, quantization and entropy coding, residue information can be obtained to the final image encoded data. Then every image cluster consists of the information of one reference image, N − 1 residue images and N − 1 motion vectors sets, shown in Fig. 3.

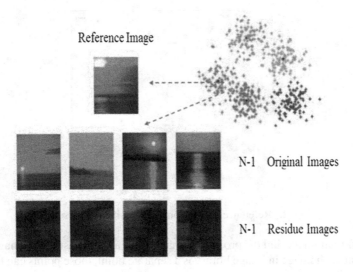

Fig. 3. The results of block-matching in each cluster

3   Feature Extraction and Image Classification

3.1   Feature Extraction

The key of classification lies on selecting appropriate image features, which greatly influence the accuracy of the classification and the efficiency of the coding process. Bag of features (BOF) is a popular model in image classification as extracting the combination of features to represent a complete image. Usually, three steps are needed to construct the occurrence histogram: descriptor extraction, learning vocabulary and coding of descriptors [11].

First of all, SIFT descriptor is used to describe an image for generating visual words. Let $q_j \in R_p$ denote a p dimensional descriptor. The feature vector usually is a 128-dimension vector, mainly containing the direction and scale information of image interest point.

Secondly, a visual vocabulary is learned on extracted descriptors by some methods such as k-means. Manhattan distance standard is commonly used to measure the distance between descriptor q_j and descriptor p_j as Eq. (3).

$$L = \sum_{j=1}^{d} \left| q_j - p_j \right| \tag{3}$$

All descriptors are divided into clusters, and centroids in each cluster are called visual vocabulary.

Thirdly, the coding of descriptors assigns these descriptors to their corresponding visual words in the vocabulary with corresponding coefficients. The number of visual words and the value of coefficient vary with different coding schemes. Let U_{ij} denote the coding coefficient of descriptor x_i to visual word. An image can be represented as a set of visual words histogram as shown in Fig. 4 by counting the frequency of the visual vocabulary.

Fig. 4. Histogram of visual words

3.2 Image Classification

Image classification technology can divide images into clusters where pictures are relevant just like consecutive frames in a video. Support Vector Machine (SVM) is one of the typical supervised algorithms. Studies show that SVM have better performance compared with traditional classifiers [12]. The application of kernel function contributes to the good performance for SVM, thus optimal classification plane can be constructed in the case of that data in higher dimension space is linearly inseparable.

We set $x, z \in x$, and input x from $R(n)$ space to the feature space $\emptyset$, through a nonlinear function ϕ, where $\emptyset$ is a part of $R(m)$, and $n << m$:

The kernel function is defined as:

$$K(x, z) = \langle \emptyset(x), \emptyset(z) \rangle \tag{4}$$

We choose RBF kernel function for the features:

$$K_{d-RBF}(x, y) = e^{-\rho d(x,y)} \tag{5}$$

Where $d(x, y)$ can be selected for any distance in the feature space, and assume x_i and y_i represent the visual words of the BOF histogram. Function γ^2 is appropriate for distance:

$$d_{\gamma^2}(x, y) = \sum_i \frac{(x_i - y_i)^2}{x_i + y_i} \tag{6}$$

4 Experiments

We processed images from INRIA Holiday dataset, which has 1491 images in total, for our experiments in this paper. There are multiple images in the same scene captured at different viewpoints and focal length, and its composition is similar with phone's album. As shown in Fig. 5, ten types of images are selected to test. For convenience, we denote them in this paper from "a" to "j" as ten clusters.

Fig. 5. The selected images as inputs in our experiments, denoted as "*a*" to "*j*"

In the proposed framework, the features of all images are taken as SVM inputting vectors, after classification, images with higher similarity in terms of visual content are

Fig. 6. Experimental results of image classification

divided into 10 classes. As shown in Fig. 6. Two pictures are under the threshold, they are not contributed to any class generated, shown as Fig. 7.

Fig. 7. Unclassifiable images

Each picture in the 10 classes will get a MSE value after loop computation in its own cluster. The picture with the minimum MSE value is selected as reference picture by comparing every MSE value of the pictures in one cluster. The residue images of the other images in each cluster can be acquired by using the reference image, then transform to the final encoded data after a series processing. Limited by the pages, only the residue images of group "j" are shown in Fig. 8.

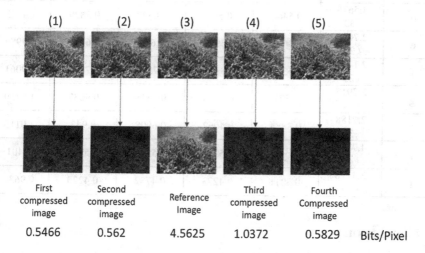

Fig. 8. Compressed images of experimental results in classes "j"

In our experiment, original images take up 607884364 bits' storage space, compared to 199159425 (with compressed data 184208217 bits and motion vector data 14942208 bits.) after processing of images coding method we proposed with the reduction percentage up to 66.24%. In terms of data size of per pixel, the average of data size needed after processing is approximately one third of the original.

According to the Table 1 above, in the classes of the "e", "f", "h" and "j" marked in blue color, the compression effect is rather ideal with compression ratio up to 10:1. The main reason is the highly content-correlated between images. On the contrary, in the classes of "a" and "c" marked in yellow color, the compression ratio just only reached 3:1, which caused by the difference in pixels level between reference image and original one. In general, the proposed coding method can effectively reduce the content redundancy with the help of images database we designed. Especially for a database with abundant information, our method can reduce the data size after compression to a considerable extent.

Table 1. Experimental data of coding in pixel (numbers with brackets in the second columns are the reference images)

Image Classes	Reference data	First compressed image	Second compressed image	Third compressed image	Fourth compressed image	Average data
	Bits/pixel	Bits/pixel	Bits/pixel	Bits/pixel	Bits/pixel	Bits/pixel
a	3.4688 (1)	0.4338	0.4389	1.4915	None	1.4583
b	2.75 (2)	0.3948	0.6498	0.9946	None	1.1973
c	5.0833 (3)	0.6726	0.6036	1.6292	1.6856	1.9349
d	4.5625 (3)	0.5466	0.562	1.0372	0.5829	1.4583
e	2.7605 (2)	0.3626	0.5933	0.662	0.6144	0.9986
f	2.1459 (2)	0.5305	0.3135	0.7574	0.7831	0.9061
g	2.7917 (2)	0.377	0.5258	0.8311	0.9037	1.0859
h	2.7188 (3)	0.3884	0.4062	0.6008	0.943	1.0115
i	4.7740 (4)	0.594	0.5332	0.5246	0.5788	1.401
j	3.1128 (3)	0.3811	0.4273	0.4732	0.4225	0.9634

5 Conclusion

In this paper, we propose an image coding method based on content similarity analysis. Our method is mainly applied to the database where images possess relatively high content correlation, the phone album is appropriate for this situation. In our compression framework, images are interpreted by BOF descriptors and then similar images are processed after classification. Through selecting the image which has most abundant information in each class as reference image, other images can be compressed based on the reference image. The experiments demonstrate that the storage space used by images can be significantly reduced compared to the original JPEG format.

The relevance between images plays the most important role in the coding efficiency. For an input image, if we cannot find highly correlated images in the database, the scheme cannot output an excellent result. Although mobile photos are discussed as an exemplified application in this paper, it is still need to improve the classification accuracy to find highly correlated images available is the next research. In addition, a reference picture for each cluster may vary when a set of pictures is updated by adding new entities. Since the database maybe dynamical, we should further consider to re-compress all pictures in the proposed scheme.

References

1. Kranthi Kumar, T., Reddy, D.H.: An overview of new trends in image compression. Int. J. Emerg. Trends Technol. Sci. **04**, 314–329 (2015)
2. Pennebaker, W., Mitchell, J.: JPEG, Still Image Data Compression Standard. Van Nostrand, New York (1993)
3. Mu, Y., Murali, B., Ali, A.L.: Embedded image coding using zerotrees of wavelet coefficients for visible human dataset. In: Proceedings of IEEE Conference Record of the Thirty-Ninth Asilomar Conference on Signals, Systems and Computers, Pacific Grove, CA, pp. 276–280 (2005)
4. Adams, M.D.: The JPEG2000 Still Image Compression Standard, ISO/IEC JTCI/SC 29/WG 1 N2412, 1 September 2001
5. Omari, M., Jaafri, S.O., Karour, N.: Image compression based on exploiting similarities in a group of pictures. In: Proceedings of IEEE International Conference on Industrial Informatics and Computer Systems (CIICS), Sharjah, pp. 1–5, March 2016
6. Yue, H., Sun, X., Yang, J., Wu, F.: Cloud-based image coding for mobile devices—toward thousands to one compression. Proc. IEEE Trans. Multimedia **15**, 845–857 (2013)
7. dan Song, X., Peng, X., Xu, J., Shi, G., Wu, F.: Cloud-based distributed image coding. Proc. IEEE Trans. Circuits Syst. Video Technol. **25**(12), 1926–1940 (2015)
8. Bachu, S., Chari, K.M.: A review on motion estimation in video compression. In: Proceedings of IEEE International Conference on Signal Processing and Communication Engineering Systems, Guntur, pp. 250–256 (2015)
9. El-Naqa, I., Yang, Y., Wernick, M.N., Galasanos, N.P., Nishikawa, R.M.: A support vector machine approach for detection of microcalcifications. In: Proceedings of IEEE International Conference on Image Processing, vol. 21, no. 12, pp. 953–956 (2002)
10. Sivic, J., Zisserman, A.: Video Google: a text retrieval approach to objects matching in videos. In: Proceedings of 9th International Conference on Computer Vision, vol. 2, pp. 1470–1477 (2003)
11. Yang, Z., Kurita, T.: Improvements to the descriptor of SIFT by BOF approaches. In: Proceedings of 2nd Asian Conference on Pattern Recognition, Naha, pp. 95–99 (2013)
12. Yan, F., Wang, Y., Wang, W., Gao, W.: SVM for image classification and retrieval in natural content image. J. Comput. 1261–1265 (2004)

Block of Interest Based AVS to HEVC Transcoding with Resolution Conversion

Malik Asfandyar[✉], Mehmood Nawaz[✉], Xie Rong, Liang Zhang,
and Muddsser Hussain

Department of Information and Communication Engineering,
Shanghai Jiao Tong University, Shanghai, China
{Asfi0044,mehmoodnawaz,xierong,mudd_umz}@sjtu.edu.cn,
liang.zhang@ieee.org

Abstract. Video transcoding technique is widely used in many multi-media applications. There are many transcoding techniques have been proposed in recent decade in which we map the advanced video coding standard (AVS) to high efficiency video coding (HEVC). To improve the visual efficiency of transcoding, we pro-posed a super resolution block based technique. By using this technique we improve the low resolution AVS video to high definition (HD) video. As Human eyes are more sensitive to moving objects in video contents. Where moving objects can be estimated in terms of coding by decoded motion vectors (MV), macroblock (MB) modes and transform coefficients. By using these information, proposed method classify each frame into two types of blocks, one is the most block of interest (MBOI) and second is the less block of interest (LBOI). After classification of blocks, we apply super resolution method on decoded low resolution blocks with different parameters values. The experimental results show that our method save 20% to 40% time than full frame super resolution while keeping the same visual quality in terms of PSNR and SSIM index.

Keywords: Super resolution · Block of interest · AVS · HEVC

1 Introduction

For better performance of ultra-high definition video, a new coding standard has been formulated known as high efficiency video coding (HEVC). HEVC is a com-bined effort of two groups joint collaborative team on video coding (JCT-VC) and moving picture expert group (MPEG). Various video coding standards have been developed by international telecommunication union (ITU-T) video coding expert group (VCEG), ISO/IEC moving picture expert group (MPEG) and HEVC [1]. The cisco data traffic predicts that 80–90% of global internet traffic in 2017 will be of high definition video contents. With rapid development in multimedia applications, demand for high resolution videos and better visual experience is increasing. Hence many video compression standards like HEVC,

© Springer Nature Singapore Pte Ltd. 2017
X. Yang and G. Zhai (Eds.): IFTC 2016, CCIS 685, pp. 296–306, 2017.
DOI: 10.1007/978-981-10-4211-9_29

H264 and AVS etc. are required to minimize the large video data. HEVC standard aims to reduce the bitrate up to 50%, compared with H264/AVC while giving equivalent visual quality. Besides that HEVC introduces significant new features like extended range of block sizes, rather than a fix macro blocks.

Transcoding is the technique which converts a compressed bit stream (source bit stream) to another compressed bit stream (transcoded bit stream) [2,3]. Now a days with fast developing and emerging video coding standards, video transcoding provides multimedia contents to various consumers [4]. To meet the requirements of the network and consumer devices, every service provider use different transcoder to save the bitrate or resolution of different videos. The H.264/AVS standard is very popular and it is used for physical media, internet streaming, broadcasting and cable television services. HEVC is a new standard which reduce more bit rate than others standards on same visual quality. In heterogeneous transcoder, source bit stream is convert to a different coding standards bit stream like H.264/AVC to HEVC. There are many challenges for applying this technique, one of them is quadtree structure used by HEVC. Quadtree use larger CU sizes (64×64) for motion estimation where as H.264/ AVS use (16×16). And other challenge is the use of main anchor profiles for the HEVC which used fast motion estimation technique instead of full motion estimation. It achieve better performance close to the full motion estimation, at lower complexity cost for HD videos [5,6]. If complexity is not an issue, we can also use other techniques like fast ME with more reference frames and rate distortion (RD) optimization module which allow to test more quantization parameters (QPs). We can easily reduce the complexity of HEVC by using above two techniques with higher potential gain.

Several algorithms have been proposed for AVS to HEVC transcoding. Liu et al. proposed motion based optimization scheme with decoded motion information extraction method for visual characteristics [7]. Zhang et al. introduce fast transcoder by using inter and intra modes [8]. He used H.264 intra coding modes for macro blocks and HEVC inter coding modes for power spectrum based on rate optimization (PS-RDO). Peixoto et al. proposed a transcoder which is based on complexity-scalability from H.264 to HEVC [9]. S.F. Huang et al. proposed a method of transcoding where ROI is implemented during segmentation of frames by applying bayesian theorem threshold [10]. R. Luo et al. proposed a ROI method using decoded information of motion vectors and transform coefficient, while keeping the fix search depth for detected CUs [11]. P. Xing et al. proposed an HEVC transcoder which applied to video surveillance [12]. In this work, each coding unit (CU) is classified in different categories: background, foreground and hybrid etc. Different strategies of CU partition termination, prediction Unit (PU) candidate selection and motion estimation simplification are used to reduce the complexity in the transcoding process [11,13].

In this paper, a block of interest based transcoding with super resolution (SR) method is proposed. As Human eyes are more sensitive to moving objects in video contents. Where moving objects can be estimated by decoded motion vectors (MV), macroblock (MB) modes and transform coefficients. By using these information, pro-posed method classify each frame into two types of blocks, one is the most block of interest (MBOI) and second is the less block of interest (LBOI). After classification of blocks, we apply super resolution method on decoded low resolution blocks with different parameters values. Most block of interest (MBOI) take more time than less block of interest (LBOI) due to more number of iterations in less block of interest [14]. By this way we can save 20% to 40% time than full frame super resolution while keeping the same visual quality in terms of PSNR and SSIM index.

The rest of the paper contains following sections. Section 2 represents the detection of region of interest, Sect. 3 describe super resolution of MBOI and LBOI. Section 4 shows the experimental results and Sect. 5 represents the brief conclusion.

2   Detection of Regions of Interests

In reality, human being pay more attention to the region of interest. The sensitivity of visual system is more important for image block classification. In video, rich texture blocks or moving objects both are more attractive to the viewers. Those blocks are called the most block of interest (MBOI). Usually background objects or less texture blocks are less attractive from the observer. They are defined as less block of interest (LBOI). The video quality of MBOI and LBOI can be well maintained by higher super resolution algorithms [6] and lower super resolution algorithms respectively. Regions of newly integrated objects and fast moving objects or camera motion can be find by transform coefficients and motion vectors (MVs). In image, we can easily detect different regions of interest by using coding parameters. In AVS, video frames are encoded by macroblocks (MBs) where each macroblock dimension is 16×16 fixed. For the transcoding from AVS to HEVC transcoding, 16 macroblocks (MBs) each having a size of 16×16 pixels are grouped into one CTU with a size of 64×64 pixels. We will evaluate MB's encoding information to decide the classification of each CTU.

While each frame macroblocks are encoded in either intra or inter mode. In detection of blocks a video image is divided into two types of blocks as discussed above. The number of MBs which are encoded with intra mode within one frame is used for further decision either for intra or inter mode. Let α_i be used for indication for the ith MB within one frame,

$$\alpha_i = \begin{cases} 0, & \text{if MB is encoded for Intra mode} \\ 1, & \text{if MB is encoded for inter mode.} \end{cases} \quad (1)$$

Then, formula for threshold is;

$$\sum_{1=1}^{16} \alpha_i \geq T \quad (2)$$

Which is further used for BOI classification. Equation 1 is used as a criteria for the classification of a CTU into an intra/inter-encoded CTU, where "T" is

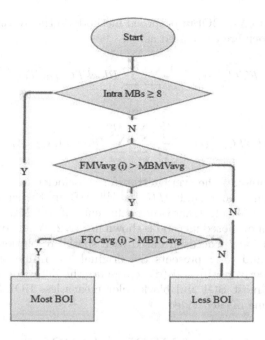

Fig. 1. BOI detection algorithm flowchart

used as thresh-old and its value during experiment is 8 because it gives maximum output at value of 8 as shown in Fig. 1. So for classification of current frame, motion vectors are calculated as:

$$Fmv_{avg}(i) = \frac{1}{N} \sum_{k=1}^{N} \sum_{l=1}^{M} MBlockmv_{MBk}(l) \tag{3}$$

where Fmv_{avg} represents the average motion of frame, "i" belongs to index of current frame and MB_k is k^{th} MB in the current frame and $Blockmv_{MBk}(l)$ presents the magnitude of motion vectors which is defined as:

$$Blockmv_{MBk}(l) = \sqrt{Bmvx^2(l) + Bmvy^2(l)} \tag{4}$$

where $Bmvx^2(l)$ and $Bmvy^2(l)$ are the horizontal and vertical motion vectors (MV) components, respectively. An average MV of current MB in frame is calculated as:

$$MBmv_{avg}(i) = \frac{1}{NF} \sum_{k=1}^{NF} \sum_{l=1}^{M} MBlockmv_{MBk}(l) \tag{5}$$

where "NF" represents the number of MB in a current frame and an image background is measured by transform coefficient "TC". Figure 1 represents the flow chart of detection of BOI in proposed method. So the average TC for frame and for current block are calculated as:

$$FTC_{avg}(i) = \frac{1}{N} \sum_{k=1}^{N} \sum_{l=1}^{M} BlockTC_{MBk}(l) \qquad (6)$$

$$MBTC_{avg}(i) = \frac{1}{NF} \sum_{k=1}^{NF} \sum_{l=1}^{M} BlockTC_{MBk}(l) \qquad (7)$$

where FTC_{avg} represents the average transform coefficient of frame, "i" belongs to index of current frame and MB_k is k^{th} MB in the current frame and $BlockTC_{MBk}(l)$ represents transform coefficients of kth MB. An example for detection of BOI in proposed method is shown in Fig. 2. Where original test video sequence HoneyBee and Cactus are used with spatial resolution of 1920×1080.

In Fig. 2, (a) and (c) represents the original 3rd frame of HoneyBee and cactus video respectively (b) and (d) represents the detection of blocks; where grey color means most BOI and black color means less BOI. These BOI vary from frame to frame in each video.

3 Super Resolution of MBOI and LBOI

We used sparse linear regression and iterative back projection method [14] to improve the visual quality of low resolution MBOI and LBOI. First of all, we divide the down sample frame into two blocks like MBOI and LBOI on the base of visual characteristic as discussed in Sect. 2. Figure 2, grey color blocks represent the most block of interest (MBOI) and black color are the less block of interest (LBOI). We apply sparse linear regression and iterative back projection method to get the high quality MBOI and LBOI. Mainly three types are implemented for upsampling; first type is 2K-to-4K, second type is 1K-to-4K and third type is 1K- to-2K upsampling. In 2K-to-4K, we used (1920×1080) low resolution input video and upsampled it up to (3840×2160) high resolution video by using super resolution method. For example, Fig. 3(a) represents the low resolution MBOI of HoneyBee image and (b) represents the high resolution MBOI. In Fig. 3, (c) shows the low resolution less block of interest (LBOI) and (d) represents upsampled high resolution LBOI. We can easily classify the visual difference between high and low block of interest.

In 1K-to-4K upsampling, we used (960×544) low resolution input and upsampled it up to (3840×2160) by using super resolution method. In 1K-to-2K upsampling, we used (960×540) low resolution input and upsampled it up to (1920×1080) by using super resolution method [14]. In generally, low resolution $(N \times N)$ is up sampled to $(2N \times 2N)$ in 2K to 4K, low resolution $(N \times N)$ is up sampled to $(4N \times 4N)$ in 1K to 4K and low resolution $(N \times N)$ is up sampled to $(2N \times 2N)$ in 1K to 2K by using super resolution on each MBOI and LBOI, respectively. Where the value of "N" should be the multiple of 16. Different super

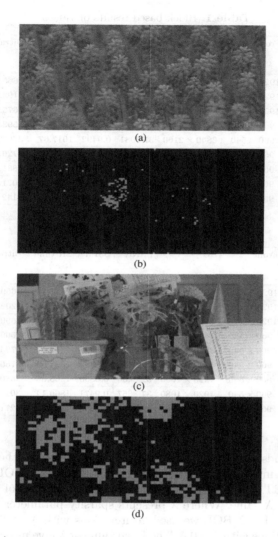

Fig. 2. (a) and (c) represents the original video sequence frame, (b) and (d) Block of Interest: grey color represents the most BOI and black color represents the less BOI

Fig. 3. (a) low resolution MBOI (b) high resolution MBOI (c) low resolution LBOI and (d) high resolution LBOI

Table 1. Block based results of videos

Video sequence	From	To	PSNR	SSIM	SR Time (Sec)	Bitrate	HEVC encoding time (Sec)
HoneyBee	1920 × 1080	3840 × 2160	38.7043	0.9345	4171.90	1665.63	10130.64
Bosphorus	1920 × 1080	3840 × 2160	39.6410	0.9592	3649.80	3193.76	14652.55
Jockey	1920 × 1080	3840 × 2160	39.2736	0.9438	4790.18	2675.47	9324.05
HoneyBee	960 × 540	3840 × 2160	37.4774	0.9294	1548.80	1593.00	11288.62
Bosphorus	960 × 540	3840 × 2160	37.7081	0.9492	1017.67	3767.36	15616.37
Jockey	960 × 540	3840 × 2160	37.9340	0.9383	1137.79	3726.01	10924.37
Cactus	960 × 540	1920 × 1080	32.8428	0.8801	1228.84	3831.21	4500.52
Kimono	960 × 540	1920 × 1080	37.8653	0.9469	1313.90	3021.42	4553.62
BOTerrace	960 × 540	1920 × 1080	29.4451	0.8695	1020.25	7142.20	4783.99

Table 2. Frame based results of videos

Video sequence	From	To	PSNR	SSIM	SR time (Sec)	Bitrate	HEVC Encoding time (Sec)
HoneyBee	1920 × 1080	3840 × 2160	38.7134	0.9346	7456.26	1659.34	7157.30
Bosphorus	1920 × 1080	3840 × 2160	39.6489	0.9593	4850.50	3202.68	11082.82
Jockey	1920 × 1080	3840 × 2160	39.2649	0.9436	5520.03	2690.54	10778.62
HoneyBee	960 × 540	3840 × 2160	37.4784	0.9293	1843.21	1600.73	7111.07
Bosphorus	960 × 540	3840 × 2160	37.7084	0.9492	1312.07	3795.72	11492.01
Jockey	960 × 540	3840 × 2160	37.9478	0.9382	1624.99	3756.54	12360.79
Cactus	960 × 540	1920 × 1080	32.8406	0.8800	1565.66	3880.83	8049.17
Kimono	960 × 540	1920 × 1080	37.8657	0.9471	1860.14	3018.84	8802.40
BOTerrace	960 × 540	1920 × 1080	29.4715	0.8699	1361.43	7271.20	4791.19

resolution methods have been used in transcoder to convert the low resolution video bit stream into high resolution bit stream [6,15]. In MBOI, the super resolution time (SRT) increase because we used more number of iterations than LBOI as well as λ value. Where λ presents sparsity parameter used for sparse linear regression. For MBOI, we used 20 iterations with $\lambda = 0.2$ but for LBOI, we used 10 iterations with $\lambda = 0.4$. The large value of λ give more accurate result with high computational time that is the reason we used different value of λ in proposed method.

4   Experimental Results

The proposed transcoder algorithm is based on AVS reference software RM52j-r1 and HEVC reference codec HM10.1 for the attainment of ultra-high definition (UHD) videos evaluation. The SR techniques are implemented by using MATLAB 2014a on BOI. All simulations are carried out on Intel(R) Core™i5-4590 CPU@ 3.3 GHZ with 8 GB RAM, with spatial resolutions of 3840 × 2160 used for performance evaluation. All frames are encoded using low delay-P-main config-uration file. While performance is measured in terms of image quality ΔPSNR, bitrate Δ Bit-rate and computational complexity Δ T as follows:

$$\Delta PSNR = PSNR_{proposed} - PSNR_{anchor} \tag{8}$$

$$\Delta Bitrate = \frac{Bitrate_{proposed} - Bitrate_{anchor}}{Bitrate_{anchor}} * 100\% \tag{9}$$

$$\Delta T = \frac{T_{proposed} - T_{anchor}}{T_{anchor}} * 100\% \tag{10}$$

$PSNR_{proposed}$, $Bitrate_{proposed}$ and $T_{proposed}$ represents the PSNR, bitrate and encoding time for the proposed algorithm respectively. $PSNR_{anchor}$, $Bitrate_{anchor}$ and T_{anchor} represents the PSNR, bitrate and encoding time of anchor software HM10.1 respectively. Experimental results of block based super resolution are more efficient and has less SR computational time as compared to frame base super resolution results as shown in Tables 1 and 2. In 2K to 4K upsampling results shows that our proposed method save 44% time as compared to frame based super resolution with rare difference of PSNR as well as SSIM index. In 1K to 4K upsampling, block based HoneyBee save 18% time with sim-ilar SSIM index as well as similar PSNR than frame based super resolution. In 1K to 2K upsampling, Kimono save 29.36% SR time than frame base value. The experimental results show that proposed method give better results on 2K and 4K videos.

Table 3 shows the comparison values between frame based and block based 2K and 4K upsampling videos. The negative sign in table represents the decrement and positive sign shows the increment in values. In Table 3, HoneyBee PSNR decreased 0.0091 dB than frame based value but Cactus has PSNR increased 0.001 dB than frame based result. If we compared the results in terms of bitrate, BQTerrace gain maximum bitrate reduction of 1.78% than frame based value and Kimono gain minimum bitrate reduction of 0.085% than frame based value.

Table 3. Comparison values between frame based and block base

Video sequence	From	To	PSNR	SR time (%)	Bitrate (%)	HEVC Encoding time (%)
HoneyBee	1920 × 1080	3840 × 2160	−0.0091	−44.04	0.3790	41.54
Bosphorus	1920 × 1080	3840 × 2160	−0.0079	−24.75	0.2785	32.20
Jockey	1920 × 1080	3840 × 2160	0.0087	−13.22	−0.5601	−13.49
HoneyBee	960 × 540	3840 × 2160	−0.0010	−15.97	−0.4829	58.74
Bosphorus	960 × 540	3840 × 2160	−0.0030	−22.43	−0.7471	35.88
Jockey	960 × 540	3840 × 2160	−0.0138	−29.98	−0.8127	11.62
Cactus	960 × 540	1920 × 1080	0.0022	−21.51	−1.2780	43.54
Kimono	960 × 540	1920 × 1080	−0.0040	−29.36	0.0854	48.26
BQTerrace	960 × 540	1920 × 1080	−0.0264	−25.06	−1.7741	0.1502

The HEVC encoding time in Table 3 indicates that maximum average encoding time saving in "HoneyBee" is (58.74%) while minimum encoding time in "BQTer-race" is (0.15%). However the obtained average encoding time saving is 28.7% as compared to the anchore software HM10.1. All the experimental results of proposed method save maximum SR time as well as maximum visual quality at pedestal videos where camera move back and forth. In pedestal video, back ground remain stable but object remain in motion.

Figure 4, shows the results of frame based super resolution (a) represents the frame based output of 2K HoneyBee (b) represents the frame based value of 2K Jockey and (c) represents the frame based value of 2K Cactus video respectively. Figure 4, shows the results of block based super resolution (a) represents the block based output of 2K HoneyBee (b) represents the block based value of 2K Jockey and (c) represents the block based value of 2K Cactus video frame respectively. If we compared our results in terms of SR time, bitrate, HEVC encoding and PSNR, the results are efficient and reliable.

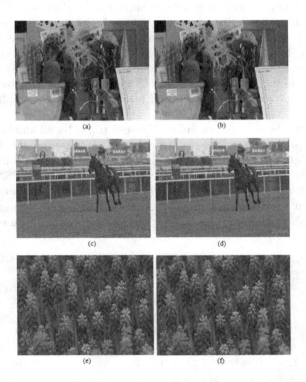

Fig. 4. (a) represents the frame based output of 2K Cactus video (b) represents the super resolution block based value of 2K Cactus (c) represents the frame based value of 2K Jockey video (d) shows the results of block based super resolution of 2K Jockey (e) represents the frame based output of 2K HoneyBee video frame and (f) represents the block based value of 2K HoneyBee video frame respectively

5   Conclusion

This paper presents the block based super resolution method which reduced 20% to 40% complexity. The proposed transcoder classify BOI with decoded information into MBOI and LBOI. The used of same SR algorithms on BOI with different number of parameters, the time complexity of 4K videos decreased. Experimental results of 2K and 4K videos show that the propose transcoder can reduce computational complexity 20% to 40% than full frame super resolution while keeping the same visual quality in terms of PSNR(dB) and SSIM(index).

Acknowledgement. This work is partially supported by National Natural Science Foundation of China (No: 61521062 and No: 61420106008).

References

1. Sullivan, G.J., Ohm, J.-R., Han, W.-J., Wiegand, T.: Overview of the High Efficiency Video Coding (HEVC) standard. IEEE Trans. Circ. Syst. Video Technol. **22**(12), 1649–1668 (2012)
2. Ahmad, I., Wei, X., Sun, Y., Zhang, Y.-Q.: Video transcoding: an overview of various techniques and research issues. IEEE Trans. Multimedia **7**(5), 793–804 (2005)
3. Björk, N., Christopoulos, C.: Transcoder architectures for video coding. In: IEEE International Conference on Acoustics Speech and Signal Processing, vol. 5. Institute Of Electrical Engineers Inc. (IEE), pp. V-2813 (1998)
4. Vetro, A., Christopoulos, C., Sun, H.: Video transcoding architectures and techniques: an overview. IEEE Sig. Process. Mag. **20**(2), 18–29 (2003)
5. Bossen, F., Bross, B., Suhring, K., Flynn, D.: HEVC complexity and implementation analysis. IEEE Trans. Circ. Syst. Video Technol. **22**(12), 1685–1696 (2012)
6. Prendergast, R.S., Nguyen, T.Q.: A block-based super-resolution for video sequences. In: 2008 15th IEEE International Conference on Image Processing, pp. 1240–1243. IEEE (2008)
7. Pengyu, L., Kebin, J.: Fast extraction method for video motion region of interest combining visual characteristics. In: 2011 International Conference on Computer Science and Service System (CSSS), pp. 3939–3944. IEEE (2011)
8. Zhang, D., Li, B., Xu, J., Li, H.: Fast transcoding from H.264 AVC to high efficiency video coding. In: 2012 IEEE International Conference on Multimedia and Expo, pp. 651–656. IEEE (2012)
9. Peixoto, E., Shanableh, T., Izquierdo, E.: H. 264/AVC to HEVC video transcoder based on dynamic thresholding and content modeling. IEEE Trans. Circ. Syst. Video Technol. **24**(1), 99–112 (2014)
10. Huang, S.-F., Chen, M.-J., Li, M.-S.: Region-of-interest segmentation based on Bayesian theorem for H.264 video transcoding. In: 2011 IEEE Visual Communications and Image Processing (VCIP), pp. 1–4. IEEE (2011)
11. Luo, R., Xie, R., Zhang, L.: IEEE International Symposium on Broadband Multimedia Systems and Broadcasting, pp. 1–6. IEEE (2014)
12. Xing, P., Tian, Y., Zhang, X., Wang, Y., Huang, T.: A coding unit classification based AVC-to-HEVC transcoding with background modeling for surveillance videos. IEEE Visual Commun. Image Process. (VCIP) **2013**, 1–6 (2013)

13. Wee, S.J., Apostolopoulos, J.G., Feamster, N.: Field-to-frame transcoding with spatial and temporal downsampling. In: 1999 International Conference on Image Processing, ICIP 1999. Proceedings, vol. 4., pp. 271–275. IEEE (1999)
14. Nawaz, M., Xie, R., Zhang, L., Asfandyar, M., Hussain, M.: Image super resolution by sparse linear regression and iterative back projection. In: IEEE International Symposium on Broadband Multimedia Systems and Broadcasting (BMSB), pp. 1–6. IEEE (2016)
15. Pantoja, M., Ling, N.: Transcoding with resolution conversion using super-resolution and irregular sampling. J. Sig. Process. Syst. **60**(3), 305–313 (2010)

Fast Intra Coding in an Efficient HEVC Multi-rate Encoding System Based on x265

Dongbin Cheng[(✉)], Xiaoyun Zhang, and Zhiyong Gao

Shanghai Jiao Tong University, Shanghai 200240, China
{windcdb,xiaoyun.zhang,zhiyong.gao}@sjtu.edu.cn

Abstract. To meet the needs of various video service under different network conditions, multi-rate encoding using HEVC is in substantial demand. Although the efficient HEVC encoder x265 is developed with many optimization skills, it still performs slowly in intra coding. In this paper, we focus on multi-rate coding which simultaneously outputs several compressed bitstreams with different bitrates for one input source video. By analyzing the correlation and similarity of CU depth and PU prediction mode between multi-rate HEVC streams, an efficient HEVC multi-rate encoding system is proposed. Early-skip depth decision and fast intra mode decision are presented for reducing the coding complexity of the slave encoders by utilizing heuristic coding information obtained from the master encoder. Experimental results show that the proposed method can averagely reduce 52.45% total encoding time, in comparison with independent x265 encoders, with only 0.86% BDBR performance degradation. The time saving can reach up to 71.52% for only slave encoders.

Keywords: HEVC · Multi-rate video encoding · x265 · Intra coding · CU depth · PU prediction mode

1 Introduction

Video streams should meet all kinds of network conditions while being transmitted from the source end to the user end. These network factors include, but not limited to, network connection mode, network bandwidth, the network occupancy rate and so on. Thus the video service provider often needs to encode the same video sequence for several times with different bitrates to adaptively meet users' demand.

HEVC is the newest block-based video encoding standard to replace H.264/AVC, and it's also designed to encode videos of higher resolutions [1]. HEVC can save 50% bitrate at the same visual quality when compared to H.264/AVC but it leads to the substantial increase in coding complexity. It is worth emphasizing that the coding tree structure in HEVC becomes more flexible and introduces the concepts of coding unit (CU) and prediction unit (PU) to block partition.

Considering the heavy computation burden of HEVC, x265 is designed to be the world's fastest and most computationally efficient HEVC encoder by utilizing many accelerating methods [2], which make it the best choice for HEVC encoding in practical applications. Besides, different profiles and presets, from *ultrafast* preset to *medium* preset and so on, are added to x265 to meet practical demand. Although the

© Springer Nature Singapore Pte Ltd. 2017
X. Yang and G. Zhai (Eds.): IFTC 2016, CCIS 685, pp. 307–317, 2017.
DOI: 10.1007/978-981-10-4211-9_30

average encoding speed of x265 is fast enough, it performs badly while encoding intra frames, which leads to intolerable latency in real-time video communication applications.

In recent years, a lot of research has been done to reduce the HEVC intra coding complexity [3, 4]. The majority of them focus on simplifying the processes of CU depth decision and PU mode decision, which are the most time-consuming parts in intra coding. But those work is all conducted on HEVC reference software (HM) and no related work is based on practical x265 encoder [2] yet. On the other hand, only few recent research about multi-rate video encoding has been proposed [5, 6]. [5] claimed the block structure similarity between streams of different bitrates, and it reused the block structure from a high quality reference encoder. Similar ideas are proposed in [6]. Furthermore, some work like [7, 8] involves in transcoding between different video coding standards. They both reduce the encoding complexity by referring already existing streams of another encoding standard.

In this paper, we propose an efficient HEVC multi-rate video encoding system developed based on x265 which is consisted of several encoders for coding different bitrate streams. The encoders can be classified into a master encoder, which collects and exports coding information, and other slave encoders which imports the coding information from the master encoder and utilize them. The coding information includes CU depth and PU modes of every block in each frame. Based on the coding information from the master encoder, an early skip algorithm of CU depth decision and a fast PU prediction mode decision method are proposed for the slave encoders. The proposed system can reduce 52.45% total coding time for all encoders with only 0.86% BDBR performance decrease, and the time saving even reaches 71.52% for the slave encoders.

The remainder of this paper is organized as follows. In Sect. 2, the analysis about the correlation and similarity between streams of different bitrates is fully expounded. Then the framework of the proposed system, as well as the fast intra coding algorithms are presented in Sect. 3. The experimental results are shown in Sect. 4 and finally this paper is briefly concluded in Sect. 5.

2 Block Similarity and Correlation

2.1 CU Depth Correlation Among Different Bitrates

The hierarchical quadtree block structure is believed to be one of the most important characteristics of HEVC beyond previous video coding standards. Every frame is divided to many coding tree units (CTU) with size of 64 × 64 in HEVC main profile [1]. CTU comprises a hierarchical quadtree-structure, in which every leaf node is called a coding unit (CU). The height of the node in the quadtree is defined as CU depth, and the size of CU ranges from 64 × 64 to 8 × 8, with corresponding depth as 0 to 3. The principle of determining the block partition is rate-distortion optimization (RDO), which recursively calculate and compare to choose the best CU depth and the best PU mode. And RDO is considered to be the most time consuming part in HEVC [9].

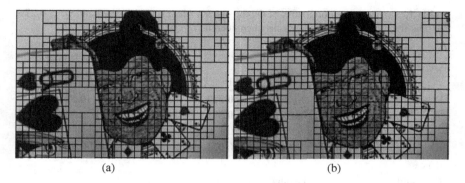

Fig. 1. Similar CU partition in streams of different QPs, (a) QP = 27 (b) QP = 32

Firstly, a example of the CU partition details are illustrated for the streams of QP 22 and 27 using Elecard HEVC Analyzer. As shown in Fig. 1, the partition of most blocks in (b) are same with (a) and the rest are partitioned with less details than that of (a). It intuitively shows the strong block similarity between streams at different bitrates and the tendency that the partition tend to be deeper with bigger depth while QP is smaller.

Furthermore, to make more precise analysis, one stream is taken as the reference stream, and its QP is labeled as QP_m. Similarly, another stream is regarded as slave stream to be analyzed, and its QP is labeled as QP_s. The CU partition depths are respectively referred as $Depth_m$ and $Depth_s$. Thus the depth correlation between different QPs or bitrates can be divided into two situations: (1) $QP_s < QP_m$, (2) $QP_s > QP_m$.

In order to quantify the block similarity, we analyze the first 10 frames of Cactus and BasketBallDrive and count the depth of every CU for the streams of different QP. Then a right stochastic matrix is calculated for every situation and it has been shown in Table 1. The statistical data is used to estimate and represent the CU depth transition possibilities from the depth of reference stream to that of the analyzed stream. The boldfaced data denotes the principal components of the transition possibilities. In detail, it's confirmed in Table 1 (a) that lower QP leads to deeper depth levels, i.e., $Depth_s > Depth_m$. On the contrary, the bold data in Table 1 (b) show that, in most cases, the $Depth_s$ value belongs to $[Depth_m-1, Depth_m]$. The above rules are shown in Eq. 1.

$$Depth_s \in \begin{cases} [Depth_m, 3] & QP_s < QP_m \\ [\max(Depth_m - 1, 0), \ \max(Depth_m, 1)] & QP_s > QP_m \end{cases} \tag{1}$$

2.2 Intra PU Mode Local Similarity Between Different Rates

PU is the basic unit to predict in intra and inter, and the intra prediction mode in HEVC is extended to 35 (33 directional modes, DC and Planar mode). The mode decision

Table 1. (a) The transition matrix of depth between streams of $QP_s = 22$ and $QP_m = 27$ (b) The transition matrix of depth between streams of $QP_s = 32$ and $QP_m = 27$

(a)

$QP_s < QP_m$		$Depth_s$			
		0	1	2	3
$Depth_m$	0	**0.125**	**0.379**	**0.220**	**0.227**
	1	0.059	**0.391**	**0.225**	**0.325**
	2	0.018	0.139	**0.366**	**0.477**
	3	0.002	0.021	0.109	**0.868**

(b)

$QP_s > QP_m$		$Depth_s$			
		0	1	2	3
$Depth_m$	0	**0.521**	**0.419**	0.059	0.001
	1	**0.265**	**0.617**	0.106	0.012
	2	0.145	**0.360**	**0.451**	0.044
	3	0.025	0.155	**0.343**	**0.477**

process mainly consists of two steps: rough mode decision (RMD) and RDO, respectively using criterion J_{RMD} and J_{RDO} [1, 2]. The cost function is given in Eqs. 2 and 3:

$$J_{RMD} = SATD + \lambda \cdot R_{MODE} \tag{2}$$

$$J_{RDO} = SSE + \lambda \cdot R_{MODE} \tag{3}$$

where SATD denotes the Hadamard transformed SAD and SSE denotes the sum of squared difference between the original and reconstructed PU. λ is the Lagrangian multiplier which is dependent on quantization parameter (QP), and R_{MODE} represent the required coding bits for the current prediction mode.

Since SSE requires the entropy coding process, the calculation of J_{RDO} is far more complex than J_{RMD} but it achieves more accurate R_{MODE}. A predefined number (5 to 7 in x265 *medium* preset) of modes form the RDO mode candidates, which consist of the modes with smallest J_{RMD} and the most probable modes (MPM) [1], derived from spatial neighboring PUs.

$$BMD = |BM_s - BM_m| \tag{4}$$

In order to investigate the best PU mode similarity between streams of different bitrates, we also collect the best modes of every PU. The best mode in the reference stream is labeled as BM_m, with the best mode in the analyzed stream labeled as BM_s. The distance between modes (BMD) are defined as the absolute value of the difference between BM_s and BM_m, which is formulated in Eq. 4.

For different QP_s and QP_m, no matter which one is bigger, similar result is observed and shown in Fig. 2. It illustrates the probability distribution of BMD by statistical data. It shows that at over 60% of the difference between BM_s and BM_m is no more than 2 and the left 40% of the difference almost averagely distributes from 3 to 34 but with two obvious peaks which are centered around the horizontal mode (mode value 10) and the vertical mode (mode value 26). Figure 2 has proven the strong local similarity of best PU prediction modes between streams of different bitrates and the proposed multi-rate system will take the advantages of this characteristic, along with consideration of the two peaks around the horizontal and vertical directional modes.

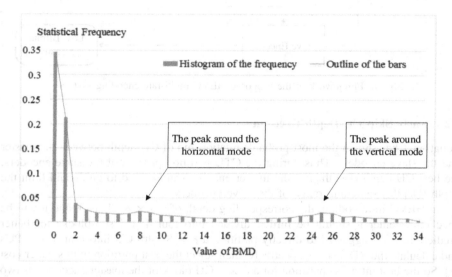

Fig. 2. The frequency distribution of the BMD by statistical data

3 The Proposed Multi-rate Encoding System

3.1 Multi-rate Encoding System Architecture

Figure 3 illustrates the framework of the proposed HEVC multi-rate encoding system. As shown in Fig. 3, the system consists of a master encoder and several slave encoders. The master encoder is the original x265 encoder only with an attached function of collecting coding information, which includes the best CU depth and the best PU prediction modes [1]. Slave encoders obtain the coding information from the master encoder and then utilize it to decrease the calculation of their own CU partition and PU mode decision, which is the most time-consuming part in HEVC coding [9].

The analysis in [5] shows that as the quantization parameter (QP) or bitrate distance increases, the correlation between different streams also tend to be weaker. Since the practical demand of multi-rate coding may range from low bitrate to high bitrate, we choose medium bitrate stream as the reference stream to keep the most correlation. The correlation includes two situations: the low bitrate streams refer the medium and the high bitrate streams refer the medium, as shown in Fig. 3.

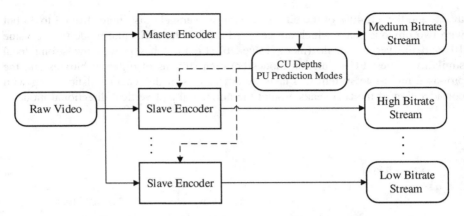

Fig. 3. Framework of the proposed HEVC multi-rate encoding system

3.2 Early Skip CU Depth Decision

Equation 1 has shown the most probable relationship of CU depth between the master and the slave encoders. Thus during the CTU partition process of the slave encoders, the best CU depth ($Depth_m$) of the master encoder can be used to guide and limit the depth ($Depth_s$) searching range of the slave encoders.

In HEVC intra coding, the corresponding depth of a 8 × 8 CU is 3, and it will be checked whether it should be further divided into four 4 × 4 sub-blocks for better prediction. It is suggested to directly partition a 8 × 8 intra CU into four 4 × 4 PUs and calculate the RDO cost respectively, then select the best partition with smaller cost [1]. So the best intra CU partition for a 8 × 8 CU block of the master encoder has two possible decision results: a whole 8 × 8 block or four 4 × 4 sub-blocks. In the proposed multi-rate system, we define the 4 × 4 sub-block as the depth of 4. Thus the depth range for intra coding is extended from [0, 3] to [0, 4]. And, the depth searching range for the slave encoders in our system are given in Eq. 5, which is a more efficient extension compared with Eq. 1:

$$Depth_s \in \begin{cases} [Depth_m, \ \min(Depth_m + 1, \ 4)] & QP_s < QP_m \\ [\max(Depth_m - 1, 0), \ \max(Depth_m, 1)] & QP_s > QP_m \end{cases} \quad (5)$$

where $Depth_m$ belongs to [0, 4] and QP_m and QP_s are the quantization parameter for the same CTU in master and slave encoders. During the depth decision process of the slave encoders, instead of searching depth from 0 to 4, the proposed system only searches the limited depth range according to Eq. 5 and early skips the unlikely depths.

3.3 Fast PU Mode Decision

As has been illustrated in Fig. 2, a strong local similarity of the best intra prediction modes truly exists between the streams of different bitrates, which can be exploited to reduce the calculation of PU mode decision of the slave encoders. However, the

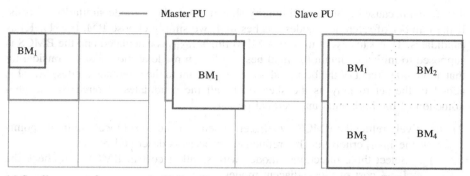

(a) Smaller, one reference mode (b) Equal, one reference mode (c) Larger, four reference modes

Fig. 4. The size relationship between slave PU and master PU

utilization of the prediction modes from the master encoder is more complicated than CU depth sharing, because the PU size of the slave encoders may be larger, equal or smaller compared with the corresponding PU in the master encoder, as shown in Fig. 4.

Thus, the number of reference modes from the master encoder (BM_m), defined as K, is different for the above situations. It can be seen that K = 1 when slave PU is smaller than or equal to master PU, and K = 4 when slave PU is larger.

It has been stated that the original PU mode decision process of x265 *medium* preset deserves the calculation of 35 times J_{RMD} and 5–7 times J_{RDO}. In the proposed multi-rate system, the fast intra prediction mode decision algorithm is mainly consisted of the following three steps:

1) Check the J_{RMD} cost of the best mode candidate set (BMCS) shown in Eq. 6:

$$BMCS = \{BM_mS \cup MDM \cup MPM\} \qquad (6)$$

where MDM represents the five main directional modes 2, 10, 18, 26 and 34, which indicate the prediction directions of lower left, horizontal left, upper left, vertical upper and upper right respectively. MPM is the most probable modes defined by HEVC standard and BM_mS means the best reference modes set got from the master encoder. Moreover, number K determines the BM_mS in the way formulated in Eq. 7:

$$BM_mS = \begin{cases} \{Planar, DC\} & \textit{if } K = 1 \textit{ and } BM_1 \textit{ is Planar or DC} \\ \{x|x \in [\max(2, BM_1 - 1), \min(BM_1 + 1, 34)]\} & \textit{if } K = 1 \textit{ and } BM_1 \textit{ is directional} \\ \{BM_i|i \in [1, K]\} & \textit{if } K = 4 \end{cases} \qquad (7)$$

where BM_i (i = 1...K) is the reference mode from the master encoder as shown in Fig. 4.

In Eq. 7, when slave's PU is smaller or equal to the master's PU, i.e., K = 1, since Planar mode (0) and DC mode (1) are not directional modes and not adjacent to any other mode, BM_mS is also set as Planar and DC mode if BM_1 is Planar or DC mode. The left and right mode of the directional BM_i are added to the set when BM_1 is directional because of the local similarity shown in the above mode similarity analysis. If the number of reference modes reaches to 4, we simply choose BM_i (i = 1...K) as candidates. That's to say, at most 9 + MPM times J_{RMD} is calculated and the BMCS is supposed to initially contain the final best prediction mode at most cases. Considering that about 40 percent of the best modes aren't adjacent to the reference modes, MDM is added to the set to play as the skeleton of all the candidates inspired by the phenomenon of the horizontal and vertical peak.

2) Iteratively refine the BMCS by adjacent extension and select local minimum points with the J_{RMD} criterion. This refinement process is described below:

    I. Select three directional modes with smallest cost in BMCS and check the J_{RMD} cost of their adjacent modes.

    II. Replace current mode with their adjacent modes and update into BMCS if their adjacent cost is smaller.

    III. Repeat step I and step II until the best three modes in BMCS keep unchanged.

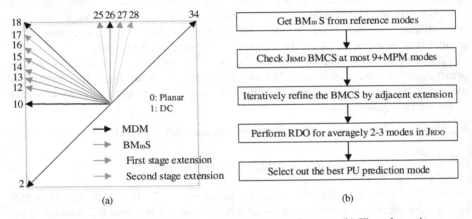

Fig. 5. (a) An example of the BMCS and the iteratively refinement (b) The schematic process of the proposed fast intra mode decision algorithm

An example of the initial BMCS and a two stage refinement process is illustrated in Fig. 5 (a). MDM and BM_mS are initially selected and BM_mS contains mode [13,15] if the reference mode is 14. Then, mode 12, 16, 25 and 27 are the first stage extensional modes when mode 13, 15 and 26 have smallest J_{RMD} cost. A further second stage searching will be conducted for mode 17 and 28 if mode 16 and 27 turn out to be better than mode 15 and 26 respectively. The purpose of the iteratively refinement is to select local minimum modes based on J_{RDM} criterion into BMCS, since the local minimum PU modes tends to be the best mode, which has been proved and utilized in [4].

3) Check the J_{RDO} cost of the modes in truncated BMCS and skip the adjacent modes.

In the more time consuming RDO process, 5–7 candidates (same with x265) with smallest J_{RMD} cost in BMCS are selected as RDO candidates and they are sorted orderly with smaller J_{RMD} cost in the front. The J_{RDO} cost is checked for every RDO candidate one by one and skip the mode if it's adjacent to the candidate modes which have been checked in the front. Since at most cases, we put the adjacent modes of reference modes into BMCS, the experimental results show that only 2–3 (2.69 averagely) modes are actually checked in the RDO process thus a great amount of computational complexity is reduced.

In general, the proposed fast intra mode decision algorithm is shown in Fig. 5 (b). It takes use of the mode local similarity between master and slave encoders by selecting adjacent modes of the reference mode as candidates, and some other modes are added initially to maintain the coding quality. The main strategy of simplification is to find modes with smallest cost by local iteratively refinement at first, and to skip the adjacent modes of local minimum points secondly. Thus only 9 + MPM times J_{RMD} and 2–3 times J_{RDO} calculation are conducted except the iteratively refinement process, which will be terminated rapidly at most cases because of the existence of MPM candidates.

4   Experimental Results

The proposed HEVC multi-rate encoding system is developed and implemented on x265 v1.8, and the platform is a workstation of Intel(R) Xeon(R) CPU E5-2697 v2 @ 2.70 GHz with 24 cores. Five HD video sequences from class A, including Baketball-Drive, BQTerrance, Cactus, Kimonol, and ParkScene, are encoded at default medium preset of x265 v1.8 and all the frames are encoded in intra mode. In the comparison test, four independent original x265 encoders without any information sharing are running at the same time with setting QP as 22, 27, 32 and 37 respectively. For the proposed multi-rate system, one master encoder with QP 27, as well as three slave encoders with setting QP as 22, 32 and 37 respectively, are encoded simultaneously. The performance of the proposed system is evaluated by BDBR [10] and BDPSNR [11]. The reduction of the computational complexity from the comparison test to the proposed system is given by the global time saving rate (TS). Besides, the time saving rate for only slave encoders (Slave TS) is provided if both excluding the time of QP = 27 encoder.

The results in Table 2 show that the proposed multi-rate system can reduce about half computational complexity for high-resolution videos with only 0.86% BDBR increase. What's more, it can be seen that the global time saving will be greater if we increase the number of slave encoders, because the time saving for the slave encoders can reach 71.52% at present settings. Since the complexity of the master encoder is almost not changed, the proposed system succeed to encode three video streams with the complexity of one by sharing and reusing CU depths and PU modes information.

Table 2. The performance of the proposed system compared with independent x265 encoders

Sequences	BDBR (%)	BDPSNR (dB)	TS (%)	Slave TS (%)
BasketballDrive	0.992	-0.040	52.67	71.43
BQTerrace	0.952	-0.057	50.39	69.72
Cactus	0.791	-0.042	50.71	69.82
Kimono1	0.798	-0.022	57.52	77.57
ParkScene	0.743	-0.037	50.97	69.03
Average results of the proposed	**0.855**	**-0.039**	**52.45**	**71.52**
The results provided in [5]	**0.56**	**-0.02**	**27.05**	\

5   Conclusion

In this article, an efficient HEVC multi-rate encoding system is proposed based on the analysis of the correlation and local similarity between the streams of different bitrates. An innovative "master to slave" mechanism is put forward to reuse the CU depths and PU modes information in HEVC intra coding. Furthermore, an early skip CU depth decision algorithm and a fast intra PU mode decision algorithm are proposed based on the above similarity. Experimental results show that the proposed multi-rate system can averagely reduce 52.25% computational complexity for HD sequences with only BDBR 0.86% performance degradation, compared with independent x265 encoders. The time saving rate can reach 71.52% for only slave encoders.

Acknowledgement. This work was supported in part by National Natural Science Foundation of China (61133009, 61301116, 61221001), the Shanghai Key Laboratory of Digital Media Processing and Transmissions(STCSM 12DZ2272600).

References

1. Sullivan, G.J., et al.: Overview of the high efficiency video coding (HEVC) standard. IEEE Trans. Circuits Syst. Video Technol. **22**(12), 1649–1668 (2012)
2. The x265 website.https://bitbucket.org/multicoreware/x265/wiki/Home
3. Shen, L., Zhang, Z., An, P.: Fast CU size decision and mode decision algorithm for HEVC intra coding. IEEE Trans. Consum. Electron. **59**(1), 207–213 (2013)
4. Shi, Y., et al.: Local saliency detection based fast mode decision for HEVC intra coding. In: IEEE 15th International Workshop on Multimedia Signal Processing (MMSP 2013). IEEE (2013)
5. Schroeder, D., Rehm, P., Steinbach, E.: Block structure reuse for multi-rate high efficiency video coding. In: IEEE International Conference on Image Processing (ICIP 2015). IEEE (2015)
6. Finstad, D.H., et al. Improved multi-rate video encoding. In: IEEE International Symposium on Multimedia (ISM 2011). IEEE (2011)
7. Chen, Y., et al.: Efficient software H. 264/AVC to HEVC transcoding on distributed multicore processors. IEEE Trans. Circuits Syst. Video Technol. **25**(8), 1423–1434 (2015)

8. Zhang, J., Dai, F., Zhang, Y., Yan, C.: Efficient HEVC to H.264/AVC transcoding with fast intra mode decision. In: Li, S., Saddik, A., Wang, M., Mei, T., Sebe, N., Yan, S., Hong, R., Gurrin, C. (eds.) MMM 2013. LNCS, vol. 7732, pp. 295–306. Springer, Heidelberg (2013). doi:10.1007/978-3-642-35725-1_27
9. Bossen, F., et al.: HEVC complexity and implementation analysis. IEEE Trans. Circuits Syst. Video Technol. **22**(12), 1685–1696 (2012)
10. Bjontegaard, Gisle: Improvements of the BD-PSNR model. ITU-T SG16 Q 6, p. 35 (2008)
11. Bjontegaard, Gisle: Calcuation of average PSNR differences between RD-curves. Doc. VCEG-M33 ITU-T Q6/16, Austin, TX, USA, 2–4 April 2001

3D Holoscopic Images Coding Scheme Based on Viewpoint Image Rendering

Ling Yang[1,2], Ping An[1,2(✉)], Deyang Liu[1,2], and Ran Ma[1,2]

[1] School of Communication and Information Engineering,
Shanghai University, Shanghai 200072, China
`anping@shu.edu.cn`
[2] Key Laboratory of Advanced Displays and System Application,
Ministry of Education, Shanghai 200072, China

Abstract. 3D holoscopic imaging can provide immersive 3D viewing experiences, which is considered to be a promising 3D acquisition and display solution. However, in order to proper storage and delivery such particular type of image, efficient coding schemes are of great importance. Therefore, in this paper, we propose a new coding scheme based on viewpoint image rendering. All the viewpoint images are rendered firstly from the 3D holoscopic contents. The total rendered viewpoint images are then arranged into a video sequence. HEVC inter coding method is utilized to remove the redundancy among the rendered viewpoint images. Experimental results show that the proposed coding scheme can achieve average 2.70 dB quality improvements for holoscopic images compared to HEVC intra standard.

Keywords: 3D holoscopic images · Viewpoint image rendering · Image coding · HEVC

1 Introduction

Holoscopic imaging, also referred to as integral imaging, light field imaging or plenoptic imaging, derives from Integral Photography proposed by G. Lippmann in 1908 [1]. With the development of high quality microlens arrays and high-resolution photoreceptor, holoscopic imaging technology becomes realizable. Comparing with most of the existing 3D display systems, it has three advantages. Firstly, 3D holoscopic imaging technology is able to provide three dimensional images with full parallax and continuous viewpoint, which can bring audience more strong visual experience. Secondly, in the simplest form, the holoscopic imaging system with full parallax consists of a lens array mated to a digital sensor. Therefore, the holoscopic content capturing device is simple and portable. Thirdly, holoscopic imaging can provide a glass-free and fatigue-free viewing to more than one person, independent of the viewers' positions.

Holoscopic image is composed of a lot of micro-images (MIs) recorded through different microlens. Each MI is similar to a traditional 2D image and represents a different view of the 3D scene. Owing to the specific structure of holoscopic images, the state-of-the-art HEVC standard does not comprise adequate coding tools for this

X. Yang and G. Zhai (Eds.): IFTC 2016, CCIS 685, pp. 318–327, 2017.
DOI: 10.1007/978-981-10-4211-9_31

type of images. Therefore, in order to successfully introduce this technology into the consumer market, some new coding technologies that can efficiently handle 3D holoscopic images are needed. The recent 3D holoscopic image coding schemes can be classified into two categories: Non-local spatial predictive image coding and viewpoint image (VI) rendering based image coding. The two kinds of coding schemes are briefly reviewed as follows.

In non-local spatial predictive image coding schemes, new intra prediction algorithm is incorporated into HEVC to exploit the inherent characteristics of 3D holoscopic image content to improve the coding efficiency. The self-similarity (SS) based prediction mode is proposed and introduced into H.264 [2] and HEVC [3] to improve the performance for 3D holoscopic image coding. The SS mode is similar to the block copying (BC) mode in HEVC range extension, which is proposed for screen content coding [4]. Locally linear embedding (LLE)-based prediction algorithm is proposed and incorporated into the HEVC encoder to handle the 3D holoscopic images in [5]. A disparity compensation based prediction scheme for 3D holoscopic image coding is proposed in [6], in which disparities between MIs are exploited to improve the accuracy of the prediction. Although the non-local spatial predictive coding algorithms are efficient in most cases, they ignore the high spatial correlation exists among the rendered VIs from holoscopic images which can also be used to compress the 3D holoscopic image. Viewpoint image rendering based image coding schemes are derived from rendering algorithms of holoscopic images. Owing to the specific structure of holoscopic images, MIs can't directly display on the 2D displays, for which the rendering methods that convert 3D holoscopic formats into general 2D image formats (referred to "viewpoint images" in this paper) are required [7–9]. The rendered viewpoint images (VIs) are similar to the natural 2D images, which can be easily compressed with the existing coding standard. In some rendering methods, these rendered 2D images can be reversely converted into 3D holoscopic image formats. The conversion technology provides a new way to encode the holoscopic images. In [10, 11], holoscopic images are decomposed in VIs, and the obtained VIs are arranged as a multi-view video by different scanning order. Then the organized multi-view video is encoded by multi-view coding standard. In these schemes, rendered VIs appear strong blocking artifacts which will influence coding performance. In [12], a display scalable coding scheme is proposed. VIs rendering algorithms are used to generate the content for the first two scalability layers which aim to compatible with legacy 2D and 3D displays. In the third layer, an inter-layer prediction scheme is applied to improve the coding efficiency by exploiting the existing redundancy between the VIs in the first two layers and the 3-D holoscopic content in the third layer. A holoscopic image coding scheme based on VIs rendering is improved in [13]. This coding scheme improves the rendering algorithm used in [12] and optimizes coding parameters, achieving better compression efficiency than [12]. In [12, 13], residual information between VIs and the original holoscopic images is obtained and encoded at the encoder. The used bitrate for encoding residual information is large and account for largest percentage of the final bitstream. Moreover, the process is very complex and not efficient enough for improving compression efficiency in all cases for holoscopic coding.

In order to palliate aforementioned shortcomings, an efficient compression scheme based on VI rendering for holoscopic image is proposed in this paper. In the proposed scheme, holoscopic images are decomposed into VIs totally and the redundancy between adjacent VIs is removed by using HEVC inter prediction method. The proposed coding scheme not only uses the characteristics of VIs which are less costly to encode, but also retains the complete characteristics of original holoscopic images. As a result, the proposed method can achieve a better coding efficiency for the 3D holoscopic images.

This paper is organized as follows. The VIs rendering methods are described in Sect. 2. Section 3 presents the proposed coding scheme. The experimental results are presented and analyzed in Sect. 4. Conclusions and discussions are drawn in Sect. 5.

2   Viewpoint Images Rendering

Holoscopic imaging becomes a prospective glassless 3D technology to provide a more immersive multimedia experience to the end user. However,its displays are not compatible with stereoscopic displays and Multiview displays. To solve this problem, many methods that converting 3D holoscopic formats into 2D and 3D image formats are proposed. In these methods, the most crucial process is to obtain high-quality VIs from holoscopic images through some holoscopic image process. VIs are the 2D versions of the holoscopic images and easier to be encoded by the existing standard encoder.

Three simple and efficient patch based rendering approaches are developed by Todor Georgiev [7]: Basic Rendering, Depth-Based Rendering and Blending Rendering. These three rendering approaches are based on the particular optical structure of holoscopic image capture system, in which microlens arrays are placed between the image sensor plane and the main lens image plane. Holoscopic images from this capture process are composed of numerous MIs and each MI is conceptually similar to a traditional 2D image. To retain both angular information and spatial information of a scene in each MI and across MIs, each MI represents a small portion of the scene and contents of MIs are similar to their neighbors, as illustrated in Fig. 1.

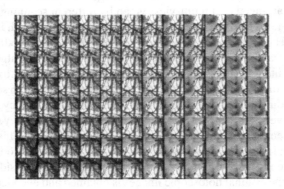

Fig. 1. Close-up on micro images-*Jeff*

In the basic rendering algorithm, the same size patches from the same position of each MI are extracted and then stitched together to construct a VI. The rendering process is illustrated in Fig. 2. The position of patch decides viewing angle of the rendered VI.

By varying the relative position of the extracted patches in MIs, a set of VIs with different horizontal and vertical viewing angles can be generated. The size of patch decides the depth plane in the scene on which the rendered VI will be focused: the lager the patch size, the closer the focus plane. In basic rendering algorithm, obvious block artifacts will be apparent in out of focus planes of VIs, as we can see in Fig. 3. To solve this problem, more advanced methods are proposed to reduce the block artifacts, such as Depth-Based Rendering and Blending Rendering. Although the last two algorithms can acquire artifact-free VIs, the information of holoscopic image is revised during the process of rendering and the holoscopic image can't be reconstructed by these rendered VIs, which will affect the coding efficiency. Therefore, in this paper, the basic rendering algorithm is selected to render VIs.

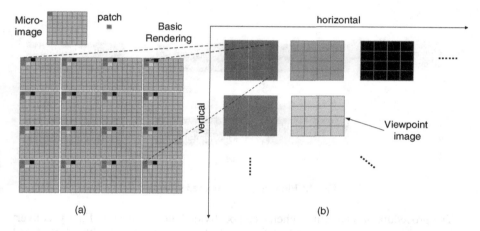

Fig. 2. Viewpoint images rendering: (a) micro-image array of holoscopic image; (b) generating a set of viewpoint images from the holoscopic image

Fig. 3. Rendered viewpoint image using basic algorithm and the presence of artifacts in the out-of-focus regions-*Jeff*

3 Proposed Coding Algorithm

In this section, the proposed coding scheme is described. In this scheme, holoscopic images are converted into VIs at the encoder and holoscopic images are reconstructed from those decoded VIs. To avoid the complex process of obtaining residual information, holoscopic images are converted into VIs completely. In other words, the set of rendered VIs from every holoscopic image contains all the information of the holoscopic image and the holoscopic image can be constructed from these VIs. Because the amount of data in VIs set is enormous, the proposed coding method aims to improve the coding efficiency by exploring the correlations between the adjacent rendered VIs. Figure 4 presents the overview diagram of the proposed encoding and decoding scheme.

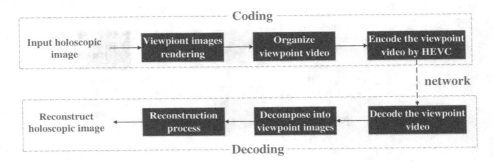

Fig. 4. Flow chart of proposed scheme

The procedure of our coding scheme can be divided into three steps. Firstly, convert the holoscopic image into a set of VIs through the basic rendering algorithm introduced in Sect. 2. Secondly, arrange the extracted VIs as a VI video. Finally, encode the VI video by using the HEVC inter coding method. Correspondingly, at the decoder side, the decoded VI video should be decomposed into VIs and the holoscopic image is reconstructed by the decomposed VIs. The reconstruction process is the inverse process of VI rendering.

In the process of generating VIs, the holoscopic image is divided into some adjacent and non-overlapped patches which are used to generate VIs, as shown in Fig. 2(a). Patches at the same position from different MIs are stitched together to render VIs according to the basic rendering algorithm, as shown in Fig. 2(b). To remove the redundancy among the rendered VIs to the utmost extent, we consider organizing the set of VIs as a VI video and using the inter prediction to encode the video. We arrange these VIs as an array and the position of every VI in the array corresponds to the position of patch being used to extract this VI, as shown in Fig. 2(b). During the process of constituting the VI video, VIs from different viewing angles are scanned in broken line order in order to minimize the motion compensation between them, as illustrated in Fig. 5.

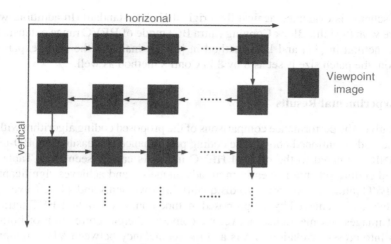

Fig. 5. Converting VIs into a VI video

We convert the holoscopic image into the VIs completely for two reasons. Firstly, the coding complexity can be decreased. At the encoder, we don't need the complex process of computing the residual information which will cost much coding time in [12, 13]. Secondly, the coding performance can be improved. Rendering all the information can retain the whole optic structure information of the holoscopic image as well as reduce the estimation errors in the reconstruction process at the decoder. The HEVC inter coding can efficiently to remove the redundancy of the VI video and improve the compression rate.

4 Experimental Results

4.1 Experimental Conditions

Six 3D holoscopic test image [14] (Bike, Fountain, Jeff, Laura, Seagull and Zhengyun1) are used in our experiments. The original images have a resolution of 7240 by 5433, and each micro-image is of 75 by 75. To the convenience of our experiment, we crop the center of each micro-image out with a size of 64 by 64 and remove incomplete micro-images to form the preprocessed 3D holoscopic images with the resolution 6080 by 4544 according to [15]. All images were transformed into YUV 4:2:0 formats.

To convert holoscopic images into VI videos, basic rendering algorithm is used and the patch size is 8 by 8. Therefore, every holoscopic image can generate 64 VI images can be derived from each 3D holoscopic image with the resolution 760 by 568. The obtained VI images from one holoscopic image are then arranged as a VI video sequence. Encoding of the VI videos is performed under HEVC reference software (HM 16.0 is used to encode the VI sequence.). Since the VI videos are encoded by HEVC inter coding, the configuration parameter is set as "lowdelay main" with POC being set to 8. Four commonly used tested Quantization Parameters 22, 27, 32 and 37 are used. We evaluate the coding performance with the rate distortion curve which is PSNR against the bit rate. BD-PSNR and BD-Rate is also computed. The performance of the proposed coding scheme is evaluated against the original HEVC standard. In addition, we also compare with the intra Block Copying (intra BC) mode of HEVC range extension [16], Conti's method in [12] and liu's method in [6]. To maintain the same experimental condition, the patch size is set as 8 by 8 in Conti's method as well.

4.2 Experimental Results

Table 1 gives the performance comparisons of the proposed coding algorithm with other three methods mentioned above. The coding performance is measured by BD-rate and BD-PSNR compared to the original HEVC intra. As can be seen from Table 1, the proposed coding scheme is clearly more advantageous and achieves significant gains over HEVC intra. An average 2.70 dB quality improvements and 44.32% average bit-rate reduction is achieved by the proposed method compared to the HEVC intra for all the test images. As mentioned above, we convert inherent correlation of holoscopic images into cross-correlation of VIs and the redundancy between VIs is removed by HEVC inter. As expected, the bit rate reduction is witnessed by using our scheme. It can be also observed that the proposed coding scheme is able to consistently achieve an advantage over the three newly proposed efficient coding schemes.

Table 1. Coding efficiency comparisons in terms of BD-PSNR and BD-rate

Image	HEVC intra BC		Liu's method		Conti's method		Proposed	
	BD-PSNR (dB)	BD-rate (%)	BD-PSNR (dB)	BD-rate (%)	BD-PSNR (dB)	BD-rate (%)	BD-PSNR (dB)	BD-rate (%)
Bike	1.69	−24.58	1.63	−23.21	1.01	−16.86	2.48	−37.44
Fountain	1.84	−27.33	1.77	−26.25	0.94	−16.28	2.60	−39.32
Jeff	1.81	−29.22	1.61	−26.28	0.92	−17.45	2.45	−42.58
Laura	1.88	−25.36	1.69	−22.80	1.18	−17.92	3.10	−42.15
Seagull	2.56	−39.23	2.24	−35.32	1.37	−25.06	3.54	−56.08
Zhengyu n1	1.37	−29.01	1.32	−27.88	0.96	−24.48	2.05	−48.36
Average	**1.86**	**−29.12**	**1.71**	**−26.96**	**1.06**	**−19.68**	**2.70**	**−44.32**

Figure 6 shows rate-distortion curves for the six test image using five coding scheme mentioned above. The results in Fig. 6 further show our scheme performs better than the other four schemes steadily and the results are consistent for the tested images. That is to say, our scheme always outperforms the other four schemes at all QPs and all the tested images. Our scheme achieves relative steady improvement of coding performance corresponding to other proposed method because all the information of the holoscopic image is encoded and the rendering information are arranged to more adaptive to the HEVC encoder.

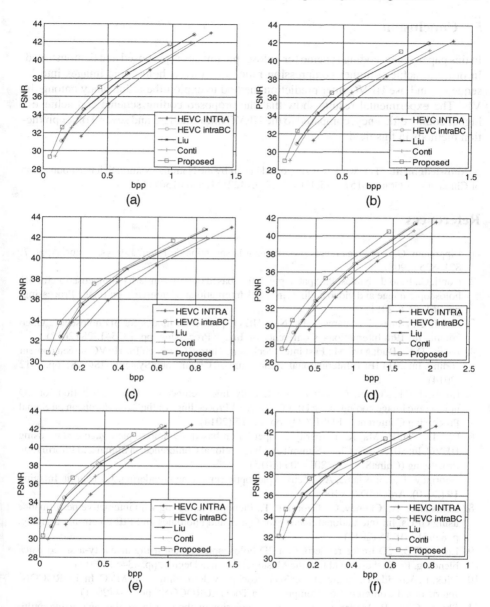

Fig. 6. Rate-distortion curves for the six test image: (a) Bike; (b) Fountain; (c) Jeff; (d) Laura; (e) Seagull; (f) Zhengyun1

5   Conclusion

In this paper, a new coding scheme for holoscopic images is proposed and demonstrated. In order to achieve higher compression ratio, we convert holoscopic images into VI sequence and use HEVC inter prediction method to exploit the redundancy among the VIs. The experimental results show that the proposed coding scheme can achieve a higher coding efficiency, compared to the HEVC intra standard and several other prediction methods in this field.

Acknowledgment. This work was supported in part by the National Natural Science Foundation of China, under Grants 61571285, U1301257, 61422111, and 61301112.

References

1. Lippmann, G.: Epreuves reversibles donnant la sensation du relief. J. Phys. Theor. Appl. **7**, 821–825 (1908)
2. Conti, C., Lino, J., Nunes, P.: Spatial prediction based on self-similarity compensation for 3D holoscopic image and video coding. In: 2011 International Conference on Image Processing, pp. 961–964 (2011)
3. Conti, C., Nunes, P., Soares, L.D.: New HEVC prediction modes for 3D holoscopic video coding. In: 19th International Conference on Image Processing, pp. 1325–1328 (2012)
4. Kwon, D.K., Budagavi, M.: Fast intra block copy (IntraBC) search for HEVC screen content coding. In: 2014 IEEE International Symposium on Circuits and Systems (ISCAS), pp. 9–12 (2014)
5. Lucas, L.F.R., Conti, C., Nunes, P.: Locally linear embedding-based prediction for 3D holoscopic image coding using HEVC. In: 2014 Proceedings of the 22nd European on Signal Processing Conference (EUSIPCO), pp. 11–15 (2014)
6. Liu, D., An, P., Ma, R.: Disparity compensation based 3D holoscopic image coding using HEVC. In: 2015 IEEE China Summit and International Conference on Signal and Information Processing (ChinaSIP), pp. 201–205 (2015)
7. Georgiev, T., Lumsdaine, A.: Focused plenoptic camera and rendering. J. Electron. Imaging **19** (2010). ArticleID 021106
8. Lumsdaine, A., Chunev, G., Georgiev, T.: Plenoptic rendering with interactive performance using GPUs. In: International Society for Optics and Photonics on SPIE Electronic Imaging, p. 829513-01-15 (2012)
9. Lino, J.F.O.: 2D image rendering for 3D holoscopic content using disparity-assisted patch blending. Ph.D. thesis to obtain the Master of Science Degree, pp. 43–54 (2013)
10. Dick, J., Almeida, H., Soares, L.D.: 3D holoscopic video coding using MVC. In: EUROCON-International Conference on Computer as a Tool (EUROCON), pp. 1–4 (2011)
11. Shi, S., Gioia, P., Madec, G.: Efficient compression method for integral images using multi-view video coding. In: 2011 18th IEEE International Conference on Image Processing, pp. 137–140 (2011)
12. Conti, C., Nunes, P.: Inter-layer prediction scheme for scalable 3-D holoscopic video coding. IEEE Sig. Process. Lett. **20**, 819–822 (2013)
13. Dricot, A., Jung, J., Cagnazzo, M.: Integral images compression scheme based on view extraction. In: Signal Processing Conference (EUSIPCO), pp. 101–105 (2015)
14. Todor Georgiev, August 2013. http://tgeorgiev.net/

15. Li, Y., Sjöström, M., Olsson, R.: Coding of plenoptic images by using a sparse set and disparities. In: 2015 IEEE International Conference on Multimedia and Expo (ICME), pp. 1–6 (2015)
16. Flynn, D., Sole, J., Suzuki, T.: High Efficiency Video Coding (HEVC) range extensions text specification: Draft 4, Joint Collaborative Team Video Coding (JCT-VC), document JCTVC-N1005 (2013)

A Fast Inter-frame Prediction Algorithm for AVS2 Based on Mode Complexity

Fang Chen[✉], Guoping Li, Guozhong Wang, and Haiwu Zhao

School of Communication and Information Engineering,
Shanghai University, Shanghai 200444, China
cf515827@163.com

Abstract. The complexity of inter-frame prediction is increasing in the new generation video standard AVS2 by introducing the technology of quad-tree division. To solve the problem, a fast inter-frame prediction algorithm based on mode complexity is proposed which consists of prediction mode decision and reference frame selection. Since there is a strong correlation between CU and its optimal referenced block, information of the optimal referenced block can be utilized to measure the mode complexity of the current CU so as to make an early termination for prediction modes. Meanwhile, based on a bottom-to-up visiting structure in the quad-tree of AVS2, the reference information of sub-CUs can be extracted to distribute the appropriate candidates of reference frame for the current CU. Experimental results show that, the proposed algorithm can reduce the coding time by 44.29% on average, with a 2.03% increase of Bjontegaard delta bit rate (BD-Rate) and a 0.07 dB decrease of Bjontegaard delta peak signal-to-noise rate (BD-PSNR).

Keywords: AVS2 · Prediction mode · Mode complexity · Reference frame

1 Introduction

In order to meet the requirement of higher video compression ratio, Chinese AVS working group has developed a new generation of video coding standard named AVS2 with independent intellectual property rights in the last three years [1]. AVS2 provides significant improvements on the coding efficiency relative to the preceding H.264/AVC and AVS1 standard. And compared with H.265/HEVC, AVS2 can achieve more efficient compression for certain applications such as surveillance as well as low-delay communication such as video conference [2].

A more flexible partition structure is adopted by AVS2 which consists of Coding Unit (CU), Prediction Unit (PU), and Transform Unit (TU). An image consists of multiple coding tree units (CTUs) which can be divided into a series of CUs as an iterative quad-tree structured method. CU is the basic unit of inter/intra prediction whose size ranges from 8×8 to 64×64, and it can be split into one or more PUs and TUs. As shown in the Fig. 1, intra-prediction has

© Springer Nature Singapore Pte Ltd. 2017
X. Yang and G. Zhai (Eds.): IFTC 2016, CCIS 685, pp. 328–337, 2017.
DOI: 10.1007/978-981-10-4211-9_32

four PU partition types: 2N × 2N, N × N, 0.5N × 2N and 2N × 0.5N, while inter-prediction has eight PU partition types: four symmetric partitions (2N × 2N, 2N × N, N × 2N, N × N) and four asymmetric partitions (2N × nU, 2N × nD, nL × 2N and nR × 2N). Specifically, CU in inter-frame includes anther two modes: SKIP mode and DIRECT mode [2]. The partition for SKIP and DIRECT is 2N × 2N when the size of CU is 8 × 8, and the partition is N × N for other CU sizes. The mode decision process in AVS2 is performed among all above modes to find the best one with least rate distortion (RD) cost.

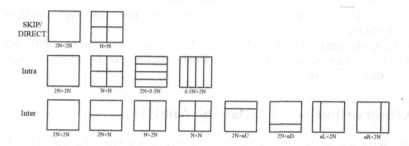

Fig. 1. The prediction modes of AVS2

Although the recursive quad-tree structure improves the coding performance significantly, it occupies intensive computational complexity, which restricts the popularization of AVS2 on the real time applications. However, rare works were applied on AVS2 encoder to reduce the computational complexity. In this paper, a novel algorithm is presented to accelerate inter-frame prediction for AVS2 based on the relationship between CU and its relevant block in the reference frame. What's more, the optimal reference frame selected by PUs in the CU of neighboring depth is highly related. It is unnecessary to try all candidates in the reference list.

The rest of the paper is organized as follows. An overview for related works is presented in Sect. 2. Statistical analysis is displayed in Sect. 3. Section 4 introduces the fast algorithm particularly. Section 5 shows the overall algorithm. Experimental results are given in Sect. 6. Paper is concluded in Sect. 7.

2 Related Works

Recently, many fast algorithms have been proposed to reduce computational complexity, which can be roughly classified into two categories: fast intra prediction approaches and fast inter prediction approaches.

The fast intra prediction approaches focus on fast intra mode decision. In [3], the Hadamard cost was calculated to roughly select the potential intra prediction modes instead of all candidates, and the RD cost was employed to terminate the CU split early. The neighboring direction information was exploited in [4] to draw a gradient mode histogram so that the number of candidate modes was limited. However, the coding time occupied by intra prediction is so less that the consumed time of these algorithms is limited.

The fast inter prediction approaches are designed to speed up inter mode decision and reference frame selection. By comparing the Manhattan distance of the motion vectors difference among adjacent PUs in AVS2, the optimal reference frame was gotten in [5]. In [6], the depth information of the collocated CU was utilized to reduce CU depth. In [7], the coding information correlation between the depth level and spatiotemporal correlation among adjacent CUs was used jointly to accelerate mode decision. However, when CU is located in the boundary of moving object or it moves fast, the accuracy of these fast algorithms will be greatly reduced.

Besides, the majority of methods are based on statistical characteristics of the HEVC encoder, which cannot be directly applied on the AVS2 encoder due to the different coding structures.

3   Observation and Statistical Analysis

To reduce the coding bit rate, simple prediction modes are always selected by the CU with simple texture and gentle motion. While complex prediction modes are usually preferred for the CU with complex texture and fast motion to increase the accuracy of prediction.

In [7], all the available prediction modes in HEVC are classified into several classes based on their different complexities. According to different characteristics of motion and texture, a mode complexity factor (MCF) is distributed for each prediction mode in AVS2. As shown in Table 1, the simple prediction mode corresponds to a smaller MCF, while the complex prediction mode corresponds to a larger MCF.

Table 1. Classification of prediction modes and the corresponded MCF

Class	Prediction mode	Motion and texture	MCF
C1	SKIP	Motionless or homogeneous motion	0
C2	DIRECT, $2N \times 2N$	Simple motion and texture	1
C3	$2N \times N$, $N \times 2N$	Moderate motion and texture	2
C4	$2N \times nU$, $2N \times nD$, $nL \times 2N$, $nR \times 2N$, $N \times N$	Fast motion, highly-textured region or new object	4
C5	$0.5N \times 2N$, $2N \times 0.5N$	Most highly-textured region	5

Generally, all the prediction modes can be roughly classified into three types according to the value of MCF, which are simple modes (SM), moderate modes (MM) and complex modes (CM), respectively. The specific classification is shown as follows,

$$\mathbf{CU} \subseteq \begin{cases} SM, MCF \leq 1; \\ MM, 1 < MCF < 4; \\ CM, MCF \geq 4 \end{cases} \qquad (1)$$

It is analyzed in [7] that the majority of best prediction modes after mode decision in inter-frames are within SM. To characterize this feature, we test sequences with different motion activities and texture features in AVS2.

Statistical percentages of different modes are demonstrated in Fig. 2. It can be seen from Fig. 2 that the percentage of SM is highest compared with other modes and it also increases with quantization parameter (QP) increasing. If the mode complexity of CU is identified as early as possible, it will avoid the unnecessary process of performing other modes.

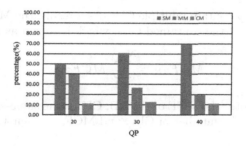

Fig. 2. The percentage of SM, MM and CM under different QP

Similar to mode decision process, the reference frame selection also examines all frames to find the best one, which brings high computational cost. In fact, the probability of each reference frame selected as the optimal one is different. It is analyzed in [8] that the nearest reference frame is always selected as the optimal one. To verify this trait, different sequences are tested under the condition that the maximum number of reference frames is 4. The distributions of the optimal frame are listed in Figs. 3 and 4. It can be obtained that the highest proportion of optimal reference frames is ref1 which denotes the nearest frame. And the percentage of ref1 increases with QP increasing.

4   Proposed Algorithm

4.1   Fast Prediction Mode Decision

In the AVS2 inter prediction, motion estimation is applied on the reference frames to search the optimal referenced block. As the $2N \times 2N$ mode is firstly checked (except SKIP and DIRECT) in the process of traversing all prediction modes, we define the optimal referenced block as the relevant block (RB) for the current CU. As shown in Fig. 5, the simple RB may contain only one CU, while

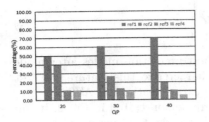 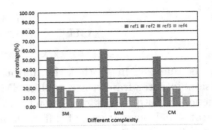

Fig. 3. The distribution of reference frames under different QP

Fig. 4. The distribution of reference frames under SM, MM, CM

the complex RB may contain multiple CUs. As a result, the MCF of RB is equal to the sum of MCF of the contained CUs, which is shown as follows,

$$MCF_{RB} = \sum_{i=1}^{N_{CUr}} MCF_{CU_{ri}} \tag{2}$$

where MCF_{RB} denotes the MCF of the RB, CU_r is the same-sized CU contained in the RB, N_{CUr} is the number of CU_r, and MCF_{CUri} denotes the MCF of the ith specific CU_r.

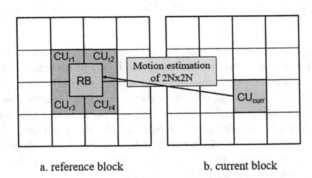

a. reference block   b. current block

Fig. 5. Location of the RB

To search the correlation between CUs and the corresponding RB in terms of mode complexity, we define four conditional probabilities which are shown in formulas (3) to (6).

$$P1 = P(CU_{curr} \in SM | RB \in SM) = \frac{P(CU_{curr} \in SM, RB \in SM)}{P(RB \in SM)} \tag{3}$$

$$P2 = P(CU_{curr} \in MM | RB \in MM) = \frac{P(CU_{curr} \in MM, RB \in MM)}{P(RB \in MM)} \tag{4}$$

$$P3 = P(CU_{curr} \in CM | RB \in CM) = \frac{P(CU_{curr} \in CM, RB \in CM)}{P(RB \in CM)} \quad (5)$$

$$P4 = P(CU_{curr} \in (SM \cup MM) | RB \in MM)$$
$$= \frac{P(CU_{curr} \in (SM \cup MM), RB \in MM)}{P(RB \in MM))} \quad (6)$$

We test several sequences in AVS2, and the results are shown in Table 2.

Table 2. The probability of P1, P2, P3, P4

Sequence	BQSquare	BasketballPass	BQMall	BasketballDrill	City	SlideEditing
P1(%)	86.76	97.64	95.23	92.63	81.68	97.24
P2(%)	26.29	28.33	20.36	9.17	12.06	4.81
P3(%)	13.19	16.39	14.13	9.40	9.40	4.52
P4(%)	96.41	95.55	96.11	97.59	97.13	98.37

From Table 2, we can know that the current CU would probably choose the simple mode as its optimal prediction mode when the RB belongs to SM, and the optimal prediction modes are usually within MM and SM when the RB belongs to MM. As a result, appropriate prediction modes can be allocated according to the mode complexity of the RB.

In order to reduce the erroneous judgment and ensure the quality of coding, the predicted RD_0 is set as the threshold to further determine whether the next prediction mode is performing. The value of RD_0 is calculated by the mean of RD cost of the CU contained in RB. Formula is shown as below,

$$RD_0 = \frac{1}{N_{CU_r}} \sum_{i=1}^{N_{CU_r}} RD\cos t_{CU_{ri}} \quad (7)$$

where N_{CU_r} denotes the number of CU_r, $RDcost_{CU_{ri}}$ is the RD cost of the ith CU_r.

As a result, the core idea of fast prediction mode decision is concluded as follows. Firstly, for SKIP and DIRECT mode, the specific RB and RD_0 are inferred by their own predicted motion vectors. Make an early termination if the RB belongs to SM and the RD cost is less than the RD_0. Secondly, for the remaining prediction modes, the RB and RD_0 are exploited by the motion vector of 2N × 2N mode, and then the kind of RB is determined by the formula (1). Make an early termination if the current prediction mode and the RB both belong to SM and the RD cost of this mode is less than the RD_0. When the RB belongs to MM and the current prediction mode belongs to MM or SM, also the RD cost of this mode is less than the RD_0, the rest of prediction modes are not checked.

4.2   Fast Reference Frame Decision

CU is always homogeneous when all sub-CUs belong to SM, so it is unnecessary to traverse all reference frames. To prove this characteristic, we define Ω_{sub} and Ω_{curr} as the set of best reference frames for the current CU and sub-CUs, respectively. As the nearest frame is always selected as the optimal one, Ω_{cand} is defined as the union of Ω_{sub} and the nearest frame, which is shown as below,

$$\Omega_{cand} = \Omega_{sub} \cup \{0\} \tag{8}$$

where 0 denotes the index of the nearest frame.

And we calculate the probability that Ω_{curr} is distributed in the Ω_{cand} when all sub-CUs belong to SM. The experimental conditions are similar to the above. Results are shown in the Table 3.

$$P = P(\Omega_{curr} \subseteq_{cand} | CU_{sub\_all} \in SM) \tag{9}$$

where CU_{sub_all} denotes all of the sub-CUs.

Table 3. The probability of Ω_{curr} distributed in the interval of Ω_{cand}

Sequence	BQSquare	BlowingBubbles	PartyScene	BasketballDirve	Crew	SlideShow
P(%)	81.05	90.35	89.96	91.14	88.23	96.7

It is different from the CU traversal order of HEVC that AVS2 traverses CU from the bottom depth to the upper depth gradually. As a result, the best reference frames of sub-CUs are known before coding the current CU.

Demonstrated by Table 3, there is a strong correlation between Ω_{curr} and Ω_{cand} when sub-CUs belong to SM. The current CU only tries the reference frames in the Ω_{cand} under this circumstance.

5   Overall Algorithm

According to the above analysis, the algorithm proposed in this paper includes two parts. The detail steps of the algorithm are presented as follows:

Step one: the predicted motion vectors of SKIP and DIRECT mode are utilized to get the RB and RD_0, and calculate the RD cost for each modes. If the RB belongs to SM and the RD cost is less than the RD_0, jump to Step six, otherwise go to Step two;

Step two: exploit the RB and RD_0 for 2N × 2N which are also used in the remaining prediction modes, and then calculate the RD cost of this mode. If the RB belongs to SM or MM and the RD cost is less than the RD_0, jump to step six, otherwise go to step three;

Step three: calculate the RD cost of 2N × N. If the RB belongs to MM and the RD cost is less than the RD_0, jump to step six, otherwise go to step four;

Step four: calculate the RD cost of N × 2N. If the RB belongs to MM and the RD cost is less than the RD_0, jump to step six, otherwise go to step five;

Step five: traverse the rest of complex inter modes and intra modes.

Step six: select the prediction mode with minimum cost as the best one. End inter frame prediction for the current CU.

Meanwhile, the reference list tried by step two to step five consists of the nearest reference frame and the optimal ones selected by sub-CUs when all sub-CUs belong to SM.

6   Experimental Results

To evaluate the performance of the proposed fast inter prediction algorithm, the proposed algorithm is implemented on the recent AVS2 reference software (RD14.2). Sequences with different motion activities and texture features are tested. The specific configuration of the experiment is shown in Table 4, which is according to the general test conditions for AVS2 [9]. The Bjontegaard delta peak signal-to-noise rate (BD-PSNR) and the Bjontegaard delta bit rate (BD-Rate) [10] are used to represent distortion and compression efficiency, respectively.

Table 4. Experimental test conditions

Hardware platform	ProcessorIntel(R) Xeon(R) CPU x5647 @2.93 GHz Memory16.0 GB
Frame architecture	IPPPPP
Test sequence	Resolution: 832 × 480, 1280 × 720, 1920 × 1080
	Sequence: BasketballDrill, RaceHorses, City, Crew, Cactus, Kimonol
QP	27, 32, 38, 45
The maximum number of reference frames	4
CTU	64 × 64

And △T represents the reduced coding time, which is calculated as below,

$$\Delta T = \frac{T_{pro} - T_{RD}}{T_{RD}} \times 100\% \tag{10}$$

where T_{pro} and T_{RD} denote the coding time of the proposed algorithm and the conditional method of RD14.2, respectively.

Table 5 shows the performance results of the proposed algorithm. It can be seen from Table 5 that the proposed approach can reduce the coding time by

44.29% on overage, with only a 2.03% BD-Rate increase and a 0.07 dB BD-PSNR decrease. "Vidyo3" achieves the highest time reduction by 63.36% for its simple background. For the sequence with complex motion like "RaceHorses", our algorithm displays a good performance, achieving a 30.25% time reduction with a negligible loss. Compared with [5], our proposed algorithm achieves a better performance, it reduces more than 8.18% of the coding time, with a 0.89% BD-Rate decrease and a 0.03 dB BD-PSNR increase. All the results verify that the presented algorithm is effective.

Table 5. Experimental test results

Resolution	Sequence	[5]			The proposed algorithm		
		BD-Rate(%)	BD-PSNR(dB)	$\triangle T(\%)$	BD-Rate(%)	BD-PSNR(dB)	$\triangle T(\%)$
832 × 480	BasketballDrill	3.96	−0.14	−33.93	1.96	−0.07	−48.04
	PartyScene	3.03	−0.13	−39.40	2.32	−0.10	−37.47
	RaceHorses	1.88	−0.09	−20.90	1.25	−0.05	−30.25
1280 × 720	City	3.30	−0.12	−31.78	2.81	−0.08	−36.67
	Johnny	2.59	−0.09	−32.52	2.04	−0.05	−63.34
	Vidyo3	2.46	−0.10	−57.25	2.38	−0.08	−63.36
1920 × 1080	Cactus	2.52	−0.06	−39.42	2.38	−0.06	−47.27
	Kimonol	3.75	−0.10	−36.11	0.75	−0.03	−32.44
	Taishan	2.78	−0.11	−33.71	2.40	−0.08	−39.76
Average		2.92	−0.10	−36.11	2.03	−0.07	−44.29

Figures 6 and 7 describe the RD curves of City and Kimonol whose BD-Rates are highest in the result. It can be seen from the figures that the two RD curves are basically coincident. As a result, it verifies that the proposed algorithm can achieve almost the same RD performance compared with the original encoder.

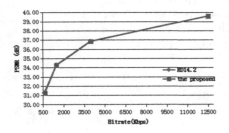

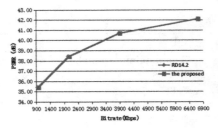

Fig. 6. The RD curve of City   **Fig. 7.** The RD curve of Kimonol

7   Conclusion

Combine with the specific coding structure in AVS2, we propose a low complexity coding scheme to promote the industrialization of AVS2 in this paper. It firstly utilizes the strong correlation among relevant blocks to skip unnecessary prediction modes. Furthermore, the traversal of prediction modes can be terminated in advance by using statistical characteristics of RD cost. At the same time, the reference frames selected by sub-CUs are provided as the candidates for the current CU when sub-CUs are simple modes. Experimental results show that, the algorithm can reduce time by 44.29% on average, with a 2.03% increase of BD-Rate and a 0.07 dB decrease of BD-PSNR.

Acknowledgment. This work is supported by National Science Foundation of China under Grant No. 61271212. National High-tech R&D Program (863 Program) under Grant No. 2015AA015903.

References

1. He, Z., Yu, L., Zheng, X. et al.: Framework of AVS2-video coding. In: IEEE International Conference on Image Processing, pp. 1515–1519. IEEE (2013)
2. Ma, S., Huang, T., Reader, C., et al.: AVS2? Making video coding smarter [standards in a Nutshell]. IEEE Signal Process. Mag. **32**(2), 172–183 (2015)
3. Zhang, H., Ma, Z.: Fast intra mode decision for high efficiency video coding (HEVC). IEEE Trans. Circ. Syst. Video Technol. **24**(4), 660–668 (2014)
4. Jiang, W., Ma, H., Chen, Y.: Gradient based fast mode decision algorithm for intra prediction in HEVC. In: 2012 2nd International Conference on Consumer Electronics, Communications and Networks (CECNet), pp. 1836–1840. IEEE (2012)
5. Lin, Q., Zhao, H., Wang, G., et al.: Fast inter prediction algorithm for AVS2. Digital Video **38**(17), 76–79 (2014)
6. Lee, H.S., Kim, K.Y., Kim, T.R., et al.: Fast encoding algorithm based on depth of coding-unit for high efficiency video coding. Opt. Eng. **51**(6), 067402:1–067402:11 (2012)
7. Shen, L., Zhang, Z., Liu, Z.: Adaptive inter-mode decision for HEVC jointly utilizing inter-level and spatiotemporal correlations. IEEE Trans. Circ. Syst. Video Technol. **24**(10), 1709–1722 (2014)
8. Shang, X., Wang, G., Fan, T., et al.: Statistical and spatiotemporal correlation based low-complexity video coding for high-efficiency video coding[J]. J. Electron. Imaging **24**(2), 023006–023006 (2015)
9. Zhen, X.: General test conditions for AVS-P2[EB/OL], August 2104. ftp://124.207.250.92/public/avsdoc/1406_Dalian/avs/
10. Bjontegaard, G.: Calcuation of average PSNR differences between RD-curves. Doc. VCEG-M33 ITU-T Q6/16, Austin, TX, USA, 2–4 April 2001

Content Oriented Video Quality Prediction for HEVC Encoded Stream

Kanghua Zhu[1], Yongfang Wang[1(✉)], Jian Wu[1], Yun Zhu[1], and Wei Zhang[2]

[1] School of Communication and Information Engineering,
Shanghai University, Shanghai 200072, China
zhukanghuashu@163.com
[2] Department of Electronics and Information Engineering, Huazhong
University of Science and Technology, Wuhan 430074, Hubei, China

Abstract. In this paper, a novel content-oriented video quality prediction model for HEVC encoded video stream is proposed, which takes into account of quantization parameter (QP) and the newly proposed content based video metric. Firstly, the proposed content type metric is developed by combining temporal and spatial information as well as the standard deviation of bitrates. By extensive experiments, we find there exist logarithmic relationship between the content type metric and video quality. Then we set up a content-oriented video quality prediction model based on above experiments. The experimental results demonstrate the proposed prediction model can achieve an overall correlation coefficient of 98% with the training sequences and 97% with the testing sequences.

Keywords: Content type · HEVC · Video complexity · Video quality prediction

1 Introduction

Video content has a significant impact on perceptual video quality. Different video quality assessment (VQA) results can be produced under the same coding parameters setting such as frame rate and spatial resolution. Given that the dependence of video quality on content type, it is important to take the different content of video into consideration for quality prediction.

The common objective metrics for perceptual video quality estimation include two main groups: human vision model based metrics [1, 2] and video parameters based metrics [3, 4]. In order to reduce the video quality metrics complexity, it is necessary to take full advantage of the encoded bitstream, extracting features accurately without any information about the reference frames.

Common approaches of determining video content types are extracting motion features from the encoded bitstream and computation of pixel-wise differences between frames. Authors in [5] presented a new reference free approach for quality estimation based on motion features including amount and direction of the motion between two scene changes. [6] proposed a more accuracy model taking content classification into account using an impairment detection model modified from H.264. Content adaptive parameters and classification, were presented to estimate video quality in [7], which was

© Springer Nature Singapore Pte Ltd. 2017
X. Yang and G. Zhai (Eds.): IFTC 2016, CCIS 685, pp. 338–348, 2017.
DOI: 10.1007/978-981-10-4211-9_33

determined by MV information and pixel-wise SAD. In [8], quality of experience (QoE) content type, sender bitrate, block error rate and mean burst length were considered in the model, but no motion characteristics or content type were taken into account. Researchers in [9] proposed a video prediction algorithm based on spatial and temporal content, but the type of the frame (e.g. I frame and P frame) was not considered. Objective and subjective tests on video sequences were carried out to investigate the impact of video content type and encoding parameter settings on HEVC in [10], in which a motion amount (MA) metric was defined to determine the video content type of encoded stream, and combined with multiplication of quantization parameter to predict video quality, but without considering the frame type of each frame and the variation of bits among frames, which will not present the video quality precisely.

In this paper, we proposed a content-based video quality prediction model by exploring complexity of spatial and temporal of video sequences, as well as the standard deviation of bitrates. Firstly we give the definition of video content type in terms of motion activities and video complexity derived from the encoded stream that predicts the video exactly. Then based on above content type metric, content based video quality model established.

The rest of the paper is organized as follows: Sect. 2 describes the proposed content type definition process. The proposed content based video quality prediction model is presented in Sect. 3. Section 4 shows experimental results. Section 5 concludes the paper.

2 Content Type Definition

Figure 1 illustrates the block diagram of the system designed for an investigation of the effect of encoding parameters on video quality prediction. The key components of the system are: encoding/decoding, feature extraction (spatial/temporal complexity), and the modelling of the prediction model.

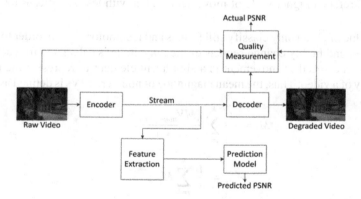

Fig. 1. Block diagram of the system for video quality prediction mode

Human Visual System (HVS) is sensitive to sharp changes in the videos, in temporal and spatial domain [11]. Therefore, we define the spatial-temporal complexity of the video by making use of the parameters derived from the encoded bitstream.

2.1 Temporal Complexity

The motion activity is the most common motion feature, which describes the intensity of activity whether motion is low, normal or high in a video sequence. Motion Vectors (MV), which represent a coding block in a picture based on the position of this block (or a similar one) in a reference picture, are used as basic element on the assumption that motion is the primary indication of the temporal complexity.

If the matching block is found at the same location as the target block, then the magnitude of the MV should be zero, the motion vector is known as the zero MV, which means there has no movement on the block. The percentage of zero MVs in a frame represents the proportion of the frame that does not change between two consecutive frames. Thus, the non-zero MV ratio $\overline{C}$ for the video, which indicates the feature of temporal complexity, can be defined as follows.

$$C_i = \frac{count_i(MV_{non-zero})}{count_i(MV)} \tag{1}$$

$$\overline{C} = \frac{1}{N} \sum_{i=1}^{N} C_i \tag{2}$$

where $count_i(MV_{non-zero})$ represents the number of non-zero MVs in the ith frame, $count_i(MV)$ represents the total number of MVs in ith frame, and N represents the number of frames encoded. This feature detects the proportion of a mobile region: the higher value of $\overline{C}$ refers a higher scale of movement region with less significant local movement [12].

The value of $\overline{C}$ can only classify still frames and locomotor ones, in order to discriminate slowly and highly change sequences the magnitude is calculated for each coding unit (CU). The speed of movement is a significant element to represent the temporal complexity of a video. Thus, the mean magnitude of non-zero MVs is defined as follows:

$$M_i = \frac{1}{K_i} \sum_{i=1}^{K_i} \frac{|MV_{non-zero}|}{w \bullet h} \tag{3}$$

$$M_{arg} = \frac{1}{N} \sum_{i=1}^{N} M_i \tag{4}$$

$$|MV_{non-zero}| = \sqrt{(\Delta x)^2 + (\Delta y)^2} \tag{5}$$

where K_i represents the number of non-zero MVs in the ith frame, $|MV_{non-zero}|$ represents the magnitude of motion vector, Δx and Δy are the horizontal and vertical component of MV. w and h represent the width and height of the frame respectively, in order to eliminate the influence of the spatial resolution, we normalize the magnitude of MV by dividing frame size. M_i is the mean magnitude of non-zero MVs in the ith frame, so temporal complexity M_{arg} can be calculated by averaging all M_i of N frames in the sequence.

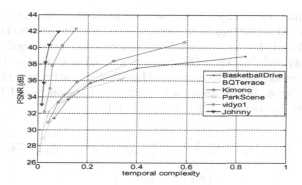

Fig. 2. The relationship between temporal complexity and PSNR

In order to convert the spatiotemporal complexity into video quality measure, the average bit rate parameter is defined.

$$B_{ave} = \frac{1}{N} \sum_{i=1}^{N} Bits_i \tag{6}$$

where $Bits_i$ represents the output bits of the ith frame, and N represents the frame number of the sequence.

Then we combine $\overline{C}$, M_{arg} and B_{ave} to make a definition of the temporal complexity.

$$T_{info} = \frac{B_{ave}}{\overline{C} \cdot M_{arg}} \tag{7}$$

Because $\overline{C}$ can be used to indicate the proportion of region where motion exists, M_{arg} can be used to indicate the average motion amplitude of the same region, hence the multiplicative term $\overline{C} \cdot M_{arg}$ stands for the amount of motion, which is the most important temporal information.

For a constant average bitrates, temporal distortion increase with more vigorous activity. Similarly, videos share the same temporal motion activity, video quality increase with average bitrates. So divide B_{ave} by $\overline{C} \cdot M_{arg}$ can describe temporal complexity, which closely related with video quality.

The temporal complexity monotone decreasing with increased QP, because the redundancy between successive frames decreased with increased QP by reducing the amount of motion. Figure 2 illustrates the relationship between temporal complexity and Peak Signal to Noise Ratio (PSNR). According to the trend of the curves, there exist a nearly logarithmic relationship between temporal complexity and PSNR.

2.2 Spatial Complexity

The average picture complexity metric is selected to quantify the spatial information of a video sequence, which derived from different encoded video frames (I frame, P frame and B frame). As it is known that, the bitrates of encoded frame highly related to the spatial complexity under the same QP setting. The result of evaluation [13] shows that bits of every frame decrease with QP increased, while different frame expressed different tendency of variation. In the paper, we optimize the spatial model [13] as spatial complexity metric by consider all frame types as follows

$$S_{info} = \left(\left(\frac{1}{L}\sum_{i=1}^{L}\frac{bits_{I_i}}{Max_{bits}}\cdot\frac{1}{QP_{I_i}}\right)\cdot\left(\frac{1}{M}\sum_{j=1}^{M}\frac{bits_{P_j}}{Max_{bits}}\cdot\frac{1}{QP_{P_j}}\right)\cdot\left(\frac{1}{K}\sum_{k=1}^{K}\frac{bits_{B_k}}{Max_{bits}}\cdot\frac{1}{QPs_{B_k}}\right)\right)^{\alpha} \tag{8}$$

$$\alpha = \frac{(Bits_{QP_n} - Bits_{QP_m})}{Bits_{QP_n}} \tag{9}$$

where α represents the percentage of bits reduction calculated by average number of bits reduction when QP increased. α is 0.11 in the paper according to the extensive experiment results. $Bits_{QP_n}$ and $Bits_{QP_m}$ represent the bits of previous and current QP setting, respectively. L, M and K indicate the number of encoded frame of I, P and B. $bits_*$ and QP_* represent the corresponding bits and QP set for different frames. Max_{bits} denotes the maximum possible number of bitrates in the video, used to normalize the spatial complexity, for the purposes of eliminating the influence of spatial resolution.

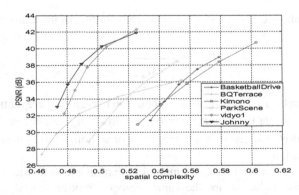

Fig. 3. The relationship between spatial complexity and PSNR

The spatial complexity decrease with increased QP, as QP increased, some of the detail is aggregated so that the spatial complexity drops as well as video quality. Figure 4 shows the relationship between spatial complexity and PSNR, which indicates the video quality increase with increased spatial complexity for the same sequence. These curves show the relationship between spatial complexity and PSNR may follow logarithmic function (Fig. 3).

2.3 Standard Deviation of Bits

The temporal and spatial complexity defined in (7) and (8) may be deficient in predicting the overall quality without considering the variation of bits among frames. We define the standard deviation of bitrates (SDB) as follows

$$B_{dev} = \sqrt{\frac{1}{N} \sum_{i=1}^{N} (Bits_i - B_{ave})^2} \tag{10}$$

where B_{ave} represents the average bits of a sequence (showed in (6)), $Bits_i$ represents the encoded bits of the ith frame.

SDB decreases with increased QP, since the difference of bitrate of every frame trend to be small. Now that the video quality degrades with increased QP, SDB and PSNR have a positive correlation in some degree. Figure 4 shows the relationship between the SDB and PSNR. Results indicate that the video quality increase with increased standard deviation of bitrates.

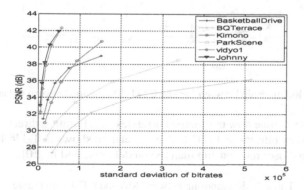

Fig. 4. The relationship between SDB and PSNR

2.4 Content Type Metric

In general, the redundancy between successive frames decreased with increased QP by reducing the amount of motion and associated bitrates.

We propose to combine with the above three features, namely S_{info}, T_{info} and B_{dev} to establish a content type metric (CTM), using the following regression formulation.

$$CTM = a + b \cdot T_{\text{inf}o} + c \cdot S_{\text{inf}o} + d \cdot B_{dev} \qquad (11)$$

where $a = 633400.310$, $b = 4716.647$, $c = -1350204.437$, and $d = 13.7133$ are regression coefficients that apply to all video sequences.

3   Proposed Video Quality Prediction Model

As we have known, at the encoding process, under the same QP setting, the output bitrates and video quality are different with different videos owing to different spatial and temporal complexity. What means there exits some relationship among CTM and video quality.

Experiment results show that the relationship between QP and CTM following a logarithmic-like growth mode, with same grow trend between QP and bitrates as shows in Fig. 5.

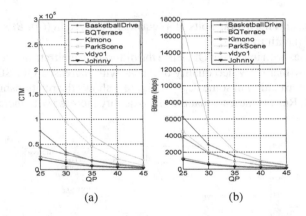

(a)   (b)

Fig. 5.   (a) Relationship between QP and CTM (b) Relation between QP and bitrates

In order to determine how our metric correlates with bitrate, a direct correlation was calculated between bitrates and CTM. The correlation shows in Table 1, it's seen that our metric has a closer relationship than the model presented in [10].

Table 1.   Relationship between MA and CTM with bitrate

Correlation coefficient	Correlation between MA and Bits [10]	Correlation between CTM and Bits
R2	0.816	0.836

It's a common sense that video quality degrades with decreased bitrate. Now that the metrics of CTM has a linear relationship with bitrate, there should be a correlation between CTM and PSNR. The relationship between calculated CTM and pixel-wised PSNR is analysed using the HM encoder in Fig. 6.

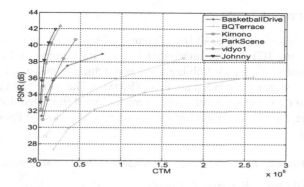

Fig. 6. The relationship between CTM and PSNR

As can be seen, the CTM of all the sequences has logarithmic relationship with PSNR, which is similar to the relationship between bitrates and PSNR. This is important for us to establish a quality prediction model by applying the metric of CTM.

Based on the analysis above, CTM can be used to predict initial video quality without decode the sequence. The calculated CTM decreases with increased QP, and PSNR decreases with increased QP. Therefore, video quality can be predicted with CTM and QP as follows

$$PSNR = f(QP, CTM) \tag{12}$$

Figure 6 shows that the CTM has a logarithmic relation with PSNR. While PSNR has a linear relation with QP [10]. So, we propose the quality prediction model as follows

$$PSNR = \phi + \gamma \cdot QP + \eta \cdot \ln(CTM) \tag{13}$$

where $\phi = 96.241$, $\gamma = -0.787$, $\eta = -2.528$ are coefficients derived from regression process, which can be used for all sequences.

4 Experimental Results and Analysis

4.1 Experiment Environment

In order to test the performance of the proposed model, we implement the proposed model for HEVC encoded stream at HM 14.0 encoder. We compress the original video sequences into the bit stream with the random access main profile GOP pattern. Quantization parameters are chosen with 20, 25, 30, 35 and 40; respectively; frame rate of 30 fps, spatial resolution of sequences are 1280 × 720 and 1920 × 1080 respectively. We do not use rate control and the scalable layer coder technology in the encoding.

4.2 Training Process

Six sequences (BasketballDrive, Vidyo1, Johnny, BQterrace, Kimono and ParkScene) were encoded using JCT-VC recommended settings for training. Table 2 shows the prediction performance of each training sequence, which is measured by correlation coefficients (R^2) and Root Mean Square Error (RMSE). The correlation coefficient can be up to 0.995 for an average level, when compared with full reference PSNR measurements. Figure 7 shows the impact of QP on actual and predicted PSNR for training video sequences.

Table 2. Model prediction performance for training sequences

Cor. Coef.	Basketball Drive	BQTerrace	Kimono	ParkScene	Vidyo1	Johnny
R2	0.9886	0.9976	0.9960	0.9984	0.9965	0.9940
RMSE	0.3750	0.2393	0.5665	0.4088	0.1540	0.3458

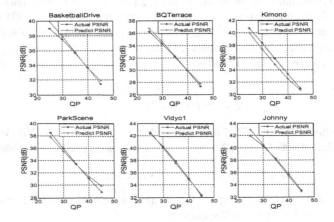

Fig. 7. Actual and predicted PSNR for training video sequences

4.3 Testing Process

In order to test the performance of the proposed model, the CTM and QP from video sequences bitstream that not used in model training process are extracted. Testing sequences include ChinaSpeed, FourPeople, Cactus and KristenAndSara. Figure 8 displays the impact of QP on actual and predicted PSNR for training video sequences. It's clear that we have a better fitting performance than the algorithm proposed in [10]. Figure 9 demonstrates the scatter plot of actual PSNR vs. predicted PSNR for training and testing video sequences. The scatter plot says our proposed method can predict the video quality effectively, owing to making use of the information of encoded video stream. Table 3 shows the prediction performance for testing sequences.

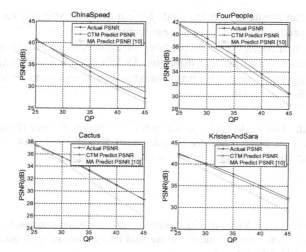

Fig. 8. Actual and predicted PSNR for testing video sequences

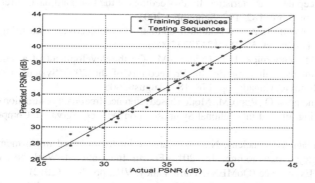

Fig. 9. Actual vs. Predicted PSNR for training and testing video sequences

Table 3. Model prediction performance for testing sequences

Cor. Coef	MA [10]	CTM
R2	0.9375	0.9764
RMSE	1.3175	0.4127

5 Conclusion

In this paper, we proposed an content based perceptual quality prediction metric for the most frequent content types for HEVC encoded streams. We defined a novel video content metric CTM, which bases on spatial and temporal complexity and the standard deviation of bitrates. We proposed a new video quality prediction model using the CTM and QP, which can predict the video quality accurately. Experiment results show the proposed video prediction model has a great accuracy.

Future work will focus on the relationship of influence of video quality reduction caused by transmission and quality estimation. And the deep learning method should be applied to training more features such as context and environment to build a more accurate quality prediction model.

Acknowledgment. This work was supported by National Natural Science Foundation of China (61671283, 61301113), Natural Science Foundation of Shanghai (13ZR1416500), and Open Project of Key Laboratory of Advanced Display and System Application.

References

1. Winkler, S., Dufaux, F.: Video quality evaluation for mobile applications. In: Proceedings of SPIE Conference on Visual Communications and Image Processing, Lugano, Switzerland, vol. 5150, pp. 593–603, July 2003
2. Ong, E.P., Lin, W., Lu, Z., Yao, S., Yang, X., Moschetti, F.: Low bit rate quality assessment based on perceptual characteristics. In: Proceedings of the International Conference on Image Processing, vol. 3, pp. 182–192, September 2003
3. Pinson, M.H., Wolf, S.: A new standardized method for objectively measuring video quality. IEEE Trans. Broadcast. **50**(3), 312–322 (2004)
4. Kusuma, T.M., Zepernick, H.J., Caldera, M.: On the development of a reduced-reference perceptual image quality metric. In: Proceedings of the 2005 Systems Communications (ICW05), Montreal, Canada, pp. 178–184, August 2005
5. Ries, M., Nemethova, O., Rupp, M.: Motion based reference-free quality estimation for H.264/AVC video streaming. In: 2nd International Symposium on Wireless Pervasive Computing, February 2007
6. Van Wallendael, G., Staelens, N.: No-reference bitstream-based impairment detection for high efficiency video coding. In: 2012 Fourth International Workshop on Quality of Multimedia Experience (QoMEX), Yarra Valley, VIC, pp. 7–12 (2012)
7. Ries, M., Nemethova, O., Rupp, M.: Video quality estimation for mobile H.264/AVC video streaming. J. Commun. **3**(1), 41–50 (2008)
8. Khan, A., Sun, L., Ifeachor, E.: QoE prediction model and its application in video quality adaptation over UMTS networks. IEEE Trans. Multimedia **14**(2), 431–442 (2012)
9. Konuk, B., Zerman, E.: A spatiotemporal no-reference video quality assessment model. In: 2013 IEEE International Conference on Image Processing, Melbourne, VIC, pp. 54–58 (2013)
10. Anegekuh, L., Sun, L.: Encoding and video content based HEVC video quality prediction. Multimedia Tools Appl. **74**(11), 3715–3738 (2015)
11. Amirshahi, S.A., Larabi, M.: Spatial-temporal video quality metric based on an estimation of QoE. In: International Workshop on Quality of Multimedia Experience (QoMEX), pp. 84–89 (2011)
12. Ries, M., Gardlo, B.: Audiovisual quality estimation for mobile video services. IEEE J. Sel. Areas Commun. **28**(3), 501–509 (2010)
13. Anegekuh, L., Sun, L., Jammeh, E.: Content-based video quality prediction for HEVC encoded videos streamed over packet networks. IEEE Trans. Multimedia **17**(8), 1323–1334 (2015)

Fast Mode Decision Algorithm for Quality Scalable HEVC

Mengmeng Kang[1,2], Ran Ma[1,2(✉)], Zefu Li[1,2], Xiangyu Hu[1,2], and Ping An[1,2]

[1] School of Communication and Information Engineering,
Shanghai University, Shanghai 200072, China
maran@shu.edu.cn
[2] Key Laboratory of Advanced Displays and System Application,
Ministry of Education, Shanghai 200072, China

Abstract. In order to adapt networks and various devices, the Joint Collaborative Team on Video Coding (JCTVC) develops scalable HEVC (SHVC), which is an extension of HEVC. It is important to reduce the complexity of SHVC because of its high computational time, which may not be suitable for real-time application scenarios. In this paper, we exploit the correlation between the current CU and nearby CUs to skip some unnecessary mode. Meanwhile, we also use the correlation between base layer and enhancement layer to reduce the coding complexity. Experimental results show that our proposed coding algorithm can reduce the coding complexity by 37.7%, with a slight decrease in PSNR of 0.01 dB in base layer and 0.004 dB in enhancement layer, respectively. In the meantime, the R-D performance of luma and chroma is degraded about 0.7% on average.

Keywords: SHVC · Mode decision · R-D performance

1 Introduction

In the process of the standardization of video coding, MPEG and ITU-T make a significant contribution, which formulate and publish a series of international standards and gradually make the video coding technology more mature. As high-resolution video applications and services are becoming increasingly more popular, JCT-VC have developed the next generation video coding standards, called High Efficiency Video Coding (HEVC) [1]. HEVC uses the hybrid coding framework and offers a variety of advanced coding technology. Under the same visual quality, HEVC can save about 50% of the rate in comparison to H.264/AVC [2, 3]. However, due to the different communication capability of different networks (such as cable networks and wireless networks), the compressed video stream should adapt different network transmission characteristics and meet different requirements. Scalable video coding is a very attractive method to solve this problem, in which the original video is encoded at various qualities and resolutions into a single bit stream. The output stream includes one base layer and more than one enhancement layer. JCT-VC is developing a new coding standard called SHVC as a scalable extension of HEVC, which is based on HEVC and extended on the syntax and the tool sets [4]. HEVC provides high coding efficiency while also brings high

© Springer Nature Singapore Pte Ltd. 2017
X. Yang and G. Zhai (Eds.): IFTC 2016, CCIS 685, pp. 349–357, 2017.
DOI: 10.1007/978-981-10-4211-9_34

coding complexity. Similarly, SHVC also has higher coding complexity. So it is very necessary to reduce the encoding complexity of SHVC.

In order to reduce the high coding complexity, many fast methods have been proposed for SHVC. R. Tohidypour used the correlation between base layer and enhancement layer to select proper motion search-range for the enhancement layer, which reduced the coding complexity to a certain extent [5]. R. Tohidypour's method had a good reflect on video with fast motion. However, the effect was not obvious for video with flat motion. Ge proposed two fast algorithms based on the CU depth for base layer and enhancement layer respectively [6]. The proposed algorithm can reduce the time complexity very well, but it brought a very high loss of R-D performance. Bailleul proposed fast mode decision for the quality enhancement layer mode restriction and gained great time-saving in enhancement layer while limiting the loss of the rate-distortion performance of the encoder [7]. However, Bailleul directly copied the base layer CU split flags to enhancement layer or disallowed intra modes, which brought a lot of loss in R-D performance. Although these methods can achieve some gains in reducing the complexity, they don't fully take into account the strong correlation between base layer and enhancement layer.

As we all know, base layer and enhancement layer have the same resolution for quality scalability, so there is a strong correlation between base layer and enhancement layer in mode decision. In addition, due to the consistency of image motion, current frame and reference frame also have a strong correlation. For the above reasons, we propose a fast mode decision for quality scalability.

This paper is organized as follows: Sect. 2 overviews the coding frame of SHVC. Section 3 presents the proposed compression scheme. Section 4 presents the considered test condition and experimental results. Conclusions and discussions are drawn in Sect. 5.

2   Overview of SHVC

Figure 1 shows typical architecture of a two-layer Quality SHVC encoder. In the Quality SHVC encoder, the input video sequence has the same resolution, which means there is a lot of redundant information between base layer and enhancement layer, such as texture and movement information. In order to improve the coding efficiency of enhancement layer, Interlayer prediction (ILP) is employed in SHVC. ILP uses many kinds of information from a reference layer to predict the current enhancement layer, such as the reconstructed texture, mode and motion information. In enhancement layer, the reconstructed picture from the reference layer in the same access unit is regarded as a long-term reference picture, which is inserted into both the forward reference list and backward reference list. And along with other temporal reference pictures in the same layer, the reconstructed picture is assigned a reference index in the reference list.

Seen from Fig. 1, base layer and enhancement layer share the same coding framework with the exception of ILP, which means that the input video sequence of the two layers is still coded by the framework of HEVC. Although HEVC achieves a great increase in rate-distortion (R-D) performance, it comes with intensive computational complexities.

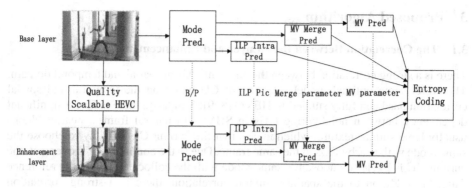

Fig. 1. The architecture of an SHVC encoder

Especially, the optimal mode decision takes up a lot of time consumption. HEVC allows a very flexible block size by adopting a quad-tree structure based coding tree unit (CTU). The coding blocks are named as coding unit (CU), which is a basic coding unit similar to macroblock in H.264/AVC and has a variable size from 64×64 to 8×8. One CTU may be split into four CUs of identical size, and each CU can also be further split unless it reaches the smallest allowable CU size. After splitting CU, mode decision process is performed as in Fig. 2 to seek for the prediction mode and partition size. During the process, R-D optimization is checked in a recursive manner for all the CU sizes to obtain the optimal mode, which undoubtedly increases the time consumption. Therefore, if the number of execution of mode decision process is reduced, the encoding complexity can be reduced.

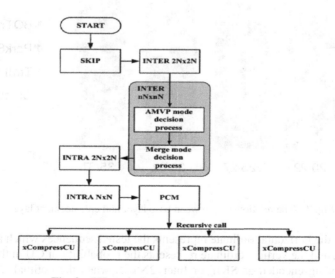

Fig. 2. PU mode decision without fast methods.

3   Proposed Algorithm

3.1   The Correlation Between Base Layer and Enhancement Layer

There is a strong correlation between the adjacent CUs in spatial and temporal domain. Therefore, some optimal model selection of CU based on the temporal and spatial correlation has been fully studied in HEVC [8, 9]. Similarly, there is also a significant dependency between neighboring CUs in SHVC. In natural frames, nearby blocks usually have similar texture, which means that the current CU is likely to choose the same mode with nearby CUs in the same frame. Due to the continuity of movement, the current CU is likely to choose the same mode with the collocated CU in the reference frame. In addition to the spatial-temporal correlation, there is a strong correlation between the layers in SHVC.

In general, base layer is first encoded independently, followed by the enhancement layer. In case of quality scalability, the input video of the different layers is generated at different QP from the same original video source. Because of the highly correlated content, the optimal mode of enhancement layer is strongly correlated with that of base layer. In order to illustrate the mode relationship between base layer and enhancement layer, we analyze the probability of CU in the enhancement layer being encoded as SKIP or Inter_2N×2N when the optimal mode of the collocated CU in base layer is also SKIP or Inter_2N×2N. Figure 3 shows the statistical analysis result of four video sequences.

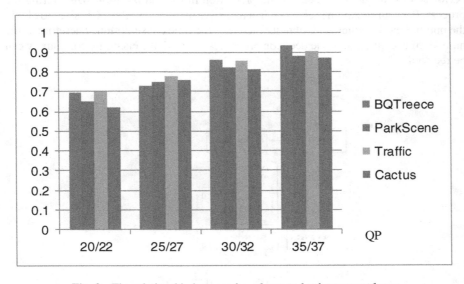

Fig. 3.   The relationship between base layer and enhancement layer

In Fig. 3, the horizontal ordinate represents the tested sequences which are set with different QP, and the vertical ordinate represents the probability of CU in the enhancement layer being encoded as SKIP or Inter_2N×2N when the optimal mode of the collocated CU in base layer is also SKIP or Inter_2N×2N. Obviously, there is a strong correlation between base layer and enhancement layer. Especially, when the QP increases, the probability is greater.

Therefore, the spatial-temporal correlation and the correlation between different layers provide the basis for the choice of the optimal mode.

3.2   The Proposed Fast Mode Decision Algorithm

In our proposed algorithm, the mode cost function of the current CU is defined to skip unnecessary mode decision. Obviously, the mode cost function should be related to mode type and the above two kinds of correlation, so the mode cost of the current CU can be predicted as follows,

$$\mod e_{\cos t} = \sum_{i=0}^{N-1} \omega_i * \alpha_i \tag{1}$$

where N is the number of neighboring CUs.

In our proposed algorithm, the four neighboring CUs are chosen and called Left CU, Up CU, Left-up CU and the collocated CU respectively, shown as Fig. 4. The nearby CUs and the collocated CU of the current CU are also assigned by a weighing factor α_i based on their location. The weighing factor of the Left CU and Up CU is set to 0.3. The weighing factor of Left-up CU and the collocated CU is set to 0.2, just shown in Table 1.

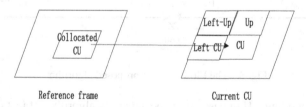

Fig. 4. The nearby CUs and the collocated CU of the current CU

Table 1. Weighting factor of different CUs based on its location

CU	Left CU	Up CU	Left-up CU	Collocated CU
α_i	0.3	0.3	0.2	0.2

Each mode type is assigned by a weighing factor ω_i based on its importance of mode type, e.g., Intra is the highest priority and SKIP is assigned the lowest priority. Different weighing factor is shown in Table 2.

Table 2. Weighing factor of different mode

Mode	SKIP	Inter_2N×2N	SMP	AMP	Inter_N×N	Intra
ω_i	0	1	2	3	4	5

Figure 5 presents the flowchart of the proposed fast mode decision algorithm. The coding procedure can be divided into two main parts according to the different layers.

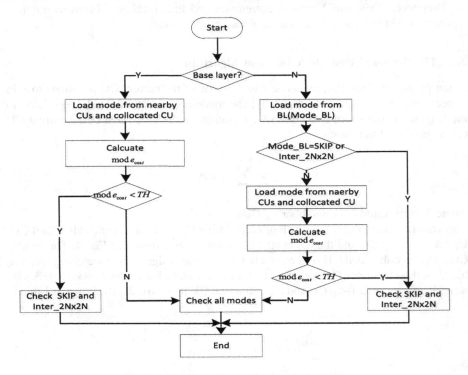

Fig. 5. The Flow chart of proposed algorithm

In case of encoding CU in base layer, the generally algorithm of fast mode decision flow is as follows.

Step1, get the optimal mode of the Left CU, Up CU, Left-up CU and the collocated CU.

Step2, compute the mode cost of the current CU according to (1).

Step3, judge whether the mode cost of the current block less than the threshold we define or not. If so, the encoder only checks the mode of SKIP and Inter_2N×2N. Otherwise, it checks all kinds of mode to choose the optimal mode.

In case of encoding CU in enhancement layer, the generally algorithm of fast mode decision flow is as follows.

Step1, get the optimal mode of the collocated CU in base layer. If the mode is SKIP or Inter_2N×2N, the encoder only checks the mode of SKIP and Inter_2N×2N. Otherwise, go to step2.

Step2, get the optimal mode of Left CU, Up CU, Left-up CU and the collocated CU.

Step3, compute the mode cost of the current block according to (1).

Step4, judge whether the mode cost of the current block less than the threshold we define or not. If so, the encoder only checks SKIP and Inter_2N×2N. Otherwise, it checks all kinds of mode to choose the optimal mode.

4   Experimental Results

4.1   Experimental Conditions

To validate the proposed fast mode decisional algorithm for Quality SHVC, we implement the proposed method into the SHVC reference software (SHM5.0) in Random Access (RA) mode. Two classes of different resolutions video sequences (2560×1600, 1920×1080) are tested, which are shown in Table 3. In the experiment, TH is set to 0.4.

Table 3. The resolution of tested sequences

Resolution	Sequence
2560×1600	PeopleOnStreet
2560×1600	Traffic
1920×1080	BasketballDive
1920×1080	BQTerrace
1920×1080	Cactus
1920×1080	Kimono
1920×1080	ParkScene

The coding block has a fixed size of 64×64 pixels. The maximum depth level is 4, resulting in the minimum CU size of 8×8 pixels. The performance of the proposed algorithm is compared against the original SHM5.0, which are both evaluated with QPs 20, 25, 30 and 35 in base layer and 22, 27, 32 and 37 in enhancement layer, respectively.

The encoding time saving is calculated according to (2).

$$TS(\%) = \frac{Enc.time(SHM5.0) - Enc.time(Proposed)}{Enc.time(SHM\,5.0)} \bullet 100\% \qquad (2)$$

Coding efficiency is measured with bit rate and PSNR. BDBR (%) is used to represent bitrate differences [10]. R-D performance is separately calculated using BDR on total bitrate (BL + EL) for luma and chroma components, where negative value indicates performance gain. $BDR(YUV)$ is the weighted average of the BDR values of three components, and is calculated by using (3).

$$BDR(YUV) = \frac{8 * BDR_Y + BDR_U + BDR_V}{10} \qquad (3)$$

$DPSNR(dB)$ is used to represent PSNR differences. Its positive value indicates performance gain, and is calculated by using (4).

$$DPSNR = PSNR_Y(Proposed) - PSNR_Y(SHM5.0) \qquad (4)$$

4.2   Experimental Results

Table 4 gives the time saving performance comparisons of the proposed algorithm with original SHM5.0. As can be seen in Table 4, under different QP, the proposed algorithm saves about 24%–54% of the time overhead, and the average time saving is approximately 37.7%. It can be also observed that the higher time saving is gained with the higher QP. The reason is that when the QP increases, the higher probability of SKIP or Inter_2N×2N is selected.

Table 4. Compare of time saving

Sequence	TS				
	QP				Average
	20/22	25/27	30/32	35/37	
PeopleOnStreet	24.2%	27.8%	30.4%	34.4%	29.2%
Traffic	35.1%	42%	46.8%	51.3%	43.8%
BasketballDive	29.4%	33.3%	37.9%	41.3%	35.5%
BQTerrace	29.8%	40.4%	49.3%	54.1%	43.4%
Cactus	30.7%	36.8%	41.5%	46.6%	38.9%
Kimono	25.3%	28.4%	33.2%	39.3%	31.6%
ParkScene	32.8%	39.2%	45.3%	49.8%	41.8%
Average	–	–	–	–	37.7%

As shown in Table 5, there is no obvious performance loss for the proposed algorithm. A slight BD-rate increment is only 0.7%. And there is a slight PSNR loss for base layer and enhancement layer, which are 0.01 and 0.004, respectively.

Table 5. Compare of Bit-rate increment and PSNR loss

Sequences	BDR (YUV)	DPSNR_BL	DPSNR_EL
PeopleOnStreet	0.64%	−0.025	−0.0075
Traffic	1.0%	−0.01	−0.0025
BasketballDive	0.62%	−0.005	−0.005
BQTerrace	0.39%	−0.0125	−0.0025
Cactus	0.6%	−0.01	−0.0025
Kimono	0.81%	0	−0.0025
ParkScene	0.83%	−0.01	−0.005
Average	0.7%	−0.01	−0.004

5   Conclusion

In this paper, a fast mode decision algorithm for quality SHVC is proposed and demonstrated. In addition to the traditional spatial-temporal correlation, through the experimental analysis of the correlation between different layers, we find that there is a strong correlation between base layer and enhancement layer, which can be used to reduce the number of candidate mode of enhancement layer. In addition, we use the strong relationship between the current block and the nearby blocks to predict the optimal mode of the current mode. In this way, we formulate the mode cost of the current CU, which will be judged by a threshold to choose the candidate mode of current CU. The results reveal that encoding complexity can be reduced efficiently by using the proposed method, and the PSNR and the R-D performance of luma and chroma are only slightly decreased at the same time.

Acknowledgment. This work was supported in part by the National Natural Sicence Foundation of China, under Grants 161301112.

References

1. Sullivan, G.J., Ohm, J.R., Han, W.J., Wiegand, T.: Overview of the high efficiency video coding (HEVC) standard. IEEE Trans. Circ. Syst. Video Technol. **22**(12), 1649–1668 (2012)
2. ITU-T: Recommendation H.264 Advanced Video Coding for Generic Audiovisual Services, Rec. H.264 and ISO/IEC 14496-10 Version 1 (2003)
3. ITU-T: Recommendation H.264 Advanced Video Coding for Generic Audiovisual Services, Rec. H.264 and ISO/IEC 14496-10 Version 8 (2007)
4. Jill, M., Boyce, Y., Chen, J.L., Adarsh, K.: Overview of SHVC: scalable extensions of the high efficiency video coding standard. J. IEEE Trans. Circ. Syst. Video Technol. **26**, 20–34 (2016)
5. Tohidypour, H.R., Pourazad, M.T., Nasiopoulos, P.: Adaptive search range method for spatial scalable HEVC. In: IEEE International Conference on Consumer Electronics (ICCE), pp. 191–192 (2014)
6. Ge, Q.Y., Hu, D.: Fast encoding method using CU depth for quality scalable HEVC. In: Advanced Research and Technology in Industry Applications, pp. 1366–1370 (2014)
7. Bailleul, R., Cook, J.D.: Fast mode decision for SNR scalability in SHVC digest of technical papers. In: IEEE International Conference on Consumer Electronics (ICCE), pp. 193–194 (2014)
8. Shen, L.Q., Zhang, Z., Liu, Z.: Adaptive inter-mode decision for HEVC jointly utilizing inter-level and spatiotemporal correlations. IEEE Trans. Circ. Syst. Video Technol. **24**(10), 1709–1722 (2014)
9. Shi, N.D., Ma, R., Li, P.: An, P.: Efficient mode decision algorithm for scalable high efficiency video coding. In: SPIE-Optoelectronic Imaging and Multimedia Technology, vol. 9273 (2014)
10. Bjontegaard, G.: Calculation of average PSNR differences between RD-Curves. ITU-T SG16 Q.6 Document, VCEG-M33 (2001)

A Novel Rate Control Algorithm for Low Complexity Frame Compression System

Junqing Gong, Li Chen$^{(\boxtimes)}$, Jia Wang, and Zhiyong Gao

School of Electronic Information and Electrical Engineering,
Shanghai Jiao Tong University, Shanghai 200240, China
{gongjq,hilichen,jiawang,zhiyong.gao}@sjtu.edu.cn

Abstract. Many low-complexity intra-frame compression algorithms
are designed to solve existing memory access problems caused by ultra-
high definition digital video applications. Among them, Apple ProRes is
widely used in industry, which can effectively reduce the data memory
access. Compared with traditional intra-frame compression algorithm,
such as JPEG-LS, ProRes can provide much lower computing complexity and better parallelism. However, the ProRes encoding algorithm is
proprietary. In this paper, we propose a low complexity video compression implementation whose bitstreams are compatible with ProRes. The
proposed algorithm can provide higher PSNR and less computing complexity than Kostya ProRes, meanwhile keeping comparable accuracy in
rate control.

Keywords: Rate control · Low complexity · Frame compression

1 Introduction

Traditional video compression schemes aim at reducing tremendous data sizes
for storing the video. The state-of-the-art video compression technology is
H.264/Advanced Video Coding (AVC) [1] and High Effective Video Coding
(HEVC) [2]. They both take advantage of complex technology, such as motion
estimation and arithmetic coding, massively reducing the data size. As those traditional video compression schemes need very high computing complexity, they
are not appropriate for some special applications. The codecs used within professional camcorders or for professional video editing trend to maintain high visual
quality as well as low complexity, which can lead to better performance for real-
time video editing. Frame recompression technology is usually used to compress
the reference frame in the process of complex video technology, such as H.264
and HEVC, so as to reduce large amount of memory access [3–5]. Frame recompression algorithms are characterized by low complexity and high visual quality.
For reducing the complexity as much as possible, coding blocks are regarded as
independent coding unit. In the coding process, pixels in the independent unit
can not utilize other information outside the unit. Another kind of video compression method is called Embedded Compression [6], which usually bases on

X. Yang and G. Zhai (Eds.): IFTC 2016, CCIS 685, pp. 358–367, 2017.
DOI: 10.1007/978-981-10-4211-9_35

some traditional intra-frame compression algorithm such as JPEG-LS [7]. The purpose of embedded compression algorithm is to reduce data access bandwidth during the transmission process. Compared with frame recompression algorithm, embedded compression algorithm can achieve higher compression efficiency but higher computing complexity.

Apple ProRes is one of the most popular codecs in professional post-production. Compared with other codecs, Apple ProRes features excellent image quality as well as low complexity, providing better performance for real-time video editing [8]. Unfortunately, although Apple ProRes is the most widely used intra-frame compression algorithm, it has not been disclosed as a proprietary technology. Thus, it is meaningful to propose a low complexity video compression implement whose bitstreams are compatible with ProRes decoder. The bitstream syntax of Apple ProRes and its decoding process has been disclosed in [9]. Based on the bitstream syntax, it is possible to implement the codec whose bitstreams are compatible with ProRes decoder. FFmpeg software [10] published under GNU (General Public License) has already implemented an encoder whose name is Kostya ProRes, however, the quantization steps of the encoded frame vary a lot. This paper proposes a novel low complexity frame compression implementation, which can supply higher PSNR and much less lower complexity than Kostya with comparably accurate rate control.

The remaining of this paper is organized as follows: Kostya implementation and our proposed algorithm are introduced in Sect. 2; Experiments and results analysis are presented in Sect. 3; Concluding remarks are given in Sect. 4.

2 Low Complexity Frame Compression System

2.1 Basic Framework of ProRes Algorithm

Slice Segmentation. In the encoding progress of ProRes, a frame is divided into lots of independent code unites named slice. A slice is composed of several macroblocks, the maximal number of macroblocks in a slice is usually set as 8. For 422 format video, a macroblock contains four luma blocks and two chroma blocks. The size of every block is 8×8. If the number of pixels can not be divided by 16, the edge of frame will be filled with neighbouring pixels so as to ensure the integrity of macroblocks.

DCT. In the input of encoder, the blocks in a slice are input to DCT, which turns geometric distribution of space pixels to frequency dimension. DCT can centralize most energy in low-frequency coefficients.

Quantization. Through Quantization to DCT coefficients, large amount of dispensable information can be reduced with acceptable visual quality loss. The quantization matrices of luma and chroma are stored in the frame header of bitstream.

Entropy Coding. The ProRes standard combines run-length coding with golomb coding. Every coding method has many different codebooks to adjust coding strategy adaptively. Exponential-golomb coding and golomb-rice coding are used alternatively according to current chosen codebook and the magnitude of encoding coefficient.

2.2   Rate Control Algorithm in Kostya

The idea of Kostya's rate control algorithm is limiting the maximal bit numbers of every row of slices, so that the total bit numbers of the encoded frame are below a constant. The process of Kostya's rate control algorithm can be summarized as follows.

In the process of choosing quantization step of encoding slice, several nodes are used to record coding information corresponding to different quantization steps, the structure of one node can be described as

```
struct Node{
    int prev_node;
    int quant;
    int bits;
    int score;
};
```

In the node information, $quant$ denotes quantization step used in the node, $bits$ denotes the bit numbers generated by encoded slices, $score$ is the estimated error of encoded slices, $prev\_node$ denotes the previous node which makes the $score$ minimal when quantization step (QS) is set as $quant$. The number of the nodes for a slice is $max\_quant - min\_quant + 2$, $quant$s of first $max\_quant - min\_quant + 1$ nodes are set from min_quant to max_quant while the $quant$ of the last node is set as the minimal value which satisfies two conditions: (1) large than or equal to min_quant; (2) the generated bit numbers is less than or equal to the maximal permitted bit numbers of a slice. The choosing of the quantization steps is conducted after all the nodes of the row of slices are recorded, whose pseudo code is described in Algorithm 1. In the pseudo code, $slice\_bits[qs]$ denotes the generated number of bits when the quantization step of current slice is qs. $slice\_error$ is the sum of the error of DCT coefficients, which reflected the quality distortion to some extent.

After all the slices in the current row are encoded, the quantization step of the last slice chooses the $quant$ of the node whose $score$ is the least. Because the quantization step of previous slice can be inferred by the pre_node of current slice, we can get all the quantization steps through inverse iteration.

Through setting more than one node for every slice, Kostya algorithm can achieve lower error with the same bit numbers to some extent. In addition, as every slice iteration has limited the maximal number of bits through line 5 in Algorithm 1, the total number of bits in the frame is under control. However, the Kostya algorithm also has disadvantages. On one hand, because a slice is encoded

---

Algorithm 1. The choosing of the quantization steps in Kostya algorithm

---

1: **for** each $prev \in [min\_quant, max\_quant + 1]$ **do**
2:     **for** each $cur \in [min\_quant, max\_quant + 1]$ **do**
3:         $bits \leftarrow slice_j.nodes[pq].bits + slice\_bits[cur]$
4:         $error \leftarrow slice\_score[cur]$
5:         **if** $bits > bits\_limit$ **then**
6:             $error \leftarrow +\infty$
7:         **end if**
8:         $new\_score \leftarrow slice_{j-1}.nodes[prev].score + error$
9:         **if** $slice_j.nodes[cur]$ is initial **or**
10: $slice_j.nodes[cur].score > new\_score$ **then**
11:             $slice_j.nodes[cur].bits \leftarrow bits$
12:             $slice_j.nodes[cur].score \leftarrow new\_score$
13:             $slice_j.nodes[cur].prev\_node \leftarrow prev$
14:         **end if**
15:     **end for**
16: **end for**

---

by many times for different quantization steps, the computing complexity of the algorithm can be further reduced by optimizing the algorithm. On the other hand, the quantization errors of neighbouring slices varies a lot.

2.3 The Proposed Rate Control Method

In this paper, a new rate control algorithm is proposed. Different from Kostya ProRes, the proposed rate control algorithm combines with a new bits allocation scheme, which can provides higher PSNR and less computing complexity than Kostya ProRes. For some complex slices, the number of bits generated by same quantization will be larger than other simple slices. If the slice-level rate control is used, the complex slice will distort more details with the same bit numbers restriction. This situation will lead to serious quality loss in some part of the frame. Therefore, the distribution of quantization steps are desired to centralize as much as possible. A variable named *offset* is introduced to adjust slice-level rate control while still keeping fame-level rate control strictly. It demonstrates that at the early stage of an entire rate-control process, the bit allocation can be more flexible which allows allocating more bits to a slice with complex content and less bits to a slice with simple content respectively. The *offset* can be defined as

$$offset(q,j) = \begin{cases} -(slice\_cnt - j) \times c & q \leqslant q_0 \\ 0 & q_0 < q \leqslant q_1 \\ (slice\_cnt - j) \times c & q > q_2 \end{cases} \tag{1}$$

where $slice\_cnt$ represents the slice numbers of a row of slices in the rate control process. j is the position of current slice, c is a constant. With the increasing of j, the offset would drop off to zero so as to guarantee the accurate fame-level rate control. Linearity model is used for simplification, which can be replaced with more accurate model in future work without increasing computing complexity.

Algorithm 2. The choosing of the quantization steps in our proposed algorithm

---

Input: The quantization step of previous slice q_{prev}
Output: The quantization step of current slice q_{cur}

1: $q_{cur} \leftarrow q_{prev}$
2: **repeat**
3:     $TR \leftarrow slice\_bits(q) + offset(q, j)$
4:     **if** $TR < LB$ **then**
5:         $q_{cur} \leftarrow q_{cur} + 1$
6:     **else if** $TR > UB$ **then**
7:         $q_{cur} \leftarrow q_{cur} - 1$
8:     **end if**
9: **until** $LB \leqslant TR \leqslant UB$

The pseudo code of choose quantization steps in our proposed algorithm is described in Algorithm 2. The target bit numbers for a row of the slices in the frame is computed as:

$$T_i = \frac{bit\_rate}{2 \times frame\_rate \times slice\_height} \tag{2}$$

where bit_rate is the target bit rate, $frame\_rate$ is the frame rate of the video. $slice\_height$ is the number of the slice rows in the frame.

TR is the target bit rate for the current slice, which is computed as:

$$TR = \frac{T_i - B_{j-1}}{slice\_cnt - (j-1)} \tag{3}$$

where B_j is the number of bits generated by encoding all slices in the row of slices up to and including j.

Considering that the quantization step of current slice has a high possibility of being equal to previous slice, the initial q value is set as the chosen quantization step of previous slice. Offset decided by q and j is added to the estimated size in order to offset the effect of slice-level rate control. LB and UB respectively represent the lower boundary and upper boundary for the presence of slice-level rate control error. q_j would be output when TR is between HB and LB.

3   Experiment Results

3.1   Comparison Between JPEG-LS and Our Proposed Algorithm

JPEG-LS is a traditional intra-frame compression algorithm which can provide near-lossless compression. In this experiment, the rate-distortion performance and algorithm complexity are compared between the proposed algorithm and JEPG-LS. Figure 1 shows the rate-distortion performance. For a fair comparison, frames in different scenes are used in the experiment. The compression performance of JPEG-LS is slightly better than our proposed algorithm when the bitrate is high while it is worse than our proposed algorithm when the bitrate is low. Figure 2 compares the encoding time of two algorithms under the same condition. Although the compression performance of our proposed algorithm does not outperform JPEG-LS, it can provide lower complexity and better parallelism.

3.2 Comparison Between Kostya and Proposed Algorithm

Since Apple ProRes is one of the most popular codecs in professional post-production, it is used to compress 4K, 10-bit, 4:2:2 raw videos. Apple ProRes has several different bit-rate formats. For 4k, 10-bit, 30 fps video, the target bit rate of Apple ProRes 422 HQ widely adopted across the video post-production industry is approximately 884 Mb/s [8]. To fairly compare the prediction performance, all algorithms are implemented based on the common reference software, FFmpeg 2.8.4, under the same condition. In FFmpeg, 422 HQ profile is chosen in Kostya codec, whose bit rate is almost the same with Apple ProRes.

In this experiment, we test first 100 frames of five video sequences, which represent different scenes. Rate-distortion performance and algorithmic complexity are used to evaluate these two rate-control algorithms. As we keep the same bit rate, we just need to compare the PSNR of those two algorithms. Average encoding time of the video sequence is measured to reflect the complexity of algorithm.

Figure 3 records the PSNR of 100 frames of sequence Fountains and sequence Marathon respectively. We can see that the proposed algorithm outperforms Kostya algorithm in every frame. Table 1 shows the average bit rate, PSNR and encoding time of five video sequences with Kostya and proposed algorithm. From the table, we can observe that the proposed algorithm provides higher PSNR and much less encoding time with the same bit rate. In addition, the rate control in our proposed algorithm provides comparable accuracy compared with Kostya.

Table 1. The comparision between Kostya and proposed algorithm

Sequences	Kostya			Proposed		
	RB (Mbps)	PSNR	Encoding time (ms)	RB (Mbps)	PSNR	Encoding time (ms)
Fountains	886.1	48.39	2480	885.2	49.24	629
Dancers	886.2	50.48	1883	885.3	50.63	575
Library	885.5	49.10	1856	885.0	49.33	574
Marathon	883.2	45.05	3064	885.3	45.16	572
Bosket	884.3	43.47	1763	885.3	43.67	845

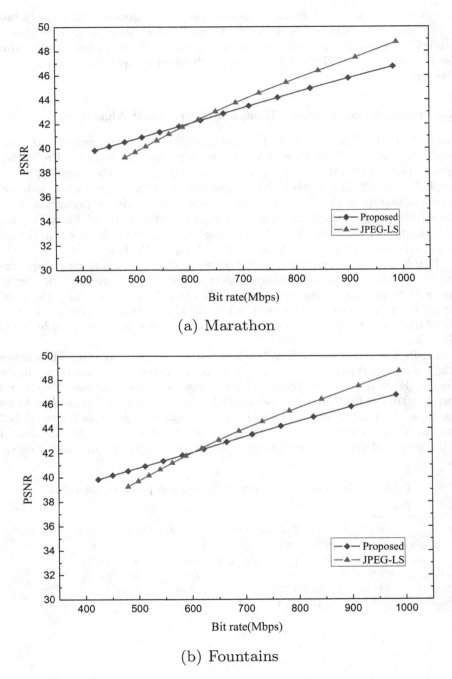

(a) Marathon

(b) Fountains

Fig. 1. The rate-distortion performance of JEPG-LS and our proposed algorithm.

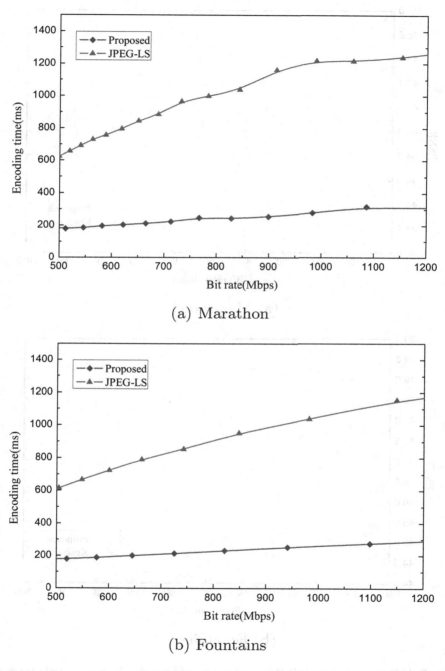

(a) Marathon

(b) Fountains

Fig. 2. The encoding time performance of JEPG-LS and our proposed algorithm.

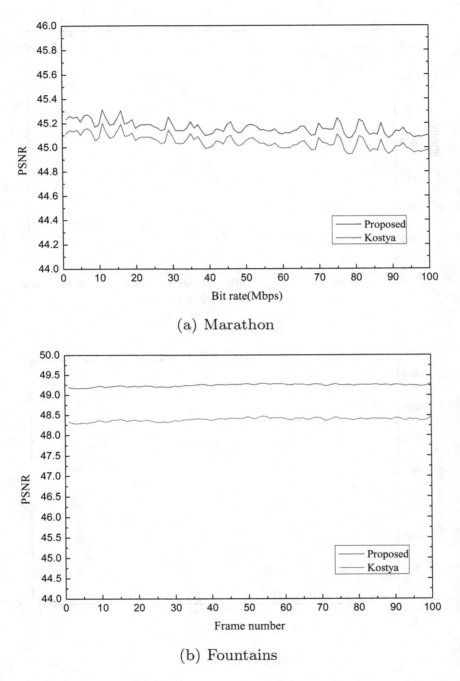

(a) Marathon

(b) Fountains

Fig. 3. Comparison of the PSNR of first 100 frames encoded by Kostya and proposed algorithm.

4   Conclusions and Future Work

In this paper, a low complexity frame compression implementation is proposed, which uses a new rate control algorithm. The key idea of the proposed algorithm is introducing offset to slice-level rate control, which can obtain more flexible bit allocation. Before we determine the quantization step of current slice, the target bits of current slice will be offset so as to get a smoother quantization steps distribution. Experimental results demonstrate that our proposed algorithm not only enhances the PSNR but also reduce the algorithm complexity with the same bit rate compared with Kostya algorithm. In our future work, the relationship between content activity of the slice and the generating bit numbers will be researched and incorporated into our rate control algorithm so as to further reduce the complexity of the algorithm.

Acknowledgement. This work was supported in part by Chinese National Key S&T Special Program (2013ZX01033001-002-002), National Natural Science Foundation of China (61133009, 61221001, 61301116), the Shanghai Key Laboratory of Digital Media Processing and Transmissions (STCSM 12DZ2272600).

References

1. Wiegand, T., Sullivan, G.J., Bjontegaard, G., Luthra, A.: Overview of the H.264/AVC video coding standard. IEEE Trans. Circ. Syst. Video Technol. **13**(7), 560–576 (2003)
2. Sullivan, G.J., Ohm, J.R., Han, W.J., Wiegand, T.: Overview of the high efficiency video coding (HEVC) standard. IEEE Trans. Circ. Syst. Video Technol. **22**(12), 1649–1668 (2012)
3. Lee, Y., Rhee, C.E., Lee, H.J.: A new frame recompression algorithm integrated with H.264 video compression. In: 2007 IEEE International Symposium on Circuits and Systems. pp. 1621–1624. IEEE (2007)
4. Guo, L., Zhou, D., Goto, S.: A new reference frame recompression algorithm and its VLSI architecture for UHDTV video codec. IEEE Trans. Multimedia **16**(8), 2323–2332 (2014)
5. Fan, Y., Shang, Q., Zeng, X.: In-block prediction-based mixed lossy and lossless reference frame recompression for next-generation video encoding. IEEE Trans. Circ. Syst. Video Technol. **25**(1), 112–124 (2015)
6. Hwang, Y.T., Lyu, M.W., Lin, C.C.: A low-complexity embedded compression codec design with rate control for high-definition video. IEEE Trans. Circ. Syst. Video Technol. **25**(4), 674–687 (2015)
7. Weinberger, M.J., Seroussi, G., Sapiro, G.: The LOCO-I lossless image compression algorithm: principles and standardization into JPEG-LS. IEEE Trans. Image Process. **9**(8), 1309–1324 (2000)
8. Apple ProRes White Paper (2014). http://www.apple.com/final-cut-pro/docs/Apple_ProRes_White_Paper.pdf
9. SMPTE Registered Disclosure Doc - Apple ProRes Bitstream Syntax and Decoding Process. RDD 36:2015, pp. 1–39 (2016)
10. FFmpeg. https://ffmpeg.org/

Telecommunications

L-Band Land Mobile Satellite Channel Characteristic Analysis for Geosynchronous Satellite

Guangmin Wang, Dazhi He[✉], Yin Xu, Yunfeng Guan,
Wenjun Zhang, and Yihang Huang

Cooperative Medianet Innovation Center, Shanghai Jiao Tong University, Shanghai, China
{1466225873,hedazhi,xuyin,yfguan69,zhangwenjun}@sjtu.edu.cn

Abstract. Comparing with the traditional mobile communication system, there is a strong line-of-sight (LOS) component in satellite to mobile communication. In fact, LOS and diffuse scattered component are both influenced by shadowing and obstacles. In this paper, a theoretical model for a land mobile satellite channel is analyzed in various shadowing situations. Since LOS and diffuse scattered component are both considered, the angles of arrival are not uniformly distributed in a given azimuth sector. So a kind of asymmetrical Doppler power spectrum is proposed in the paper. Then, in order to effectively respond to the actual channel environment, the different state length L_{frame} in each state is presented and simulated, the minimum state length should be shorter in the environment, which the channel changes intensely. Finally, numerical simulations in four-state Markov model indicate that the proposed asymmetrical Doppler power spectrum and the various L_{frame} are reasonable.

Keywords: Land mobile satellite channel · Doppler power spectrum · Markov channel model

1 Introduction

The transmission performance of land mobile satellite (LMS) services are mainly impaired by rapid amplitude and phase fluctuations of the received signal. Such fluctuations are caused by multipath rays propagation as well as time-varying attenuation due to shadowing. The statistical properties of these signal variations are closely related to the elevation angle and propagation environment in which vehicle is located. There may be more than one system using the geostationary orbit (GEO) or other orbits providing

This paper is supported in part by National Natural Science Foundation of China (61420106008, 61521062), National High Technology Research and Development Program (2015AA015802), 111 Project (B07022), Shanghai Key Laboratory of Digital Media Processing (STCSM12DZ2272600), and Scientific and Innovative Action Plan of Shanghai (15DZ1100101).

higher elevation angles for satellite-to-mobile transmissions. Thus, elimination of shadowing effects of fabricated or natural features in the vicinity of mobile terminal becomes important increasingly.

The shadowing channel with multipath in LMS communication can be modelled using different strategies, namely an empirical approach, a physical-geometrical approach, finally, a statistical approach. Compared with the former two approaches, statistical approach makes reasonable assumption for the real-world situations in multipath rays propagation, which makes it easy to implement. Thus, this paper will concentrate on statistical modelling techniques.

Statistical models associate a given statistical distribution and its parameters to possible environment type plus elevation angle combination. The parameters in statistical models must be obtained experimentally. The famous representation of statistical models for land mobile satellite channels are the classical Rice process, Rayleigh process and Loo process. A complex envelope channel simulator based on these models is also described in this paper. A four-state Markov chain model is implemented [1]. This approach for modelling LMS propagation channel has also been used by a number of other researchers [2–4]. Markov chain is used to describe the long-term received signal variation caused by shadowing. Four models (Rice model, Loo model, Loo model, Rayleigh model respectively) are used for short term in each state.

Using four-state Markov chain statistical modelling approach, a more detailed representation of the received signal may be available in a system manager. The fine structure of both the shadowing and fading phenomena encountered by a mobile receiver would be apparent, as it traverses a given environment for any elevation angle.

Besides, there are also several technical merits should be considered in L-band high-power synchronous satellite system.

- In previous research, the angles of arrival rays are assumed to be uniformly distributed in a given azimuth sector. In fact, this is not accurate in real-world situations with multipath rays propagation, To obtain a more accurate Doppler power spectrum, the angles of arrival rays are assumed to be non-uniformly distributed in this paper. It is worth noting that the elevation angle is related to latitude, that the shadowing degree will decrease with higher elevation.

- A minimum state length L_{frame} is the duration of each state in the Markov chain. It represents the short shadowing event arise. Among the previous researches, the parameter is constant, which is improper in different environment.

In this paper, specific model analysis of arrival rays angles are proposed and some simulations are presented with various minimum state length L_{frame}. This paper is organized as follows. In Sect. 2, we analyze the distribution of the angles of arrival, and deduce the Doppler power spectrum. Section 3 gives the reasonability about four-state Markov model and investigates the influence of minimum state length in LMS propagation environment. Then, Sect. 4 presents the simulation of LMS channel model using four-state Markov chain. Section 5 concludes the paper and gives some future outlook.

2 Doppler Power Spectrum

The common statistical modelling approach used to describe the LMS propagation environment is known as above. And these models also need to be complemented with geometrical information. The distribution of arrival angles can be deduced for this purpose.

2.1 The Azimuth and Angles of Arrival

The signal variations corresponding to each model parameters in each state are generated geometrically considering the arrival angles of both LOS and multipath components shown in Fig. 1. Because the earth tangent plane AB, parallels to the moving direction of terminal, elevation angle α approximately equals to angle of LOS arrival. Relationship between the elevation and the latitude is as following:

$$L^2 = R^2 + H^2 - 2RH \cos \theta \tag{1}$$

$$\frac{L}{\sin \theta} = \frac{H}{\sin(90° + \alpha)} \tag{2}$$

$$\alpha = \arccos \frac{H \sin \theta}{L} \tag{3}$$

where the latitude $\theta \subset (3°, 54°)$ for China, R and H is the earth radius and satellite altitude from the sphere center, respectively. It can be seen that elevation is approximately linear growth with the latitude during $\theta \subset (3°, 54°)$.

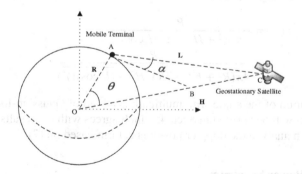

Fig. 1. Communication connection between satellite and terminal

Continuing with the geometrical approach to describe the multipath structure, typically, near echoes are considered to be uniformly distributed in azimuth whereas multipath echoes with longer delays tend to be concentrated around given directions shown in Fig. 2. Azimuth angle sector is represented by its width ξ, and by its center α, for which significant multipath rays are received. supposing that the transmitter power is P, the incidence angle spectrum is

$$p(\alpha) = \frac{P}{4\pi L^2} \tag{4}$$

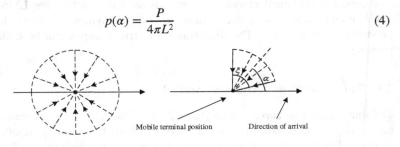

Mobile terminal position   Direction of arrival

Fig. 2. Azimuth and angles of arrival

From (1), the receiver angle spectrum can be expressed as follows:

$$
\begin{aligned}
p(\alpha) &= \frac{P}{4\pi L^2} \\
&= \frac{P}{4\pi(R^2 + H^2 - 2RH\cos\theta)}
\end{aligned}
\tag{5}
$$

From (2), it can be deduced that

$$\cos\theta = \frac{\sqrt{H^2 - (L\cos\alpha)^2}}{H} \tag{6}$$

So, the receiver angle spectrum is

$$
\begin{aligned}
p(\alpha) &= \frac{P}{4\pi(R^2 + H^2 - 2RH\cos\theta)} \\
&= \frac{P}{4\pi(R^2 + H^2 - 2R\sqrt{H^2 - (L\cos\alpha)^2})}
\end{aligned}
\tag{7}
$$

The distribution of the angle with multipath is a kind of Gaussian-like distribution. This assumption will be verified in Sect. 4, which agrees with the results of Loo Model [2]. Then we can analyze the doppler power specturm based on (7).

2.2 Doppler Power Spectrum

The classical U-shape spectrum is widely used in modelling LMS channel [5, 6]. As premise, there are three terms:

(1) The transmission happens in two-dimensional plane, and the receiver is located in the center of scattering region.
(2) The angles of arrival subordinates to the uniform distribution.
(3) Omnidirectional antenna in receiver.

More, it assumes:

1. $[0, 2\pi)$, angular range of a number N of arrival.
2. $p(\alpha)d\alpha$, the incidence power at $\alpha \sim \alpha + d\alpha$.
3. $G(\alpha)$, the receiver antenna gain.
4. f_c, f_m, the carrier frequency and the max Doppler frequency shift, $f_m = v/\lambda$, v is terminal velocity.

So, the receiver power is $b \cdot p(\alpha) \cdot G(\alpha) \cdot d\alpha$, where b is mean power of receiver antenna, $p(\alpha) = 1/2\pi(-\pi \le \alpha \le \pi)$. When $N \to \infty$, $p(\alpha)d\alpha$ becomes continuous distribution, and the receiver power is:

$$P_r = \int_0^{2\pi} b \cdot p(\alpha) \cdot G(\alpha) \cdot d\alpha \tag{8}$$

Doppler frequency shift is:

$$f = f(\alpha) = f_c + f_m \cos \alpha = f(-\alpha) \tag{9}$$

Thus, the receiver power spectrum:

$$S(f)|df(\alpha)| = b \cdot |p(\alpha) \cdot G(\alpha) + p(-\alpha) \cdot G(-\alpha)| \cdot d\alpha \tag{10}$$

Differential (9),

$$|df(\alpha)| = f_m|- \sin \alpha||d\alpha| \tag{11}$$

and

$$\alpha = \arccos \frac{f - f_c}{f_m} \tag{12}$$

for (12),

$$\sin \alpha = \sqrt{1 - \left(\frac{f - f_c}{f_m}\right)^2} \tag{13}$$

Finally, the Doppler power spectrum is

$$\begin{aligned} S(f) &= \frac{b \cdot [p(\alpha) \cdot G(\alpha) + p(-\alpha) \cdot G(-\alpha)]|d\alpha|}{|df(\alpha)|} \\ &= \frac{b \cdot [p(\alpha) \cdot G(\alpha) + p(-\alpha) \cdot G(-\alpha)]}{f_m \sqrt{1 - \left(\frac{f - f_c}{f_m}\right)^2}} |f - f_c| < f_m \end{aligned} \tag{14}$$

However, when any of the above three terms is not satisfied, that angle of arrival can not be uniformly distributed, as mentioned above. The revised Doppler power spectrum under the condition of Gaussian distribution of incidence angle is:

$$
\begin{aligned}
S(f) &= \frac{b \cdot [p(\alpha) \cdot G(\alpha) + p(-\alpha) \cdot G(-\alpha)]}{f_m \sqrt{1 - \left(\dfrac{f - f_c}{f_m}\right)^2}} \; |f - f_c| < f_m \\[4mm]
&= \frac{P}{4\pi(R^2 + H^2 - 2R\sqrt{H^2 - (L \cos \alpha)^2})} \cdot \frac{b \cdot (G(\alpha) + G(-\alpha))}{\sqrt{f_m^2 - (f - f_c)^2}}
\end{aligned}
\tag{15}
$$

It can be seen apparently that the Doppler power spectrum is related to elevation.

Theoretical investigation has proved that Doppler power spectrum will seriously deviate from the classical shape in frequency selective fading condition where bandwidth is generally more than 10 kHz, and it will be in close proximity to the Gaussian distribution [5].

3   The Four-State Markov Chain

Different from the terrestrial communication system, the LMS communication system propagation is too wide and fickle to be described by single state distribution which has been discussed in the previous sector. A finite-state machine, usually with three or four propagation states, represents the large-scale model. Multi-state Markov model with four states is used to cover different degree shadowed states in Fig. 5. The finite-state machine is controlled by the time duration in each state, where single model generates the fade statistics within a state. So, two key points are considered in this model:

- Choice of single state distribution
- Duration in each state

Combining with each state parameter, the three important components of Markov channel modeling are surveyed.

3.1   Markov Multi-state Models

The objective of the work presented in this sector is to improve the channel state duration statistics, where the states include open, light shadow, intermediate shadow and the blockage condition.

Areas with homogeneous environmental properties can be represented with several models tuned to the specific areas. As the mobile terminal moves, it is necessary to distinguish various environmental properties. This can be modeled as state machine switching between different single state model. The state machine is usually modeled as a Markov process with two to four states [6–8]. The basic idea of Markov chain is shown in Figs. 3 and 4 illustrates the four-state Markov chain considered for this LMS channel model, the number of states, four for each environment, is selected by trading off model complexity and received signal dynamic range for the environments.

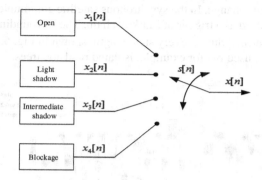

Fig. 3. Generation of the observed sequence

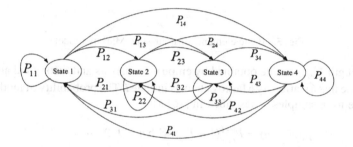

Fig. 4. State transition diagram of a Markov chain

A Markov-chain model can be described that the next state is determined by a transition probability without any knowledge of the previous state. The chain is a random process taking on only discrete values satisfying the condition [9, 10]

$$P\Big[\big(s[n] = s_n\big)\Big|\big(s[n-1] = s_{n-1}\big), \big(s[n-2] = s_{n-2}\big), \cdots\Big]$$
$$= P\Big[\big(s[n] = s_n\big)\Big|\big(s[n-1] = s_{n-1}\big)\Big]$$

(16)

when $s[n] = s_i$, the Markov chain is in state i and the conditional $P_{i,j}(n) = P\big[(s[n] = j)|(s[n-1] = i)\big]$ is known as the state-transition probabilities, $\sum_{j=1}^{4} P_{i,j} = 1$ $i = 1, 2, 3, 4$.

Four-state Markov transition probability can also be theoretically obtained by Newton-Gaussian fitting method for various environment in some research.

3.2   The Different State Length

Switching of Markov chain state is the precondition for modelling satellite mobile channel characteristics change. In the synchronous satellite communication system, the state length L_{frame} is used as a trigger of Markov chain. The surrounding environment of mobile terminal is verified during every state length, shown in Fig. 5. State-4 occurs in blockage condition caused by, for example, isolated roadside trees.

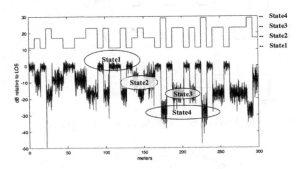

Fig. 5. Basic elements of Four-state Markov model

State length L_{frame} can be obtained by empirical analysis and theoretical argumentation. Assume that a stationary Markov chain is in state i. The probability of model staying in that state for n samples is described in [10] as

$$p_i(N = n) = P_{i,i}^{n-1}(1 - P_{i,i}) \text{ with } n = 1, 2, \cdots \tag{17}$$

The cumulative duration distribution for each state in the Markov chain becomes

$$P_i(N \leq n) = (1 - P_{i,i}) \cdot \sum_{j=1}^{n} P_{i,i}^{j-1}, \, n = 1, 2, \cdots \tag{18}$$

where the duration becomes n times the sampling period or sampling distance. The model stays within a state for a certain time, or equivalently, a distance. This distance is directly to the size of the objects and the spacing between them and called the state length.

In most previous research, the L_{frame} is considered to be constant, for example, in [6], an average minimum state length value of 7.5 m was obtained from the analysis of the experimental data set. However, as building size is increasingly various, the environment where terminal is located changes more acutely than before. Therefore, it is improper to consider state length as constant. Generally, it will switch more frequently when the terminal is located in urban area, than in suburb. Supposing that state length is 7.5 m in open area, then it would be less in shadow area since the located environment becomes more complex and the multipath effect turns to be more prominent. This analysis is consistent with [12], in which the S-band channel behavior is presented.

4   Simulation Results

After the theoretical analysis stage described in the previous section, some simulation results are shown in this section.

Figure 6 presents the arrival angle distribution in the situation where arrival angle does not conform to uniform distribution. The simulation result indicates that the distribution of arrival angle follows a Gaussian-like (0, 2) distribution, which agrees with research [11]. Especially the radian ranges from 0 to 0.5 and the simulation curve is more consistent with theory in China.

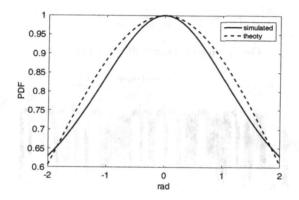

Fig. 6. Distribution of alfa

The simulation platform is based on a 4-state Markov model with four distribution (Rayleigh/Rician/Loo). The main parameters extracted from a comprehensive experimental campaign (Table 1). Simulation results using Markov state sequences, which are generated by the transition probability, are presented in Figs. 7, 8, 9, 10, 11 and 12. And each minimum state length is 7.5 m, 6.3 m, 4.5 m and 4.3 m, respectively [12]. The signal envelope presented in Figs. 8 and 9 are similar to measured signal, and both of them are acceptable. But from Figs. 7, 8 and 9, we can conclude that a 4-state Markov model is more consistent with actual environment than 3-state Markov model. Figure 10 describes different PDF compared between 4-state and 3-state simulation. It further shows the advantage of 4-state Markov model in a real system. In fact, the number of states can be chosen by trading off between simulated complexity and received signal dynamic range for various environments.

Table 1. Four-state parameters

	State 1			State 2			State 3			State 4		
	α	MP	ψ	α	MP	ψ	α	MP	ψ	α	MP	ψ
40°	−2.25	−21.2	0.13	−15.0	−13.0	5.9	−19.0	−10.0	4.0	−24.2	−19.0	4.5
60°	−1.40	−23.1	0.25	−3.8	−13.2	0.34	−10.8	−10.0	2.7	−15.2	−24.8	5.0
70°	−0.75	−23.24	0.37	/	/	/	−7.5	−7.0	2.0	−12.3	−16.0	4.1
80°	−0.72	−22.0	0.27	−4.25	−25.0	3.0	−8.0	−7.0	5.0	−11.0	−24.2	8.75

The missing parameters are due to the lack of sufficient data.

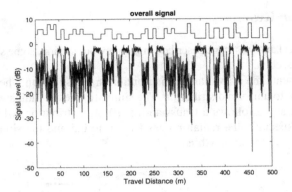

Fig. 7. Measured signal, 40° elevation angle

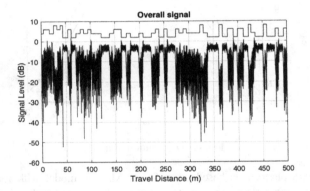

Fig. 8. Simulated time series using four-state Markov model, 40° elevation angle

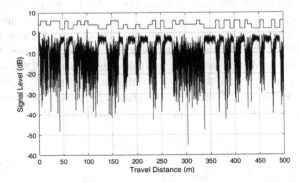

Fig. 9. Simulated time series using three-state Markov model, 40° elevation angle

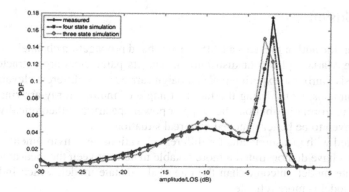

Fig. 10. PDF comparison with simulation and measured signal

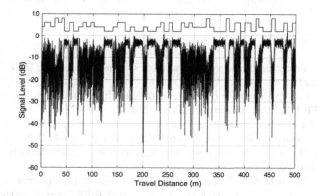

Fig. 11. Simulated time series with linear interpolated, 40° elevation angle

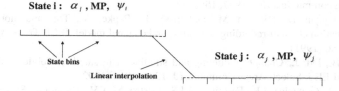

Fig. 12. Smoothing algorithm

To maintain the continuity of phase and amplitude during transitions, and to avoid sharp changes, interpolated samples are padded in to produce more realistic results. Figures 8 and 11 present the time series with and without smoothing, respectively. Linear interpolation is used for the α, MP and ψ parameter starting in the middle of the last bin of one state and finishing in the middle of the first bin of next state, shown in Fig. 12.

5   Conclusion

In this paper, the author presents a LMS narrow-band propagation channel model based on a 4-state Markov plus four distribution. And its parameters are extracted from a comprehensive airborne experimental campaign carried out at different elevation angles and environments. Considering the fact that angle of multipath ray arriving does not conform to uniform distribution, the Doppler power spectrum is theoretically analyzed and it is proven to be better matched with real situation.

Compared with measurements for different elevations and environments, the simulation results have demonstrated a more notable match between the measured data and the four-state model outcome than the one of three-state model, which indicates the enhanced model is more reliable.

Considering the future research, it would be interesting to analyze new sets of measurements using the proper approach to capture measured data in more areas and scenario.

References

1. Papoulis, A.: Probability, random variables and stochastic processes. IEEE Trans. Acoust. Speech Signal Process. **20**(1), 135 (1967)
2. Vucetic, B., Du, J.: Channel modeling and simulation in satellite mobile communication systems. IEEE J. Sel. Areas Commun. **10**(8), 1209–1218 (1992)
3. Sforza, M., Buonomo, S., Martini, A.: Channel modeling for land mobile satellite systems: Markov chain approach. In: Proceedings of PIERS 1994, pp. 35–43 (1994)
4. Lutz, E.: A Markov model for correlated land mobile satellite channels. Intl. J. Satell. Commun. **14**(4), 333–339 (1996)
5. Fontan, F.P., Castro, M.A.V., Kunisch, J., et al.: A versatile framework for a narrow-and wide-band statistical propagation model for the LMS channel. IEEE Trans. Broadcast. **43**(4), 431–458 (1997)
6. Markov model based simulator for the narrow-band LMS channel [J]. International journal of satellite communications, 1997, 15: 1–15
7. Lutz, E., Cygan, D., Dippold, M., Dolainsky, F., Papke, W.: The land mobile satellite communication channel-recording, statistics, and channel model. IEEE Trans. Veh. Techol. **40**, 375–386 (1991)
8. Vucetic, B., Du, J.: Channel modeling and simulation in satellite mobile communication systems. IEEE J. Select. Areas Commun. **10**, 1209–1218 (1992)
9. Fontan, F.P., Gonzalez, J.P., Ferreiro, M.J.S., Castro, M.A.V., Buonomo, S., Baptista, J.P.: Complex envelope three-state Markov model based simulator for the narrow-band LMS channel. Int. J. Satellite Comm. **15**, 1–15 (1997)
10. Rabiner, L.R.: A tutorial on hidden Markov models and selected applications in speech recognition. Proc. IEEE **77**, 257–286 (1989)
11. Bråten, L.E., Tjelta, T.: Semi-Markov multistate modeling of the land mobile propagation channel for geostationary satellites. IEEE Trans. Antennas Propag. **50**(12), 1795–1802 (2002)
12. Perez-Fontan, F., Vazquez-Castro, M.A., Buonomo, S., et al.: S-band LMS propagation channel behaviour for different environments, degrees of shadowing and elevation angle. IEEE Trans. Broadcast. **44**(1), 40–76 (1998)

Low-Complexity Soft-Decision Decoder Architecture for BCH Code in the BeiDou System

Chaoyi Zhang[1,2(✉)], Haiyang Liu[1], Songlin Ou[1], Jinhai Li[1],
Jinhai Sun[1], and Yuepeng Yan[1]

[1] Institute of Microelectronics of Chinese Academy of Sciences, Beijing, China
zhangchaoyi@ime.ac.cn
[2] University of Chinese Academy of Sciences, Beijing, China

Abstract. In order to improve the performance of the traditional hard-decision decoding of BCH code in the BeiDou satellite navigation System, a low-complexity soft-decision decoder architecture is designed and implemented in this paper. The designed decoder is based on the syndrome-assisted soft-decision decoding algorithm. A non-uniform quantization scheme and a ROM reduction strategy based on cyclic property are proposed to reduce the hardware resources. Simulation results show that the performance of designed decoder is closed to that of the optimal soft-decision decoding. Compared with the traditional hard-decision decoder, the hardware resource increment is very small, which suggests the designed decoder is a suitable choice in practice.

Keywords: BeiDou system · BCH code · Low-complexity · Soft-decision decoding algorithm · Hardware implementation

1 Introduction

Nowadays, BeiDou satellite navigation system (BeiDou system for short) can provide continuous passive positioning, navigation and timing services to China and surrounding areas [1]. The accuracy of navigation message is very important for a satellite receiver providing precise positioning results. In the BeiDou system, a cyclic BCH code is used to enhance the accuracy of navigation message [2]. Hence, it is important to design and implement efficient decoder for the BCH code in the BeiDou system.

Traditionally, the BCH code in the BeiDou system is decoded by the hard-decision algorithm, which is recommended by the BeiDou interface document [2]. Although simple and easy to implement, the performance of hard-decision decoding is relatively poor, since only single bit error in the navigation message can be corrected. In practice, however, the received navigation message may contain more than one bit error, especially in the low signal-to-noise ratio (SNR) environments. In order to achieve better performance, the soft-decision decoding algorithms can be used.

C.Y. Zhang—The research is supported by National Natural Science Foundation of China with Grant No. 61271423.

X. Yang and G. Zhai (Eds.): IFTC 2016, CCIS 685, pp. 383–391, 2017.
DOI: 10.1007/978-981-10-4211-9_37

Generally speaking, the soft-decision decoding of linear block codes can be divided into two classes: optimal algorithms and sub-optimal algorithms. The optimal algorithms have optimal decoding performance at the expense of daunting complexity, which makes them impractical. In contrast, the sub-optimal algorithms usually have a good tradeoff between the performance and complexity, especially for codes with short lengths. These merits make sub-optimal algorithms suitable for practical purposes.

In this paper, a soft-decision decoder is designed and implemented for BCH Code in the BeiDou System based on the low-complexity syndrome-assisted (SA) algorithm presented in [3]. The cyclic property of the BCH code is exploited to reduce the memory requirements of the designed decoder. In addition, a non-uniform quantization scheme is further proposed to reduce the hardware resources of the designed decoder. Simulation results suggest that the performance of the designed decoder is closed to that of the optimal soft-decision decoding. Compared with the traditional hard-decision decoder, the hardware resource increment is small. In conclusion, the designed decoder is very suitable for practical BeiDou navigation receiver.

The rest of this paper is organized as follows. Section 2 presents background knowledge. In Sect. 3, the designed soft-decision decoder architecture is provided. The simulation and implementation results on the decoder are given in Sect. 4. Finally, Sect. 5 concludes the paper.

2   Background

2.1   BCH Code in the BeiDou System

BCH code is an important class of linear block codes that is widely used in the coding theory. In the BeiDou system, a cyclic BCH(15,11) code is used as the forward error correction code, whose code length and information length are 15 and 11, respectively. The generator polynomial of BCH(15,11) code is

$$g(X) = X^4 + X + 1 \tag{1}$$

Because of the cyclic property, the encoding of BCH code can be easily implemented by the linear shift register circuit in practice [2]. It is straightforward to check that the minimum Hamming distance of BCH(15,11) code is 3, which means that any single error can be corrected by the code under hard-decision decoding, such as the syndrome-based look-up table method recommended in [2]. However, the probability of more than one error in a hard-decision vector is not negligible at the range of moderate SNRs [4]. In this situation, the hard-decision algorithm is unable to correct the errors in the received vector. As a result, the coding gain of the hard-decision decoding is relatively small.

2.2   Soft-Decision Algorithm

The key difference between the hard-decision decoding and the soft-decision decoding is the decoder input. More specifically, each position of the received vector is quantized into 0 or 1 in the hard-decision decoding. In contrast, the received vector is unquantized or quantized into multi-levels in the soft-decision decoding. In general, the soft-decision decoding can offer better performance than the hard-decision decoding for a given code, since the hard-decision results in information losses [5].

Due to the nice structural properties of BCH codes, the soft-decision decoding of this class of codes has been investigated in the literature [3, 6]. In particular, the SA soft-decision decoding algorithm presented in [3] has near optimal decoding performance. Besides, the operations in the algorithm are relatively simple and easy to implement. As a result, the algorithm is selected in the design and implementation of the decoder of BCH(15,11) code in the BeiDou system. In the following, a brief description of the algorithm is given.

Suppose the codeword $c = [c_0, c_1, \cdots, c_{14}]$ in BCH(15,11) code is transmitted and the binary phase-shift keying (BPSK) modulation is used. The bipolar sequence $x = [x_0, x_1, \cdots, x_{14}]$ after the modulation is given by

$$x_i = 2c_i - 1 \quad (i = 0, 1, \cdots, 14) \tag{2}$$

Suppose x is transmitted over the channel and $r = [r_0, r_1, \cdots, r_{14}]$ is the received soft-decision vector, which is given by

$$r_i = x_i + n_i \quad (i = 0, 1, \cdots, 14) \tag{3}$$

where n_i is the noise in the i-th position.

The hard decision result $v = [v_0, v_1, \cdots, v_{14}]$ is given by

$$v_i = \text{sgn}(r_i) \quad (i = 0, 1, \cdots, 14) \tag{4}$$

Based on v, the syndrome s can be calculated, which can be implemented by a linear shift register circuit [2].

The SA soft-decision decoding algorithm is to generate a list of error patterns for each syndrome and store them in advance. In the decoding process, each error pattern is correlated with the reliability of the received soft-decision vector, $l = [l_0, l_1, \cdots, l_{14}]$, which is given by

$$l_i = |r_i| \quad (i = 0, 1, \cdots, 14) \tag{5}$$

The correlation value d is calculated by

$$d = \sum_{i=0}^{14} l_i e_i \tag{6}$$

where $e = [e_0, e_1, \cdots, e_{14}]$ is the error pattern vector. The error pattern with the minimum correlation value is used for error correction, since the pattern has the highest probability of a correct decoding.

It can be shown that the number of error patterns for each syndrome is crucial, since it directly affects the decoding performance and complexity. For each syndrome, the error patterns of weights one and two are considered in our design, which is due to the fact that the probability of received vector with one or two errors is relatively high compared with that of more than two errors [4]. It can be calculated that each syndrome has eight error patterns whose weight is less than or equal to two [3, 4]. Overall, the detailed procedure is described as follows:

Sub-optimal soft-decision decoding algorithm for BCH(15,11) code

Input: Error pattern lists. Each list corresponds to a syndrome and contains eight error patterns. The soft-decision vector r.

Output: Decoded codeword $\hat{c}$.

Step 1: Calculate the hard-decision vector v and the reliability vector l.

Step 2: Calculate the syndrome s based on v.

Step 3: Select the corresponding error pattern list $E = \{e^{(1)}, e^{(2)}, \cdots, e^{(8)}\}$.

Step 4: Calculate the correlation values, $d^{(1)}, d^{(2)}, \cdots, d^{(8)}$, for error patterns.

Step 5: Choose the error pattern $e^{(k)}$ with the minimum correlation value.

Step 6: Calculate $\hat{c} = e^{(k)} + v$.

---

3   Proposed Decoder Architecture

In this section, a decoder for BCH(15,11) code is designed based on the SA soft-decision decoding algorithm introduced in Sect. 2.2.

3.1   Overall Architecture

The overall architecture of the proposed BCH(15,11) decoder is described in Fig. 1. First, the soft-decision vector r is obtained by quantizing channel outputs into fixed width. In order to reduce the hardware resources of the decoder, a non-uniform quantization scheme is developed based on simulations. The details of the quantization scheme will be given in the next subsection. The data preprocessing unit calculates the sign and the absolute value of each entry in r. As a result, the hard-decision vector v and reliability vector l are obtained, respectively. Afterwards, the syndrome s is calculated by putting hard-decision vector v into the linear shift register circuit orderly. Next, the error pattern list E is selected by the error pattern selection unit based on the calculated s. As discussed in the previous section, the list E contains a total of eight patterns in our design. Each of the eight error patterns is correlated with the reliability vector l. The basic operations in the correlation process are multiplication and accumulation, which can be performed effectively by adding up the two values in the reliability vector l whose corresponding positions are 1 in the error pattern. After that, the pattern e with the minimum correlation value is selected by the comparison unit for error correction. Two kinds of structures can be chosen for the design of comparison unit, the parallel structure and the serial structure. The former has fast computational speed whereas the latter can save more resources. Since the serial structure only causes eight more clocks' delay, which can be arranged in the gap between the adjacent received vectors, it is the better choice. Finally, the decoder output is calculated by $\hat{c} = e + v$.

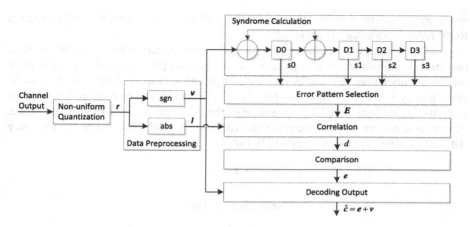

Fig. 1. Overall architecture of the designed decoder for BCH(15,11) code

3.2 Non-uniform Quantization Scheme

The quantization width of the soft-decision values is an important parameter that affects the logical resources and the performance of the designed decoder. In order to reduce the logical resources while maintaining the performance, non-uniform quantization can be applied [7]. Based on computer simulations, a non-uniform quantization scheme is developed, in which each soft-decision value is quantized into five bits (one sign bit and four bits for magnitude). The basic idea of the scheme is as follows: The quantization step should be small in the small magnitude value range in order to keep the precision. In contrast, the quantization step can be large in the large magnitude value range in order to reduce the quantization width. The developed quantization scheme is summarized in Table 1. In order to further illustrate the scheme, consider the following example. Assume the reliability vector is [1.15 0.89 1.43 0.51 0.76 1.06 0.80 0.54 1.48 0.36 0.64 1.07 1.76 1.17 1.18]. The quantization result is [13 12 14 9 11 12 11 9 14 7 10 12 15 13 13].

Table 1. The developed non-uniform quantization scheme

Magnitude range before quantization	Quantization step	Magnitude range after quantization
[0, 1/8)	1/32	0–3
[1/8, 3/8)	1/16	4–7
[3/8, 7/8)	1/8	8–11
[7/8, 13/8)	1/4	12–14
[13/8, +∞)	–	15

3.3 ROM Reduction Strategy

The error pattern lists are stored in the ROM resources in advance. Every list contains 8 error patterns, each of which has 15 bits. Since there are a total of 15 different syndromes, the size of the ROM should be $15 \times 15 \times 8 = 1800$ bits. In the following, a ROM reduction strategy is provided.

Since the maximum Hamming weight of the error pattern is two, there are at most two error positions in each error pattern. Hence, the error patterns can be stored by error positions rather than the whole vector. Each position ranging from 0 to 14 can be presented by 4 bits. Therefore, the size of one error pattern can be reduced from 15 bits to 8 bits. In addition, by taking advantage of the cyclic property of BCH(15,11) code, fifteen error pattern lists can be generated from one list, which is called the reference list. The detailed process is described in Fig. 2.

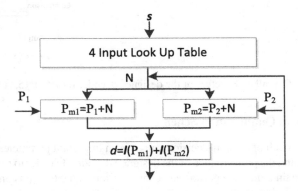

Fig. 2. The flowchart of ROM reduction strategy

Due to the cyclic property, the error patterns from one list can be obtained by cyclic shifting of error patterns in another list. A 4-input look-up table provides the mapping from the syndrome s to the bit shifting number N, as shown in Table 2. Here the syndrome $s = [s_0, s_1, s_2, s_3]$ is represented in the decimal format. Since $s = 0$ means the received vector has no errors, the table does not include this case. Take $s = 1$ as an example. In this case, the bit shifting number is 14.

Table 2. The mapping from syndrome to bit shifting number

s	1	2	3	4	5	6	7	8	9	10	11	12	13	14	15
N	14	13	10	12	6	9	4	11	0	5	7	8	1	3	2

The list corresponding to $s = 9$ is selected as the reference list, whose error patterns are stored in the ROM. The two error positions P_1 and P_2 for each pattern are showed in Table 3.

Table 3. The positions stored in the ROM

Error pattern index	0	1	2	3	4	5	6	7
P_1		1	2	3	5	6	7	11	0
P_2		12	9	4	10	8	13	14	X

The notation X in last column means the error pattern has weight one. Instead of shifting the error pattern, the modified positions can be simply obtained by addition operation. First, the bit shifting number N is read from the look-up table. Second, the positions P_1 and P_2 are read from the ROM. Third, the modified positions P_{m1} and P_{m2} are calculated by $P_{m1} = \mod(P_1 + N, 15)$ and $P_{m2} = \mod(P_2 + N, 15)$. Afterwards, the values in reliability vector whose positions are P_{m1} and P_{m2} are added. The above process is repeated until all the eight error patterns in the list are calculated.

It can be seen that only 64 bits are required if the ROM reduction strategy is applied, which is only 3.56% of the case when no reduction strategy is applied. Meanwhile, the extra logical resources brought by the strategy are two adders and one 4-input look-up table, which is negligible compared with the memory resources.

4 Simulation and Implementation Results

4.1 Simulation Results

The floating point and fixed point bit error rate (BER) performances of the proposed BCH(15,11) decoder are given in Fig. 3. For comparison purposes, the performances of hard-decision decoding and optimal maximum-likelihood (ML) soft-decision decoding are also included. It is known from the figure that the SA soft-decision decoding algorithm significantly outperforms the traditional hard-decision decoding algorithm. For example, the proposed algorithm achieves about 1.2 dB and 2 dB coding gain at

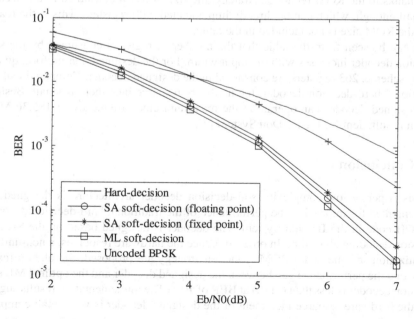

Fig. 3. BER performance of BCH(15,11) code with different decoding algorithms

BER $= 10^{-3}$ compared with the traditional hard-decision decoding and the uncoded BPSK, respectively. It is also worth mentioning that the performance gap between the SA soft-decision decoding algorithm and the optimal ML soft-decision decoding is less than 0.1 dB at BER of 10^{-3}. However, the soft-decision decoding is much more complicated than the proposed algorithm, which is difficult to implement in practice. In addition, it is known from the figure that the performance loss caused by the proposed non-uniform quantization scheme is very little, which suggests the effectiveness of the scheme.

4.2 Implementation Results

The proposed architecture is described by Verilog HDL, simulated by Modelsim, synthesized with Quartus II, and implemented on a Cyclone 5C target FPGA device. The implementation results are given in Table 4. For comparison purposes, the hard-decision decoding based on the method recommended in [2] is also implemented.

Table 4. Implementation results of designed decoder

Decoder type/width	Number of registers	Clock frequecy/MHz
Hard-decision	45	648.51
Soft-decision/4bit	240	181.19
Soft-decision/5bit	263	185.36
Soft-decision/6bit	305	176.90

Thanks to the ROM reduction strategy, the size of ROM consumed in the decoder is small enough, which can be directly implemented with registers. This is the reason why the ROM size is not included in the table.

It can be seen from the table that the number of registers consumed by the soft-decision decoder increases with the input width. For the designed non-uniform quantization scheme, 263 registers are consumed in the designed decoder. Compared with the traditional hard-decision decoder, the hardware resource increment is small. Besides, the designed decoder can operate at the maximum clock frequency of 185.36 MHz, which is sufficient for the BeiDou System [2].

5　Conclusion

In this paper, a low-complexity soft-decision decoder architecture is designed and implemented for improving the performance of the traditional hard-decision decoding of BCH code in the BeiDou System. The decoder is designed based on the SA soft-decision decoding algorithm. In order to reduce the hardware resources, a non-uniform quantization scheme and a ROM reduction strategy are proposed. Simulation results show that the performance gap between the designed decoder and the optimal ML soft-decision decoder is less than 0.1 dB at BER of 10^{-3}. The implementation results suggest that the hardware resource increment of the designed decoder is very small compared with the traditional hard-decision decoder, which indicates the designed decoder is suitable for practical BeiDou satellite navigation receiver.

References

1. Report on the Development of BeiDou Navigation Satellite System (Version 2.2), China Satellite Navigation Office (2013)
2. BeiDou Navigation Satellite System Signal in Space Interface Control Document: Open Service Signal B1I (Version 2.0), China Satellite Navigation Office (2013)
3. Müller, B., Holters, M., Zölzer, U.: Low complexity soft-input soft-output hamming decoder. In: Fitce Congress, pp. 1–5 (2011)
4. Zhu, J.F., An, J.P., Wang, A.H.: Syndrome-assisted list decoding for BCH codes of China Beidou navigation signal (in Chinese). J. Electron. Inf. Technol. 36(4), 1013–1016 (2014)
5. Lin, S., Costello, D.J.: Error Control Coding: Fundamentals and Applications, 2nd edn. Prentice-Hall, Englewood Cliffs (2004)
6. Vardy, A.: Be'Ery, Y.: Maximum-likelihood soft decision decoding of BCH codes. IEEE Trans. Inform. Theor. 40(2), 546–554 (1994)
7. Proakis, J.G.: Digital Communications, 5th edn. McGraw-Hill, New York (2007)

Author Index

Printed in the United Sta...
By Bookmasters

Printed in the United States
By Bookmasters